Fodo

Arizona

Fodor's Travel Publications, Inc.
New York • Toronto • London • Sydney • Auckland

ISBN 0-679-02260-0

Fodor's Arizona

Editor: Jillian L. Magalaner
Editorial Contributors: Ron Butler, Suzanne Carmichael, William Hafford, Mark Hein, Edie Jarolim, Pattie Johnston, Marcy Pritchard, Trudy Thompson Rice
Creative Director: Fabrizio LaRocca
Cartographer: David Lindroth
Illustrator: Karl Tanner
Cover Photograph: Peter Guttman

Design: Vignelli Associates

Special Sales

Fodor's Travel Publications are available at special discounts for bulk purchases (100 copies or more) for sales promotions or premiums. Special editions, including personalized covers, excerpts of existing guides, and corporate imprints, can be created in large quantities for special needs. For more information, write to Special Marketing, Fodor's Travel Publications, 201 E. 50th Street, New York, NY 10022. Inquiries from Canada should be sent to Random House of Canada, Ltd., Marketing Department, 1265 Aerowood Drive, Missauga, Ontario L4W 1B9. Inquiries from the United Kingdom should be sent to Fodor's Travel Publications, 20 Vauxhall Bridge Road, London, England SW1V 2SA.

MANUFACTURED IN THE UNITED STATES OF AMERICA
10 9 8 7 6 5 4 3 2 1

Contents

Maps

Foreword

While every care has been taken to ensure the accuracy of the information in this guide, the passage of time will always bring change, and consequently the publisher cannot accept responsibility for errors that may occur.

All prices and opening times quoted here are based on information supplied to us at press time. Hours and admission fees may change, however, and the prudent traveler will avoid inconvenience by calling ahead.

Fodor's wants to hear about your travel experiences, both pleasant and unpleasant. When a hotel or restaurant fails to live up to its billing, let us know and we will investigate the complaint and revise our entries where the facts warrant it.

Send your letters to the editors of Fodor's Travel Publications, 201 E. 50th Street, New York, NY 10022.

Highlights '93 and Fodor's Choice

Highlights '93

The Grand Canyon State has hit the headlines with quirks, controversy, and incredible caverns. The construction of futuristic Biosphere 2, the defeat of Martin Luther King, Jr., Day, and the acquisition of the spectacular Kartchner Caverns continue to be widely discussed topics, hotly debated issues, and long-awaited events, respectively, that not only keep this state in the news but will have long-term economic ramifications—both good and bad. Other new developments include major revitalization projects and added recreational choices.

Phoenix The defeat of Proposition 302, which would have established Martin Luther King, Jr., Day as a paid state holiday, took with it a big chunk of revenue earmarked for the Arizona coffer when major organizations relocated scheduled events to other states. Phoenix, however, took the biggest loss when the NFL pulled Super Bowl XXVII, an event that would have brought a projected $200 million into the local economy, off the city's 1993 calendar.

The Arizona Center, a $515 million multiphase development encompassing an eight-block stretch, has become downtown's trendiest meeting and people-watching place. More than 150,000 square feet of restaurants, shops, and entertainment facilities are already open and operating, with a movie theater given a spring 1993 completion date. When finished, this massive complex will house a three-acre urban plaza, a 600-room hotel, and millions more square feet of commercial and retail space.

The $89 million America West Arena, which opened June 1, 1992 is home to the National Basketball Association Phoenix Suns. It also stages popular music concerts. The city is also hoping the new stadium will help in its bid for a National Hockey League expansion franchise.

Patriot Square Park, in the center of downtown, has turned on its new laser light system, a beckoning beam that can be seen for miles in the clear night sky.

Tucson The world will be watching the eight paid-volunteer "biospherians" sealed inside Biosphere 2, one of the most important and challenging ecological research projects of the 1990s. Located 35 miles northeast of Tucson, the three-acre, self-sustaining enclosure encompasses seven ecological systems within its airtight structure, including tropical rain forest, savannah, marine, marsh, desert, and intensive agricultural areas. Biospherians will live within the "mini earth" for two-year stints, studying ecological management for what is hoped will be a prototype for future space colonies. Built with private funds by Space Biospheres Ventures, the facility anticipates a half-million visitors annually to come peek inside from one of the viewing platforms.

In 1974, spelunkers Randy Tufts and Gary Tenen accidentally uncovered Arizona's largest known cave on the privately owned Kartchner ranch, yet managed to keep their discovery secret for 14 years. The spectacularly colorful wet limestone cave, with crystals still growing within, measures more than 2 miles long and is thought to be millions of years old. Recently acquired by the state, Kartchner Caverns State Park, near Benson, about 45 miles east of Tucson, is scheduled to open to the public in the 1994–95 season, just as soon as planners have devised a way to keep visitors from destroying this rare and fragile find. A park campground should be open by the end of 1993.

Grand Canyon Want to jump on the environmental bandwagon? Just hop on the Grand Canyon Railway, which travels from Williams to the South Rim, and the railway will make a donation to the Grand Canyon Trust, a nonprofit organization committed to protecting, preserving, and managing the public lands and other natural resources of the canyon.

Scottsdale The glitzy, ritzy $123 million Scottsdale Galleria, opened in late 1991, isn't just your average shop-and-eat mall. Developers relegated some $10 million for the construction of Undersea World America, a two-story acquarium with more than 100 species of marine life.

For the ultimate aerial tour, take to the skies in a replica of an open cockpit, two-winged Waco barnstormer biplane. Passengers are treated to all the accoutrements associated with this post–World War I flying machine, including 1930s goggles, helmet, and—for daredevils—acrobatics.

Flagstaff The natural history of the Colorado Plateau (encompassing northern Arizona and the Four Corners Region) is the subject of two new exhibits at the Museum of Northern Arizona. Opened on September 5, 1992, these permanent shows illustrate the geology, paleontology, and biology of the plateau using state-of-the-art equipment, including a life-size skeletal model of a carniverous dinosaur found only in northern Arizona. Also at the museum, "Native Peoples of the Colorado Plateau" is an award-winning permanent anthropology exhibit documenting 12,000 years of human plateau-occupation distributed throughout four small galleries.

Springerville The announcement in May 1991 of the discovery of a group of catacombs—the first found in the United States—at the Casa Malpais ruins has excited archaeologists and residents of the nearby town of Springerville. The find is expected to shed light on the culture of the Mogollon people, who had mysteriously vanished from the area by the year AD 1450; the underground burial chambers are part of a complex that includes a multifamily dwelling and a large kiva. Residents of Springerville hope the discovery will bring tourists to their small town (population 2,000) near the New Mexican border, some four to five hours from the nearest large city; they've already opened a small museum on Main Street offering tours of the ruins.

Fodor's Choice

No two people will agree on what makes a perfect vacation, but it's fun and helpful to know what others think. We hope you'll have a chance to experience some of Fodor's Choices yourself in Arizona. For detailed information about each entry, refer to the appropriate chapter.

Activities

A mule ride or hike to the bottom of the Grand Canyon

A raft trip on the Colorado, white water or quiet water, Grand Canyon

The East Rim Tour, along the Grand Canyon's South Rim

Lake Powell excursion to Rainbow Bridge, Northeast Arizona

Picnic in Monument Valley, The Northeast

Hiking tour to Betatakin Ruin, Navajo National Monument, The Northeast

Hiking into Canyon de Chelly National Monument, The Northeast

Looking through the telescope at Lowell Observatory, North-Central Arizona

Hiking along the rim of a volcano at Sunset Crater National Monument, North-Central Arizona

A llama trek in Sedona, North-Central Arizona

An early morning walk through the Desert Botanical Gardens, Phoenix

Climbing Squaw Peak at sunset, Phoenix

Casa Grande Ruins National Monument, Phoenix

San Xavier del Bac Mission, Tucson and Southern Arizona

Arizona–Sonora Desert Museum, Tucson and Southern Arizona

The Copper Queen Mine, Bisbee, Tucson and Southern Arizona

Scenic Drives

The 210-mile drive from the South Rim to the North Rim, Grand Canyon

The dirt-road drive to Point Sublime, North Rim, Grand Canyon

West Rim Drive, South Rim, Grand Canyon

Petrified Forest National Monument—U.S. 163 from Kayenta to the Goosenecks of the San Juan River, The Northeast

AZ 264 across the Hopi Mesas, The Northeast

Flagstaff to Sedona via Oak Creek Canyon, North-Central Arizona

Sedona to Jerome, North-Central Arizona

Phoenix to Prescott and Wickenburg, Phoenix and Central Arizona

Along I–10 east of Benson through Texas Canyon, Tucson and Southern Arizona

Tucson to Kitt Peak, Tucson and Southern Arizona

Shopping

Cameron Trading Post, Grand Canyon

Desert View Trading Post, South Rim, Grand Canyon

El Tovar Gift Shop, South Rim, Grand Canyon

Hubbell Trading Post, The Northeast

Navajo Arts and Crafts Enterprise in Cameron and Window Rock, The Northeast

Museum of Northern Arizona gift shop, Flagstaff, North-Central Arizona

Tlaquepaque Mall, Sedona, North-Central Arizona

The Mercado and Arizona Center, Phoenix and Central Arizona

The Heard Museum gift shop, Phoenix and Central Arizona

Main Street, Scottsdale, Phoenix and Central Arizona

Old Town Artisans, Tucson and Southern Arizona

San Xavier Plaza, Tucson and Southern Arizona

Tubac, Tucson and Southern Arizona

Dining

Vincent Geurithault's on Camelback, Phoenix and Central Arizona (*Very Expensive*)

El Tovar Dining Room, South Rim, Grand Canyon (*Expensive–Very Expensive*)

La Hacienda, Phoenix and Central Arizona (*Expensive–Very Expensive*)

Compass Room, Phoenix and Central Arizona (*Expensive*)

L'Auberge de Sedona, North-Central Arizona (*Expensive*)

Tack Room, Tucson and Southern Arizona (*Expensive*)

El Charro, Tucson and Southern Arizona (*Moderate*)

Grand Canyon Lodge Dining Room, North Rim, Grand Canyon (*Moderate*)

Rustler's Rooste, Phoenix and Central Arizona (*Moderate*)

Oak Creek Owl, Sedona, North-Central Arizona (*Moderate*)

Rainbow Room at Wahweap Lodge, Lake Powell, Northeast Arizona (*Moderate*)

Adrian's, Phoenix and Central Arizona (*Inexpensive*)

Café Poca Cosa, Tucson and Southern Arizona (*Inexpensive*)

Lodging

Loews Ventana Canyon, Tucson and Southern Arizona (*Very Expensive*)

El Tovar Hotel, South Rim, Grand Canyon (*Expensive–Very Expensive*)

The Pointe Hilton on South Mountain, Phoenix and Central Arizona (*Expensive–Very Expensive*)

Westcourt in the Buttes, Phoenix and Central Arizona (*Expensive–Very Expensive*)

Arizona Inn, Tucson and Southern Arizona (*Expensive*)

Enchantment Resort, Sedona, North-Central Arizona (*Expensive*)

Thunderbird Lodge at Canyon de Chelly, Northeast Arizona (*Expensive*)

Wahweap Lodge at Lake Powell, Northeast Arizona (*Expensive*)

Best Western Grand Canyon Squire, South Rim, Grand Canyon (*Moderate–Expensive*)

Grand Canyon Lodge, North Rim, Grand Canyon (*Moderate*)

Little America of Flagstaff, North-Central Arizona (*Moderate*)

The Lodge on the Desert, Tucson and Southern Arizona (*Moderate*)

West Coast Executive Park, Phoenix and Central Arizona (*Moderate*)

Sky Ranch Lodge, Sedona, North-Central Arizona (*Inexpensive–Moderate*)

Ambassador Inn, Phoenix and Central Arizona (*Inexpensive*)

Days Inn Downtown, Tucson and Southern Arizona (*Inexpensive*)

Hopi Cultural Center Motel at Second Mesa, Northeast Arizona (*Inexpensive*)

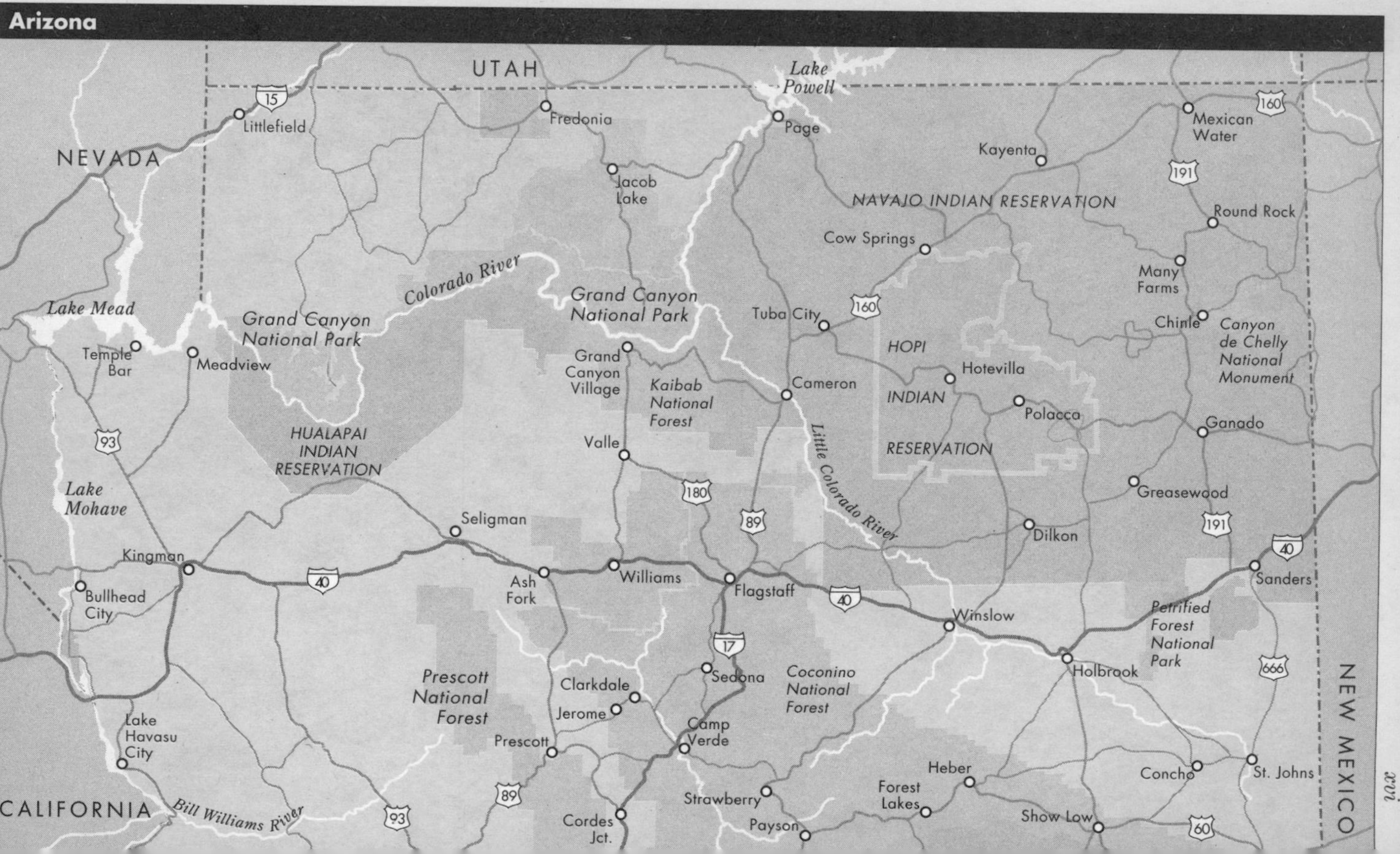
Arizona
UTAH
NEVADA
CALIFORNIA
NEW MEXICO
Lake Powell
Lake Mead
Lake Mohave
Colorado River
Little Colorado River
Bill Williams River
Grand Canyon National Park
Grand Canyon National Park
NAVAJO INDIAN RESERVATION
HOPI INDIAN RESERVATION
HUALAPAI INDIAN RESERVATION
Kaibab National Forest
Coconino National Forest
Prescott National Forest
Petrified Forest National Park
Canyon de Chelly National Monument
Littlefield
Fredonia
Page
Kayenta
Mexican Water
Round Rock
Many Farms
Chinle
Cow Springs
Jacob Lake
Tuba City
Cameron
Hotevilla
Polacca
Ganado
Greasewood
Dilkon
Temple Bar
Meadview
Grand Canyon Village
Valle
Seligman
Kingman
Bullhead City
Ash Fork
Williams
Flagstaff
Winslow
Holbrook
Sanders
Sedona
Clarkdale
Jerome
Camp Verde
Prescott
Lake Havasu City
Cordes Jct.
Strawberry
Payson
Forest Lakes
Heber
Show Low
Concho
St. Johns
15
160
191
93
180
89
40
17
666
60

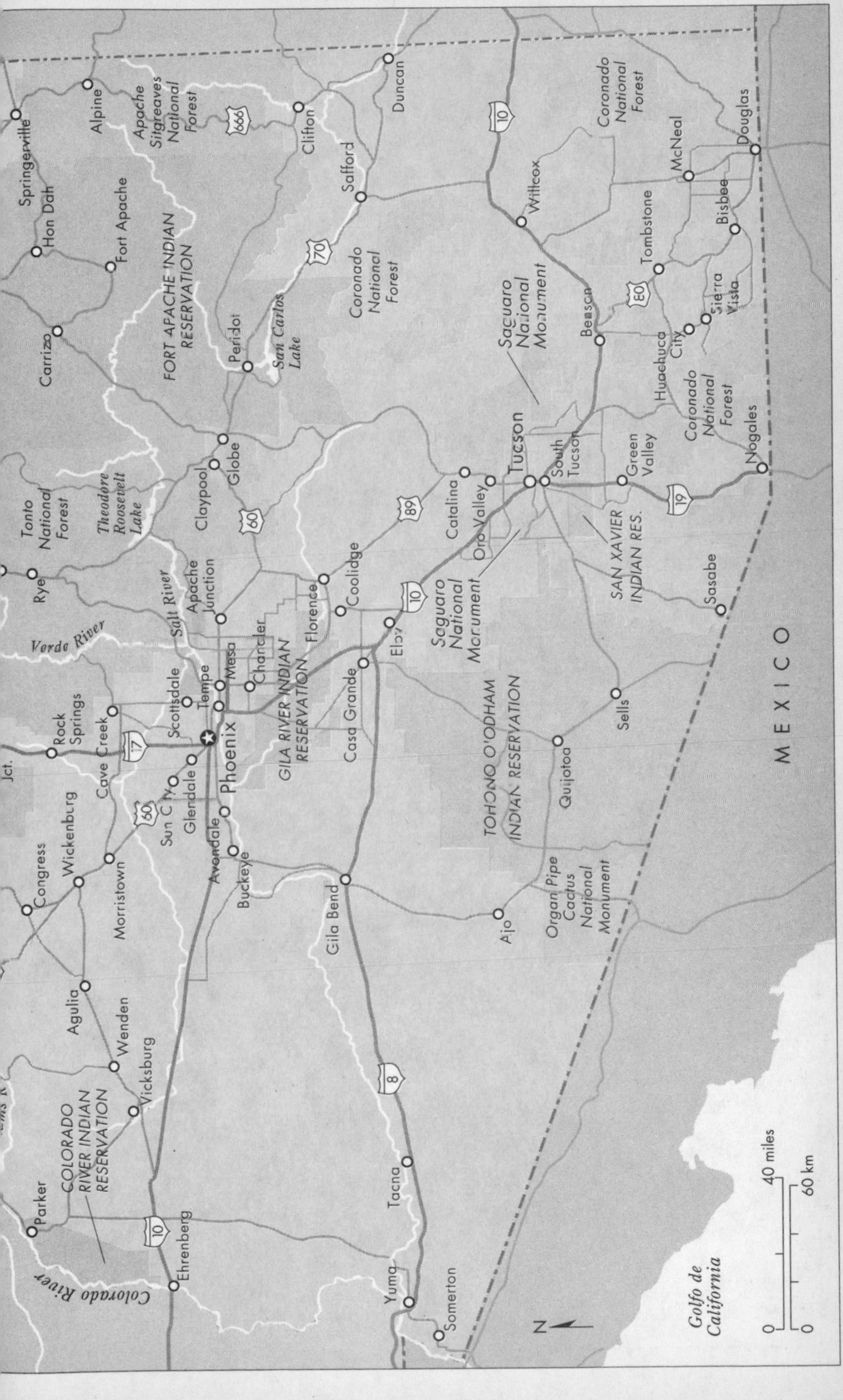

Jct.
Parker
Colorado River
COLORADO RIVER INDIAN RESERVATION
Congress
Agulia
Wickenburg
Rock Springs
Wenden
Morristown
Cave Creek
Vicksburg
10
Ehrenberg
60
17
Sun City
Glendale
Scottsdale
Avondale
Phoenix
Tempe
Mesa
Buckeye
Chandler
Verde River
Salt River
Apache Junction
Rye
Tonto National Forest
Theodore Roosevelt Lake
Claypool
Globe
60
GILA RIVER INDIAN RESERVATION
Florence
Coolidge
Casa Grande
Gila Bend
Yuma
Tacna
8
Somerton
Eloy
10
89
Saguaro National Monument
Catalina
Oro Valley
Tucson
South Tucson
TOHONO O'ODHAM INDIAN RESERVATION
Ajo
Organ Pipe Cactus National Monument
Quijotoa
Sells
SAN XAVIER INDIAN RES.
Green Valley
19
Sasabe
Nogales
N
Golfo de California
0
40 miles
0
60 km
MEXICO
Carrizo
Hon Dah
Springerville
Alpine
Fort Apache
FORT APACHE INDIAN RESERVATION
Apache Sitgreaves National Forest
666
Peridot
San Carlos Lake
70
Clifton
Safford
Coronado National Forest
Duncan
10
Saguaro National Monument
Willcox
Benson
80
Tombstone
Huachuca City
Coronado National Forest
Sierra Vista
Bisbee
McNeal
Douglas
Coronado National Forest

The United States

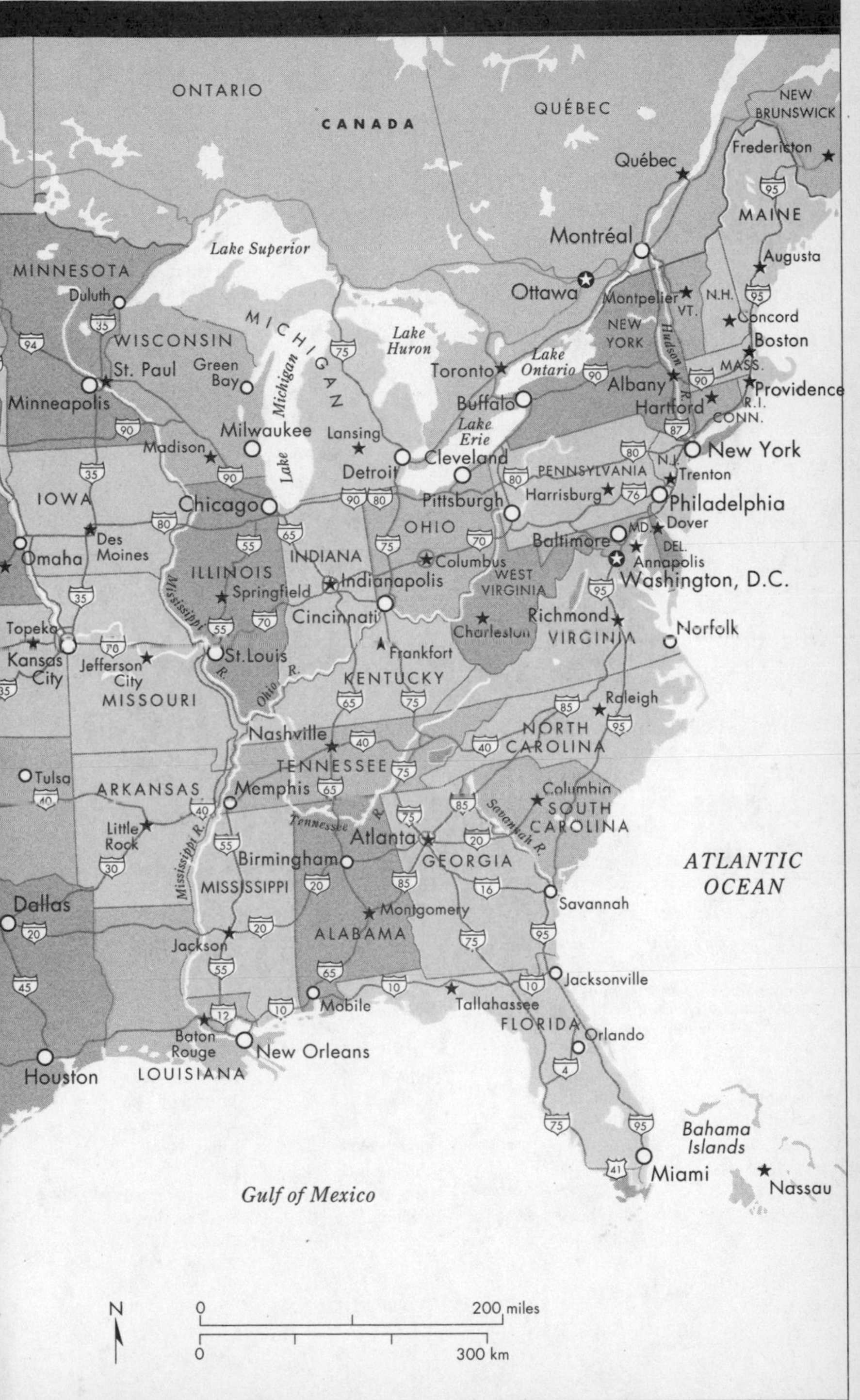
ONTARIO
CANADA
QUÉBEC
NEW BRUNSWICK
Fredericton
Québec
MAINE
Montréal
Ottawa
Augusta
Lake Superior
MINNESOTA
Duluth
WISCONSIN
MICHIGAN
Lake Michigan
Lake Huron
Montpelier
VT.
N.H.
Concord
NEW YORK
Hudson R.
St. Paul
Minneapolis
Green Bay
Toronto
Lake Ontario
Boston
MASS.
Albany
Providence
Buffalo
Hartford
R.I.
CONN.
Milwaukee
Lansing
Lake Erie
Madison
Cleveland
New York
Detroit
N.J.
PENNSYLVANIA
Trenton
IOWA
Chicago
Pittsburgh
Harrisburg
Philadelphia
OHIO
Dover
Des Moines
Omaha
INDIANA
Baltimore
MD.
DEL.
Columbus
Annapolis
ILLINOIS
WEST VIRGINIA
Washington, D.C.
Springfield
Indianapolis
Mississippi R.
Cincinnati
Richmond
Topeka
Charleston
VIRGINIA
Norfolk
Kansas City
Jefferson City
St. Louis
Frankfort
Ohio R.
MISSOURI
KENTUCKY
Raleigh
Nashville
NORTH CAROLINA
TENNESSEE
Tulsa
ARKANSAS
Memphis
Columbia
SOUTH CAROLINA
Tennessee R.
Savannah R.
Little Rock
Atlanta
Birmingham
GEORGIA
ATLANTIC OCEAN
MISSISSIPPI
Dallas
Savannah
Montgomery
ALABAMA
Jackson
Jacksonville
Mobile
Tallahassee
FLORIDA
Baton Rouge
New Orleans
Orlando
Houston
LOUISIANA
Bahama Islands
Miami
Nassau
Gulf of Mexico
N
0
200 miles
0
300 km

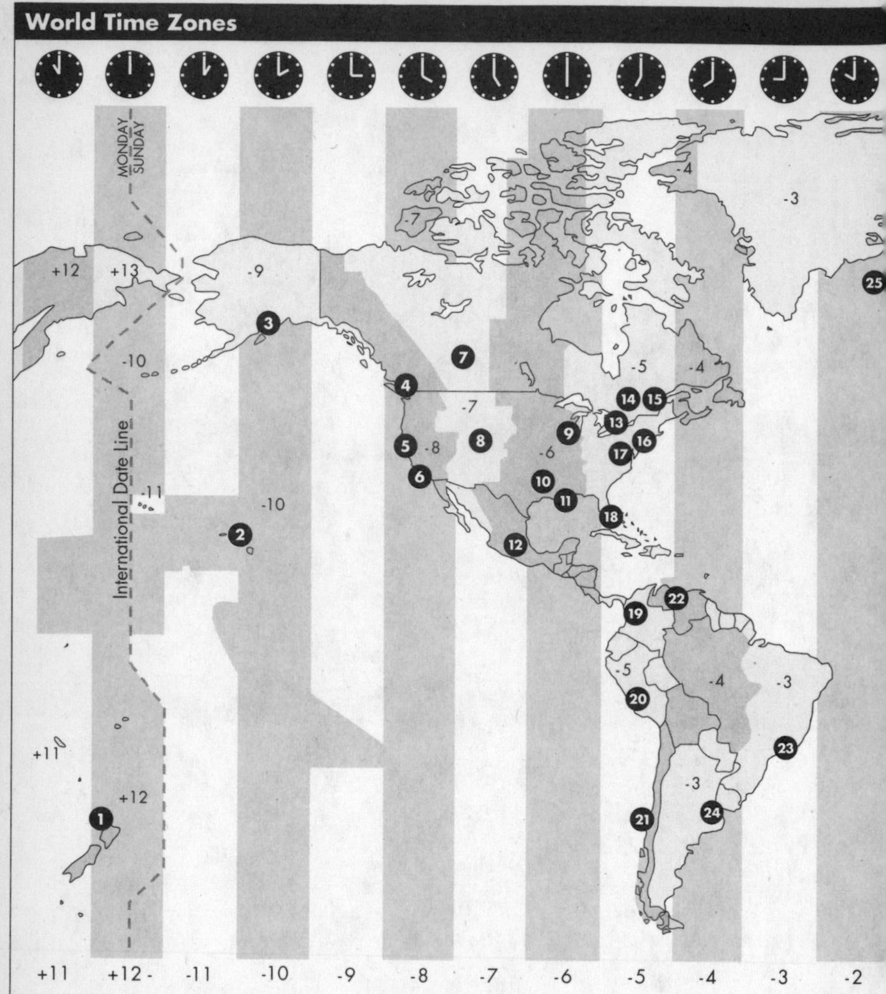

Numbers below vertical bands relate each zone to Greenwich Mean Time (0 hrs.).
Local times frequently differ from these general indications,
as indicated by light-face numbers on map.

Algiers, **29**
Anchorage, **3**
Athens, **41**
Auckland, **1**
Baghdad, **46**
Bangkok, **50**
Beijing, **54**
Berlin, **34**
Bogotá, **19**
Budapest, **37**
Buenos Aires, **24**
Caracas, **22**
Chicago, **9**
Copenhagen, **33**
Dallas, **10**
Delhi, **48**
Denver, **8**
Djakarta, **53**
Dublin, **26**
Edmonton, **7**
Hong Kong, **56**
Honolulu, **2**
Istanbul, **40**
Jerusalem, **42**
Johannesburg, **44**
Lima, **20**
Lisbon, **28**
London (Greenwich), **27**
Los Angeles, **6**
Madrid, **38**
Manila, **57**

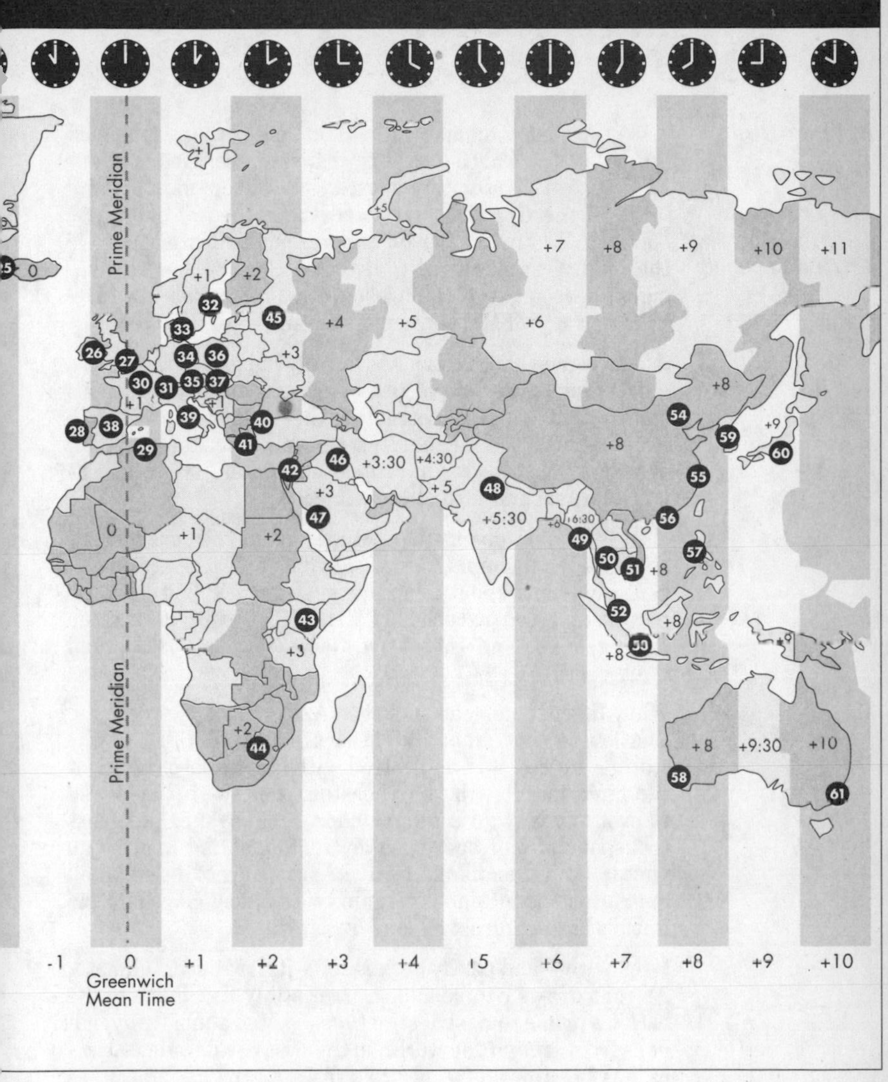

Mecca, **47**
Mexico City, **12**
Miami, **18**
Montréal, **15**
Moscow, **45**
Nairobi, **43**
New Orleans, **11**
New York City, **16**

Ottawa, **14**
Paris, **30**
Perth, **58**
Reykjavík, **25**
Rio de Janeiro, **23**
Rome, **39**
Saigon (Ho Chi Minh City), **51**

San Francisco, **5**
Santiago, **21**
Seoul, **59**
Shanghai, **55**
Singapore, **52**
Stockholm, **32**
Sydney, **61**
Tokyo, **60**

Toronto, **13**
Vancouver, **4**
Vienna, **35**
Warsaw, **36**
Washington, D.C., **17**
Yangon, **49**
Zürich, **31**

Introduction

By Mark Hein

Mark Hein is an editor and a writer in the features department of the Arizona Republic.

Arizona is an ancient land, etched with the long past of the Earth and of the human race. Aeons of our planet's story are written in the deep, multicolored walls of the Grand Canyon and the cathedral-like stone spires of Monument Valley. Ages of human history echo in the hidden grandeur of Canyon de Chelly, the "sky villages" perched atop Hopi reservation mesas, and the prehistoric ruins of Montezuma Castle and Casa Grande.

At the same time, Arizona is a lively hub of modern life, a quickening center in the emerging web of communications and trade, travel and recreation that links western North America with the Pacific Rim. Phoenix, the state's capital and the Southwest's metropolitan center, is America's ninth-largest and fastest-growing city.

Visitors to Arizona usually wonder about the desert: How hot is it? What should we wear? Is it safe? These are intelligent questions about a land where summer daytime temperatures often exceed 100°F (38°C), major rivers run underground, and the native flora are spiny cactus and thorny scrub.

What few people realize is that Arizona has two deserts. The low desert (roughly the southwestern third of the state) is indeed arid and dotted with tall saguaro cacti, but the high desert—the northeastern tier, with the Grand Canyon and Navajo and Hopi lands—is a savannalike plain, thousands of feet above sea level and mantled in snow all winter. And the middle third of Arizona is not desert at all but rather mountainous terrain, with alpine lakes and the world's largest forest of ponderosa pines.

Even with—and partly because of—its low-desert climate, Arizona draws people almost irresistibly. Long one of the nation's prime tourist destinations, visited annually by millions from around the world, in the past two decades Arizona has been one of America's fastest-growing states, as tens of thousands of immigrants arrive each year.

That growth has transformed Phoenix from a farming town of 60,000 people in 1940 to an urban center of 1 million in 1990; it has also doubled and redoubled the population of Tucson, the "Old Pueblo" in the southern part of the state. Yet Arizona remains a place of boundless vistas, with more than 80% of its land in U.S. and state parks and preserves or Indian reservations. Whether they are in the deserts or the mountains, Arizona's small towns still have vast spaces between them.

Arizona has also retained much of its rich Indian and Hispanic heritage. More Native Americans live here than in any other state, and the Hopi village of Oraibi is the oldest continually inhabited community in North America. Hispanic families arrive daily from Mexico and Central America, many following routes opened by Spanish explorers a century before the Pilgrims landed; numerous Tucson families trace their lineage to Mexican pioneers who arrived in the days of the American Revolution.

Visitors can readily see some of the gifts modern Arizona has received from these ancient cultures: the Indian and Spanish names on most of its mountains and rivers, plants, and animals, even its streets; the pervasive influence of Hopi and Mexican architecture in homes and public buildings. Other aspects of this heritage appear only after some study: the canals that carry Arizona's mountain streams into the low desert, the legal system that gives husband and wife equal shares in their "community property."

One part of Arizona's cultural heritage that almost everyone gets to share is the relaxed pace and style of living: In almost everything, from clothing to art, from home decor to meals, the desert dwellers of each era have learned to prize the unhurried and the informal, to accept the calming lessons of the heat and the majestic landscape. Leave your tie and tails at home and, even if you're on business, plan to take time out: Lean back for a leisurely late lunch during the hottest part of the day; stretch out under a patio awning beside a pool or fountain during the long, cool evenings.

And wherever you take your siesta, cast your eye toward the horizon: You'll see deep skies and luminous, gold-edged sunsets; the towering silhouettes of buttes and mountain ranges, their rugged surfaces subtly alive with shifting shadows and pastel colors; a forest of widely spaced saguaros, standing like many-armed sentinels amid sketchy bushes of creosote and ocotillo, while birds and lizards dart from one spiny haven to the next; the long, green bowl of a mountain meadow, dusted with poppy clusters and blue lupine beds, edged in shimmering aspens. Arizonans and visitors alike never tire of watching the play of sun and shadows on some corner of this magnificent land.

1 Essential Information

Before You Go

Visitor Information

Even if you're not the type to plan your Arizona vacation down to the last cactus, golf ball, or canyon vista, why not do a bit of reading and research anyway? A descriptive passage, a colorful photo, or a historical reference might inspire an unexpected turn or spontaneous twist in your itinerary. With knowledge gleaned and imagination triggered, you'll find even preplanned vacations can take on an aura of adventure.

Information on all parts of the state is available in a comprehensive tourist kit from the **Arizona Office of Tourism** (1100 W. Washington, Phoenix 85007, tel. 602/542–TOUR).

The **Hopi Tribe Office of Public Relations** (Box 123, Kykotsmovi 86039, tel. 602/734–2441) can inform you of upcoming ceremonies on the mesas. For Navajo tribal activities, obtain literature and events calendars from **Navajo Tourism Department** (Box 663, Window Rock 86515, tel. 602/871–6659). For information on the 12 other tribal councils in the state, contact the Arizona Office of Tourism for a map of Indian reservations and a list of addresses and phone numbers.

For more pretrip literature, *see* Further Reading, *below*.

Tour Groups

Care to visit the Grand Canyon, glimpse the legendary red rocks of Sedona, drive through Monument Valley, and still have time for 18 holes of golf? Then you might want to consider an escorted tour of Arizona. Creative itineraries abound, hitting the traditional tourist spots as well as out-of-the-way places you might not be able to get to on your own. Tour groups also tend to save you money on airfare and hotels. Keep in mind, though, that you can spend only as much time in one place as the tour itinerary allows. If freedom and flexibility are important to you, consider an independent package. Most major airlines offer economical fly/drive deals.

When evaluating any tour, be sure to find out exactly what expenses are included (particularly tips, taxes and service charges, side trips, additional meals, and entertainment); ratings of all hotels on the itinerary and the facilities they offer; cancellation policies for both you and the tour operator; and, if you are traveling alone, the cost of a single supplement.

Listed below is a sampling of operators and packages to give you an idea of what is available. For additional resources, contact your travel agent or the Arizona Office of Tourism. Most tour operators request that bookings be made through a travel agent—there is no additional charge for doing so.

General-Interest Tours

Bixler Tours (Box 37, Hiram, OH 44234, tel. 216/569–3222 or 800/325–5087) offers a week-long trip to Arizona as well as a 14-day "Wonders of the West" tour that takes in Arizona, Colorado, Wyoming, and Utah.

Two of the western itineraries offered by **Domenico Tours** (751 Broadway, Bayonne, NJ 07002, tel. 201/823–8687 or 800/554–TOUR) include stops in the Grand Canyon State.

Gadabout Tours (700 E. Tahquitz Canyon Way, Palm Springs, CA 92262, tel. 619/325–5556 or 800/952–5068) offers a choice of four escorted tours of the state, ranging from five to six days in length. "Arizona Indian Summer" explores the Canyon de Chelly and other sights on the Navajo and Hopi reservations, while "Tucson Holiday" concentrates on southern Arizona. Other tours highlight the scenic red rocks of Sedona and the Grand Canyon.

In eight days, **Maupintour** (Box 807, Lawrence, KS 66044, tel. 913/843–1211 or 800/255–4266) covers many of Arizona's natural scenic wonders, including the Grand Canyon, Petrified Forest, Painted Desert, Monument Valley, and Oak Creek Canyon. "Arizona Adventure" offers a more in-depth introduction to the state, visiting all the top tourist spots in 14 days. Several other tours combining Arizona with New Mexico, Colorado, and Utah are also available.

In eight days, **Talmage Tours** (1223 Walnut St., Philadelphia, PA 19107, tel. 215/923–7100) hits the major parks of the Southwest, including Arizona's famed Grand Canyon, and Bryce Canyon and Zion national parks in Utah.

Tauck Tours (Box 5027, Westport, CT 06881, tel. 203/226-6911 or 800/468–2825) has an eight-day tour of Arizona's famous resorts, as well as one of the canyon lands of Arizona, Utah, and Nevada.

Special-Interest Tours

Art

Customized art tours of galleries and artists' studios are arranged by **Sedona Spectrum Group International** (Box 2091, Sedona 86336, tel. 602/282–9013). **Painted Desert Productions** (3533 N. 70th St., Suite 201, Scottsdale 85251, tel. 602/946–8860) specializes in Southwestern art and cultural adventures.

Cycling

Take a three-, five-, or seven-day bike tour with **Cycling Arizona** (4466 E. Haven La., Tucson 85712, tel. 602/322-0984). Groups are limited to 12 cyclists, and tours include hotels and most meals.

Fishing

Half-, one-, or two-day guided fishing trips on Arizona's desert lakes, in groups of up to 40, are organized by **Neal's Fishing Guide Service** (8715 E. Amelia Ave., Scottsdale 85251, tel. 602/945–6122).

Gold Panning **Arizona's Old West Tours** (841 E. Paradise La., Phoenix 85022, tel. 602/942–3361) arranges gold- and silver-panning expeditions, as well as Jeep outings to mountains and deserts.

History **The Dons of Arizona** (201 N. Central Ave., Phoenix 85004, tel. 602/258–6016) is a service club that organizes tours emphasizing Southwestern history and folklore.

Package Deals for Independent Travelers

United Vacations (tel. 800/328–6877) and **American Airlines Fly AAway Vacations** (tel. 800/321–2121) both offer fly/drive packages combining special rental car and hotel rates in Arizona.

GoGo Tours (69 Spring St., Ramsey, NJ 07446; book through your local travel agent) has three- to seven-night packages in Phoenix, Scottsdale, Sedona, and Tucson. All include a rental car with unlimited mileage.

Tips for British Travelers

Tourist Information The **United States Travel and Tourism Administration** (Box 1EN, London W1A 1EN, tel. 071/495–4466) has information and brochures.

Passports and Visas You will need a valid 10-year passport to enter the United States (cost: £15 for a standard 32-page passport, £30 for a 94-page passport). Application forms are available from most travel agents and major post offices and from the **Passport Office** (Clive House, 70 Petty France, London SW1H 9BR, tel. 071/279–4000 or 071/279–3434 for recorded information). You do not need a visa if you are visiting on either business or pleasure, are staying for 90 days or less, have a return ticket or an onward ticket, are traveling with a major airline (in effect, any airline that flies from the United Kingdom to the United States), and complete a visa waiver I–94W, which is supplied either at the airport of departure or on the plane. If you fail to comply with any of these requirements, you will need a visa. Apply to a travel agent or the **United States Embassy Visa and Immigration Department** (5 Upper Grosvenor St., London W1A 2JB, tel. 071/499–7010 or 071/499–3443 for recorded information). Visa applications to the U.S. Embassy must be made by mail, not in person. Visas can be given only to holders of 10-year passports, although visas in expired passports remain valid. If you think you might stay longer than three months, you must apply for a visa before you travel.

Customs Entering the United States, a visitor age 21 or over can bring in 200 cigarettes or 50 cigars or 2 kilograms smoking tobacco; 1 liter of alcohol; and duty-free gifts to a value of $100. You may not bring in meat or meat products, seeds, plants, or fruit.

Returning to the United Kingdom, a traveler age 17 or over can take home (1) 200 cigarettes or 100 cigarillos or 50 cigars or 250 grams of tobacco; (2) 1 liter of alcohol over 22% volume or 2 liters of alcohol under 22% volume (fortified or sparkling wine) or 2 liters of table wine; (3) 2 more liters of table wine; (4) 60 milliliters of perfume and 250 milliliters of toilet water; (5) other goods to a value of £32, but not more than 50 liters of beer or 25 cigarette lighters.

Insurance We recommend that you take out insurance to guard against health problems, motoring mishaps, theft, flight cancellation, and loss of luggage. Most major tour operators offer holiday insurance, and details are given in brochures. For free general advice on all aspects of holiday insurance, contact the **Association of British Insurers** (51 Gresham St., London EC2V 7HQ, tel. 071/600–3333). A proven leader in the holiday insurance field is **Europ Assistance** (252 High St., Croydon, Surrey CRO 1NF, tel. 081/680–1234).

Tour Operators The following is a selection of companies that offer tour packages to Arizona and the Southwest. For details on these and other resources, consult a travel agent.

Bales Tours Ltd (Bales House, Junction Rd., Dorking, Surrey RH4 3HB, tel. 0306/76881) offers a 10-day deluxe coach tour of the scenic canyons and lakes of Arizona and Utah, taking in Phoenix, Sedona, and Navajo Indian lands.

Cosmos (Ground floor, Dale House, Tiviot Dale, Stockport, Cheshire SK1 1TB, tel. 061/480–5799) includes the Grand Canyon and other Arizona highlights on several of its coach tours of the western states.

Greyhound International Travel Inc (Sussex House, London Rd., East Grinstead, West Sussex RH19 1LD, tel. 0342/317317) offers inclusive flight/coach tours of Arizona resorts and canyonlands, and can arrange independent itineraries using regularly scheduled bus services. Flights to the United States must be booked separately.

Jetsave Travel Ltd (Sussex House, London Rd., East Grinstead, West Sussex RH19 1LD, tel. 0342/312033) offers a 15-day "Mountains & Canyons" coach tour featuring Denver, Salt Lake City, the Grand Canyon, and several national parks, as well as self-drive packages, rail tours, and ranch holidays in Colorado or southern Arizona.

Kuoni Travel (Kuoni House, Dorking, Surrey RH5 4AZ, tel. 0306/742222) has a 15-day "Great West" tour by coach that includes Phoenix, the Grand Canyon, Monument Valley, Lake Powell, and national parks in Utah and California, as well as packages for the independent traveler.

British Airways Holidays (Atlantic House, Hazelwick Ave., Three Bridges, Crawley, West Sussex RH10 1NP, tel. 0293/611611) features a 17-day "Western Discovery" coach tour that includes the Grand Canyon and other Arizona highlights.

Airlines and Airfares Flying time varies considerably with the airline booked and the length of plane changes made in various hub cities; approximate flying time to Phoenix from London is 13½ hours.

The major airport for Arizona is in Phoenix. It can be reached via connecting flights from the hub cities of most major airlines:

American (tel. 0800/010151) via Dallas, Miami, or Chicago; **Continental** (tel. 0293/776464) via Denver or Houston; **Delta** (tel. 0800/414767) via Atlanta or Cincinnati; **Northwest** (tel. 0345/747800) via Boston or Minneapolis; **Pan Am** (tel. 071/409–3377) via New York, Miami, or Washington, DC; **TWA** (tel. 071/439–0707 or 0800/222222 outside London) via New York or St. Louis; **United** (0800/888555) via New York, Chicago, or Los Angeles; **USAir** (tel. 0800/777333) via Charlotte, NC. Many of these airlines offer air-pass programs for two or more flights within the United States, as does **America West** (tel. 071/633–9293).

Airfares vary enormously, depending on the type of ticket you buy and the time of year you travel. Ticket agencies such as the **American Travel Center, Jetsave Travel, Trail Finders,** and **STA** offer good deals.

When to Go

Depending on whether you prefer scorching desert or snowy slopes, elbow-to-elbow resorts or wide-open territory, some area of this diverse state will be perfect at any time. In general, the best seasons to visit are spring and autumn, when the temperatures are milder and the crowds have thinned out.

Winter is prime time in the central and southern parts of the state. The weather is sunny and mild, the deserts are in bloom, and the cities are abustle with travelers seeking to escape their cold climes. Conversely, northern Arizona—including the Grand Canyon—can be blizzardlike, with snow, freezing rain, and subzero temperatures.

The desert regions throughout Arizona sizzle in summer, and travelers and their vehicles should be adequately prepared for the blistering heat. Practically every restaurant and accommodation is equipped with air-conditioning. Summer, however, is a delightful time to visit northern Arizona's high-country region, when temperatures are 18°–20°F lower than they are down south.

Climate Phoenix boasts 300 sunny days and an average 7 inches of precipitation annually. Tucson gets all of 11 inches of rain each year, and the high mountains see about 25 inches. The Grand Canyon is usually cool on the rim, about 20°F warmer on the floor. During winter months, approximately 6–12 inches of snow fall on the North Rim, while the South Rim receives half that amount.

The following average daily maximum and minimum temperatures for two major cities in Arizona offer a representative range of temperatures in the state.

Tucson									
Jan.	64F	18C	**May**	89F	32C	**Sept.**	96F	36C
	37	3		57	14		68	20
Feb.	68F	20C	**June**	98F	37C	**Oct.**	84F	29C
	39	4		66	19		57	14
Mar.	73F	23C	**July**	100F	38C	**Nov.**	73F	23C
	44	7		73	23		44	7
Apr.	82F	28C	**Aug.**	96F	36C	**Dec.**	66F	19C
	51	11		71	22		39	4

Flagstaff								
Jan.	41F	5C	**May**	66F	19C	**Sept.**	71F	22C
	14	-10		33	1		41	5
Feb.	44F	7C	**June**	77F	25C	**Oct.**	62F	17C
	17	- 8		41	5		30	- 1
Mar.	48F	9C	**July**	80F	27C	**Nov.**	51F	11C
	23	- 5		50	10		21	- 6
Apr.	57F	14C	**Aug.**	78F	26C	**Dec.**	42F	6C
	28	- 2		48	9		15	- 9

Current weather information for foreign and domestic cities can be obtained by calling The Weather Channel Connection at 900/WEATHER from a touch-tone phone. In addition to offering the weather report, The Weather Channel Connection offers local time and travel tips as well as hurricane, foliage, and ski reports. The call costs 95¢ per minute.

Time

The state of Arizona does not go on daylight saving time. During the daylight saving portion of the year, Arizona time will be the same as Pacific daylight time and two hours earlier than central daylight time. However, if you're traveling to the vast Navajo and Hopi reservations in the northeastern section of Arizona, be aware that Indian country (although in Arizona) *is* on daylight saving time.

Festivals and Seasonal Events

Arizona's sunny days, sporty lifestyle, fiesta atmosphere, and rich Native American heritage are natural components of a multitude of spirited festivals, musical celebrations, and competitive sporting events. Following is a list of perennial favorites. For a comprehensive calendar and specific details, contact the **Arizona Office of Tourism** (*see* Visitor Information, *above*).

January **Phoenix Open Golf Tournament,** Scottsdale. Big names both play and attend this PGA tournament, with a $200,000 purse, held at the Tournament Players Club of Scottsdale.

Northern Telecom Tucson Open, Tucson. The other top PGA event, this is played at the Tournament Players Club at StarPass.

Southern Arizona Square and Round Dance Festival, Tucson. Dancers from all over the state participate in this four-day event.

January–February **Hashknife Pony Express Ride,** Holbrook. Each year a sheriff's posse transports the U.S. mail from Holbrook to Scottsdale over the Mogollon Rim.

Parada del Sol Rodeo and Parade, Scottsdale. This popular state attraction on Scottsdale Road features lots of dressed-up cowboys and cowgirls, plus horses and floats.

February **Quartzsite Pow Wow Gem and Mineral Show,** Quartzsite. This gigantic, 10-day flea market attracts more than 100,000 buyers and sellers of rocks, minerals, gems, and related crafts and supplies.

O'odham Tash, Casa Grande. Indian tribes from around the country host parades, native dances, a rodeo, costume displays, and food stands.

Wickenburg Gold Rush Days, Wickenburg. History comes to life when this Old West town puts on a rodeo, dances, gold-panning demonstrations, a mineral show, and other activities.

La Fiesta de los Vaqueros, Tucson. The world's longest "nonmechanized" parade—horses pull the floats and carry the dignitaries—launches this four-day rodeo at the Tucson Rodeo Grounds.

Tucson Gem and Mineral Show. Rock hounds–amateur and professional–from all over the world come to buy, sell, and display their geological treasures at this huge downtown event, which includes lectures and competitive exhibits.

March **LPGA Samaritan Turquoise Classic,** Phoenix. Top women players compete for the $150,000 purse.

Pioneer Days, Tucson. Celebrating the era before Arizona became a state, this two-day festival features military reenactments as well as western crafts displays.

Heard Museum Guild Indian Fair and Market, Phoenix. This prestigious juried show of Native American arts and crafts brings together participants from all over the Southwest; visitors can also enjoy Native American foods, music, and dance here.

April **International Mariachi Conference,** Tucson. The Tucson Convention Center is the setting for four days of mariachi music, plus cultural and educational exhibits, for mariachi music lovers.

Route 66 Fun Run Weekend, Seligman/Topock. The historic road between Chicago and Los Angeles is feted with classic car rallies, hot rod and antique-car shows, and various other events—including a 1950s hop.

San Xavier Pageant and Fiesta, Tucson. A reenactment of the establishment of the famous "White Dove of the Desert" mission, this event features mariachi music, a bonfire procession, and fireworks.

La Vuelta de Bisbee, Bisbee. Arizona's largest bicycle race attracts top racers from around the country.

May **Cinco de Mayo,** Phoenix, Tucson. A variety of festivities commemorate Mexico's 1863 victory over France.

Bill Williams Mountain Men Parade and Rodeo, Williams. The events of the mid-1800s are reenacted by the townspeople, who dress in period costume for the occasion.

May–June **Trappings of the American West Festival,** Flagstaff. The featured attraction at this two-week festival is cowboy art—everything from painting and sculpture to cowboy poetry readings.

June **Pine Country Rodeo,** Flagstaff. Southwestern cowboys compete in this weekend event at Fort Tuthill.

All Indian Powwow and **Native American Arts Fair,** Flagstaff. On the weekend before July 4, tribes from all over the world hold dance performances and competitions, while an international array of crafts are displayed and sold.

July **Prescott Frontier Days and Rodeo,** Prescott. Billed as the world's oldest rodeo, this event sees big crowds and an equally big party on downtown Whiskey Row.

Loggers Festival, Payson. Loggers from the United States and Canada test their skills and strength.

August **Payson Rodeo,** Payson. Top cowboys from around the country compete.

Festival in the Pines, Flagstaff. Painters, potters, and other artists from around the United States compete with musicians, carnival rides, and food vendors for the crowd's attention.

September **Jazz on the Rocks Festival,** Sedona. Six or seven ensembles perform in a striking outdoor setting.

Navajo Nation Annual Tribal Fair, Window Rock. The world's largest Native American fair includes a rodeo, traditional Navajo music and dances, food booths, and an intertribal powwow.

October **Arizona State Fair,** Phoenix. This massive event, at the state fairgrounds, features entertainment, games, rides, exhibits, livestock, art shows, and more.

Tombstone Helldorado Days, Tombstone. The town relives the spirited Wyatt Earp era and the shoot-out at the OK Corral.

London Bridge Days, Lake Havasu City. A triathlon, parade, kinetic-sculpture races, and other contests are part of this 10-day event.

November **Heard Museum Native American Art Show,** Phoenix. Exhibits feature fine tribal arts and crafts from across the state.

Havasu Classic Outboard World Championships, Lake

Havasu City. Various classes of racing boats compete for prize money and trophies.

Thunderbird Invitational Balloon Race, Glendale. One hundred or more balloons participate in a colorful race.

December **Luminaria Night,** Phoenix. A candlelight ceremony on the Desert Botanical Garden walkways celebrates the Christmas season.

Indian Market, Phoenix. A good selection of Native American arts and crafts is displayed and sold at Pueblo Grande Museum.

Tempe Old Town Festival, Tempe. The downtown area closes to traffic for three days of art exhibits, food booths, musical performances, and other entertainment.

All Indian Fair, Navajo Country. Native dances, food, and crafts exhibits constitute this national event.

What to Pack

Casual clothing and resort wear fit in well with Arizona's climate and attractions. T-shirts, polo shirts, sundresses, and lightweight shorts, trousers, skirts, and blouses are just right for summer. Cotton fabrics and light colors will help to keep you cool.

Larger city restaurants, as well as dining rooms in the high-class resorts, require diners to be appropriately attired. Women may want to pack several dresses with day-to-evening accessories, while men should include a dinner jacket, dress shirt, and tie in their suitcases.

Sun hats, swimsuits, sandals, and sunscreen are mandatory warm-weather items. In winter be sure to include a sweater and a warm jacket, particularly for high-country travel. Jeans and sneakers or sturdy walking shoes are important year-round items.

Naturally, if you plan to participate in a sport, bring along the appropriate gear. Tennis, golf, ski, and horseback-riding equipment are readily available for rental.

A camera and film, sunglasses, an extra pair of prescription glasses, and any necessary medications should also be tucked into your suitcase. Be sure to leave room for new purchases—perhaps a pair of hand-tooled western boots or a piece of handcrafted silver jewelry.

Carry-on Luggage Passengers aboard U.S. major carriers are usually limited to two carry-on bags. Bags stored under the seat must not exceed 9 inches by 14 inches by 22 inches. Bags hung in a closet can be no larger than 4 inches by 23 inches by 45 inches. The maximum dimensions for bags stored in an overhead bin are 10 inches by 14 inches by 36 inches. Any item that exceeds the specified dimensions will generally be rejected as a carryon and handled as checked baggage. Keep in mind that an airline can adapt these rules to circumstances; on an especially crowded flight, you may be allowed to bring only one carry-on bag aboard.

In addition to two carryons, passengers may also bring aboard a handbag, an overcoat or a wrap, an umbrella, a camera, a reasonable amount of reading material, an infant bag, and crutches, braces, a cane, or other prosthetic device upon which the passenger is dependent. Infant-child safety seats can also be brought aboard if parents have purchased a ticket for the child or if there is space in the cabin.

Checked Luggage Luggage allowances vary slightly among airlines. Many carriers allow three checked pieces; some allow only two. It is best to consult with the airline before you go. In all cases, check-in luggage cannot weigh more than 70 pounds per piece or be larger than 62 inches (length plus width plus height).

Getting Money from Home

Cash Machines

Withdrawals It's easy to use automated-teller machines (ATMs) to withdraw money from your checking account with a bank card. Just get the names of affiliated cash-machine networks before your departure. (For locations for two of the larger networks, Cirrus and Plus, call 800/4-CIRRUS or 800/THE-PLUS.) Note that you may be charged a fee for withdrawals away from your home turf. Of course, you need to get a personal identification number (PIN) if you don't have one already.

Cash Advances You can also use ATMs to get cash advances on your credit card, providing you have a PIN number for your card. As with cash advances from tellers, you pay interest from the day of posting, and some banks tack on an additional service charge.

For both withdrawals and cash advances, there are usually limits on the amount you can access within given time periods. Know before you go.

Bank Transfers Call your local bank and have money sent to a bank in the area you're visiting. It's easiest to transfer money between like branches of the same bank; otherwise, the process may take longer and cost more.

American Express Cardholder Services The company's Express Cash system links your U.S. checking account to your Amex card. You can withdraw up to $1,000 in a 7-day period (more if your card is Gold or Platinum). For each transaction there's a 2% fee (minimum $2, maximum $6). Call 800/227-4669 for information.

Cardholders can also cash personal or counter checks at any American Express office for up to $1,000, of which $500 may be claimed in cash and the balance in traveler's checks carrying a 1% commission.

Wiring Money To send or receive up to $10,000, you can use an American Express MoneyGram, and you don't have to have an American Express card. The sender goes to an American Express MoneyGram agent, specifies an amount, pays up to $1,000 with a credit card (anything over that in cash), and telephones the receiver with the reference number he is given. The receiver goes to the nearest MoneyGram agent, presents identification and the reference number, and picks up cash. Fees are 5% to 10%, depending on the amount and method of payment (AE, D, MC, V are accepted). For agent locations, call 800/543–4080.

Traveling with Film

If your camera is new, shoot and develop a few rolls before leaving home. Pack some lens tissue and an extra battery for your built-in light meter. Invest about $10 in a skylight filter: It will protect the lens and reduce haze.

Film doesn't like hot weather, so if you're driving in summer, don't store film in the glove compartment or on the shelf under the rear window. Put it behind the front seat on the floor, on the side opposite the exhaust pipe.

On a plane trip, never pack unprocessed film in check-in luggage; if your bags are X-rayed, your film could be ruined. Always carry undeveloped film with you through security and ask to have it inspected by hand. (It helps to keep your film in a plastic bag, ready for quick inspection.) Inspectors at American airports are required by law to honor requests for hand inspection. The newer airport scanning machines used in all U.S. airports are safe for anything from 5 to 500 scans, depending on the speed of your film.

Traveling with Children

Many of the big resorts and dude ranches offer special activities just for children, and many offer baby-sitting services. Children of all ages are enthralled by the Wild West flavor around Tucson and the southeastern part of the state, with Tombstone ranking as a particular favorite. If you're driving some of the long desert stretches, take along plenty of games and thirst-quenching snacks.

Publications ***Family Travel Times*** is a newsletter published 10 times a year by TWYCH (Travel with Your Children, 45 W. 18th St., 7th Floor Tower, New York, NY 10011, tel. 212/206–0688). A one-year subscription costs $35 and includes access to back issues. The organization also offers a free phone-in service with advice and information on specific destinations.

Great Vacations with Your Kids, by Dorothy Jordan and Marjorie Cohen, offers complete advice on planning your trip with children, from toddlers to teens ($12.95 paperback, E. P. Dutton, 375 Hudson St., New York, NY 10014, tel. 212/366–2000).

"Kids and Teens in Flight," a useful brochure about children flying alone, is available from the U.S. Department of Transportation. To order a free copy, call 202/366–2000.

Getting There On domestic flights, children under age 2 not occupying a seat travel free. Various discounts apply to children 2–12 years of age, so check with your airline when making reservations.

Regulations about infant travel on airplanes are in the process of being changed. Until this happens, however, if you want to be sure your infant is secure, you must bring your own infant car seat and buy a separate ticket. Check with the airline in advance to be sure your seat meets the required standard. If possible, reserve a seat behind one of the plane's bulkheads, where there's usually more legroom and enough space for a bassinet (which is available from the airlines). The booklet "Child/Infant Safety Seats Acceptable for Use in Aircraft" is available from the **Federal Aviation Administration** (APA-200, 800 Independence Ave. SW, Washington, DC 20591, tel. 202/267–3479). If you opt to hold your baby on your lap, do so with the infant outside the seat belt rather than inside it so he or she doesn't get crushed in case there's a sudden stop.

When reserving tickets, also ask about special children's meals or snacks. The February 1990 and 1992 issues of *Family Travel Times* include TWYCH's "Airline Guide," which contains a rundown of the children's services offered by 46 different airlines.

Getting Around

By Train On all Amtrak routes, children under age 2 ride for free (provided they don't occupy a seat), children age 2–14 accompanied by an adult pay half-price, and children 15 or older pay the full adult fare. For information on routes and reservations, call **Amtrak** (tel. 800/USA–RAIL).

By Bus On Greyhound buses, one child under age 2 travels free on an adult's lap, and one child 2–4 pays 10% of the adult fare; children 5–11 pay half the adult price, and children 11 or older pay full fare. For further information, call your local **Greyhound/Trailways** station.

Hotels All **Holiday Inns** (tel. 800/465–4329) allow children age 12 or under to stay free when sharing a room with an adult, and some offer family plans, providing the same privileges for children 18 or under. The **Westin La Paloma Hotel** in Tucson (tel. 800/228–3000) offers year-round, supervised activities for children ages 6 months to 12 years, as well as professional child care. The fee is $3 per child per hour. Every day during the summer holiday season (Memorial Day–Labor Day), and weekends throughout the year, the **Hyatt Regency** in Scottsdale (tel. 800/233–1234) offers a full-day Kamp Kachina recreation and activity program for children ages 3–12. The schedule includes traditional summer-camp activities, such as arts and crafts, supervised sports, and off-property excursions for older children. The charge for each full day of activities is $25, or $5 per activity. Baby-sitting is also available.

Hints for Disabled Travelers

General Information

Most of the region's national parks and recreation areas have accessible visitor centers, rest rooms, campsites, and trails, and more are being added every year. For information on accessible facilities at specific parks and sites in northeastern Arizona, contact the **National Park Service, Southwest Regional Office** (tel. 505/988–6375); for sites in southwestern Arizona, contact the **Western Regional Office** (tel. 415/744–3929).

All blind or disabled U.S. citizens and permanent residents are entitled to a free lifetime pass to all federally operated parks, monuments, historic sites, recreational areas, and wildlife refuges that charge entrance fees. The **Golden Access Passport,** which must be obtained in person from a federally operated park or recreational area, also provides a 50% discount on federal fees charged for facilities and services, such as camping, boat launching, and parking.

Group tours for travelers with disabilities are regularly scheduled by the **Arizona Recreation Center for the Handicapped** (1550 W. Colter St., Phoenix 85015, tel. 602/230–2226).

The **Information Center for Individuals with Disabilities** (Fort Point Pl., 1st floor, 27–43 Wormwood St., Boston, MA 02210, tel. 617/727–5540) offers useful problem-solving assistance, including lists of travel agents who specialize in tours for the disabled.

Mobility International USA (Box 3551, Eugene, OR 97403, tel. 503/343–1284 voice and TDD) is an internationally affiliated organization with 500 members. For a $20 annual fee, it coordinates exchange programs for disabled people around the world and offers information on accommodations and organized study programs.

Moss Rehabilitation Hospital Travel Information Service (1200 W. Tabor Rd., Philadelphia, PA 19141, tel. 215/456–9603) provides information on tourist sights, transportation, and accommodations in destinations around the world for a small fee.

The **Society for the Advancement of Travel for the Handicapped** (347 5th Ave., Suite 610, New York, NY 10016, tel. 212/447–7284) has access information and lists of tour operators specializing in travel for the disabled. Annual membership costs $45, or $25 for students and senior citizens. Send $2 and a self-addressed envelope for information on a specific destination.

Getting Around

By Train

Amtrak (tel. 800/USA–RAIL or TDD 800/523–6590) offers all disabled passengers a 15% discount on the lowest available fare. A disabled children's fare is also available. All trains and all large stations have accessible toilets, though some of the region's smaller, unmanned stations do not. Reserve tickets 48 hours in advance to be sure of special seats, individually prepared meals, and wheelchair assistance. For a free copy of *Access Amtrak*, a guide to special services for elderly and disabled travelers, write to Amtrak (Passenger Services, 60 Massachusetts Ave. NE, Washington, DC 20002).

By Bus Although Greyhound buses have no special facilities for disabled passengers, an attendant can ride for free. For additional information, contact **Greyhound/Trailways** (tel. 800/345–3109).

By Car **Avis** (tel. 800/331–1212), **Hertz** (tel. 800/654–3131), and **National** (tel. 800/328–4567) can provide hand controls on some of their rental cars if they have advance notice.

Publications The **Arizona Easter Seal Society** (903 N. 2nd St., Phoenix 85004, tel. 602/252–6061) publishes three comprehensive booklets of travel tips for disabled visitors to Arizona. *Access Valley of the Sun* covers Phoenix and environs; *Access Tucson & Green Valley* focuses on the southeastern region; *Access Northern Arizona* encompasses Flagstaff and surrounding communities.

Arizona Accommodations Directory, published by the **Arizona Hotel and Motel Association** (1110 E. Missouri Ave., Suite 720, Phoenix 85014, tel. 602/264–6081), supplies listings of hotels and motels throughout the state that are equipped with facilities for the disabled.

The Itinerary (Box 2012, Bayonne, NJ 07002, tel. 201/858–3400) is a bimonthly travel magazine for the disabled. Call for a subscription ($10 for one year, $20 for two years); it's not available in stores.

Travel Industry and Disabled Exchange (TIDE, 5435 Donna Ave., Tarzana, CA 91356, tel. 818/368–5648) publishes a quarterly newsletter and a directory of travel agencies and tours catering specifically to the disabled. The annual membership fee is $15. Nautilus Tours, Inc., which can be contacted through TIDE, is a company that arranges tours for disabled travelers.

Twin Peaks Press (Box 129, Vancouver, WA 98666, tel. 206/694–2462 or 800/637–2256 for orders only) specializes in books for the disabled. *Travel for the Disabled*, by Helen Hecker, offers helpful hints as well as a comprehensive list of guidebooks and facilities geared to the disabled. *Wheelchair Vagabond*, by John G. Nelson, contains valuable information for independent travelers planning extended trips in a car, van, or camper.

Twin Peaks also offers a Traveling Nurses Network, which provides registered nurses to accompany and assist disabled travelers.

Hints for Older Travelers

The state's healthful environment and many retirement communities make it a popular destination for older travelers. As such, Arizona has a multitude of recreational, sports, and entertainment facilities geared especially to senior citizens' needs and interests. In addition, discounts are offered on public transportation, museum entrance fees, fishing and hunting licenses, cinemas, musical and theatrical performances, and a wide variety of other services. The minimum age limit varies between 55 and 65 years old. If you fall into this age group, be sure to inquire about discounts before putting your money on the counter; savings can be substantial.

Seven Arizona college and university campuses participate in Elderhostel (*see below*). Some scheduled classes include Native American Archaeology, Geology of the Grand Canyon, Flora and Fauna of the Sonoran Desert, Astronomy, and Cowboys and the Old West.

General Information

The **Golden Age Passport** is a free lifetime pass to all parks, monuments, and recreation areas run by the federal government. Permanent U.S. residents age 62 or older may pick one up in person at any of the national parks that charge admission. The passport covers the entrance fee for the holder and anyone accompanying the holder in the same private vehicle. It also provides a 50% discount on camping, boat launching, and parking charges. Proof of age is required.

The **American Association of Retired Persons** (AARP, 601 E St. NW, Washington, DC 20049, tel. 202/434–2277) has two programs for independent travelers: (1) the Purchase Privilege Program, which offers discounts on hotels, airfare, car rentals, recreational vehicle (RV) rentals, and sightseeing; and (2) the AARP Motoring Plan, provided by Amoco, which furnishes emergency road-service aid and trip-routing information for an annual fee of $33.95 per person or couple. The AARP also arranges group tours, cruises, and apartment living all over the world through **AARP Travel Experience from American Express** (400 Pinnacle Way, Suite 450, Norcross, GA 30071, tel. 800/927–0111). Members of AARP must be 50 or older; annual dues are $5 per person or couple.

If you qualify to use an AARP or other senior-citizen identification card to obtain a reduced hotel rate, mention it at the time you make your reservation rather than when you check out. At participating restaurants, show your card to the maître d' before you're seated, because discounts may be limited to certain menus, days, or hours. When renting a car, be sure to ask about special promotional rates that might offer greater savings than the available discount.

Elderhostel (75 Federal St., 3rd floor, Boston, MA 02110, tel. 617/426-7788) is an innovative, low-cost educational program for people age 60 or older. Participants live in dorms on some 1,600 campuses around the world. Mornings are devoted to lectures and seminars; afternoons to sightseeing and field trips. Fees for two- to three-week international trips—including room, board, tuition, and round-trip transportation—range from $1,800 to $4,500.

Mature Outlook (6001 N. Clark St., Chicago, IL 60660, tel. 800/336-6330), a subsidiary of Sears, Roebuck and Co., is a travel club for people over age 50 that provides hotel and motel discounts and publishes a bimonthly newsletter. Annual membership is $9.95; there are 800,000 members currently. Instant membership is available at Sears stores and participating Holiday Inns.

National Council of Senior Citizens (1331 F St. NW, Washington, DC 20004, tel. 202/347-8800) is a nonprofit advocacy group with some 5,000 local clubs across the United States. Annual membership (no age restriction) is $12 per person or couple. Members receive a monthly newspaper with travel information and an ID card for reduced-rate hotels and car rentals.

Saga International Holidays (120 Boylston St., Boston, MA 02116, tel. 800/343-0273) specializes in group travel for people over age 60. A selection of variously priced tours allows you to choose the package that meets your needs.

September Days Club (tel. 800/241-5050) is run by the moderately priced Days Inns of America. The $12 annual membership fee for individuals or couples over age 50 entitles them to reduced-rate car rentals and to reductions of 15% to 50% at most of the chain's more than 350 motels.

Getting Around

By Train

Amtrak (tel. 800/USA-RAIL) offers all passengers 62 and older a 15% discount on the lowest available coach fare (effective Monday through Thursday). For a free copy of *Access Amtrak*, a guide to its services for elderly and disabled travelers, write to Amtrak (Passenger Services, 60 Massachusetts Ave., NE, Washington, DC 20002).

By Bus

Greyhound/Trailways (tel. 800/752-4841) offers senior citizens (age 64 or older) a 5% reduction on all regular fares.

Publications

The Senior Citizens Guide to Budget Travel in the United States and Canada, by Paige Palmer, is available for $5.95 (including shipping) from Pilot Books (103 Cooper St., Babylon, NY 11702, tel. 516/422-2225).

Further Reading

General History

Arizona Cowboys, by Dane Coolidge, is an illustrated account of the cowboys, Indians, settlers, and explorers of the early 1900s. Originally published in 1878, *The Handbook to Arizona, Its Resources, History, Towns, Mines, Ruins and*

Scenery, by Richard J. Hinton, gives insight into Arizona then and now. Buried-treasure hunters will be inspired by *Lost Mines of the Great Southwest*, by John D. Mitchell, which is just enough of a nibble to start you sketching maps and planning strategy. First printed back in 1891, *Some Strange Corners of Our Country*, by Charles F. Lummis, takes readers on a century-old journey to the Grand Canyon, Montezuma Castle, the Petrified Forest, and other Arizonan "strange corners." *In the House of Stone and Light*, by J. Donald Hughes, follows the history of the Grand Canyon, via many illustrations, from Indian occupation to tourist park. Trace the region's cultures from the early natives to the present dwellers and learn about archaeologists' techniques in *Southwestern Archaeology*, by John C. McGregor. Dude ranches, ghost towns, saloons—read all about them in *The Best of the Old West, An Indispensable Guide to the Vanishing Legend of the American West*, by Ron Butler.

Native American History *The Anasazi: Prehistoric Peoples of the Four Corners Region*, by J. Richard Ambler, is an intriguing study of this area and its early inhabitants. *Hohokam Indians of the Tucson Basin*, by Linda Gregonia, offers an in-depth look at this prehistoric tribe. In *Hopi*, by Susanne Page and Jake Page, the daily, ceremonial, and spiritual life of the tribe are explored in detail. Study up on the history of Hopi silversmithing techniques in *Hopi Silver*, by Margaret Wright. *Spider Woman Stories*, by G. M. Mullett, is a collection of tales from Hopi tribal mythology. *Hopi Kachinas: The Complete Guide to Collecting Kachina Dolls*, by Barton Wright, describes these special dolls and their function. Navajo homes, ceremonies, crafts, and tribal traditions are kept alive in *The Enduring Navajo*, by Laura Gilpin. Navajo legends and trends from early days to present time are collected in *The Book of the Navajo*, by Raymond F. Locke.

Natural History *A Guide to Exploring Oak Creek and the Sedona Area*, by Stewart Aitchison, provides natural-history driving tours of this very scenic district. All rock hounds will treasure *Mineral and Gem Localities in Arizona*, by Lee Hammons, with its specific locations of rocks, minerals, and gems, plus statewide color maps. In *100 Desert Wildflowers in Natural Color*, by Natt N. Dodge, you'll find a color photo and brief description of each of the flowers included. Also written by Natt N. Dodge, *Poisonous Dwellers of the Desert* gives precise information on both venomous and nonvenomous creatures of the Southwest. *Cacti of the Southwest*, by W. Hubert Earle, depicts some of the best-known species of the region with color photos and descriptive material. *Where Water Flows: The Rivers of Arizona*, by Lawrence Clark Powell, is a beautifully photographed coffee-table book about seven of the state's waterways. For comprehensive information on Grand Canyon geology, history, flora and fauna, plus hiking suggestions, pick up *A Field Guide* *to the Grand Canyon*, by Steve Whitney. *Common Edible and Useful Plants of the West*, by Muriel Sweet, gives the layperson descriptions of medicinal and other plants and shrubs, most of which were first discovered by Native Americans.

Crafts *The Traveler's Guide to American Crafts: West of the Mississippi*, by Suzanne Carmichael, gives browsers and buyers alike a useful overview of Arizona's traditional and contemporary handiwork.

General Interest *Arizona Highways*, a monthly magazine, features exquisite color photography of this versatile state. *Travel Arizona* and *Travel Arizona—The Back Roads*, both published by Arizona Highways, describe a variety of scenic tours.

Arriving and Departing

By Plane

Most major domestic airlines fly into Phoenix and Tucson from all parts of the United States. Busy Phoenix Sky Harbor International, about 3 miles east of the city center, also serves as the hub for flights to other parts of the state. Tucson International Air Terminal is located about 8½ miles south of the downtown area. Both facilities offer a number of different transportation services into the city, from minivan shuttles to stretch limousines.

Air carriers to Arizona are **Alaska** (tel. 800/426–0333), **American** (tel. 800/433–7300), **America West** (tel. 800/247–5692), **Continental** (tel. 800/525–0280), **Delta** (tel. 800/221–1212), **Northwest** (tel. 800/225–2525), **Southwest** (tel. 800/531–5601), **TWA** (tel. 800/221–2000), **United** (tel. 800/241–6522), and **USAir** (tel. 800/428–4322).

Within the state, **America West** and **Skywest** (tel. 800/453–9417) operate regularly scheduled flights among Phoenix, Tucson, Flagstaff, and Yuma; Skywest also flies to Page/Lake Powell.

When choosing a flight, be sure to distinguish among (1) nonstop flights, with no stops or changes of aircraft; (2) direct flights, which make one or more stops but require no change of aircraft; and (3) connecting flights, which require at least one change of aircraft and possibly several stops as well. A good travel agent can advise you on special package deals and excursion fares.

Smoking It is best to request a no-smoking seat at the time you book your ticket. If a U.S. airline representative tells you there are no seats available in the no-smoking section, insist on one: Department of Transportation regulations require U.S. flag carriers to find seats for all nonsmokers on the day of the flight, provided they meet check-in time restrictions. On foreign carriers, ask for a seat far from the smoking section.

Lost Luggage On domestic flights, airlines are responsible for up to $1,250 per passenger in lost or damaged property. If you're carrying valuables, either take them with you on the plane or purchase additional insurance for lost luggage. Some airlines issue luggage insurance when you check in, but many do not. Insurance for lost, damaged, or stolen luggage is available through travel agents or directly through various insurance companies. Luggage-loss coverage is usually part of a comprehensive travel-insurance package that includes personal accident, trip cancellation, and sometimes default and bankruptcy. Companies that issue luggage insurance include **Tele-Trip** (Box 31685, 3201 Farnam St., Omaha, NE 68131–0618, tel. 800/228–9792), a subsidiary of Mutual of Omaha, and **The Traveler** (Ticket and Travel Dept., 1 Tower Sq., Hartford, CT 06183–5040, tel. 203/277–0111 or 800/243–3174), **Access America, Inc.,** a subsidiary of Blue Cross–Blue Shield (Box 11188, Richmond, VA 23230, tel. 800/334–7525 or 800/284–8300), and **Near Services** (450 Prairie Ave., Suite 101, Calumet City, IL 60409, tel. 708/868–6700 or 800/654–6700). Rates vary according to the length of the trip.

By Car

Major approaches from the east and west are I–40, I–10, I–8, and U.S. 60. Main north–south routes are I–17, I–10, and U.S. 89. Other artery roads are U.S. 70 and U.S. 64 (U.S. 160 in Arizona) from the east.

Most highways into the state are good to excellent, with easy access, roadside facilities, rest stops, and scenic views. The speed limit is 65 miles per hour, but even though it may be tempting to let the speedometer needle fly in the wide-open desert, beware—police use sophisticated detection systems to nab violators.

Hazards to desert drivers include dust storms and flash floods. Dust storms usually occur mid-July to mid-September (the monsoon months), just before thunderstorms hit, causing extremely low visibility. If you're on the highway, pull as far off the road as possible, turn off your headlights, and wait for the storm to subside. Flash floods strike low-lying areas during both the monsoon and winter rainy seasons. Dry washes, which fill quickly with running water, are particularly dangerous and should not be crossed until you can see the bottom.

Vehicles and passengers should be well equipped for searing summer heat in the low desert. Always carry plenty of water, a good spare tire, a jack, and emergency supplies. If you get stranded, stay with your vehicle and wait for help to arrive.

At some point you will probably pass through one or more of the state's 23 Indian reservations. Roads and other areas within reservation boundaries are under the jurisdiction of reservation police and governed by separate rules and regulations. Observe all signs and respect residents' privacy.

For more information on the state's highways and byways, contact the Arizona Department of Transportation (tel. 602/255–7011); for weather conditions, call 602/252-1010, ext. 7623.

Car Rentals

Most of the big-name car-rental firms are represented in Arizona. Many have airport counters or will drop cars off at your hotel or resort. Inquire about special weekly rates that include unlimited mileage.

A variety of rates and vehicles are offered by **Alamo** (tel. 800/327–9633), **Avis** (tel. 800/331–1212), **Budget** (tel. 800/527–0700), **Dollar** (tel. 800/800–4000), **Hertz** (tel. 800/654–3131), **National** (tel. 800/227–7368), and **Thrifty** (tel. 800/367–2277). If a prearrangement has been made, many companies will supply four-wheel-drive vehicles, trucks, and a range of campers.

By Train

The *Southwest Chief* operates daily between Los Angeles and Chicago, stopping in Kingman, Flagstaff, and Winslow. The *Sunset Limited* travels three times each week between Los Angeles and New Orleans, with stops at Yuma, Phoenix, Tempe, Coolidge, Tucson, and Benson. Both services connect with trains to eastern destinations. For details, contact **Amtrak** (tel. 800/USA–RAIL).

By Bus

Greyhound/Trailways provides service to many Arizona destinations from most parts of the United States. For information outside of Arizona, call 602/248–4040; local numbers are 602/271–7426 in Phoenix, 602/792–0972 in Tucson, 602/774–4573 in Flagstaff, 602/445–5470 in Prescott.

Staying in Arizona

Shopping

Many tourists come to Arizona for no other reason than to purchase fine **Native American jewelry and crafts.** Collectibles include Navajo rugs and sand paintings, Hopi kachina dolls (intricately carved and colorful representations of Hopi spiritual beings) and pottery, Tohonó O'odham (Papago) basketry, and Apache beadwork, as well as the highly prized silver and turquoise jewelry produced by several different tribes. Many of these items are sold in big-city shops and malls, though going directly to the reservation often gives shoppers additional rewards.

Museums and trading posts on the Navajo and Hopi reservations in the state's northeastern region offer introductions to crafts and their history and have gift shops where you can make purchases. Demonstrations of silversmithing, rug-weaving, and pottery-making techniques are often held on the premises. Roadside stands also offer wares for sale.

Look for the exquisite basketry and other local crafts at the Tohonó O'odham tribal headquarters in Sells, about 60 miles southwest of Tucson. Apache beadwork, baskets, wood carvings, and jewelry are sold at reservation trading posts in the eastern part of the state.

Bear in mind that the high quality of Native American arts and crafts is reflected in the prices they fetch. Bargaining is the exception, not the rule. In general, best buys are to be had in the fall, after tourists have gone home.

Highly mineralized Arizona is also a haven for **rock and mineral** collectors. An astounding variety of specimens include agate, jasper, tourmaline, petrified wood, quartz, turquoise, amethyst, precious opal, and fire agate. Buy them at specialty shops or at one of the state's year-round rock and gem shows. The largest shows, held in late January or early February, are at Quartzsite, about 19 miles from the California border, and Tucson.

Sports and Outdoor Activities

Ballooning Both Phoenix and Tucson have a large number of hot-air balloon operators, whose pilots will take you hovering above metropolitan areas as well as the Sonoran Desert. Some companies offer flights year-round, though most will fly only during the cooler months. Tours last about one hour and are followed by the customary champagne celebration.

Baseball Baseball fans visiting Arizona from late February through early April have a chance to watch major-league teams during spring training. Exhibition games begin in early March, but the eight Cactus League teams start practice at training camps as much as three weeks earlier. The free drills—held in the mornings before the exhibition games—are fun to watch, and there's a good chance you might be able to chat with the players before or after these sessions.

The Phoenix area, with five of the teams' eight stadiums within 30 miles of one another, is the best place to see Cactus League baseball: The **Chicago Cubs** play at Hohokam Park in Mesa (tel. 602/964–4467), the **Oakland Athletics** at Phoenix Municipal Stadium (tel. 602/392–0074), the **San Francisco Giants** at Scottsdale Stadium (tel. 602/990–

7972), the **Seattle Mariners** at Diablo Stadium in Tempe (tel. 602/438–8900), and the **Milwaukee Brewers** at the Compadre Stadium in Chandler (tel. 602/895–1200). The **California Angels** spend their first two weeks at various baseball fields in the valley, depending on which are available, then switch to Angel Stadium in Palm Springs, CA. The **Cleveland Indians** train in Tucson, at Hi Corbett Field (tel. 602/791–4266), and the **San Diego Padres** practice in Yuma at the Desert Sun Stadium (tel. 602/782–2567). In some cases, reserved seats sell out the fall before the season, but you can almost always get general admission seats on the day of the games. For current information on all aspects of Cactus League baseball, contact the **Mesa Convention and Visitor's Bureau** (120 North Center St., Mesa 85201, tel. 602/969–1307).

Bicycling

Cyclists can ride on city streets, desert trails, mountain passes, or the open road. Start off with a bike in good repair, a maintenance kit, a sturdy bicycle helmet, and plenty of water. If you're not used to long-distance cycling, don't push yourself. Begin with short jaunts, and, if desired, work up to longer journeys. A lightweight touring bike and extra-low gears for mountain grades will help you along. Most bicycle shops can provide you with tour guides, tips, and, if you decide to go pro, a current racing schedule. For information on bike paths in the Phoenix area, contact **Maricopa County Parks and Recreation Department** (tel. 602/506–2930).

Boating and Waterskiing

Visitors may be surprised to find so many lakes in this state noted for its desert life. Choices range from secluded, getaway-from-it-all oases to big and boisterous canyon-bound water resorts. The two national recreational areas, Glen Canyon (Lake Powell), in the north-central region, and Lake Mead (including Lake Mohave), in the northwest, offer many facilities, including marinas, launching ramps, and boat and ski rentals. At Lake Powell you can sign up for a paddle-wheeler tour or take the wheel yourself in a fully equipped houseboat. Lake Havasu, fed by the Colorado River in the western part of the state, is another favored site for boating, waterskiing, and jet-skiing; in the background is the rather surreal vision of London Bridge, which was moved block by block from England and reassembled at this lakeside resort.

Saguaro and Canyon lakes, just east of Scottsdale, offer good boating and waterskiing for those based in the Phoenix area who are looking for a convenient day trip.

For further details, contact the **Arizona Office of Tourism** (*see* Visitor Information in Before You Go, *above*).

Other Water Sports

Swimmers can take a cool plunge in a mountain lake, dive into an Olympic-size pool, or splash in the acres and acres of water at one of the recreational megaresorts. Virtually every hotel and motel has a swimming pool of some size, and nearly all Arizona cities have at least one public pool; most are heated, and in the northern region many are indoors. You can cavort in the man-made waves at a number of water parks in the Phoenix area, including Water World and Golfland/Sunsplash (in Mesa), and even **surf** the 3- to 5-foot-high waves at Big Surf in Tempe. Bring your own board, or rent one on site. **Tubing** is a popular sport along the Salt River, east of Mesa. Tubes can be rented, and a shuttle bus will pick up or drop off at any of five points, enabling you to choose the length of your float. When the breezes blow, **sailboats** and **Windsurfers** can be seen on Lakes Mead, Powell, and Havasu, as well as a few of the smaller lakes. Check ahead on availability of rental equipment, or bring your own.

Camping *See* Lodging, *below*.

Canoeing Swift currents without rapids make the daylong Topock Gorge trip on the Colorado River a favorite outing. Beginning at Topock, canoeists travel through a picturesque wildlife refuge to Castle Rock at the top end of Lake Havasu. Another route, made dramatic by the sheer Black Canyon cliffs, is along the Colorado River below Hoover Dam to Willow Beach. Canoe rentals are available at both locations.

Fishing Fish practically jump out of Arizona's cool mountain streams, major rivers, and man-made lakes and are especially plentiful at the Colorado River resorts. Rainbow, brown, brook, and cutthroat trout, as well as catfish, crappie, bass, pike, and bluegill, are the main species. San Carlos Lake is tops for bass fishing.

Fishing licenses are required and can be obtained from the **Arizona Game and Fish Department** (2221 W. Greenway Rd., Phoenix 85023, tel. 602/942–3000).

Golf Your clubs won't gather dust in Arizona. Aside from the big-draw Phoenix and Tucson opens (*see* Festivals and Seasonal Events, *above*), golfers flock to this state to tee off at the myriad top-rank private and municipal courses. The year-round desert courses offer cheaper greens fees during the summer, while those in the northern part of the state usually shut down for winter. Just about every resort has its own course or is affiliated with a private club. For a listing of Arizona's golfing facilities, contact the **Arizona Golf Association** (11801 N. Tatum Blvd., Phoenix 85028, tel. 602/953–5990).

Hiking Hikers can choose from trails that wind through the desert, head over the mountains, delve deep into the forests, or circumnavigate the cities. Whatever your choice of direction, you'll find thousands of miles of marked paths. Protect against sunburn and, if you're hiking in the desert areas, beware of heatstroke. In general, only backcountry hikers need worry about meeting up with poisonous snakes or Gila monsters.

Grand Canyon hikers should be well prepared before starting out. Summer months mean extreme heat, while the winter season can turn alternately snowy, rainy, or sunny. One of the biggest dangers of winter hikes is hypothermia, caused by exposure to cold, wet weather. In summer, hikers to the inner Canyon must head out carrying a gallon of water for each day they plan to hike. There is no shade, so a hat and sunglasses are crucial. It is not advisable to hike any remote area alone. **The Backcountry Information Line** (tel. 602/638–7888) provides hikers with trail details, weather conditions, and packing suggestions.

For hikers who prefer to travel with a group, the **Sierra Club** (tel. 602/267–1649) leads a variety of wilderness treks.

Horseback Riding Traveling by horseback through the somewhat wild West or the scenic high country is perhaps the most appropriate way to explore Arizona. Stables offer a selection of mountain- or desert-trail rides lasting a half day, two days, or as long as two weeks. In the northern regions the season is from May through October. If riding is the focus of your Arizona holiday, however, you might consider staying at a dude ranch where you can saddle up every day.

Hunting Pick your prey from deer, elk, bear, mountain lion, buffalo, and turkey in the north; dove, quail, rabbit, javelina, and other desert critters in the Phoenix area; deer, antelope, javelina, and rabbit in the western and north-central regions; and duck, goose, dove, deer, and rabbit in the south. Be sure to obtain the required permits from the **Arizona Game and Fish Department** (*see* Fishing, *above*), which will also be able to give you information about hunting seasons and permitted areas.

River Rafting Rafting and kayaking trips down the Colorado River and through the Grand Canyon are experiences that keep visitors returning year after year. Trips run from one day to two weeks and operate during the summer season. Other rafting expeditions are offered on the Salt and Verde rivers, through the Sonoran Desert, near Scottsdale. Contact the **Arizona Office of Tourism** (*see* Visitor Information, *above*) for an extensive list of operators.

Rock Hounding Arizona is rock hound heaven, its deserts and mountains laden with a dazzling variety of rocks and minerals. The **Arizona Office of Tourism** (*see* Visitor Information, *above*) produces a free *Arizona Rockhound Guide* that tells you which specimens to look for in each part of the state. Inquire about restrictions before you fill your pockets; taking rocks is illegal on the Navajo and Hopi reservations, for example.

Skiing
Cross-Country Cross-country skiing is featured at Mormon Mountain, southeast of Flagstaff, and along the miles of crisscrossing trails around Payson, Alpine, and Lakeside. Equipment

and instruction are readily available, though it's best to make reservations ahead of time for the high season.

Downhill **Sunrise Ski Resort** in McNary (tel. 602/735–7669), owned and operated by the White Mountain Apache Indians, encompasses three mountain peaks and is the state's largest ski area. Other popular resorts are at **Snow Bowl,** near Flagstaff (tel. 602/779–1951), and **Mt. Lemmon Ski Valley,** near Tucson (tel. 602/576–1400). Ski resorts cater to all levels, from beginning to expert, and provide instruction and equipment rental.

Tennis Arizona offers a multitude of tennis opportunities, from posh resorts to city parks and university campuses. Most hotels either have their own courts or are affiliated with a private or municipal facility. You can contact the local **Parks and Recreation departments** for information on municipal courts.

National and State Parks

National Parks Arizona's two national parks are the granddaddy Grand Canyon National Park (1,218,375 acres) and Petrified Forest National Park (93,533 acres). The **Grand Canyon,** northwest of Flagstaff, has achieved status as one of the Seven Natural Wonders of the World. Travelers come from all parts of the globe to hike, camp, raft, helicopter, or simply ooh and aah at the spectacular views and ever-changing colors, shadows, and light. Facilities include miles of trails, accommodations ranging from comfy rooms to primitive campsites, a comprehensive visitor center, many scheduled activities, knowledgeable park rangers, and an array of organized tours. For further information, contact Grand Canyon National Park (Grand Canyon, AZ 86023, tel. 602/638–7888).

Petrified Forest National Park, east of Flagstaff, features rainbow-colored petrified logs, tree fragments, and chunks of rock—preserved-in-stone remnants of a forest dating from the dinosaur age. Areas with the most petrified wood are Blue Mesa, Jasper Forest, Crystal Forest, Black Forest, and Rainbow Forest. Visitors come mainly to hike forest trails, which also encompass Anasazi village ruins and petroglyphs. It's illegal to collect petrified wood of any kind, but you can buy specimens at local shops. Facilities are limited to a visitor center. Overnight camping is restricted, and permits must be obtained in advance. For further information, contact the Superintendent (Petrified Forest National Park, HC 30, Box 450, Concho AZ 85924, tel. 602/524–6228).

State Parks Arizona's state parks cover wide spectrum, from relatively tiny **Slide Rock** (54 acres), near Sedona, to 13,000-acre **Lake Havasu,** comprising three separate units. Boating and water-sports enthusiasts like to congregate at **Alamo Lake State Park,** north of Wenden, while **Catalina** and **Picacho**

Peak state parks, near Tucson, are the best bets for desert activities. **Painted Rocks State Park,** west of Gila Bend, is distinctive for its Indian rock carvings. Other state parks are the evocatively named **Buckskin Mountain, Dead Horse Ranch,** and **Lost Dutchman,** as well as **Lyman Lake, Patagonia Lake,** and **Roper Lake.** All state parks have hiking trails and, except for Slide Rock, campgrounds. Most have lakes with fishing and boating facilities. For additional information, contact the **Arizona State Parks Department** (*see* Boating and Waterskiing, *above*).

Fragile Life Don't be tempted to pull any of Arizona's century-old saguaro cacti out by the roots. The state flower is protected by law, as are most of the slow-growing desert plants and flowers. Theft or vandalism carries stiff penalties.

Similarly, the dry and easily desecrated desert floor takes centuries to overcome human damage. Consequently, it is illegal for four-wheel-drive and all-terrain vehicles and motorcycles to travel off established roadways.

Indian Reservations

Individual tribes own their respective lands. If you venture off main highways that traverse the reservations, you must request permission from the village leader; any local should be able to direct you. Never take photographs without first asking consent and paying a fee, if required. Visitors are occasionally allowed to watch certain tribal ceremonies, but all cameras, tape recorders, and even sketch pads are forbidden. Remember that you are a guest on private property. If you are planning to make extensive visits to the reservations, contact the **Arizona Office of Tourism** (*see* Visitor Information, *above*) for a map of the Arizona reservations and a list of addresses and telephone numbers of the 14 tribal councils in the state.

Dining

Outside the main cities, Arizona cuisine leans mainly toward western-style steaks, barbecued ribs and beans, biscuits with gravy, and chuck wagon–type fare. The Navajo taco (beans, tomatoes, lettuce, and cheese on Indian fry bread) and a few Hopi recipes served on the reservation blend Native American and Mexican food traditions. Mexican food is plentiful everywhere in the state. Phoenix and Tucson, happily, offer fine Continental dining, an eclectic mix of ethnic eateries, and, most important, the acclaimed southwestern international–style cuisine, featuring indigenous ingredients prepared in an innovative fashion. Make advance reservations at the better restaurants and don't be misled by the casual lifestyle—ask about dress codes first to avoid being turned away at the door. Many establishments, particularly the swank resorts, require men to wear a dinner jacket and tie.

Lodging

Arizona's hotels and motels run the gamut from world-class resorts to budget chains, with historic inns, bed-and-breakfasts, mountain lodges, dude ranches, campgrounds, and RV parks providing even more options. Most nationwide and international companies are represented within the state. Big resorts, such as the Sheraton or Westin, offer extensive recreational and dining facilities, while modest motels may provide nothing more than a small swimming pool and complimentary coffee. Make reservations well in advance for the high season—winter in the desert south and summer in the high country. If you're not fussy about when you travel, tremendous bargains can be found in the off season, when even the ultraswank Ritz-Carlton cuts its rates by half.

Bed-and-Breakfasts Many areas of the state offer European-style B&B lodging, in anything from a country ranch to a city mansion. Moderate prices and personalized, homey hospitality are the hallmarks of this type of accommodation. For complete statewide listings, contact **Mi Casa Su Casa** (Box 950, Tempe 85200, tel. 602/990–0682) or **Bed and Breakfast in Arizona** (Box 8628, Scottsdale 85252, tel. 602/995–2831).

Dude Ranches Down-home western lifestyle, cooking, and activities are the focus of guest ranches, situated primarily in Tucson and Wickenburg. Some are resortlike properties where guests are pampered, while the smaller family-run ranches expect *everyone* to join in the chores. Horseback riding and other outdoor recreational activities are emphasized. Most dude ranches are closed during summer months.

Home Exchange Exchanging homes is a low-cost, relaxing way to enjoy a vacation in another part of the country, especially if you plan a lengthy visit. **Intervac U.S./International Home Exchange** (Box 590504, San Francisco, CA 94159, tel. 415/435–3497 or 800/756–4663) publishes three directories a year. The $45 membership entitles you to one listing and all three directories (there is an additional charge for postage). Including a photo of your property in the directory costs an additional $10, and listing a second home costs $10.

Loan-a-Home (2 Park La., Apt. 6E, Mount Vernon, NY 10552, tel. 914/664–7640), which publishes two directories (in December and June) and two supplements (in March and September) each year, is popular with professors on sabbatical, businesspeople on temporary assignment, and retired people on extended vacations. There is no annual membership fee or charge for listing your home, but one directory and a supplement cost $35. All four books cost $45.

Vacation Exchange Club, Inc. (Box 820, Haleiwa, HI 96712, tel. 800/638–3841) specializes in both international and domestic home exchanges. The club publishes three directories a year—in February, April, and August—and updated and late listings throughout the year. Annual membership, which includes your listing in one book, a newsletter, and copies of all publications (mailed first-class) is $50.

Camping and Campgrounds Campers can choose from a feast of federal, state, Indian, or private campgrounds in virtually all parts of the state. Facilities range from deluxe parks with swimming pools and recreation rooms to primitive backcountry wilderness sites. The majority of campgrounds provide toilets, drinking water, showers, and hookups. Camping is also permitted in Arizona's seven national forests, but be forewarned that there are no facilities whatsoever.

Campers should pack according to season, region, and length of trip. Basic gear should include a sleeping bag, a tent (optional, and forbidden in some RV parks), a camp stove, cooking utensils, food and water supplies, a first-aid kit, insect repellent, sunscreen, a lantern, rubbish disposal bags, a rope, and a tarp. In case you forget something, almost every camping item is available for sale or rent at one of Arizona's many sporting-goods shops.

Individual campgrounds should be contacted before travel for suggestions as to specific equipment to bring, as well as necessary reservations, advance deposits, and permits. Most state parks have a 15-day maximum-stay limit. For further details, contact the **Arizona Office of Tourism** or the appropriate tribal council (*see* Visitor Information in Before You Go, *above*), **National Park Service** (202 E. Earll Dr., Suite 115, Phoenix 85012, tel. 602/640–5250), **Bureau of Land Management** (3707 N. 7th St., Phoenix 85014, tel. 602/640–5547), **Arizona State Parks Department** (*see* Boating and Waterskiing, *above*), **Apache Sitgreaves National Forest** (Box 640, Springerville 85938, tel. 602/333–4301), **Coconino National Forest** (2323 E. Greenlaw La., Flagstaff 86004, tel. 602/556–7400), **Coronado National Forest** (Federal Bldg., 300 W. Congress St., Tucson 85701, tel. 602/670–6483), **Kaibab National Forest** (800 S. 6th St., Williams 86046, tel. 602/635–2681), **Prescott National Forest** (344 S. Cortez, Prescott 86303, tel. 602/445–1762), or **Tonto National Forest** (Box 5348, Phoenix 85010, tel. 602/225–5200). The **National Forest Service hotline** (tel. 602/225–5296) gives recorded information and campground updates.

Credit Cards

The following credit card abbreviations have been used: AE, American Express; D, Discover; DC, Diners Club; MC, MasterCard; V, Visa.

2 Portraits of Arizona

The What and the Why of Desert Country

By Joseph Wood Krutch

On the brightest and warmest days my desert is most itself because sunshine and warmth are the very essence of its character. The air is lambent with light; the caressing warmth envelops everything in its ardent embrace. Even when outlanders complain that the sun is too dazzling and too hot, we desert lovers are prone to reply, "At worst that is only too much of a good thing."

Unfortunately, this is the time when the tourist is least likely to see it. Even the winter visitor who comes for a month or six weeks is mostly likely to choose January or February because he is thinking about what he is escaping at home rather than of what he is coming to here. True, the still warm sun and the usually bright skies make a dramatic contrast with what he has left behind. In the gardens of his hotel or guest ranch, flowers still bloom and some of the more obstreperous birds make cheerful sounds, even though they do not exactly sing at this season. The more enthusiastic visitors talk about "perpetual summer" and sometimes ask if we do not find the lack of seasons monotonous. But this is nonsense. Winter is winter even in the desert.

At Tucson's 2,300 feet it often gets quite cold at night even though shade temperatures during the day may rise to 75° Farenheit or even higher. Most vegetation is pausing, though few animals hibernate. This is a sort of neutral time when the desert environment is least characteristically itself. It is almost like late September or early October, just after the first frost, in southern New England. For those who are thinking of nothing except getting away from something, rather than learning to know a new world, this is all very well. But you can't become acquainted with the desert itself at that time of year.

By April the desert is just beginning to come into its own. The air and the skies are summery without being hot; the roadsides and many of the desert flats are thickly carpeted with a profusion of wildflowers such as only California can rival. The desert is smiling before it begins to laugh, and October or November are much the same. But June is the month for those who want to know what the desert is really like. That is the time to decide once and for all if it is, as for many it turns out to be, "your country."

It so happens that I am writing this not long after the 21st of June and I took especial note of that astronomically significant date. This year summer began at precisely 10 hours and no minutes, Mountain Standard Time. That means that the sun rose higher and stayed longer in the sky than on any other day of the year. In the north there is often a considerable lag in the seasons as the earth warms up, but here, where it is never very cold, the longest day and the hottest are likely to coincide pretty closely. So it was this year. On June 21 the sun rose almost to the zenith so that at noon he cast almost no shadow. And he was showing what he is capable of.

Even in this dry air 109° Fahrenheit in the shade is pretty warm. Under the open sky the sun's rays strike with an almost physical force, pouring down from a blue dome unmarked by the faintest suspicion of even a fleck of cloud. The year has been unusually dry even for the desert. During the four months just past no rain—not even a light shower—has fallen. The surface of the ground is as dry as powder. And yet, when I look out of the window the dominant color of the landscape is incredibly green.

On the low foothills surrounding the steep rocky slopes of the mountains, which are actually 10 to 12 miles away but seem in the clear air much closer at hand, this greenness ends in a curving line following the contour of the mountains' base and inevitably suggesting the waves of a green sea lapping the irregular shore line of some island rising abruptly from the ocean. Between me and that shore line the desert is sprinkled with hundreds, probably thousands, of evenly placed shrubs, varied now and then by a small tree—usually a mesquite or what is called locally a cat's-claw acacia.

More than a month ago all the little annual flowers and weeds which spring up after the winter rains and rush from seed to seed again in six weeks gave up the ghost at the end of their short lives. Their hope of posterity lies now invisible, either upon the surface of the bare ground or just below it. Yet when the summer thunderstorms come in late July or August, they will not make the mistake of germinating. They are triggered to explode into life only when they are both moist and cool—which they will not be until next February or March when their season begins. Neither the shrubs nor the trees seem to know that no rain has fallen during the long months. The leathery, somewhat resinous, leaves of the dominant shrub—the attractive plant unattractively dubbed "creosote bush"—are not at all parched or wilted. Neither are the deciduous leaves of the mesquite.

Not many months ago the creosote was covered with bright yellow pealike flowers; the mesquite with pale yellow catkins. Now the former is heavy with gray seed and on the mesquite are forming long pods which Indians once ate and which cattle now find an unusually rich food.

It looks almost as though the shrubs and trees could live without water. But of course they cannot. Every desert plant has its secret, though it is not always the same one. In the case of the mesquite and the creosote it is that their roots go deep and that, so the ecologists says, there is in the desert no wet or dry season below six feet. What little moisture is there is pretty constant through the seasons of the year and through the dry years as well as the wet. Like the temperature in some caves, it never varies. The mesquite and creosote are not compelled to care whether it has rained for four months or not. And unlike many other plants they flourish whether there has been less rain or more than usual.

Those plants which have substantial root systems but nevertheless do not reach so deep are more exuberant some years than others. Thus the Encelia, or brittlebush, which, in normal years, literally covers many slopes with thousands of yellow, daisylike flowers, demands a normal year. Though I have never seen it fail, I am told that in very dry years it comes into leaf but does not flower, while in really catastrophic droughts it does not come up at all, as the roots lie dormant and hope for better times. Even the creosote bush, which never fails, can, nevertheless, profit from surface water, and when it gets the benefit of a few thunderstorms in late July or August, it will flower and fruit a second time so that the expanse which is now all green will be again sprinkled with yellow. . . .

Obviously the animals and plants who share this country with me take it for granted. To them it is just "the way things are." By now I am beginning to take it for granted myself. But being a man I must ask what they cannot: What *is* a desert and why is it what it is? At latitude 32 one expects the climate to be warm. But the desert is much more than merely warm. It is a consistent world with a special landscape, a special geography, and, to go with them, a special flora and fauna adapted to that geography and that climate.

Nearly every striking feature of this special world, whether it be the shape of the mountains or the habits of its plant and animal inhabitants, goes back ultimately to the grand fact of dryness—the dryness of the ground, of the air, of the whole sum-total. And the most inclusive cause of the dryness is simply that out here it doesn't rain very much.

Some comparisons with regions where it rains more may help us understand what that means. Take, for example, southern New England. By world standards it gets a lot—namely some 40 inches of rain per year. Certain parts of the southern states get even more: about 50 inches for east Tennessee, nearly 60 for New Orleans. Some areas on the West Coast get fantastic amounts, like the 75 inches at Crescent City, California, and the unbelievable 153 inches, or nearly four times what New York City gets, recorded one year in Del Norde County, California.

Nevertheless, New England's 40 is a lot of water, either comparatively or absolutely. The region around Paris, for instance, gets little more than half that amount. Forty inches is, in absolute terms, more than most people imagine. One inch of rain falling on an acre of ground means more than 27,000 gallons of water. No wonder that irrigation in dry regions is quite a formidable task even for modern technology.

In terms of what vegetation can use, 40 inches is ample for the kind of agriculture and natural growth which we tend to think of as "normal." It means luxuriant grass, rapid development of second growth woodland, a veritable jungle of weeds and bushes in midsummer. In inland America the rainfall tends to be less than in the coastal regions. As one moves westward from the Mississippi it declines sharply and begins to drop below 20 inches a year at about the one hundredth meridian or, very roughly, at a line drawn from Columbus, Ohio through Oklahoma City. This means too little water for most broad-leaved trees and explains why the southern Great Plains were as treeless when the white man first saw them as they are today.

Our true deserts—the Great Basin Desert in Utah and Nevada, the Chihuahuan in New Mexico, the Sonoran in Arizona, and the Mohave in California—all lie still further to the west. The four differ among themselves but they are all dry and hot and they all fulfill what is probably the most satisfactory definition of "desert"—namely a region where the ground cover is not continuous; where, that is, the earth remains bare of vegetation between such plants as manage to grow. Over these American deserts the rainfall varies considerably and with it the character and extent of the vegetation. In southern Arizona, for instance, it is about four inches at Yuma, nearly 11 near Tucson. Four inches means sand dunes which look like those pictures of the Sahara which the word "desert" calls to most people's minds. Eleven means that where the soil is suitable, well-separated individuals of such desert plants as the cacti and the paloverde trees will flourish.

But if scanty rainfall makes for deserts, what makes for scanty rainfall? To that there are two important answers. One is simply that most regions other than the mountainous ones tend to be dry if they lie in that belt of permanently high atmospheric pressure which extends some 30 or 35 degrees on each side of the equator where calms are frequent and winds erratic. Old sailors used to call this region "the horse latitudes" though nobody knows why and you can take your choice of three equally unconvincing explanations. One is that it was because horses tended to die when the ships lay long in the hot calms. Another, because the boisterous changeableness of the winds when they do come suggests unruly horses. A third is that they were originally called after the English explorer, Ross, which was mistaken by the Germans for their old word for "horse." In any event, the latitude of Tucson puts it just within the "horse latitudes." Most of the important deserts of the world, including the Sahara and the Gobi, lie within this same belt.

The other important answer to the question, "What makes for scanty rainfall?" is, "Mountains lying across the path of such moist winds as do blow." In our case the Coast Ranges of California lie between us and the Pacific. From my front porch, which looks directly across the desert to some nearer mountains of the southernmost Rockies, I can see, on a small scale, what happens. Many, many times a moisture-laden mass of air reaches as far as these closest mountains. Dark clouds form, sometimes the whole range is blotted out. Torrential rains are falling. But on me not a drop. Either the sky is blue overhead or the high clouds which have blown my way dissolve visibly as the warm air rising from my sun-drenched flats reaches them. I am in what the geographers call a "rain shadow" cast by the mountains. Up at their summit the rainfall is nearly twice as much as it is down here and they are clothed with pines beginning at 6,000 or 7,000 feet and going on up to the 19,000-foot peak. When I do get rain in midwinter and in midsummer, it is usually because winds have brought moisture up from the Gulf of Mexico by an unobstructed southern route, or because in summer a purely local thundershower has been formed out of the hot air rising from the sun-beaten desert floor. Most of the time the sun is hot, even in winter, and the air is usually fantastically dry, the relative humidity being often less than 10.

Naturally the plants and animals living in such a region must be specially adapted to survive under such conditions, but the casual visitor usually notices the strangeness of the landscape before he is aware of the flora or the fauna. And the peculiar features of the landscape are also the result of dryness, even in ways that are not immediately obvious.

The nude mountains reveal their contours, or veil them as lightly as the late Greek sculptors veiled their nudes, because only near the summits of the mountains can anything tall enough to obscure the outlines grow. A little less obvious is the fact that the beautiful "monuments" of northern Arizona and southern Utah owe their unusual forms to the sculpturing of wind-blown sand, or that sheer cliffs often rise from a sloping cone of rocks and boulders because the talus slopes can accumulate in just that way only where there is not enough draining water to distribute them over the whole surrounding plain, as they would be distributed in regions of heavier rainfall. But the most striking example of all is the greatest single scenic wonder of the region, the Grand Canyon itself. This narrow gash, cut a mile deep through successive strata until the river flows at last over some of the oldest rock exposed anywhere on earth, could have been formed only in a very dry climate.

As recently as 200 years ago the best informed observer would have taken it for granted that the river was running between those sheer walls at the bottom of the gorge simply because it had found them out. Today few visitors are not aware that the truth lies the other way around, that the river cut its own course through the rock. But most laymen do not ask the next questions: Why is Grand Canyon unique, or why are such canyons, even on a smaller scale, rare? And the answer to those questions is that a set of very special conditions was necessary.

First there must be a thick series of rock strata slowly rising as a considerable river flows over it. Second, that considerable river must carry an unusual amount of hard sand or stone fragments in suspension so that it will be able to cut downward at least as rapidly as the rock over which it flows is rising. Third, that considerable river must be flowing through very arid country. Otherwise rain, washing over the edges of the cut, will widen it at the top as the cut goes deeper. That is why broad valleys are characteristic of regions with normal rainfall; canyons, large and small, of arid country.

And Grand Canyon is the grandest of all canyons because at that particular place all the necessary conditions were fulfilled more exuberantly than at any other place in the whole world. The Colorado River carries water from a relatively wet country through a dry one, it bears with it a fantastic amount of abrasive material, the rock over which it flows has been slowly rising during several millions of years, and too little rain falls to widen very rapidly the gash which it cuts. Thus in desert country everything from the color of a mouse or the shape of a leaf up to the largest features of the mountains themselves is more likely than not to have the same explanation: dryness.

So far as living things go, all this adds up to what even an ecologist may so far forget himself as to call an "unfavorable environment." But like all such pronouncements this one doesn't mean much unless we ask "unfavorable for what and for whom?" For many plants, for many animals, and for some men it is very favorable indeed. Many of the first two would languish and die, transferred to some region where conditions were "more favorable." It is here, and here only, that they flourish. Many men feel healthier and happier in the bright dry air than they do anywhere else. And since I happen to be one of them, I not unnaturally have a special interest in the plants and animals who share my liking for just these conditions. For five years now I have been amusing myself by inquiring of them directly what habits and what adjustments they have found most satisfactory. Many of them are delightfully ingenious and eminently sensible. . . .

Men of most races have long been accustomed to speak with scorn of the few peoples who happen to live where nature makes things too easy. In the inclemency of their weather, the stoniness of their soil, or the rigors of their winter they find secret virtues so that even the London fog has occasionally found Englishmen to praise it. No doubt part of all this is mere prejudice at worst, making a virtue out of necessity at best. But undoubtedly there is also something in it. We grow strong against the pressure of a difficulty, and ingenious by solving problems. Individuality and character are developed by challenge. We tend to admire trees, as well as men, who bear the stamp of their successful struggles with a certain amount of adversity. People who have not had too easy a time of it develop flavor. And there is no doubt about the fact that desert life has character. Plants and animals are so obviously and visibly what they are because of the problems they have solved. They are part of some whole. They belong. Animals and plants, as well as men, become especially interesting when they do fit their environment, when to some extent they reveal what their response to it has been. And nowhere more than in the desert do they reveal it.

Arizona Crafts

By Suzanne Carmichael

Suzanne Carmichael is the author of The Traveler's Guide to American Crafts: East of the Mississippi and West of the Mississippi *and travel and craft articles for such publications as* The New York Times, USA Weekend, *and* Northwest Magazine.

Whether you have $10 or $1,000 to spend, shopping for crafts can make your trip to Arizona memorable, and not only for what you'll take home with you. The pursuit of local wares may take you down desert roads to remote crafts studios, introduce you to snazzy urban galleries and historic trading posts, or involve you in lively crafts festivals. Regional crafts also provide an intimate introduction to an area's history, culture, and peoples, as well as its contemporary interests and trends.

In the Southwest, several cultures have developed strong crafts traditions, some predating European contact by more than 1,000 years. Native American, cowboy, and contemporary crafts—many made from native materials or by capturing local colors, themes, and spirit—are all well developed in this region.

Native American Crafts

Arizona visitors will see Native American crafts everywhere—in specialty shops, airports, motel gift shops, drugstores, and even gas stations. The problem is finding top-notch authentic work. Some so-called Native American crafts are made in Taiwan or Mexico. Others labeled "genuine Indian made" are mass-produced with shoddy material and inferior workmanship.

If you haven't read any books on the subject, study Native American collections at the Heard Museum (Phoenix) or the Museum of Northern Arizona (Flagstaff). These museums also have their own gift shops, which sell good-quality items at reasonable prices. Long-established trading posts, galleries, and Native American dealers are another option. Most first-rate shops will have a range of prices and knowledgeable salespeople who can answer your questions. If everything in a shop is inexpensive, it's probably attributable to the poor quality of the goods rather than to a low overhead. It's a good idea to shop elsewhere.

One way to ensure authenticity and at the same time add an adventurous detour to your trip is to buy directly from craftspeople on the reservations. Look for signs that say "pottery," "rugs," or "baskets" hanging outside homes. Although visiting craftspeople is not a guarantee of quality, it does provide an opportunity to ask questions and learn about the work you are purchasing. And it's fun to watch artisans at work, to see their raw materials being turned into finished pieces.

Reservation gift shops are another option for authentic wares, although quality and prices vary tremendously. And crafts are generally sold at Native American festivals, fairs, and powwows (ceremonial gatherings), which exhibit the work of many artisans and also showcase tribal dancing, story-telling, and food. One recommended event is Flagstaff's annual six-week Festival of Native American Arts held each summer at the Coconino Center for the Arts (2300 N. Valley Rd., U.S. 180, Flagstaff, AZ, tel. 602/779–6921). This juried festival offers high-quality traditional and contemporary tribal arts, including work rarely found elsewhere, such as colorful Pueblo moccasins and miniature pottery. Visitors can also watch jewelry-making, cloth- or basket-weaving demonstrations or participate in various workshops, including one that teaches children how to make Native American masks.

Arizona's Native American crafts legacy includes distinctive tribal arts made by many of the state's 14 tribes. Although the work of the Hopi, Navajo, and Tohonó O'odham (Papago) are best known, equally fine items are produced by the Chemehuevi, Maricopa, Mojave, Paiute, and Pima tribes.

Hopi pottery, baskets, and weaving reflect ancient traditions and techniques, while the tribe's silverwork is of more recent vintage. Artisans of the Hopi tribe live on the reservation's three mesas, each one of which has a craft specialty. First Mesa is home to potters who fashion hand-coiled vessels with pale cream or deep red glazes decorated with stylized birds and figures. Second Mesa's specialty is baskets of thickly coiled yucca joined with colorfully dyed lengths of yucca leaves; wicker baskets decorated with brightly colored designs can be found on Third Mesa. When buying pottery and baskets, look for symmetrical shapes, smooth rims, and neatly painted or evenly woven designs.

Tribal artisans also create kachina dolls, colorfully costumed, masked figures embellished with feathers, textiles, and leather. Modeled after the Hopi religion's kachina ceremonial dancers, the dolls are used to teach children their religious heritage. Hopi weaving, which is done exclusively by men, creates colorful sashes and narrow decorative bands that are used on clothing. Both of these items are woven on belt looms. The vertical threads (warp) on these unusual looms stretch around one rod tied to a tree to another rod held taut by a belt wrapped around the weaver's waist. While making a sash, the weaver leans forward to loosen the warp, backward to tighten it. Although Hopi woven fabric is created primarily for personal use, some pieces are occasionally available through the reservation's crafts cooperative.

Hopi silverwork, a craft that was begun in the late 1890s, reflects a creative collaboration between contemporary silverworking techniques and ancient motifs. Hopi silversmiths use two layers of silver to create some of the Southwest's finest jewelry. Designs, which range from simple sun shapes to those depicting elaborate tribal legends, are carefully cut through the top layer, which is then soldered to the bottom layer. Tiny parallel lines are chiseled inside the design, and the piece is then oxidized to make the motif stand out from the polished silver surrounding it. The best pieces have smoothly cut patterns with neatly stamped, parallel interior lines.

Navajo jewelry traces its origin to the mid-19th century. Tribal craftsmen learned smithing from Mexican artisans, later adding their own styles and designs. Early pieces were made from hammered silver coins and decorated with stamp work. Although turquoise beads date from prehistoric times, Navajos did not combine the stone with silver until the late 1800s. Today, in addition to turquoise, artisans sometimes incorporate coral, lapis, and other semiprecious stones into their designs.

Contemporary Navajo jewelry ranges from simple rings and cast silver bracelets to massive necklaces and concha belts (named for the stamped silver disks strung together on narrow leather strips). Because there are so many variables in the quality of stones and workmanship, you should purchase Navajo jewelry only from reputable dealers. Many Indian traders and jewelry shops throughout the Southwest have one case displaying items of Native American–made jewelry that have been pawned and not retrieved by their owners. Although you can occasionally find older pieces of exquisite quality in these cases, be leery of assertions as to an item's age or caliber.

Navajos are also known for the variety and quality of their woven wool rugs. Sheepherders for centuries, Navajos learned their weaving skills from Pueblo Indians during the 18th century. At first they produced blankets and clothing in natural brown-and-white stripes. During the late 19th century, colors, particularly red, and a wide range of complex designs were added. At this time, most weavers also switched from producing items for personal use to creating rugs for traders. Today Navajo rug patterns range from traditional eye dazzlers with bold zigzag patterns and pictorials featuring animals and other figures to yei rugs that duplicate sand-painting designs and two-faced rugs with different patterns on each surface.

If you purchase a Navajo rug, make sure that it is made entirely of wool (no linen or cotton threads), that the wool is of even thickness throughout the piece, that the design is neatly woven, and that the colors are uniform throughout. A good source of Navajo rugs and other Native American crafts is the Hubbell Trading Post, a National Historic Site in Ganado, on the Navajo reservation 22 miles west of Window Rock. Established in 1878, the post looks exactly as it did in the 19th century when Navajos brought John Lorenzo Hubbell their rugs and jewelry to trade for groceries and other goods. These artisans still bring their crafts for sale or trade, but now they arrive in pickups instead of on horseback.

While Hopi and Navajo crafts are the best-known Arizona Native American arts, other tribes also produce good-quality items that provide an introduction to their cultural history. Among these are traditional Tohonó O'Odham (Papago) baskets. Tohonó O'Odham artisans create coiled, waterproof baskets with intricate designs using techniques and materials that have remained virtually unchanged for more than 11 centuries. Most baskets are broad, slightly sloping vessels with geometric patterns and are made from two Southwest desert plants. Black designs, the most highly prized, are fashioned from black devil's claw, an increasingly rare plant that yields very strong strips of jet-black fiber. Red motifs are woven with the root of banana yucca, a more common plant found in Arizona's higher elevations. One traditional Tohonó O'Odham design is the legendary Man in the Maze, a stylized male figure standing at the top of the basket, about to enter a complex white-and-black labyrinth.

Baskets are also made by the Pima and Paiute. The Pima use coils of cattail stems bound with willow and favor complex zigzag designs. Traditional Paiute baskets have plain, functional shapes, reflecting the fact that they were once used to carry water, harvest or store seeds, and cradle babies. Mojave, Maricopa, and Chemehuevi tribal arts are more difficult to find, but they are worth the effort. Mojave beadwork can be exquisite, especially large, collar-shape necklaces created in traditional network designs resembling intricate lace. Maricopa artisans specialize in cream-colored pottery, decorated with black designs that incorporate both geometric shapes and curvilinear symbols. Finely woven Chemehuevi baskets, another rare but exquisite craft, are made from coiled fiber, sometimes decorated with colorful feathers.

Cowboy Crafts

Even if you don't own horses or cattle, consider buying cowboy crafts: They can add pizzazz to your decor or an unusual flair to your wardrobe and provide an intriguing diversion as you watch them being created by talented artisans.

Arizona ranchers may use computers to keep track of their businesses, but no one has devised the technology to replace cowboys. Although his (and sometimes her) job may include time in a pickup, the daily routine is still dominated by horses, cattle, and traditional equipment rarely influenced by 20th-century innovations. The items cowboys use every day—from saddles and spurs to bridles and hats—form a crafts tradition that spans centuries. Some items originated with Native Americans, while others were adopted from Mexican or California-Spanish traditions.

Arizona cowboy crafts can be found in many shops, and even in department stores, but it's more fun to buy them directly from craftspeople or in tack shops that sell everything a horse and its rider need, from saddles to cowboy hats. Look in telephone books under tack shops, horse furnishings, or specific crafts such as saddlery or hats. For a thorough immersion, attend Flagstaff's annual 5½-week Trappings of the American West Festival, sponsored by the Coconino Center for the Arts; it runs from early May until the second week of June. The festival includes cowboy crafts demonstrations and workshops where you can learn rawhide braiding and bootmaking.

Although cowboy crafts are often decorative, they are first of all functional tools of the trade. Hats protect the wearer from weather, branches, and rocks and double as containers for carrying water and feed. Boots, designed to be pulled off easily and fit comfortably in stirrups, protect feet from mud and brush. Chaps shield the legs from prickly cactus and other hazards. The brush in Arizona is particularly heavy, so cowboys here prefer Arizona bell-bottom chaps made from very heavy leather that is flared at the bottom so they bend with the leg. The best of each? Hats made from beaver-fur felt, custom-made boots, and used chaps with that trail-worn look.

Saddles, which are custom-made to fit horse and rider, are often covered with carved or stamped designs of elaborate floral and leaf motifs. Some cowboys claim that deep carving keeps them from slipping in the saddle. For urban cowpokes, many saddlemakers create stamped or carved leather purses, belts, wallets, and even wastebaskets.

The oldest cowboy craft is leather and horsehair braiding. Conceived by Native Americans, braiding was later adopted by Mexican and American cowboys. Complex patterns decorate braided horse gear, from bridles and reins to other items whose exotic names belie their practicality: bosals and hobbles, romals and quirts. Look also for braided hatbands, belts, and bracelets.

Other cowboy accoutrements include bits and spurs with ornate inlaid designs that are seen only by the cowboy and his horse. Texas cowboys generally favor massive inlaid silver stars and geometric patterns, while California and Arizona cowboys prefer gear embellished with flowers and flourishes. Many smiths also fashion decorative silverwork for saddles, as well as buckles, money clips, and jewelry. Knives, another cowboy necessity, can be found in great variety. Look for those with handles that are made from exotic materials, engraved, or inlaid with precious metal and stones.

Contemporary Crafts

Arizona's contemporary artisans work in every medium, but particularly in ceramics, textiles, and wood. Although the focus of their work varies from abstract to functional, many of the crafts reflect Arizona colors: the splashy hues of a desert sunset, the subtle pastels of cactus flowers, the myriad reds of Sedona's cliffs. There's also a healthy dose of humor in many items: prickly ceramic cactus vases, howling wood dogs, flirty roadrunner sculptures, chairs with coyote armrests. The use of native materials is also common—for example, you may come across cactus-spine baskets or mesquite armoires.

Phoenix, Scottsdale, and Tucson offer a bonanza of contemporary crafts galleries. On a smaller scale, Tubac, an artists' community 35 miles south of Tucson, has numerous crafts studios open to the public. Tubac artisans create everything from avante-garde jewelry and textiles to copper fountains shaped like cacti. To find galleries throughout Arizona, consult *Art Life,* two comprehensive guides (one covers northern Arizona, the other southern Arizona) that describe galleries, provide detailed maps, and include indexes arranged by style, subject, and medium. Available free in many Arizona galleries, the guides can also be ordered by calling Yoakum Publishing (tel. 602/797–1271).

3 Grand Canyon Country and Lake Mead

By William E. Hafford

Updated by Edie Jarolim

Although millions of words have been devoted to describing the Grand Canyon, writers have generally conceded that the Earth's greatest gorge is beyond the scope of language. Southwestern author Frank Waters has come closer than most to capturing its power. "It is the sum total," he writes, "of all the aspects of nature combined in one integrated whole. It is at once the smile and frown upon the face of nature. In its heart is the savage, uncontrollable fury of all the inanimate Universe, and at the same time the immeasurable serenity that succeeds it. It is Creation."

To appreciate the Grand Canyon, you must see it. Not even the finest photographs pack a fraction of the impact of a personal glimpse of this vast and beautiful scar on the surface of our planet—277 miles long, 17 miles across at its widest spot, and more than a mile below the rim at its deepest point. Designated one of the Seven Natural Wonders of the World, the Grand Canyon is the quintessence of the high drama of the American western landscape.

More than 65 million years ago, a great wrenching of the earth pushed the land in the region of the canyon up into a domed tableland, today called the Colorado Plateau. Then the Colorado River, racing south through present-day Utah, began chewing at the uplifted region. The river is responsible for much of the erosion, but many side gullies and canyons were formed by melting snow and fierce rainstorms that sent water rushing into the gorge through smaller tributaries. Softer rock formations were washed away by the Colorado and carried to the distant sea; the harder formations remained as great cliffs and buttes.

The twisted and contorted layers of rock reveal a geologic profile of the Earth. The oldest exposed rock on the planet—more than 2 billion years old and formed as part of the Earth's original crust—is the Vishnu Schist at the bottom of the canyon. Today, what remains above the twisting line of river are otherworldly stone monuments with colors that range from muted pastels to deep purples, vibrant yellows, fiery reds, and soft blues. The colors shift with the hours: What you see at midmorning is repainted by the setting sun.

This is also a land of ancient peoples. In some of the deepest and most inaccessible reaches of the Grand Canyon, evidence of early human habitation exists. Stone ruins high in the cliffs reveal the archaeological secrets of a culture more than 4,000 years old. In the higher country above the rims, both north and south, are the ruins of the Anasazi, who remained in the area until about AD 1200. It is believed that they left the region during a period of harsh and sustained drought. Today's Hopi Indians, who live on high rock mesas about 150 miles east of the canyon, may be descendants of that tribe.

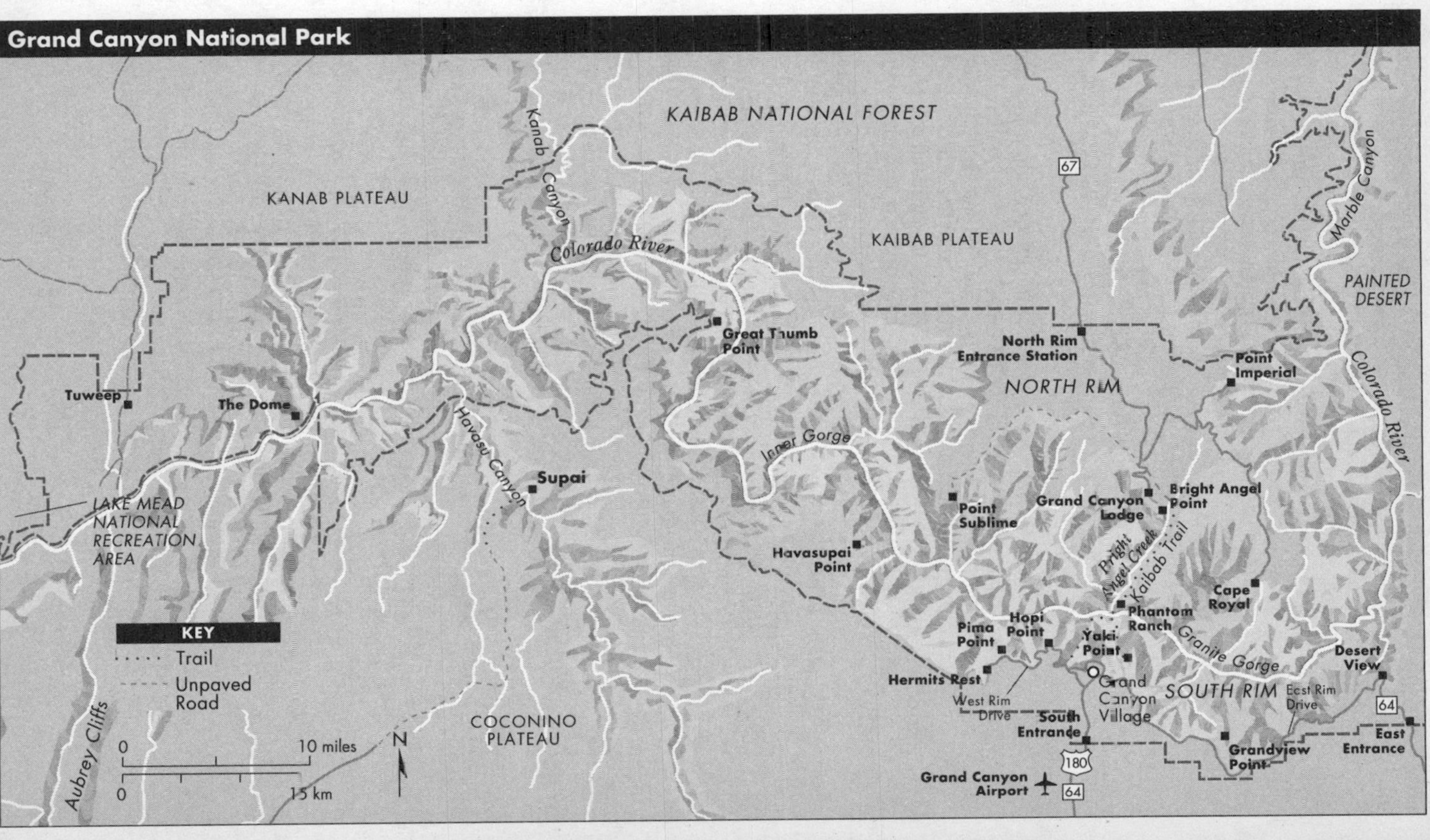
Grand Canyon National Park
KAIBAB NATIONAL FOREST
KANAB PLATEAU
KAIBAB PLATEAU
Kanab Canyon
Colorado River
67
Marble Canyon
PAINTED DESERT
Great Thumb Point
North Rim Entrance Station
Point Imperial
NORTH RIM
Colorado River
Tuweep
The Dome
Havasu Canyon
Supai
Inner Gorge
LAKE MEAD NATIONAL RECREATION AREA
Point Sublime
Grand Canyon Lodge
Bright Angel Point
Bright Angel Creek
Kaibab Trail
Havasupai Point
Cape Royal
Phantom Ranch
Pima Point
Hopi Point
Yaki Point
Granite Gorge
Desert View
Hermits Rest
West Rim Drive
Grand Canyon Village
SOUTH RIM
East Rim Drive
64
South Entrance
East Entrance
Grandview Point
180
Grand Canyon Airport
64
KEY
Trail
Unpaved Road
Aubrey Cliffs
0
10 miles
0
15 km
N
COCONINO PLATEAU

In the year 1540, a small group of Spanish soldiers under the command of Captain García López de Cárdenas became the first white men to look into the canyon. The members of the expedition, dispatched by Francisco Coronado to find an Indian village, were disinclined to stay very long—or to return. Spanish Franciscan missionary and explorer Tomás Garcés visited a Havasupai Indian village in the canyon in 1776, and Lieutenant Joseph Ives went on an official mission for the U.S. government to explore the area in 1857, but no one thought it worth much attention until 1869, when John Wesley Powell, a one-armed adventurer and scholar, put rough-hewn boats into the Colorado and let the swirling white water of the mighty river take him its length.

During the last years of the 19th century, almost all development at or near the canyon was related to mining. In fact, the earliest trails down into the canyon were built by miners searching for precious minerals. Shortly after the beginning of the 20th century, the Santa Fe Railroad completed a line to the South Rim of the canyon, ushering in the era of tourism. In 1903 Theodore Roosevelt visited and drew public interest to the site; it was declared a national park in 1919. Today nearly 4 million visitors come each year from around the world to peer into this gorge in amazement.

The Fred Harvey Company opened the world-famous El Tovar Hotel on the rim of the canyon in 1905, heralding the beginning of Grand Canyon Village. Now there are more than 850 motel and hotel rooms in Grand Canyon Village, but the ever-increasing visitor population makes even that number of accommodations insufficient during the summer months. If you can arrange it, try to visit the Grand Canyon in the fall or spring. You might encounter cold weather during those periods, but chances are good that most of the days will be clear and will range from pleasantly cool to warm. In autumn and spring, when the crowds have thinned, reservations are much easier to arrange, and, in some cases, prices drop. Or consider a winter visit. The snow on the ground only enhances the site's sublime beauty.

The North Rim, in the isolated Arizona Strip, draws only about 10% of the Grand Canyon's visitors but is every bit as gorgeous as the South Rim. From southern Arizona, there's only one highway into this area, 210 miles of lonely road to the north and west of Flagstaff. Set in deep forest near the 9,000-foot crest of the Kaibab Plateau, the North Rim is, for many visitors, worth the extra miles. But truth to tell, there's virtually no place along either rim or in the depths of the Grand Canyon that will fail to startle and impress you.

Essential Information

Important Addresses and Numbers

Tourist Information **Grand Canyon National Park Lodges** (Box 699, Grand Canyon 86023, tel. 602/638–2401), for lodging and all other tour and recreational information inside the park at the South Rim.

Grand Canyon National Park (Box 129, Grand Canyon 86023, tel. 602/638–7888), for general information.

Grand Canyon Lodge (Box 400, Cedar City, UT 84720, tel. 801/586–7686), for lodging and general information about the North Rim year-round. For information on local services during the season in which the North Rim is open (generally mid-May through late October, depending on the weather), you can phone the lodge directly (tel. 602/638–2611).

Every arriving visitor at the South or North Rim is given a detailed map of the local area. Both rims also publish a free newspaper, *The Guide*, which contains a detailed area map; it is available at the visitor center and many of the lodging facilities and stores.

The park also distributes a free *Accessibility Guide* newsletter, which details the facilities available for those with special needs.

Emergencies **Police, fire,** or **ambulance** (tel. 911).

Medical *South Rim* **Grand Canyon Health Center** (Grand Canyon Village, tel. 602/638–2551) offers physician services and receives patients weekdays 8–5:30, Saturday 9–noon. After-hours care and emergency services are also available. Dental care (tel. 602/638–2395) is offered by appointment only.

North Rim The **North Rim Clinic** (Grand Canyon Lodge, tel. 602/638–2611) is staffed by a nurse practitioner. The clinic is generally open weekdays 9–5, but 24-hour emergency service is available.

Pharmacies At the South Rim there is a well-stocked drugstore at Grand Canyon Village (tel. 602/638–2551), open weekdays 8:30–5:30. There is no pharmacy at the North Rim.

Road Service *South Rim* At Grand Canyon Village, the **Fred Harvey Garage** (tel. 602/638–2631) is a fully equipped service station and AAA garage that provides auto and RV repair, 24-hour emergency service, and propane and diesel fuel.

North Rim The **Chevron** service station (tel. 602/638–2611), offering auto repairs, is located inside the park on the access road leading to the North Rim Campground. No diesel fuel is available at the North Rim.

Food and Camping Supplies
South Rim

Babbitt's General Store (tel. 602/638–2262) has three locations in the South Rim area: at Grand Canyon Village, in the nearby village of Tusayan, and at Desert View near the east park entrance. The main store, in Grand Canyon Village, is a department store that offers a deli and a full line of camping, hiking, and backpacking supplies, in addition to groceries.

North Rim

The **North Rim General Store** (tel. 602/638–2611), located within the park and in the vicinity of the North Rim Campground, carries groceries, some clothing, and travelers' supplies.

Banks

An office of the **Valley National Bank** (tel. 602/638–2437) is located at the South Rim across from the visitor center in Grand Canyon Village. Services include a 24-hour teller machine operating with Valley National Bank, American Express, Plus (Visa), Star, Arizona Interchange Network, and Cirrus (MasterCard) access cards. The bank cashes traveler's checks and exchanges foreign currency, but does not cash personal checks. Banking hours are weekdays 10–3. No banking facilities are located within Grand Canyon National Park at the North Rim.

Arriving and Departing by Plane

Because most of Arizona's scenic highlights are many miles apart, an automobile is the most practical mode of transportation for touring the state. However, you won't really need a car if you're planning to visit only the Grand Canyon's most popular area, the South Rim. Many people choose to fly to the Grand Canyon and then hike, catch a shuttle or taxi, or sign on for bus tours or mule rides in Grand Canyon Village.

Airports

McCarran International Airport in Las Vegas (tel. 702/739–5743) is the primary air hub for flights to **Grand Canyon National Park Airport** (tel. 602/638–2446). You can also make connections into the Grand Canyon from **Sky Harbor International Airport** in Phoenix (tel. 602/273–3300). Ground transportation and air-shuttle service (*see* By Air Shuttle and By Taxi, *below*) are available from the Grand Canyon Airport either to Grand Canyon Village or to the small tourist community of Tusayan, 6 miles from the South Rim.

Airlines

The many carriers that fly to the Grand Canyon from Las Vegas include **Air Nevada** (tel. 800/634–6377), **Air Vegas** (tel. 702/736–9351), **Lang Air Service** (tel. 702/736–0031), **Las Vegas Airlines** (tel. 800/634–6851), **Las Vegas Fliers** (tel. 702/736–4554), **King Air** (tel. 702/798–0400), and **Scenic Airlines** (tel. 800/634–6801).

Twice-daily flights from Phoenix to Grand Canyon Airport are available through **Arizona Pacific Airways** (tel. 602/445–4405). Phoenix Sky Harbor Airport is served by virtually all of the major U.S. commercial airlines (*see* Chapter 6, Phoenix and Central Arizona).

Between the Airport and Grand Canyon Village/Tusayan
By Air Shuttle

Two commercial shuttle services operate between Grand Canyon Airport and the nearby towns of Tusayan and Grand Canyon Village. The **Tusayan/Grand Canyon Shuttle** (tel. 602/638–2475) makes hourly runs daily between 8:15 AM and 5:15 PM, with additional trips during the summer months. A day pass for unlimited trips costs $7 for adults and $5 for children under age 12; if you're only going one way, the cost is $4 for adults, $3 for children under 12. Children under age 6 travel free. Those with large families might consider the $20 family pass, which allows unlimited travel back and forth throughout the day. **Direct Shuttle** (tel. 602/638–2789) has unscheduled services from the airport to Tusayan and Grand Canyon Village, as well as between other points in the Grand Canyon area, but operates more like a taxi service.

By Taxi

Fred Harvey Transportation Company (tel. 602/638–2822 or 602/638–2631) offers 24-hour taxi service at Grand Canyon Airport, Grand Canyon Village, and the nearby village of Tusayan; taxis also make trips to other destinations in and around Grand Canyon National Park.

Transportation Services

During the summer, transportation services desks are maintained at **Bright Angel Lodge, Maswik Lodge,** and **Yavapai Lodge** in Grand Canyon Village; in winter only the desk at Bright Angel Lodge is open. The desks provide information and handle bookings for taxi and bus service, mule and horseback rides, Phantom Ranch (at the bottom of the Grand Canyon), and sightseeing tours. These are geared primarily to in-person visits, but you can call (tel. 602/638–2631) for additional information.

Arriving and Departing by Train or Bus

By Train

Amtrak (tel. 800/USA–RAIL) provides daily service into Arizona from both the east and west, with its most convenient stop (for Grand Canyon access) at Flagstaff. From Flagstaff, bus connections can be made for the final leg of the trip to the South Rim through **Nava-Hopi Tours** (tel. 602/774–5003).

An alternative way to complete your journey is a scenic rail trip: Take Amtrak to Williams, then continue to the Grand Canyon on an old but beautifully restored steam train on the Grand Canyon Railway (*see* Guided Tours, *below*). Currently, the trip from Flagstaff to Williams is by bus and is included in the price of the Amtrak train ticket, but negotiations for a direct rail link to Williams were in progress as we went to press.

By Bus

Greyhound/Trailways Lines provides bus service from all points in the United States to Flagstaff or Williams, both considered gateway communities to the Grand Canyon. To obtain Greyhound/Trailways travel information, use the number provided under the Greyhound/Trailways listing in your local yellow pages. This will connect you with the firm's national information center in Omaha, Nebraska.

From either Flagstaff or Williams, bus service to the South Rim of the Grand Canyon is offered by **Nava-Hopi Tours** (tel. 602/774–5003).

Getting Around

By Car If you are traveling into Arizona by car from the east, or coming up from the southern part of the state, your best access to the Grand Canyon is from Flagstaff. You can take U.S. 180 northwest (81 miles) to Grand Canyon Village on the South Rim. Or, for a scenic route with stopping points along the canyon rim, drive north on U.S. 89 from Flagstaff, then turn left at the junction of AZ 64 (52 miles north of Flagstaff) and proceed west for an additional 57 miles.

To visit the North Rim of the canyon, proceed north from Flagstaff on U.S. 89 to Bitter Springs, then take U.S. 89A to the junction of AZ 67, which leads to the North Rim, a distance of approximately 210 miles from Flagstaff.

If you are crossing Arizona on I–40 from the west, your most direct route to the South Rim is on AZ 64 (U.S. 180), which runs north from Williams for 58 miles to Grand Canyon Village.

Keep in mind that summer traffic leading to the South Rim can be quite heavy and, at times, congested in the vicinity of Grand Canyon Village and the various parking areas along the rim. If you visit from October through April, you should experience only light to moderate traffic in the vicinity of the canyon. The more remote North Rim, which reaches elevations of more than 7,000 feet, has no services available from late October through mid-May; the road is open for day use only until the first heavy snowfall of the year, at which point the roads close until spring. The South Rim stays open to auto traffic all year, though access to the West Rim is restricted during the summer because of overcrowded roads.

Rental Cars It's a good idea to make reservations in advance, particularly during the summer months. Be sure to ask about weekly rates and unlimited mileage opportunities.

Major companies serving Phoenix and Flagstaff include **Avis** (tel. 800/331–1212), **Budget** (tel. 800/527–0700), **Dollar** (tel. 800/800–4000), **Hertz** (tel. 800/654–3131), and **National** (tel. 800/227–7368). Budget and Dollar are located at Grand Canyon Airport.

By Shuttle Bus Free shuttle service offered by the **National Park Service** (tel. 602/638–7888) runs from Grand Canyon Village to Hermits Rest and Yaki Point, popular viewing areas on the

South Rim. Generally, this service, which runs approximately every 15 minutes from 6:30 AM to 6:45 PM, is available only in the summer. Also under the aegis of the National Park Service, CTS runs a year-round shuttle that takes hikers from the Backcountry Reservations Office (across from the Visitors Center), Maswik Lodge, and Bright Angel Lodge to South Kaibab Trailhead at Yaki Point; the price is $3, and there are two departures every morning. Check for times upon arrival. **Trans Canyon Van Service** (tel. 602/638–2820), a South Rim to North Rim shuttle, leaves from Bright Angel Lodge each summer day at 1:30 PM and arrives at the North Rim at about 6 PM; the return from Grand Canyon Lodge is at 7 AM, with arrival at the South Rim at about 11:30 AM. The fare is $50 each way ($85 round-trip).

Guided Tours

By Train The Grand Canyon Railway began running from Williams to the South Rim of the Grand Canyon in 1989, offering a modern version of a route that was first established in 1901. The railroad had been out of operation since 1968, but an $85 million restoration put the old steam engines and Pullman cars back in business. The ride from the renovated station in Williams, which takes about 2½ hours each way, features refreshments, commentary, and corny but fun onboard entertainment. Even if you don't take the train, stop by the Williams Depot, built in 1908. Attractions here include the locomotive and passenger car of a turn-of-the-century steam train; a small but interesting railroad museum (admission free); and a gift shop where you can find such kitschy souvenirs as a tie that plays "I've Been Working on the Railroad." *518 E. Bill Williams Ave., Williams 86046, tel. 800/THE–TRAIN. Fare: Round-trip, $54.81 adults, $31.35 children under 13; one-way, $45.08 adults, $24.86 children; for children and teens traveling with adults on the family plan, children pay half regular child fare and teens (13–19) pay approximately half adult fare. Departure from Williams June–Dec., daily 9:30 AM, return 6:30 PM; Wed.–Sun. Mar.–May and Oct.; limited schedule (generally Fri.–Sun.) Nov.–Feb.*

By Plane Flights over the Grand Canyon by airplane or helicopter are offered by a number of companies operating either from Grand Canyon Airport or from heliports in Tusayan. **Air Grand Canyon** (tel. 602/638–2618), **Grand Canyon Airlines** (tel. 800/528–2413), and **Windrock Aviation** (tel. 602/638–9591) fly small planes, while **Air Star Helicopters** (tel. 602/638–2622 or 800/962–3869), **Grand Canyon Helicopters** (tel. 602/638–2419 or 800/528–2418 outside AZ), and **Kenai Helicopters** (tel. 602/638–2412) operate whirlybirds. Prices and length of flights vary greatly with tours, but start at about $50 for short flights originating from Grand Canyon Airport. Inquiries and reservations can be made at any Grand

Canyon lodge transportation desk (*see* Transportation Services, *above*).

By Bus A free **shuttle bus service** is offered by the National Park Service (*see* By Shuttle Bus in Getting Around, *above*) in the South Rim area. This does not provide a guided tour, but you can get a good feel for the region by taking advantage of trips through Grand Canyon Village, Yavapai Museum, and Hermits Rest on the West Rim. In addition, the **Fred Harvey Transportation Company** (tel. 602/638–2822 or 602/638–2631) in Grand Canyon Village provides a veritable menu of daily motorcoach sightseeing trips along the South Rim and to destinations as far away as Monument Valley on the Navajo reservation. Prices range from $11 for the short trips to $70 for all-day tours. Children's half-price fares apply to those under 16 for in-park tours, under 12 on the longer out-of-park tours. For schedules, call the South Rim reservations number (tel. 602/638–2401) or inquire at any transportation desk (*see* Transportation Services, *above*).

By Mule Mule trips down the precipitous trails to the inner gorge of the Grand Canyon are nearly as well known as the canyon itself. But, especially for the summer season, it's very hard to get reservations unless you make them months in advance; write Reservations Department (Box 699, Grand Canyon 86023, tel. 602/638–2401). These trips have been conducted since the early 1900s, and no one has ever been killed by a mule falling off a cliff. Nevertheless, the treks are not for the faint of heart or people in questionable health. Riders must be at least 4 feet 7 inches tall, weigh less than 200 pounds, and understand English; they cannot be visibly pregnant. The all-day ride to Plateau Point costs $85 (lunch included). An overnight with a stay at Phantom Ranch at the bottom of the canyon is $255.25 ($457.50 for two) for one night, $352.75 ($599.50 for two) for two nights; meals are included in these prices.

Weather

Weather information and road conditions for both the North and South rims can be obtained by calling 602/638–7888.

In general, the South Rim, with an elevation of 7,000 feet, has summer temperatures ranging from lows in the 50s to highs in the upper 80s. There are frequent afternoon thunderstorms. Winter temperatures have average lows of around 20°F and average highs near 50°F, with the mercury occasionally dropping below zero. In spring and fall, temperatures generally stay above 32°F and often climb into the 70s. The North Rim, accessed through country that ranges in altitude from 8,000 to 9,000 feet, gets heavy winter snows and thus is open to the public only from mid-May through October. Temperatures during this open season go from lows in the 30s to highs in the 70s. It frequently rains in the afternoon; in May and October, it occasionally snows as well. As you proceed down either rim into the canyon toward the inner gorge, temperatures rise. In the summer, along the Colorado River at an elevation of about 2,400 feet, temperatures range from lows in the 70s to highs above 100°F. Winter sees lows in the 30s, highs around 50. It rarely snows at the bottom of the Grand Canyon, even in winter; the snow on the rims usually turns to rain as it falls into the inner gorge.

Telephones

It's often hard to get through to the Grand Canyon: The trunk lines into the area are limited and often overloaded with people calling this most popular of Arizona's attractions. You'll get a fast busy signal if this is the case. In addition, when you do get through to the National Park Service or South Rim Reservations numbers—which handle many of the services listed in this chapter—you'll have to punch a lot of numbers on a computer-voice system before you reach the service you want.

Safety Tips

Be careful when you or your children are near the edge of the canyon or walking any of the trails that descend into it. Guard rails exist only on portions of the rims. Infrequently, but tragically, visitors have been killed in falls from viewing points. Before engaging in any strenuous exercise, be aware that the canyon rims are more than 7,000 feet in altitude. Being at this height can cause some people to get dizzy or faint. Before hiking down into the canyon, assess the distance of the proposed hike against your physical condition. Descending into the canyon is not especially difficult, but going back up can be very strenuous. Be sure to take water on hikes into the canyon. During summer months, temperatures in the inner gorge can climb above 105°F.

Entrance Fees

The fees levied by the National Park Service vary depending on your method of entering Grand Canyon National Park. If you arrive by automobile, the fee is $10, regardless of the number of passengers. Individuals arriving by public conveyance (bus, taxi, or train) pay $4. The entrance gates are open 24 hours a day but are generally supervised from about 7 AM until 6 PM. If you arrive when there's no one at the gate, you may enter legally without paying.

Exploring the Grand Canyon

Both the South Rim and the North Rim areas of the Grand Canyon were established as recreational and sightseeing enclaves under the direction of the National Park Service. Unfortunately, most of Grand Canyon Village at the South Rim was laid out before the Park Service existed, so the area is not well prepared to accommodate the large crowds that converge on the area every summer (and, increasingly, throughout the spring and fall as well). Still, there are routes for escape everywhere, and the most trafficked spots are popular for good reason: You'll quickly forget that there's anyone nearby as you turn your gaze toward the vast abyss.

There are two ways to discover the canyon: walking or driving along the rim (Tours 1–6) and hiking down into its depths (*see* Hiking in Sports and Outdoor Activities, *below*). The first view of the canyon will stay with you a lifetime. But the truth is, after a half-dozen lookouts, one's sense of wonder begins to diminish. The problem is that it's impossible to establish a personal relationship with so much grandeur. Traveling along the rim, the visitor easily tires of putting his or her nose up against this beauty and safely, almost antiseptically, peering in. By all means stop along the rim, but we can't encourage you strongly enough to take a walk, however brief, into the canyon itself. Bright Angel Trail is easier, the South Kaibab Trail steeper but more spectacular. A 20-minute walk into the maw of this abyss will open up a totally new perspective, and permit you to develop a personal relationship with the canyon that is unattainable at the rim.

Highlights for First-time Visitors

South Rim Country

Bright Angel or Kaibab Trails (*see* Tours 2 and 3)
Desert View and The Watchtower (*see* Tour 2)
El Tovar Hotel (*see* Tour 3)
Hermits Rest Overlook (*see* Tour 4)
Lookout Studio (*see* Tour 3)
Powell Memorial (*see* Tour 4)
Visitor Center (*see* Tour 1)
Yavapai Museum (*see* Tour 2)

North Rim Country

Cape Royal (*see* Tour 6)
Grand Canyon Lodge and Bright Angel Point (*see* Tour 6)
Marble Canyon (*see* Tour 5)
Vermilion Cliffs (*see* Tour 5)

Tour 1: Approaching the South Rim

Numbers in the margin correspond to points of interest on the South Rim: Tours 1 and 2 map.

Because the approach to the South Rim of the Grand Canyon is across the relatively level surface of the 7,000-foot Coconino Plateau, you won't see the great gorge until you're practically at its edge. **Mather Point** gives you your first glimpse of the canyon from one of the most impressive and accessible vista points on the rim; it's easily reached from Grand Canyon National Park's east entrance (on AZ 64) or from the south entrance (on AZ 180). If you're arriving from the east, you might be tempted to stop at Desert View, just inside the park, but we suggest that you save this and other vista points on the eastern approach for a later East Rim tour (*see* Tour 2, *below*).

1 Located on the outskirts of Grand Canyon Village, **Mather Point** is approximately 24 miles from the east entrance and 4 miles from the south entrance. Whether you enter the park from the east or south, you'll arrive at the junction of AZ 64 and AZ 180. Proceed in the direction of Grand Canyon Village for less than a mile, and you'll see a large parking area with a sign for Mather Point.

This overlook of the canyon, named for the National Park Service's first director, Stephen Mather, affords an extraordinary view of the inner gorge of the canyon and of numerous buttes that rise out of the eroded chasm: Wotan's Throne, Brahma Temple, Zoroaster Temple, and many others. The Grand Canyon Lodge, on the North Rim, is almost directly north from Mather Point and only 10 miles away—yet you have to drive nearly 210 miles to get from one spot to the other.

After your first view of the canyon, proceed into Grand
2 Canyon Village, and stop in at the **National Park Service's visitor center,** which has something for even the most independent traveler. Not only does the center orient you to many facets of the site (history, geology, and sightseeing), but it's also an excellent place for gathering information, whether about escapist hikes or group tours. At the visitor center, you'll get an intriguing profile of the area's natural and human history. The region's first inhabitants were probably the Paleo Indians, who lived here more than 11,000 years ago. Their culture gave way to the Archaic culture. Artifacts from this civilization are on display: perfectly preserved figurines of animals, made more than 4,000 years ago from willow twigs and found in caves deep in the canyon. Sometime after AD 1, the Anasazi culture flourished, but it disappeared in about AD 1200. Exhibits give glimpses of some of the more than 2,000 Anasazi sites that have been discovered in the Grand Canyon area, including many deep within the canyon. The museum also traces the arrival of the early Spanish explorers, including Captain

The South Rim: Tours 1 and 2

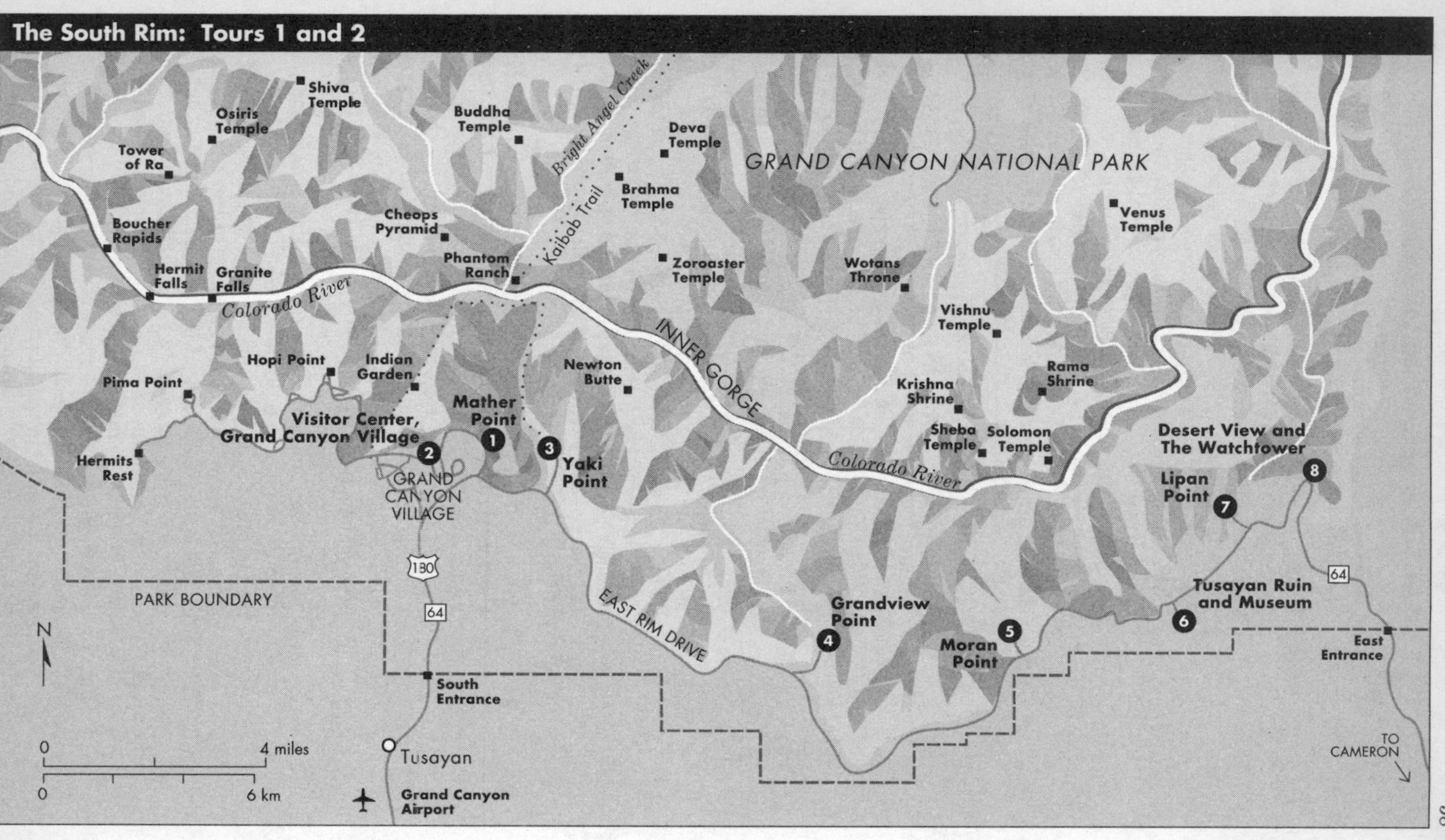

García López de Cárdenas, leader of the first expedition of white men to see the Grand Canyon (1540), and of John Wesley Powell, an American who was the first person to travel through the canyon by boat. The various crafts that have navigated the white-water rapids of the Colorado River are on display.

The visitor center also presents short movies and slide shows on the canyon, and there is a bookstore that offers a wide variety of printed matter, videotapes, and slides. Park rangers are on hand to answer questions and aid in planning Grand Canyon excursions. The center also has a schedule for ranger-guided walks along the South Rim. *East side of Grand Canyon Village, about 1 mi east of El Tovar Hotel, tel. 602/638–7888. Admission free. Open Memorial Day–Labor Day, daily 8 AM–8:30 PM; the rest of the year, daily 8–5.*

Tour 2: East Rim

This breathtaking drive on the East Rim proceeds east for about 25 miles along the South Rim from Grand Canyon Village to Desert View. Before beginning the drive, consider stopping to see the exhibits and attend the free minilectures offered by park naturalists at Yavapai Museum, three-quarters of a mile east of the visitor center. There are four signed picnic areas along the route, and rest rooms at Tusayan Museum and Desert View.

3 To get to **Yaki Point,** the first stop on the tour, from the village, head east to the junction of AZ 180 and AZ 64. Turn onto AZ 64 and continue east. From this vantage point, look to the northeast for an exceptional view of Wotan's Throne, a majestic flat-topped butte named by François Matthes, a U.S. Geological Survey scientist who developed the first topographical map of the Grand Canyon. Due north is Buddha Temple, capped by limestone; Newton Butte, with its flat top of red sandstone, lies to the east. At Yaki Point the popular Kaibab Trail starts the canyon descent to the inner gorge, crosses the Colorado over a steel suspension bridge, and wends its way to rustic Phantom Ranch, the only lodging facility at the bottom of the Grand Canyon. You might take this opportunity to hike a short distance down the Kaibab Trail, just to get a feel for a descent into the canyon. If you plan to go more than a mile, travel by water (*see* Hiking in Sports and Outdoor Activities, *below*). If you encounter a mule train, be aware that the animals have the right-of-way. Move to the inside of the trail and wait as they pass.

4 About 7 miles east of Yaki Point, **Grandview Point,** at an altitude of 7,496 feet, supports large stands of ponderosa pine, piñon pine, oak, and juniper. The view from here is one of the finest in the canyon. To the northeast is a group of dominant buttes, including Krishna Shrine, Vishnu Temple, Rama Shrine, and Shiva Temple. A short stretch of the Col-

orado River is also visible. Directly below the point and accessed by an unmaintained trail (*see* Hiking in Sports and Outdoor Activities, *below*), is Horseshoe Mesa, where you can see ruins of the Last Chance Copper Mine. Grandview Point was also the site of the Grandview Hotel, constructed in the 1890s but closed in 1908; logs salvaged from the hotel were used for the roof of the Desert View Watchtower (*see below*).

5 The next overlook is about 5 miles east at **Moran Point,** named for American landscape artist Thomas Moran, who painted Grand Canyon scenes from many points on the rim but was especially fond of the play of light and shadows from this location; he first visited the canyon with John Wesley Powell in 1873. Moran's vivid canvases helped convince Congress to create a national park at the Grand Canyon. This is also a favorite spot for photographers.

Three miles east of Moran Point on the south side of the
6 highway is the entrance to **Tusayan Ruin and Museum,** which offer evidence of early habitation in the Grand Canyon and information about the lifestyles of the Anasazi people (circa AD 1–1200). The partially intact rock dwellings here were occupied for perhaps 20 years by a group of about 30 Indian hunters, farmers, and gatherers. They left suddenly, driven to a new location, archaeologists believe, by a severe drought. The museum and bookstore feature artifacts, models of the Anasazi dwellings, and exhibits on more modern tribes of the region. *Tel. 602/638–2305. Admission free. Open Memorial Day–Labor Day, daily 8–6; rest of the year, daily 9–5.*

7 **Lipan Point,** 1 mile east of Tusayan Ruin, is the canyon's widest point. From here you can get an astonishing visual profile of the gorge's geologic history, with a view of every eroded layer of the canyon.

8 **Desert View and The Watchtower** offer a climactic final stop. At 7,500 feet, Desert View is the highest point along the tour, and the vista is spectacular. If you climb to the top of the 70-foot stone-and-mortar Watchtower, built in 1932 by the Fred Harvey Company in the style of Southwest Indian structures, you can see the muted pastel hues of the distant Painted Desert to the east and the 3,000-foot-high Vermilion Cliffs rising from a high plateau near the Utah border. You also get an extraordinary glimpse of the upper reaches of the canyon as it angles away to the north toward Marble Canyon, and at this point an impressive stretch of the Colorado River reveals itself. The Watchtower houses a glass-enclosed observatory with powerful telescopes, as well as galleries decorated with reproductions of ancient Indian pictographs, and a curio shop where paintings by contemporary Indian artists are sold. *Watchtower tel. 602/638–2736, trading post tel. 602/638–2360. Admission free, but there is a 25¢ charge to climb The Watchtower. Open Apr.–Aug., daily 8–8; Sept.–Mar., daily 9–5.*

Tour 3: The Village Rim

Numbers in the margin correspond to points of interest on the South Rim: Tours 3 and 4 map.

This is a fairly short walking tour (about 1 mile round-trip) over level ground via a paved pathway that runs along the
9 rim. The **Hopi House** is a good place to begin (if you're driving, leave your car at the nearby El Tovar parking lot). This multistoried structure of rock and mortar was modeled after buildings found in the Hopi village of Oraibi, Arizona, the oldest continualy inhabited community in the United States. Part of an attempt by the Fred Harvey Company to encourage Southwest Indian crafts at the turn of the century, Hopi House was established as one of the first curio stores in the Grand Canyon. It has the air of a museum, with some artifacts too priceless to sell today, but it remains one of the best-stocked gift shops in the vicinity (*see* Shopping, *below*).

A few yards to the west of Hopi House is the most renowned
10 hotel in the nation's National Park System, the historic **El Tovar Hotel.** Built in 1905 to resemble the great hunting lodges of Europe, this massive log structure underwent a major renovation in early 1991, but it retains the ambience of its early days. If the weather is cool, stop in front of the massive stone fireplace to warm your hands. The rustic lobby, with its numerous stuffed and mounted animal heads, is a great place for people watching.

From El Tovar, return to the rim and pick up the trail heading
11 west toward **Lookout Studio.** Built in 1914 as a lookout point, the Pueblo-style building was later used as a photography studio. Today it's a combination lookout point, museum, and gift shop, featuring an extensive collection of geologic samples from around the world as well as many fossil specimens. An upstairs loft provides another excellent overlook into the mighty gorge below.

12 Not many yards to the west of Lookout Studio is **Bright Angel trailhead,** the starting point for perhaps the best-known of all the trails that descend to the bottom of the canyon. It was originally a bighorn sheep path and was later used by the Havasupai Indians; in 1890–91 it was widened for prospectors trying to reach mining claims in the canyon. Today Bright Angel Trail is a well-maintained avenue for mule and foot traffic. If you intend to go very far—the trail descends 4,460 feet to the Colorado River—you should be prepared with proper shoes, clothing, equipment, and water (*see* Hiking in Sports and Outdoor Activities, *below*); discuss your intentions with the park service representatives at the visitor center before you go.

Bright Angel Trail is the turnaround point on this short walking tour. If you'd like to go farther west, see Tour 4: West Rim, South Rim, below. From Bright Angel Trail,

The South Rim: Tours 3 and 4

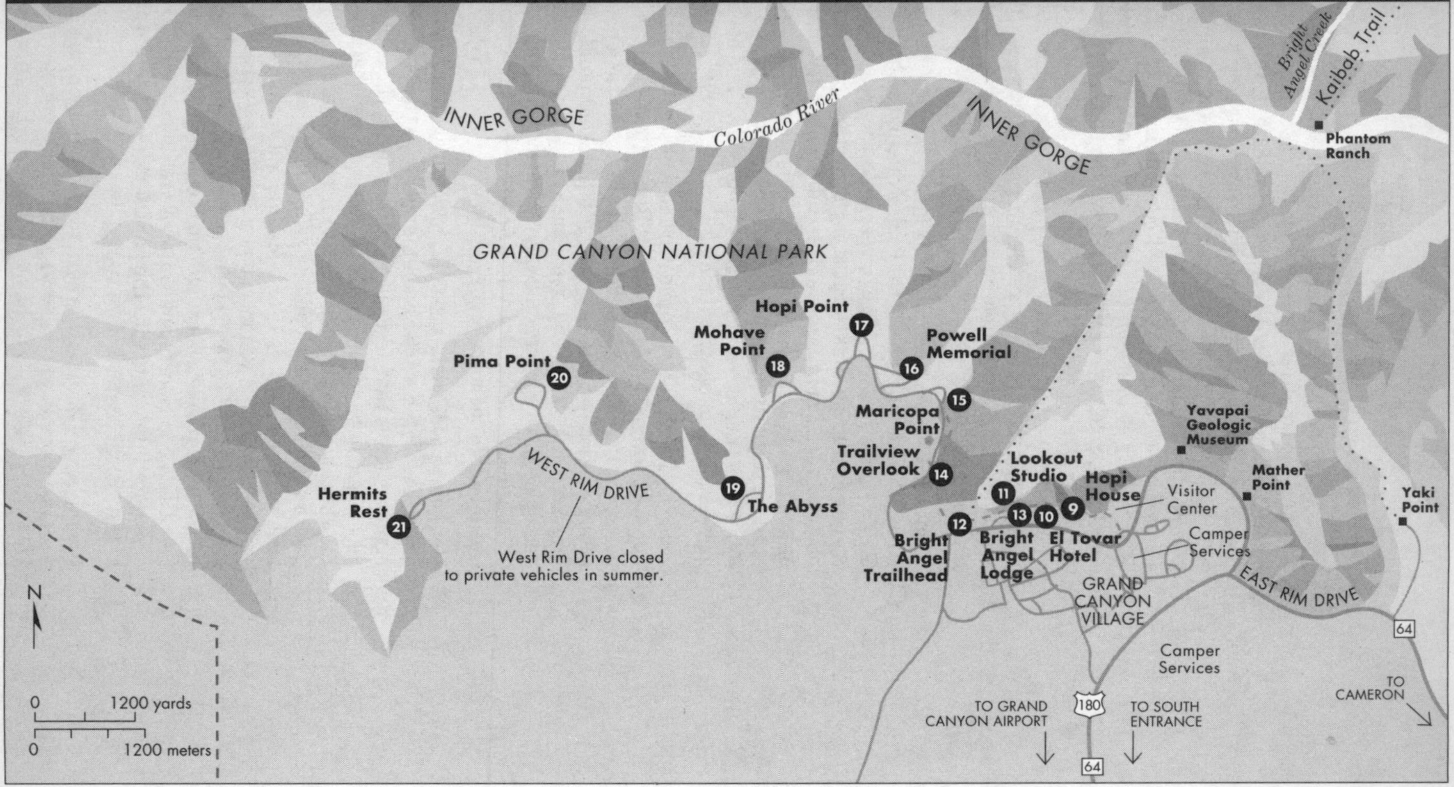

walk directly east rather than returning to the rim trail.
You'll pass the barn that houses some of the tour mules; it's
worth a brief stop, especially if children are along. Contin-
13 ue east to **Bright Angel Lodge,** which was built in 1935 of
logs and native stone, with rustic cabins set away from the
main building. It's another good place to people watch, especially in the area of the "geologic" fireplace, made of regional rocks arranged in the order in which they arelayered
in the Grand Canyon. A history room displays memorabilia
from early years at the South Rim.

Time Out For light snacks—sandwiches, ice-cream dishes, and soft drinks—try the **Soda Fountain** in the Bright Angel Lodge. *Tel. 602/638-2401. Open May–Sept., daily 11–9.*

From Bright Angel Lodge, take the village road back to your parking spot near El Tovar.

Tour 4: West Rim Drive

This tour cannot be made by car in the summer months; at that time the West Rim Road is closed to auto traffic because of congestion. From Memorial Day weekend to October 1, a free shuttle bus makes most of the stops on the described itinerary (*see* By Shuttle Bus section in Getting Around, *above*).

Originally called the Hermit Rim Road, the **West Rim Drive** was constructed by the Santa Fe Company in 1912 as a scenic tour route. Cars were banned on the road because they frightened horses pulling the open-topped touring stages. West Rim Drive today offers 10 scenic overlooks spread out over 8 miles (one-way). Consider covering half on the first leg of the trip and the others on the way back; there's easy access to the lookout points from both sides of the road.

Start out at **Bright Angel Lodge** and head west for about a
14 mile until you come to **Trailview Overlook.** If you turn and
look away from the canyon toward the south, you'll have a
wonderful, unobstructed view of the distant San Francisco
Peaks, Arizona's highest mountains (the tallest is 12,633
feet), as well as of Bill Williams Mountain (on the horizon)
and Red Butte (about 15 miles south of the canyon rim). As
its name suggests, this overlook also affords a dramatic
view of the Bright Angel and Plateau Point trails as they
zigzag down the canyon. In the deep gorge to the north
flows Bright Angel Creek, one of the few permanent tribu-
tary streams of the Colorado River in the region.

15 **Maricopa Point,** about seven-tenths of a mile from Trailview, merits a stop not only for the arresting scenery, which features a clear view of the Colorado River below, but also for its towering headframe of an early Grand Canyon mining operation. On the rim to your left, as you face the canyon, are the Orphan Mine and, in the canyon below, a

mine shaft and cable lines leading up to the rim. The copper ore in the mine, which started operations in 1893, was of excellent quality, but the cost of removing it from the canyon finally brought the venture to a halt.

About a half-mile beyond Maricopa Point, the large granite
16 **Powell Memorial** stands as a tribute to the first man to ride the wild rapids of the Colorado River through the canyon in 1869. John Wesley Powell, a one-armed Civil War hero and explorer, measured, charted, and named many of the canyons and creeks of the river. It was here that the dedication ceremony for Grand Canyon National Park took place on April 3, 1920.

17 From **Hopi Point** (elevation 7,071 feet), a half-mile down the road, you can see a large section of the Colorado River; although it appears as a thin line from here, the river is nearly 350 feet wide below this overlook. Across the canyon to the north is Shiva Temple, which, until 1937, remained an isolated section of the Kaibab Plateau. In that year, Harold Anthony of the American Museum of Natural History led an expedition to the rock formation in the belief that it supported life that had been cut off from the rest of the canyon. Imagine the expedition members' surprise when they found an empty Kodak film box on top of the temple.

18 On a windless day on **Mohave Point,** four-fifths of a mile to the west, it is possible to hear the roaring din of water crashing over Hermit Rapids on the floor of the canyon. Granite and Salt Creek rapids can also be seen from this point.

19 **The Abyss,** 1 mile farther, is one of the most awesome stops on this tour, revealing a sheer canyon drop of 3,000 feet to the Tonto Plateau in the gorge below. From this spot, you'll also see several impressive isolated sandstone columns, the largest of which is called The Monument.

20 **Pima Point,** 3 miles away, provides a bird's-eye view of the Tonto Platform and the Tonto Trail, which wends its way through the canyon for more than 70 miles. If you look down on the plateau toward the west, you may be able to see the foundations of an old tourist camp built in the first decade of the century and used until 1930. Also to the west, two dark, cone-shaped mountains—Mt. Trumbull and Mt. Logan—are visible on clear days. They rise in stark contrast to the surrounding flat-topped mesas and buttes.

21 **Hermits Rest,** the westernmost viewpoint, and the Boucher Trail that descends from it (*see* Hiking in Sports and Outdoor Activities, *below*) were named for the "hermit" Louis Boucher, a 19th-century prospector who had a number of mining claims and a roughly built home down in the canyon. Canyon views from here include Hermit Rapids and the towering cliffs of the Supai and Redwall formations. The stone building at Hermits Rest sells curios and refresh-

ments and provides the only rest rooms on the West Rim tour.

Tour 5: The Drive to North Rim

Numbers in the margin correspond to points of interest on the North Rim: Tours 5 and 6 map.

This tour is not an option during the winter, when heavy snows close highway access to, and facilities in, the North Rim.

This long excursion—about 210 miles, whether you start out from Grand Canyon Village on the South Rim of the canyon or from Flagstaff—is the best way to get to the North Rim and offers plenty to see along the way. It begins at the
22 **Cameron Trading Post,** on U.S. 89, 1 mile north of the junction with AZ 64 (which you will be on if you're coming from Grand Canyon Village) and 53 miles north of Flagstaff. Founded in 1916, this historic trading post, one of the few remaining in the Southwest, has an extensive stock of Native American jewelry, rugs, baskets, and pottery. Most of the items sold here are made by nearby Navajo and Hopi artisans, but some are created by New Mexico's Zuni and Pueblo Indians.

Time Out At the **Cameron Trading Post** restaurant (tel. 602/679–2231) you can enjoy American food that ranges from light snacks to complete dinners; if you're a hearty eater, order the huge Navajo tacos, Indian fry bread heaped with cheese, chopped meat, guacamole, and salad. You can get a sandwich and soft drink for under $6, complete meals for under $12.

The route north on U.S. 89 affords a wide and unobstructed
23 view of the **Painted Desert** off to the right. The desert, which covers thousands of square miles and extends far to the south and east, is a vision of harsh beauty, with windswept plains and mesas, isolated buttes, and barren valleys in delicate patterns of soft pastels. In the few places in which there is vegetation, it is mostly desert scrub, which provides sustenance for only the hardiest wildlife. Most of the undulating hills belong to the Chinle formation, deposited more than 200 million years ago and containing countless fossil records of ancient plants and animals—including the recently discovered remains of the oldest dinosaur ever found.

About 40 miles north of the Cameron Trading Post, the Painted Desert country gives way to soaring sandstone cliffs that run for many miles off to the right. Brilliantly hued, and ranging in color from light pink to deep orange,
24 the **Echo Cliffs** rise to well over 1,000 feet in many places. They are also essentially devoid of vegetation, but in a few isolated places high up, you'll spot thick patches of tall cot-

The North Rim: Tours 5 and 6

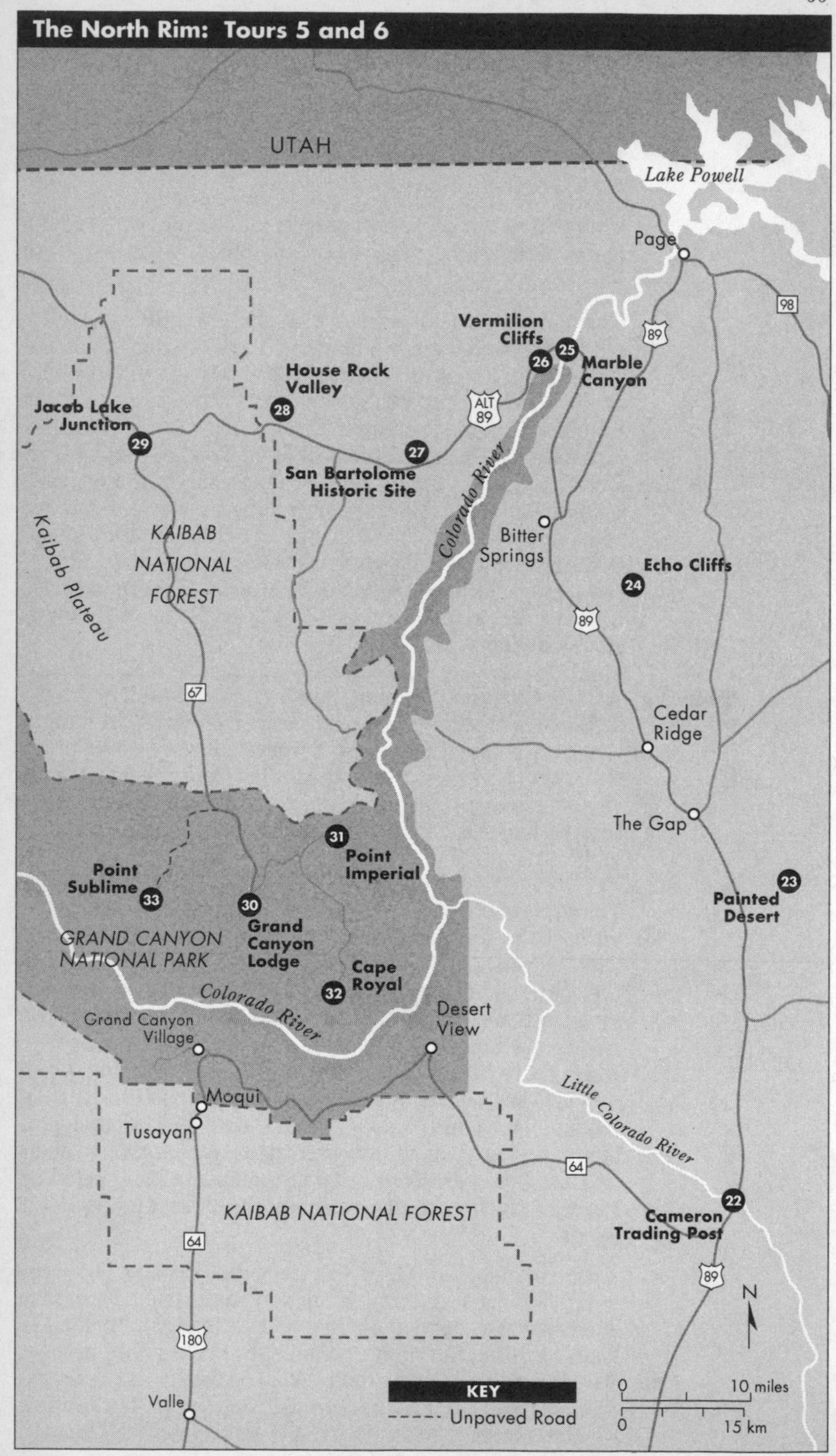

tonwood and poplar trees, nurtured by springs and water seepage from the rock escarpments.

At Bitter Springs, 60 miles north of Cameron, leave U.S. 89 and take U.S. 89A north. Fourteen miles out of Bitter
25 Springs, **Marble Canyon,** actually the beginning of the Grand Canyon, comes into view. Like the rest of the Grand Canyon, Marble Canyon has been carved by the force of the Colorado River. Navajo Bridge, the old steel bridge across the gorge, is sturdy, but many first-time visitors approach it with trepidation because of the structure's antique appearance and because it spans a chasm that's more than 500 feet deep. A visitor parking area on the north side of the bridge is a good place to stop for photographs. There's a turnoff nearby for Lees Ferry, 3 miles away, where most of the Grand Canyon river rafts put into the water. Huge trout also lurk in the river near Lees Ferry, but be sure you have an Arizona fishing license before casting a line. After crossing the Navajo Bridge, you'll be in Arizona Strip country (*see* Off the Beaten Track, *below*).

Heading west, you'll be treated to views of some of the world's most spectacular geologic formations. Rising to the
26 right of the highway are the sheer **Vermilion Cliffs,** in many places more than 3,000 feet high.

As you continue the journey to the North Rim, the immense blue-green bulk of the Kaibab Plateau stretches out before you. About 18 miles past Marble Canyon, a sign directs you
27 to the **San Bartolome Historic Site,** commemorating the Dominguez-Escalante expedition of 1776. The members of the expedition, the first non-Indians to enter the Arizona Strip area, nearly lost their lives trying to cross this harsh and forbidding land, which does not have a single permanent lake or stream. The group was saved when it found a place, farther to the east, to wade across the Colorado. The Crossing of the Fathers, as the location was later called, provided the only safe passage across the river for more than a half-century.

28 Proceeding about 2 miles west, you'll enter **House Rock Valley,** where a large sign on the road announces the House Rock Buffalo Ranch. A 23-mile dirt road leads to the home of one of the largest herds of American bison in the Southwest. You may drive out to the ranch, but be aware that you may not see any buffalo: The expanse of their range is so great that they frequently cannot be spotted from a passenger car.

About 25 miles west of Marble Canyon on U.S. 89A, you'll start climbing to the top of the Kaibab Plateau, heavily forested, rife with animals and birds, and more than 9,000 feet at its highest point. The rapid change from barren desert to lush forest is dramatic. At an elevation of 7,900 feet, the
29 **Jacob Lake junction** is a good place to stop for groceries and gas. Turn left (south) from the junction to access AZ 67.

From here to the North Rim, a distance of 44 miles, you'll be driving through one of the thickest stands of ponderosa pine in the United States. Watch for wildlife along the way. Visitors frequently see mule deer and, once in a while, catch a glimpse of rare Kaibab squirrels; you can recognize them by their all-white tails and ears with long tufts of white hair.

Tour 6: Bright Angel Point, Point Imperial, Cape Royal, Point Sublime

When you arrive at the historic Grand Canyon Lodge, you are, literally, at the end of the road; there are no meandering streets as there are at South Rim. A massive stone structure built in 1928 by the Union Pacific Railroad, the lodge is today listed in the National Register of Historic Places. Inside, the huge lounge area with hardwood floors and high, beamed ceilings affords a marvelous view of the canyon through massive plate-glass windows. On warm days, visitors sit in the sun and drink in the surrounding beauty at an equally spacious outdoor viewing deck.

The trail to Bright Angel Point, one of the most awe-inspiring overlooks on either rim, starts on the grounds of the
30 **Grand Canyon Lodge** and proceeds along the crest of a point of rocks that juts out into the canyon for several hundred yards. The walk is only 1 mile round-trip, but the trek is exciting because there are sheer drops just a few feet away on each side of the rail. At places where the route gets extremely narrow, metal railings along the path ensure visitors' safety. The trail is quite safe, but visitors have been known to clamber out to precarious perches to have their picture taken. Be very careful: There have been tragic falls at the Grand Canyon.

If you'd like to take another walk, this time through the deep forest, head for the beginning of the Transept Trail near the corner of the lodge's east patio. This 3-mile (round-trip) trail stays near the rim for part of the distance, then plunges into the forest, ending at the North Rim Campground and General Store, 1½ miles from the lodge.

Time Out Lunch, dinner, or a snack in the **Grand Canyon Lodge**'s (tel. 602/638–2611) huge, high-ceilinged, rock-and-log dining room is an integral part of the North Rim experience. The menu is varied but primarily American: breast of chicken amandine, barbecued spareribs, fresh fish, and prime rib are among the selections. Prices are moderate, dress is casual.

To get to the North Rim's most popular lookouts—Point Imperial and Cape Royal—drive north from Grand Canyon
31 Lodge and veer right at the signed fork in the road. **Point Imperial,** 11 miles from the lodge, is the highest vista point (elevation 8,803 feet) on either rim, offering magnificent

views of both the canyon and the distant country for many miles around: the Vermilion Cliffs to the north, the 10,000-foot Navajo Mountain to the northeast in Utah, the Painted Desert to the east, and the Little Colorado River canyon to the southeast.

Return west to the signed junction and turn left (south) to
32 reach **Cape Royal,** about 23 miles from your starting point at the lodge. From the parking lot at the road's end, it's a short, scenic walk on a paved road to this southernmost viewpoint on the North Rim. In addition to another large slice of the Grand Canyon, Angel's Window, a giant, erosion-formed hole, can be seen through the projecting ridge of Cape Royal. If you would like to experience a very pleasant walk in this area of the rim, drive north about ⅛ mile to Angel's Window Overlook. At this point, Cliff Springs Trail starts its 1-mile route (round-trip) through a forested ravine. The easily navigated trail passes an Anasazi ruin, winds beneath a limestone overhang, and terminates at Cliff Springs, where the forest opens on another impressive view of the canyon walls.

An excellent option for those who want to get off the beaten
33 path, the trip to **Point Sublime** is intended only for visitors driving vehicles with high-road clearance (pickups and four-wheel drive). It is also necessary to be properly equipped for wilderness road travel: Check with a park ranger or at the information desk at Grand Canyon Lodge before taking this journey. Drive north from the lodge about 2 7/10 miles to the North Rim Campground and turn left on a dirt road that winds for 17 miles through gorgeous high country to Point Sublime, an overlook that lives up to its name. You may camp here, but only after obtaining a permit from the Backcountry Reservations Office at the park ranger station (*see* Hiking in Sports and Outdoor Activities, *below*).

What to See and Do with Children

The Grand Canyon is family vacation country, and the children will enjoy essentially the same things as the adults. However, many activities at both North and South rims will appeal especially to them. It's worth checking the extensive menu of free daily programs offered by the National Park Service. The activities calendar changes seasonally, but an updated version can be found in the free Grand Canyon newspaper, *The Guide,* available to all arriving visitors at both rims. Some typical offerings are nature walks, geology talks, natural-history discussions—suitable for adults as well as children.

Animal Rides Extremely gentle horses can be rented at the **Moqui Lodge** (tel. 602/638–2424) in the village of Tusayan, South Rim. The cost is $17.50 an hour, $30 for two hours. A four-hour East Rim ride goes for $52.50, a campfire horse- and haywagon ride for $22.50. The rides operate daily from April to November.

Short mule rides suitable for children are offered on the easier trails along the North Rim. A one-hour ride, available to those 6 years of age and older, runs about $10. Half-day trips on the rim or into the canyon cost $30; the minimum age for these is 8 years. These excursions are very popular, so try to make reservations in advance at the mule rides desk at **Grand Canyon Lodge** (tel. 602/638–2292). Rides are available on a daily basis from May 15 to the end of October.

Films of the Canyon

An extraordinarily fine documentary, *Grand Canyon, Hidden Secrets*, is shown on the world's largest screen (60 feet by 80 feet) at the Imax Theater. The script is highly informative, and some of the shots—especially those of boats running the rapids—are positively dizzying. *Tusayan, tel. 602/638–2203. Admission: $7 adults, $4 children age 3–11. Open Mar. 1–Oct. 31, daily 8:30–8:30; Nov. 1–Feb. 28, daily 10:30–6:30; shows every hour starting on the half-hour.*

The computer-controlled *Over the Edge* multimedia show tells the Grand Canyon story in words and song—with the help of 12 projectors and strobe effects. The photography is often stunning. *Community Building, Grand Canyon Village, tel. 602/638–2229. Admission: $4 adults, $2 children under 16, children under 8 free. Open Apr.–Oct., daily 9–9; Nov.–Mar., daily 10–3 and 5–8; shows every 30 min.*

Off the Beaten Track

Arizona Strip

The **Arizona Strip** is the 9,000-square-mile northwestern portion of the state, cut off from the rest of Arizona by the giant scar created by the Colorado River as it comes out of Utah and winds its way through the Grand Canyon to the western border of the state. The only highway access to this area from southern Arizona is across an old steel bridge at Marble Canyon on U.S. 89A. Sometimes called the American Tibet because it's so isolated, the area boasts only one small town, the farming and lumbering community of Fredonia; otherwise, fewer than 700 permanent residents live here. To experience the strip, we suggest a one- or two-day side trip for visitors embarking from the Grand Canyon's North Rim.

The first of the two main destinations in the area is **Pipe Spring National Monument,** 90 miles from the North Rim. Head north from the rim on AZ 67, and at Jacob Lake take AZ 89A to Fredonia; continue 14 miles beyond Fredonia on the same highway (now called AZ 389). Located at Pipe Spring, one of the few reliable sources of water in the Arizona Strip, the park features a restored rock fort and ranch, with exhibits of southwestern frontier life; in the summer there are living-history demonstrations, such as ranching operations or weaving. Completed in 1871 to fend off Indian attacks (which never came because a peace treaty was signed before it was finished), the fort was originally built to protect grazing lands owned by the Mormon church. It ended up functioning mainly as headquarters for a dairy farm and later became the first telegraph station in Arizona. Also on the site are a well-stocked bookstore, a coffee shop, and exhibits in the visitor center. About a half-mile north of the monument is a campground and picnic area run by the Kaibab-Paiute tribe. *HC 65, Box 5, Fredonia 86022, tel. 602/643–7105. Admission: $1 adults, children under 17 and senior citizens over 62 free. Historic structures open daily 8–4; visitor center/museum open daily 8–4:30; closed Thanksgiving, Christmas, and New Year's Day.*

After touring the old fort, backtrack on AZ 389 for 6 miles, then take a right turn on the dirt road to **Toroweap Overlook,** a distance of approximately 60 miles. You'll be riding through starkly beautiful, uninhabited country. Toroweap, a lonely and awesome overlook of the Grand Canyon, is the narrowest stretch of the canyon (less than 1 mile across) and also the point with the deepest sheer cliff (more than 3,000 feet straight down). From this vantage point, you can see upstream to sedimentary ledges, cliffs, and talus slopes. Looking downstream, you can see miles of lava flow that forms steep deltas, some of which look like black waterfalls frozen on the cliff.

Be sure you have plenty of gas, drinking water, good tires, and a reliable car. Don't try to go in wet weather, when the dirt road is likely to be washed out. There's a ranger station near the rim as well as a primitive campground. If you plan on returning the same day, you should make motel reservations in advance at one of the Arizona Strip motels (*see* Lodging, *below*).

Havasu Canyon, South Rim

For those who want to get away from the crowds, Havasu Canyon, south of the middle part of the national park, exhibits a Shangri-la-like beauty. It is the home of some 500 Havasupai, a tribe that has populated this beautiful, isolated country for centuries. Spectacular waterfalls (one drops 200 feet) cascade over the red cliffs, spilling blue-green water into immense travertine pools surrounded by thick foliage and sheltering trees.

From Grand Canyon Village, head south on U.S. 180 (AZ 64) for 57 miles to Williams, then take I–40 west 44 miles to Seligman. From there, go 34 miles west on AZ 66 until you come to Indian Rte. 18. A drive 60 miles north will take you to the head of the 8-mile-long Hualapai Trail. You can hike into the canyon or ride a horse or mule down for about $70; the trail twists along the edges of rock walls that go straight down for hundreds of feet. The hurried—or faint of heart—can take a helicopter; **Grand Canyon Helicopters** (tel. 800/528–2418) offers round-trips for $392 per person. If you are hiking or riding, you'll want to stay overnight (*see*

Lodging, *below*). All visitors are charged a $12 fee to enter the Havasupai tribal lands. For additional information, contact Havasupai Tourist Enterprise (Supai 86435, tel. 602/448–2121 [tourist office], or 602/448-2111 [lodging]).

Lake Havasu City In case you haven't heard, London Bridge isn't in London anymore. In 1968, the historic span was dismantled stone by stone and shipped to a barren stretch of desert near Arizona's Lake Havasu, 172 miles southwest of the South Rim of the Grand Canyon. Envisioned by developer Robert McCulloch as the centerpiece for the community he had planned on the shores of the lake, the venerable structure, precisely reassembled (all 10,000 tons of it) to span a narrow arm of the lake, is indeed a focal point in a rapidly growing community of more than 32,000.

In addition to the bridge, Havasu City is known for sunshine, water sports, and fishing. The weather is wonderful in spring, fall, and winter, but summers often see temperatures that exceed 100°F. Recreational opportunities abound on and around 45-mile-long Lake Havasu: houseboat, ski-boat, jet-ski, fishing, and sailboat rentals; marinas, RV parks, and campgrounds; golf, tennis, guided fishing expeditions, and more. The area has more than 20 lodging establishments—from inexpensive roadside motels to posh resorts—and more than 40 eating places, from fast-food emporiums to fancy restaurants. To reach Lake Havasu City from Grand Canyon Village, take U.S. 180 (AZ 64) south 57 miles to Williams, then I–40 west 116 miles to Kingman; go another 35 miles to the intersection with AZ 95, and drive south for 19 miles. For more information on Lake Havasu City and its many attractions, contact the Lake Havasu Chamber of Commerce (1930 Mesquite Ave., Lake Havasu City 86403, tel. 602/453–3444 or 800/242–8278).

Shopping

At the South Rim, nearly every lodging facility and retail store offers Native American artifacts and Grand Canyon souvenirs. In truth, you'll find that after visiting a few of the curio and jewelry shops, all the merchandise begins to look alike. However, the items at most of the lodges and at major gift shops are authentic. The following are among the most interesting places for browsing or buying.

Desert View Trading Post offers a mix of traditional southwestern souvenirs and authentic Native American pottery and jewelry, plus sundries. *East Rim Dr. near The Watchtower at Desert View, tel. 602/638–2360. Open Memorial Day–Labor Day, daily 8–8; Labor Day–Memorial Day, daily 9–6.*

The historic locale of the **El Tovar Hotel Gift Shop** provides a nice atmosphere for shopping for Native American jewelry, rather expensive casual wear, and souvenir gifts. *Near the rim in Grand Canyon Village, tel. 602/638–2631, ext. 6284. Open daily 7 AM–10 PM.*

Hopi House, opened in 1905, still offers one of the widest varieties of Native American artifacts—some of museum quality and not for sale—in the vicinity of the Grand Canyon. Many are very pricey, but there are some excellent, affordable items to be found here. *East of El Tovar Hotel, tel. 602/638–2631, ext. 6587. Open May–Sept., daily 8–8; Oct.–Apr., daily 9–5.*

Cameron Trading Post is one of the Southwest's few remaining historic trading posts. Established on the Navajo reservation in 1916, this is an excellent place for fine Native American craftsmanship, including jewelry, rugs, baskets, and pottery from the Navajo, Hopi, Zuni, and New Mexico Pueblo Indians. Located near the junction of U.S. 89 and AZ 64, it's accessible to visitors coming or going to the South Rim through the east entrance and to those heading toward the North Rim. *On U.S. 89 1 mi north of junction with AZ 64, tel. 602/679–2231. Open Apr.–Oct., daily 6 AM–10 PM; Nov.–May, daily 7 AM–9 PM.*

Sports and Outdoor Activities

Participant Sports

Bicycling A few visitors to the Grand Canyon arrive on bicycles, but these are all highly conditioned and experienced long-distance cyclists. It's 80 miles from Flagstaff to the South Rim, 210 miles to the North Rim—both routes offering only limited water stops. If you wish to cycle inside the park, where there are miles of scenic thoroughfares, bring your own bike; there are no rentals available in the canyon area. Be aware that the park roads have narrow shoulders and are heavily trafficked; use extreme caution. Bicycles are not permitted on any of the trails in Grand Canyon National Park.

Camping Camping inside Grand Canyon National Park is permitted only in designated areas. (For information about campgrounds in and around the park, *see* Lodging, *below*.)

Fishing The high-plateau country of northwestern Arizona is a land of little rain and quick runoffs. Consequently, fishing opportunities are limited. However, the Colorado River in the vicinity of Lees Ferry, just across Marble Canyon Bridge on U.S. 89 (the route to the North Rim), is known for its huge trout. Before trying your luck, be sure to get an Arizona fishing license, available at most marinas and sporting-goods stores in the state. Licenses are obtainable at Babbitt's General Store at the South Rim and at Marble

Canyon Lodge, near Lees Ferry, but you won't be able to get them at the North Rim. They can also be obtained in advance from the **Arizona Game and Fish Department** (2222 W. Greenway Rd., Phoenix, AZ 85023, tel. 602/942–3000). For details on fishing regulations, check with the Backcountry Reservations Office (*see* Hiking, *below*).

Hiking Hiking trails are numerous and the scenery always spectacular in Grand Canyon country. Opportunities range from leisurely walks on well-defined paths through level or easy-rolling country to arduous treks to the bottom of the canyon—even all the way across it to the other rim. Easy hikes can be found in the Exploring section (*see* Tour 3 and Tour 6, *above*). In addition to some of the most popular trails outlined below, national park rangers or visitor center personnel will gladly provide you with hiking information and local maps of trails featuring varying degrees of difficulty.

Note: Overnight hikes require a permit that can be obtained by written request to the **Backcountry Reservations Office** (Box 129, Grand Canyon, AZ 86023, tel. 602/638–7888). Permits are limited, so it's wise to make a reservation in advance. If you arrive without one, go to the Backcountry Reservations Office at either rim: South Rim near the entrance to Mather Campground, North Rim at the ranger station.

Bright Angel Trail, South Rim One of the most popular and scenic hiking paths from the South Rim to the bottom of the canyon (9 miles), the well-maintained Bright Angel Trail was used in the late 1800s as a route to mining claims. There are rest houses for hikers at the 1½-mile and 3-mile points and at Indian Garden. Plateau Point, 1½ miles below Indian Garden, is a good turnaround point for a day hike. As the climb out is an ascent of 4,460 feet, the trip should be attempted only by those in good physical condition and is not recommended during the summer.

Hermit Trail, South Rim This 9-mile trail, which starts at Hermits Rest, 8 miles west of Grand Canyon Village, is unmaintained, steep, and suitable only for experienced long-distance hikers; a particularly tricky area is a ⅛-mile section of rock slides. No water is available along the way. The route, leading to the Colorado River, offers some inspiring views of Hermit Gorge and the Redwall and Supai formations. It's 6 miles from the head of the trail to now-abandoned Hermit Camp, operated as a tourist resort by the Santa Fe Railroad after 1912.

South and North Kaibab Trails, South and North Rims South Kaibab Trail, which begins near Yaki Point on East Rim Drive near Grand Canyon Village, connects at the bottom of the canyon (after the Kaibab Bridge across the Colorado) with the North Kaibab Trail, the only maintained trail into the canyon on the North Rim. Plan on three days if you want to hike the gorge from rim to rim. South Kaibab Trail is steep, descending 4,800 feet in just 7 miles, with no campgrounds or water and very little shade; if you're going back up to the South Rim, ascend via the Bright Angel Trail. Accommodations for hikers along the way include the campgrounds at Indian Garden and Bright Angel or Phantom Ranch (*see* Lodging, *below*).

Safety Tips Water must be carried for hikes into the inner gorge—at least 1–1½ gallons per day. To avoid dehydration, it is important to drink frequently, about every 10 minutes, especially during summer months. To avoid fatigue, take food—preferably energy snacks such as trail mix, bananas, and fig bars. Wear hiking boots or running shoes that have been broken in and proven on previous hikes. In case of a medical emergency, stay with the distressed person and ask the next hiker to go for help. Do not attempt to make the round-trip to the Colorado River in one day. The trek down is deceptively easy, the route back up very fatiguing.

Mule Trips Almost everyone who knows anything about the Grand Canyon has heard of the mule rides to the bottom of the canyon. Since they are conducted under the auspices of an experienced trail guide, these rides are profiled in the Guided Tours section, above.

Rafting Many people who have made the white-water trip down the Colorado River through the Grand Canyon say it is the adventure highlight of a lifetime. White-water trips embark from Lees Ferry, below Glen Canyon Dam near Page, Arizona. Trips that run the length of the canyon (a distance of over 200 miles) can last from three days to three weeks. Shorter trips, also starting at Lees Ferry, let passengers off at Phantom Ranch at the bottom of Grand Canyon (a distance of about 100 miles); these pass through a great amount of white water, including Lava Falls rapids (on the longer trips), considered the wildest navigable rapids in North America. For those who would like a more tranquil turn on the Colorado, there are also one-day, quiet-water raft cruises just below Glen Canyon Dam near Page. Although more than 25 companies currently offer these excursions, reservations for raft trips (excluding the smooth-water, one-day cruises) often must be made more than six months in advance. For a complete list of river-raft companies, call 602/638–7888 from a touchtone phone and press 1-3-71, or write to the River Permits Office, Grand Canyon National Park, Box 129, Grand Canyon, AZ 86023. White-water companies include **Canyoneers, Inc.** (tel. 602/526–0924), **Diamond River Adventures** (tel. 602/645–8866), **Expeditions Inc.** (tel. 602/774–8176), and **Wilderness River Adventures** (tel. 602/645–3296 or 800/992–8022). Smooth-water, one-day-trip companies include **Fred Harvey Transportation Company** (tel. 602/638–2822) and **Wilderness River Adventures** (tel. 602/645–3279). Prices for river-raft trips vary greatly, depending on type and length. Day trips on smooth water run as low as $35 per person; trips that negotiate the entire length of the canyon and take as long as 14 days can cost well over $1,000.

Skiing Though you can't schuss down into the Grand Canyon, you can hit the slopes at the nearby **Williams Ski Area** (Box 953, Williams 86046, tel. 602/635–9330), open when there's snow in the region; take South 4th Street for 2 miles, then turn right at the sign and go another 1½ miles. This is not the major Williams resort that's being planned, but it offers three groomed trails (including a beginner's run) for downhill skiiers and areas suitable for cross-country enthusiasts. Lift tickets range from $7 to $17 depending on your age and level of expertise; lessons are available on a group and individual basis.

Dining and Lodging

Dining Throughout Grand Canyon country and the vast areas of northwestern Arizona, restaurants cater to tourists who generally move from one place to another at a good clip. Therefore, most establishments offer standard American fare, prepared quickly and offered at reasonable prices. However, there are a few dining opportunities, noted below, that merit mention. In addition, for a quick meal at reasonable prices, there are cafeterias on the South Rim in Grand Canyon Village at **Yavapai Lodge** and **Maswik Lodge** (tel. 602/638–2401 for both) or at **Desert View Trading Post** (AZ 64, 23 mi east of Grand Canyon Village, tel. 602/638–2360). On the North Rim, the cafeteria is located in **Grand Canyon Lodge** (tel. 602/638–2611). Restaurants are open daily unless otherwise noted. Highly recommended restaurants are indicated by a star ★.

Category	**Cost***
Very Expensive	over $25
Expensive	$17–$25
Moderate	$10–$17
Inexpensive	under $10

**per person, excluding drinks, service, and 5% sales tax*

Lodging When it comes to lodging in Grand Canyon country, there is one thing to be aware of above all else. The popular South Rim is very crowded during the summer. The North Rim is less crowded, but that area has limited lodging facilities. You would be well advised to make reservations as soon as your itinerary has been decided, even as early as six months in advance. If you're unable to find accommodations in the immediate area of the South Rim, you might find rooms in the nearby communities of Williams (*see below*), Flagstaff (*see* Chapter 5, North-Central Arizona), or—a bit farther afield—Tuba City (*see* Chapter 4, The Northeast). For those going to the North Rim, we list three small roadside motels in the sparsely populated Arizona Strip country on the approach to the North Rim on U.S. 89A. Prices at many of the hotels and motels in Grand Canyon country are lower in spring, fall, and winter.

Highly recommended lodgings are indicated by a star ★.

Category	Cost*
Very Expensive	over $100
Expensive	$75–$100
Moderate	$50–$75
Inexpensive	under $50

**All prices are for a standard double room, excluding 5.5%–6.7% tax and service charges.*

South Rim
Dining and Lodging

★ **Bright Angel Lodge.** Designed by Mary Jane Colter for the Fred Harvey Company in 1935, this log-and-native-stone structure sits within a few yards of the canyon rim and offers rooms in the main lodge or quaint cabins (some with fireplaces) scattered among the pines. Don't come for luxury but for a historic structure that blends superbly with the spectacular natural environment in which the lodge is set. Bright Angel Restaurant is a memorable but informal spot for breakfast, lunch, or dinner. *Box 699, Grand Canyon 86023, tel. 602/638–2401 (reservations) or 602/638–2631, ext. 6015 (switchboard). 11 rooms with bath, 13 rooms with semi-bath (sink snd toilet but no bathtub or shower), 6 rooms without bath, 42 cabins with bath. Facilities: dining room, cocktail lounge, soda fountain, gift shop, TV, phones. AE, D, DC, MC, V. Moderate–Expensive.*

★ **El Tovar Hotel.** Built in 1905 of native stone and heavy pine logs, El Tovar is reminiscent of a grand European hunting lodge. Maintaining its tradition of excellent service and luxury, the hotel is, as when first built, operated by the Fred Harvey Company. Some rooms have a canyon view. For decades the hotel's world-class restaurant has enjoyed a reputation for fine food served in a classic 19th-century room of hand-hewn logs and beamed ceilings. Among the Continental dishes served with Old World style, the veal française is a long-standing favorite. The chef also prepares prime rib and fresh fish with an innovative touch. *Box 699, Grand Canyon 86023, tel. 602/638–2401 (reservations) or 602/638–2631 (switchboard). 65 rooms and 10 suites with bath. Facilities: cocktail lounge, gift shop, dining room, air-conditioning, phones, TV, room service. AE, D, DC, MC, V. Very Expensive.*

Dining

The Steak House. This is a warmly appointed, typical southwestern steak house, right down to the black-and-white-cowhide–pattern tablecloths, massive brick fireplace, displays of Native American and western art, and traditional country music on the jukebox. The John Wayne bar is lined with memorabilia of the actor. The food is well prepared, and there's plenty of it, with the menu consisting almost entirely mesquite-grilled steaks and barbecued chicken entrées; a Mexican plate is always on offer, as are specials for senior citizens and a children's menu. *Junction of U.S. 180 and AZ 64, 2 mi south of Grand Canyon entrance, directly north of the Imax Theater, tel. 602/638-2780. Reservations accepted only for parties of 8 or more. Dress: casual. AE, MC, V. Open Mar. 1–Dec. 15, daily 6:30 AM–2 PM and 5–10 PM. Inexpensive–Moderate.*

Lodging **Best Western Canyon Squire.** Located a few miles outside the national park, this motel lacks some of the charm of the older lodges at the canyon rim, but it offers a longer list of amenities. The rooms feature standard American roadside design and decor, with dark gray carpeting and orange or green floral bedspreads and drapes; all are clean and comfortable. Ask for a room with a woodside view; others face the highway. *Box 130, Tusayan 86023, tel. 602/638-2681 or 800/528-1234. 150 rooms with bath. Facilities: dining room, coffee shop, heated pool, wading pool, tennis courts, sauna, indoor whirlpool, air-conditioning, phones, TV. AE, D, DC, MC, V. Expensive.*

Fred Harvey Motels. The Fred Harvey Company has seven lodges on the South Rim. Of them, El Tovar and Bright Angel (*see above*) are outstanding, but in an area where tourist traffic is heavy and lodgings are limited, it's good to have options. Maswik Lodge, Yavapai Lodge, Moqui Lodge, Kachina Lodge, and Thunderbird Lodge do not have the antique charm of Bright Angel and El Tovar, but they are all comfortable and nicely appointed. Moqui is located on U.S. 180, just outside the national park. The others are in Grand Canyon Village. *Box 699, Grand Canyon 86023, tel. 602/638-2401 (address and reservation number for all Fred Harvey hotels on the South Rim). 855 rooms with private bath. Facilities: phones, TV, restaurant on site or close by. AE, D, DC, MC, V. Moderate–Expensive.*

Quality Inn. The design and interior of this facility in Tusayan, 6 miles south of the South Rim on U.S. 180, are typical of Quality Inns elsewhere—unpretentious, but offering a satisfactory comfort level in a land where motel vacancies are often difficult to find in the busy summer season. Rooms are done in soothing shades of light blue, peach, or tan. Unlike many other chain hotels, individual service is emphasized here. *Box 520, Tusayan 86023, tel. 602/638-2673. 177 rooms with bath. Facilities: dining room, gift shop, pool, Jacuzzi, air-conditioning, TV, phones. AE, D, DC, MC, V. Expensive.*

Camping Camping inside Grand Canyon National Park is permitted only in designated areas. Campgrounds at the South Rim are listed below.

Mather Campground in Grand Canyon Village has 97 RV and 190 tent sites (no hookups), flush toilets, water, showers, and a laundromat; the cost is $10 per site. *Box 1548, Grand Canyon 86023, tel. 602/638-7851 or reservations through MISTIX (Box 85705, San Diego, CA 92138, tel. 800/*

365–2267 or 619/452–0150 outside the U.S.. Open all year; no reservations taken from Dec. 1–Mar. 1.

Desert View Campground, 26 miles east of Grand Canyon Village off AZ 64, offers RV and tent sites, flush toilets, and water but no hookups. The cost is $10 per site, with no reservations. *Box 129, Grand Canyon 86023, tel. 602/638–7888. Open May–Oct.*

Trailer Village, in Grand Canyon Village, has 78 RV sites with full hookups for $16 per site. *Box 699, Grand Canyon 86023, tel. 602/638–2401. Open all year.*

Commercial and Forest Service campgrounds outside the park include:

Flintstone Bedrock City, 30 miles south of the park, offers 28 tent and 32 partial RV hookups. Basic rates are $12 per site for two people; add $2 for electricity hookup, $2 for water hookup, and $1.50 for each additional person. *Grand Canyon Hwy., Star Rte., Williams 86046, tel. 602/635–2600. Open mid-Apr.–Oct.*

Grand Canyon Camper Village in Tusayan, 6 miles south of the rim, has 250 RV hookups, some partial, some full ($20 for two people, plus $1 for each additional person over the age of 6) and 100 tent sites ($13 for two people). *Box 490, Grand Canyon 86023, tel. 602/638–2887.*

Ten X Campground is run by the Forest Service about 9 miles south of the park. It offers 70 family sites plus a group site (available for groups of up to 100 people), water, and pit toilets for $10 per day but no hookups. No reservations are accepted (except for the group site). *Kaibab National Forest, Tusayan Ranger District, Box 3088, Grand Canyon 86023, tel. 602/638–2443. Open May 1–Sept. 30.*

Bottom of the Canyon

Dining and Lodging

Phantom Ranch. Built on the site of an earlier hunting camp in 1932, this group of wood-and-stone buildings is set among a grove of cottonwood trees at the bottom of the canyon. For hikers (who need a backcountry permit to come down here), dormitory accommodations—20 beds for men and 20 for women—are available, as are two cabins (one sleeping four people, the other 10). There are also seven cabins reserved exclusively for mule riders; lodging, meals, and mule rides are offered as a package (*see* Guided Tours in Essential Information, *above*). The restaurant at Phantom Ranch, probably the most remote eating establishment in the United States, has a limited menu. All meals are served family style, with breakfast, dinner (including a selection for vegetarians), and box lunches available. Arrangements—and payment—for both food and lodging should be made 9 to 11 months in advance. *Box 699, Grand Canyon 86023, tel. 602/638–2401 (reservations) or 602/638–2631, ext. 6015 (switchboard). 4 dormitories for hikers with shared bath, 11 cabins for mule riders with shower outside. Facilities: dining room. AE, D, DC, MC, V. Inexpensive.*

Camping

There are two free campgrounds en route to Phantom Ranch: **Indian Garden,** about halfway down the canyon, and

Bright Angel, closer to the bottom. Both offer toilet facilities and running water (no showers). A backcountry permit is required. For information, contact Backcountry Reservations Office (Box 129, Grand Canyon 86023, tel. 602/638–7888).

Havasu Canyon
Dining and Lodging

Havasupai Lodge The lodge and restaurant at the bottom of Havasu Canyon, operated by the Havasupai tribe, offers clean, comfortable rooms at about $80 for a double (this rate is in addition to the $12 per person fee to enter the Havasupai tribal lands). The restaurant serves three meals a day, generally sandwiches and fast-food–type fare, and a special daily meal; dinner prices are around $8–$10. For information about camping in the canyon, call the Havasupai Tourist Enterprise (tel. 602/448–2121). *Supai 86435, tel. 602/448–2111 (lodge), or 602/448–2981 (restaurant). 24 rooms. No credit cards accepted at any facilities; personal checks accepted for deposit, traveler's checks or cash required upon arrival. Expensive.*

En Route to the North Rim/ Arizona Strip
Dining and Lodging

Cameron Trading Post. This guest inn, built some 60 years ago of the same native stone as the historic trading post that abuts it, offers simple but comfortable and clean rooms; some are in modern motel style; others feature the natural woods of rustic southwestern decor. Also available here is RV space. You can see fossilized dinosaur tracks left in the native stone of two of the units. A small, well-kept garden with lilacs, roses, and crabapple trees is a pleasant place in which to relax. The dining room, with its original tinwork ceilings, kiva fireplace, and beautiful oak sideboards, offers hearty meals at good prices. *Box 339, Cameron 86020, tel. 602/679–2231 or 800/338–7385. 88 units. Facilities: market, restaurant, curio shop, TV, air-conditioning. AE, D, MC, V. Inexpensive–Moderate.*

Jacob Lake Inn. This modest but clean motel, on five acres in Kaibab National Forest (at the junction of U.S. 89A and AZ 67, 45 miles north of the North Rim), is a good option for lodging in the area. Both basic cabins and standard motel-type units are available. All rooms are rustic, with simple wood furnishings; most overlook the highways. The hotel's restaurant serves American food at moderate prices. *Jacob Lake 86022, tel. 602/643–7232. 10 motel units, 28 cabins; 50 rooms with bath. Facilities: gas station, gift shop, restaurant. AE, D, DC, MC, V. Moderate.*

Dining

Vermilion Cliffs Restaurant. Located on U.S. 89A on the route to the North Rim, this small bar and grill, in a rock-and-beam building next to Lees Ferry Lodge, is a gathering place for the men and women who pilot and guide the river rafts through the Grand Canyon. The mix of local folks and tourists makes this an interesting eating place, with surprisingly good American fare—especially the steaks and seafood—served in an authentic western setting (including an old-fashioned jukebox). The hosts have lined up 89 bottles of beer (mostly imports) on the wall and are looking for another 10 to complete their collection. *Vermilion Cliffs, tel. 602/355–2231. Reservations taken only for Lees Ferry Lodge guests and large groups. Dress: casual. MC, V. Inexpensive–Moderate.*

Lodging Access to the North Rim is through the extremely unsettled Arizona Strip country on U.S. 89A. Especially during summer months, rooms at the North Rim may be difficult to acquire, unless you have made reservations in advance. The following establishments along the way are rustic, no-frills, roadside motels that range from Indian-style rock-and-mortar units to small-frame cabins, but they all are clean: **Marble Canyon Lodge** (Box 1, Marble Canyon 86036, tel. 602/355–2225); **Lees Ferry Lodge** (HC 67 Box 1, Marble Canyon 86036, tel. 602/355–2231); and **Cliff Dwellers Lodge** (HC 67 Box 30, Marble Canyon 86036, tel. 602/355–2228). These facilities are all located near the Marble Canyon crossing on U.S. 89A. All accept MasterCard and Visa. Rates for all are Inexpensive–Moderate.

Camping **Jacob Lake Campground,** at the junction of U.S. 89A and AZ 67, 45 miles north of the North Rim, has family and group RV and tent sites, but no hookups, for $10 per vehicle per day; reservations cost an additional $6. *Kaibab National Forest, North Kaibab Ranger District, Box 248, Fredonia 86022; reservations through MISTIX (Box 85705, San Diego, CA 92138, tel. 800/283–CAMP or 619/452–0510 outside the U.S.). Open May–Oct.*

North Rim *Dining and Lodging* ★

Grand Canyon Lodge. This historic property offers comfortable if not luxurious accommodations in a setting of extraordinary beauty; it's the premier lodging facility in the remote and sparsely populated North Rim area. The main building was constructed in the 1920s and exhibits massive limestone walls and timbered ceilings. Room choices include small, very rustic cabins, newer and larger cabins (some with a canyon view and some with two bedrooms), and traditional motel rooms. The hotel's huge, high-ceilinged dining room is an excellent spot for breakfast, lunch, or dinner. *TW Recreational Services, Cedar City, UT 84721, tel. 801/586–7686 (reservations). 40 rooms with bath, 54 Western cabins (for up to 5 people), 82 Frontier cabins (up to 3 people), 21 Pioneer cabins (4 or 5 people), 4 handicapped-accessible cabins. Facilities: dining room, cafeteria, cocktail lounge, gift shop, visitor center, talks and programs. AE, DC, MC, V. Moderate.*

Camping On the North Rim there is only one designated campground inside Grand Canyon National Park. **North Rim Campground,** located 3 miles north of the rim, has a total of 83 RV and tent sites, but no hookups, for $10 per day. *Box 129, Grand Canyon 86023, tel. 602/638–7888 or reservations through MISTIX (Box 85705, San Diego, CA 92138, tel. 800/365–2267 or 619/452–0150 outside the U.S). Open May 15–Oct 26.*

Forest Service campgrounds outside the park include **Demotte Campground,** 16 miles north of the rim, with 22 single-unit RV and tent sites, but no hookups, for $6 per day. No reservations accepted. *Kaibab National Forest, North Kaibab Ranger District, Box 248, Fredonia 86022, tel. 602/643–7395. Open June–Nov.*

Williams
Dining and Lodging

Mountain Side Inn & Resort. The most upscale lodging in a down-home town, this pleasant motel wouldn't be called a resort anywhere else, but its rooms are comfortable and tastefully decorated in contemporary style. On summer nights, live country-and-western bands play on the outdoor patio. The waitresses at the Dining Car restaurant will make sure you get through the copious breakfast buffet in time to catch the Grand Canyon Railroad. *642 E. Bill Williams Ave., Williams 86046, tel. 602/635–4431 or 800/462–9381. 96 rooms with bath. Facilities: restaurant, cocktail lounge, pool, spa, gift shop. AE, D, DC, MC, V. Expensive.*

Lodging

Norris Motel. This no-frills motel offers clean, comfortable rooms at good rates. You can distinguish it from the many others on the town's main drag by the British flag flown by the genial English owner. *1001 W. Bill Williams Ave., tel. 602/635–2202 or 800/341–8000. Facilities: spa. AE, MC, V. Moderate.*

Nightlife

Unless you head for nearby Williams or Flagstaff after dark, nightlife in this part of the Southwest consists of watching a full moon above the soaring buttes of the Grand Canyon, roasting marshmallows over a crackling fire, crawling into your bedroll beside some lonely canyon trail, or attending a free evening program on the history of the Grand Canyon. Dinner at **El Tovar Restaurant** (it has an excellent wine list), would be a memorable evening. In addition, the following Grand Canyon properties have cocktail lounges: **El Tovar Hotel** (piano bar), **Bright Angel Lodge** (live entertainment), **Maswik Lodge** (sports bar), **Yavapai Lodge** (dancing), and **Moqui Lodge** (live entertainment). Call 602/638–2401 for reservations and further information.

Excursion to Lake Mead and Hoover Dam

From the most popular viewing points on both the North and South rims, the Grand Canyon charts an erratic path for more than 200 miles to the west, where the wild-running Colorado River fills the dark, eroded canyons of the Black Mountains to form the largest man-made body of water in the United States, Lake Mead.

Lake Mead, which holds the equivalent of two years' runoff of the Colorado River, is held back by the massive concrete barrier of **Hoover Dam,** completed in 1935 and still considered one of the world's great engineering feats. Rising 726 feet from bedrock, the dam required 3,250,000 cubic yards of concrete poured into place by a crew of 5,000 men working in shifts around the clock. The dam is so impressive that it has drawn nearly 30 million visitors since it was completed.

Sightseeing is the number one visitor pastime in the Lake Mead area, but boating, water sports, swimming, camping, and fishing are extremely popular, too. The weather in this desert region is pleasant during winter months, ideal in spring and fall (50s to 80s), and hot in the summer (over 100°F).

Tourist Information

The best place for finding out about the Lake Mead region is the **Alan Bible Visitor Center** (601 Nevada Hwy., Boulder City, NV 89005, tel. 702/293–8906). You can also contact the **Arizona Office of Tourism** (1100 W. Washington St., Phoenix 85007, tel. 602/542–TOUR) or the Boulder City Chamber of Commerce (1497 Nevada Hwy., Boulder City, NV 89005, tel. 702/293–2034) for information about the area.

Getting There

To reach Lake Mead from Grand Canyon National Park, take U.S. 180 (AZ 64) south to Williams. Then proceed west on I–40 to Kingman, where you will veer northwest on U.S. 93 to Hoover Dam and Lake Mead. It is 184 miles from Williams to Hoover Dam.

The Lake Mead National Recreation Area and Hoover Dam can also be accessed by flying into Las Vegas's **McCarran International Airport** (tel. 702/739–5743) or by **Greyhound/ Trailways** bus (see your local yellow pages for information).

Getting Around

The only practical way to explore the vast land areas of Lake Mead is by car. Naturally, the almost endless waterways of the lake require a boat. If you aren't pulling your own, there are plenty for rent at the marinas along the shore (*see* Boating and Water Sports, *below*).

Guided Tours

By Boat A 1½-hour cruise of the Hoover Dam area on a large excursion boat is available daily through Lake Mead Cruises (Lake Mead Marina, near Boulder Beach, tel. 702/293–6180); rates are $12 adults, $5 children under 12. A motorized raft trip on the Colorado from the base of Hoover Dam down Black Canyon to Willow Beach, a distance of about 15 miles, is offered daily by Gray Line Tours (tel. 702/384-1234). Prices run about $70 per person and include lunch and transportation back.

Exploring

Numbers in the margin correspond to points of interest on the Lake Mead map.

The visual impact of the incredible mass and height of
1 **Hoover Dam** nearly compels the visitor to make this the first stop on a visit to the area. Although the highway proceeds across the dam, in order to see anything you'll need to stop in one of the two parking lots, on either the Nevada or the Arizona side, and then walk or catch a free shuttle to the dam and the small visitor center. (Expect highway delays in the area from 15 minutes up to 45 minutes because of the construction of a new visitor center.) In the blue bubble on the Nevada side, a free 35-minute movie on the building of the dam is shown; also on the Nevada side an exhibit hall has a huge topographical map displaying the drainage systems of the entire Colorado River. Tickets for guided tours, which take visitors deep into the interior of the imposing structure, can be purchased at the dam. *Tel. 702/293-8367. Admission: $1 adults, children under 16 free. Open Memorial Day–Labor Day, daily 8–7:15; Labor Day–Memorial Day, daily 9–4:15; closed Christmas.*

From Hoover Dam, head west for 3½ miles on U.S. 93 to
2 reach the **Alan Bible Visitor Center.** The best place to become acquainted with the area, the center offers films on Lake Mead and Hoover Dam, a botanical garden featuring local plant life, and a wildlife exhibit. A complete auto tour guide to the area costs 50¢ here, and free brochures provide information on recreational opportunities. *601 Nevada Hwy., Boulder City, NV 89005, tel. 702/293-8906. Admission free. Open daily 8:30–5, closed Thanksgiving, Christmas, and New Year's Day.*

Turn left outside the parking lot of the Alan Bible Visitor Center, and go down the hill to pick up Lakeshore Scenic Drive (NV 146). This route, wending its way along the shore of Lake Mead in a northwesterly direction for 9 miles,
3 also provides access to **Boulder Beach,** a favorite swimming area.

If you wish to extend your auto tour of the Lake Mead area, Lakeshore Scenic Drive intersects NV 167 about 7 miles north of Boulder Beach. You can take 167 northeast along
4 5 the Nevada shoreline to **Callville Bay** (12 miles), **Echo Bay**
6 (37 miles), or **Overton Beach** (47 miles). Marinas and campgrounds are available at all three sites, and there is a motel at Echo Bay.

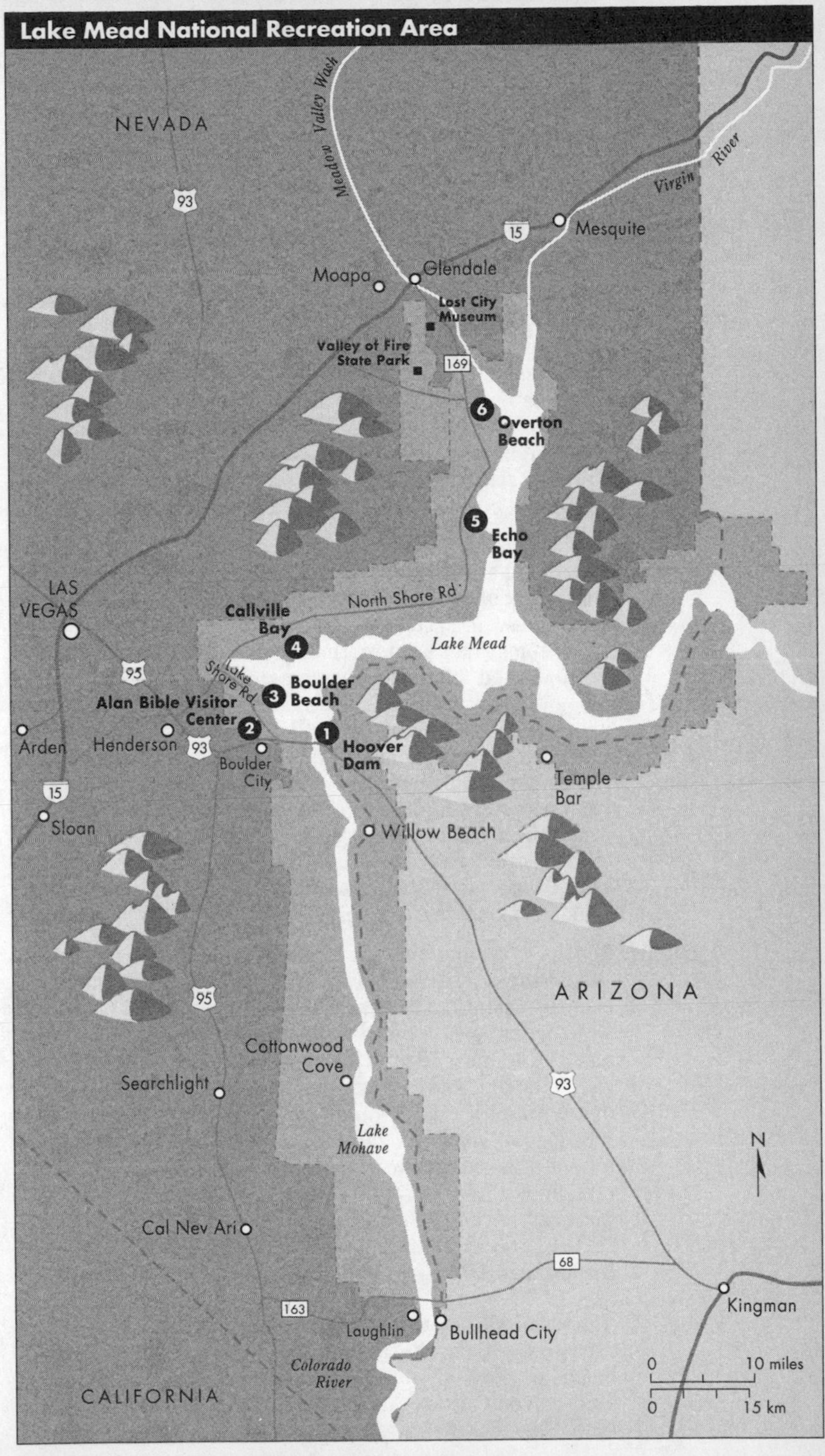
Lake Mead National Recreation Area
NEVADA
ARIZONA
CALIFORNIA
Meadow Valley Wash
Virgin River
Mesquite
Moapa
Glendale
Lost City Museum
Valley of Fire State Park
6 Overton Beach
5 Echo Bay
North Shore Rd
4 Callville Bay
Lake Mead
Lake Shore Rd
3 Boulder Beach
2 Alan Bible Visitor Center
1 Hoover Dam
LAS VEGAS
Arden
Henderson
Boulder City
Sloan
Temple Bar
Willow Beach
Cottonwood Cove
Searchlight
Lake Mohave
Cal Nev Ari
Laughlin
Bullhead City
Kingman
Colorado River
93
15
169
95
68
163
N
0
10 miles
0
15 km

Sports and Outdoor Activities

Boating and Water Sports If you have your own boat, find a marina or boat launch and put it in the water. If not, you'll have the option of choosing from a long list of rental opportunities. We suggest that you pick up a free list of all marinas at the **Alan Bible Visitor Center** (*see* Tourist Information, *above*). Houseboat rentals are available at **Callville Bay Resort and Marina** (Callville Bay, tel. 702/565–7340) or at **Echo Bay Resort** (Echo Bay, tel. 702/394–4066); prices for a boat that sleeps 10 range from about $800 to $2,700, depending on the season and the number of nights booked; the most expensive time of year is summer, and a minimum rental of three nights is required. Small boats, including patio boats, fishing boats, and ski boats, are offered at these locations and at **Lake Mead Resort** (Boulder Beach, tel. 702/293–3484), as well as at other Lake Mead locations. Prices vary greatly depending on type and size of boat. Typical price ranges for one-day rentals would be about $90 for a 16-foot skiff, $200 for a 19-foot powerboat.

Fishing Sports fishermen from far and wide travel to Lake Mead, where it's open season on all species year-round. Largemouth bass and striped bass grow to impressive sizes, the latter sometimes to more than 50 pounds. The lake has also been planted with rainbow and cutthroat trout and offers bluegill, black crappie (sometimes 5 to 6 pounds), and channel catfish. The north shore of Lake Mead is in Nevada, the south shore in Arizona. To fish from shore you must have the proper state license. From a boat, you need a license from one state and a stamp from the other. Licenses are available at most marinas and sporting-goods stores in the state. Permits can also be obtained in advance from the **Arizona Game and Fish Department** (2222 W. Greenway Rd., Phoenix 85023, tel. 602/953–5990).

Hiking You may hike anywhere within the vast Lake Mead National Recreational Area. However, most hiking is of the cross-country variety, since there are few maintained trails. For short treks, pick a place that suits you at a stopping point along the shore. But stay in sight of landmarks—this is rough, lonely, and very dry country. For longer hikes, consult with park rangers and obtain topographic maps. Taking along at least one gallon of water per day is advised for hikers. Use extreme caution in summer months. For information on trails, contact the Alan Bible Visitor Center (*see* Tourist Information, *above*).

Dining and Lodging

The resorts listed below are the main lodging options in this area. Except for the **Temple Bar Resort** (Temple Bar, AZ 86443, tel. 602/767–3211), about 39 miles south and east of Hoover Dam, there are no other lodging facilities on the lake. The closest Arizona motels are in Kingman, 73 miles south on U.S. 93. However, there are about 15 motels and numerous eating establishments (from fast-food outlets to formal restaurants) in Boulder City, Nevada, 8 miles west of Hoover Dam on U.S. 93. For information, contact the Boulder City Chamber of Commerce (tel. 702/293–2034).

Echo Bay Resort. In a remote cove of Lake Mead, away from even a hint of congestion or highway traffic, this getaway location has a sweeping panorama of the lake, rugged hills, and canyon walls. The lodge features contemporary architecture and decor. The restaurant leans heavily toward standard American fare, but the food is well prepared. A full slate of lakeside recreational activities are on offer, including ski-, patio-, and fishing-boat rentals as well as houseboat rentals, RV sites, a convenience store, a marine fueling station, and moorage. *Echo Bay, Overton, NV 89040, tel. 702/394–4000. 52 rooms with bath. Facilities: restaurant, lounge, TV, air-conditioning. MC, V. Moderate.*

Lake Mead Resort. Located near Boulder Beach, this rustic, tile-roofed lodge with a magnificent view of the lake provides comfortable rooms with a hint of southwestern decor. The resort's floating Tail o' the Whale restaurant and Pelican Perch lounge serves breakfast, lunch, and dinner; dishes are primarily American, with some Italian specialties. At the resort's marina, a mile down the road, there are many recreational facilities, including ski-, fishing-, and patio-boat rentals; a convenience store; and a marine fueling station. *322 Lakeshore Rd., Boulder City, NV 89005, tel. 702/293–2074. 42 rooms with bath. Facilities: pool, walking trails, TV, air-conditioning. MC, V. Moderate.*

4 The Northeast

Petrified Forest, Hopi and Navajo Country, Lake Powell

By William E. Hafford

Updated by Edie Jarolim

If you like wide-open spaces, you'll want to visit northeastern Arizona, a vast and lonely land of shifting red dunes and soaring buttes, where horizons capped by pure blue skies are almost always a hundred miles or more away. Covering more than 30,000 square miles, most of the northeast belongs to the Navajo and Hopi people, who have held on to their ancient cultural traditions—based on strong spiritual values and an affinity for nature—to the present day. Excellent Native Americans arts and crafts can be found in shops, galleries, and trading posts throughout the region.

The sprawling Navajo reservation (known to its people as the Navajo Nation) incorporates about 25,000 square miles of the entire northeastern corner of Arizona; in its approximate center lie the 4,000 square miles of Hopi reservation, a series of stone and adobe villages built on high mesas that overlook agricultural land. Within the stunning landscape of Navajo National Monument and Canyon de Chelly rest the mysterious ruins of the ancient Anasazi Indian tribes, who first wandered here thousands of years ago.

Outside the borders of the Navajo Nation, you'll find two of the most popular attractions in the area. Just below the southeastern boundary of the reservation, straddling I–40, is Petrified Forest National Park, an intriguing geological open book of the Earth's distant past. The park includes a large portion of the famed Painted Desert, with its stratified bands of multicolored hills in which ancient life-forms and huge fallen tree trunks have petrified over hundreds of millions of years. Above the far northwestern corner of the Navajo reservation on U.S. 89 lies Glen Canyon Dam—and behind it, more than 120 miles of Lake Powell's emerald waters held in precipitous canyons of erosion-carved stone. Many find Lake Powell one of the most serene and beautiful spots in the world.

Most of Indian country is arid land, with soil and rock formations ranging in color from delicate salmon pink to rusty orange—and sometimes nearly red. Driving for long distances, you'll generally see immense vistas of mesas, rock spires, canyons, and cliffs, but you'll also pass some impressive mountain ranges. The Chuska Mountains to the north and east of Canyon de Chelly are covered with striking stands of ponderosa pine, and Navajo Mountain to the north and west in Utah soars above 10,000 feet.

Essential Information

Important Addresses and Numbers

Tourist Information For more information regarding Indian country, contact the **Navajo Tourism Department** (Box 663, Window Rock 86515, tel. 602/871–6659 or 871–6436) and the **Hopi Tribe Office of Public Relations** (Box 123, Kykotsmovi 86039, tel.

602/734–2441). The **Page/Lake Powell Chamber of Commerce** (Box 727, Page 86040, tel. 602/645–2741) and the **National Park Service/Glen Canyon Recreation Area** (Box 1507, Page 86040, tel. 602/645-2511) are both excellent sources for Lake Powell vacation information and prices.

Emergencies

Police

Navajo tribal police: Chinle (tel. 602/674–5291), **Tuba City** (tel. 602/283–5242, **Window Rock** (tel. 602/871–6111); **Hopi tribal police: Hopi Mesas** (tel. 602/738–2233).

Hospitals/ Medical Clinics

Medical care in Indian country is not as easily accessible as in heavily populated urban areas. People with chronic medical conditions or those in frail health may wish to avoid a trip into Arizona's sparsely populated northeast. Hospital emergency care is generally not more than 60 minutes' driving time from any location on a paved highway.

Sage Memorial Hospital (tel. 602/755–3411), a public hospital located in Ganado, on the Navajo reservation, offers medical and dental services. **Monument Valley Hospital** (tel. 801/727–3241) in Utah (near Goulding's Trading Post off U.S. 163 at the Arizona–Utah border) has medical and dental services. Emergency care through the U.S. Public Health Service Indian Hospitals is available in the reservation communities of Fort Defiance (tel. 602/729-5741), Chinle (tel. 602/674-5281), Tuba City (tel. 602/283-6211), and Keams Canyon (tel. 602/738-2211). Another option in a medical emergency is to contact the Navajo or Hopi tribal police (*see* Police, *above*).

Pharmacies

There are no pharmacies on the Navajo or Hopi reservation; for emergency medical supplies, go to the private or public hospitals noted in the Hospital/Medical Clinics section, above.

Road Service

Fed Mart Automotive (AZ 264 near Window Rock, tel. 602/871–4764), **Tuba City Motors** (corner of Birch and Oak Sts., Tuba City, tel. 602/283–5330 during the day, 602/283-5300 at night), **Kayenta Discount Motor Parts** (Kayenta on Hwy. 160, tel. 602/697-3200), **Onsae Auto Repair** (Second Mesa, across from the Hopi Cultural Center, Hopi Mesas, tel. 602/734–2211).

Arriving and Departing by Plane

No major airlines fly directly to Indian country. To get closer to the northeastern part of the state, travelers will need to make flight connections in Phoenix to travel either on to Flagstaff, located on I–40 near the southwestern corner of the Navajo reservation, or the community of Page, on U.S. 89 near Lake Powell and the northern border of Arizona. At the end of your flight, you'll need to rent a car for the rest of the journey (*see* Rental Cars, *below*).

Airports and Airlines

Sky Harbor International Airport (tel. 602/273–3300) in Phoenix is the primary hub for air travel coming into Arizona from points out of state. **Flagstaff Pulliam Municipal**

Airport (tel. 602/774–1422) or **Page Municipal Airport** (tel. 602/645-2494) are both small but modern. **Sky West** (tel. 800/453-9417) has daily flights from Phoenix and Flagstaff into Page. (*See* Chapter 6, Phoenix and Central Arizona, and Chapter 5, North-Central Arizona, for information on airlines servicing those cities.)

Arriving and Departing by Train or Bus

By Train **Amtrak** (tel. 800/USA–RAIL) provides daily service into Arizona from both the east and the west. It makes scheduled stops in Flagstaff, which is a good jumping-off point for a car trip into Indian country. No passenger train enters the interior of the Navajo or Hopi reservation.

By Bus **Greyhound/Trailways** (Phoenix, tel. 602/248–4040; Flagstaff, tel. 602/774–4573) has numerous Arizona destinations, but there is no service into Indian country. If you're coming from out of state and wish to tour northeastern Arizona, you can take a bus to Phoenix or Flagstaff and then rent a car to visit Indian country.

Getting Around

By Car If you are arriving from southern California or southern Arizona, Flagstaff is the most likely entry point into northeastern Arizona. If you are coming from the north or northwest, you might choose to come in from Utah via U.S. 89, starting your tour at Page, Arizona. For those driving south from Colorado, a logical entry point would be west from Farmington, New Mexico, via U.S. 64. Gallup, New Mexico, or Flagstaff, Arizona, both located on I–40, are convenient jumping-off points for those arriving from most eastern locations.

Road Maps Because a tour of Indian country involves driving long distances among widely scattered communities, a detailed, recently published road map is absolutely essential. A wrong turn in this lonely country could send you many miles out of your way. Gas stations carry adequate state maps, but two other maps are especially recommended: the ***Arizona Highways*** magazine road map (write: Arizona Highways, 2039 W. Lewis Ave., Phoenix 85009, tel. 602/258–6641) or the excellent map of the northeastern region prepared by the **Navajo Tourism Department** (Box 663, Window Rock 86515, tel. 602/871–6659 or 6436).

Road Service and Weather It isn't easy to find a place to service your car in sparsely populated Indian country. We recommend that you make sure your car was recently inspected and serviced prior to your trip. Also, seek weather information if you see ominous rain clouds in summer or signs of snow in winter. Never drive into dips or low-lying road areas during a heavy rainstorm; they could be flooded. (For road service locations and emergency and weather information, *see* Important Addresses and Numbers, *above*, and Weather, *below*.) If you heed these simple precautions, car travel through Indian country will be as safe as travel anywhere else. Paved highways in the interior are well maintained and patrolled by trained and courteous tribal police officers.

Rental Cars Rental cars in heavily touristed Arizona are plentiful and usually available, but it's still smart to reserve a car in advance of your arrival. Phoenix is served by virtually all of the national car-rental firms and also has a number of local car-rental outlets. The major companies provide airport shuttle service or delivery, while local companies may not. For a compact with unlimited mileage, a weekly rate from these major companies will be in the $130 range.

Major companies serving Phoenix and Flagstaff include **Avis** (tel. 800/331–1212), **Budget** (tel. 800/527–0700), **Hertz** (tel. 800/654–3131), and **National** (tel. 800/227–7368). Avis and Budget also offer rentals in Page.

By Bus The **Navajo Transit System** (tel. 602/729–5449) offers regularly scheduled service on fixed routes throughout the Navajo reservation. The buses are modern, in good condition, and generally on time. However, this method of travel, across vast areas of Indian country where towns and bus stops are many miles apart, may be too slow for most visitors.

Guided Tours

Except during winter months, the **Navajo Transit System** (tel. 602/729–5457 or, at Navajo Nation Inn, tel. 602/871-4108) offers tours of Indian country departing from Window Rock, the tribal capital. Destinations include Canyon de Chelly, the Painted Desert, and the Petrified Forest. **Nava-Hopi Tours, Inc.** (tel. 602/774–5003 or 800/892-8687), an affiliate of Gray Line, schedules tours into Indian country from Flagstaff. **Crawley's Monument Valley Tours** (tel. 602/697–3463) is located on the Navajo reservation, with tours embarking from the small town of Kayenta. **Dorian Tours** (tel. 602/284–4562) provides one-day trips from Sedona to the Hopi Mesas and to various sites on the Navajo reservation. Half-day and full-day truck and Jeep tours into Canyon de Chelly on the Navajo reservation depart from nearby **Thunderbird Lodge** (tel. 602/674–5841); the half-day tours leave twice daily (when there are a minimum of six passengers) throughout the year, while full-day tours are available only from April to October.

Weather

With elevations generally between 4,500 and 6,000 feet, the region's summer temperatures average about 87°F but can climb beyond 100. Winter daytime temperatures range from the 30s to the 70s but can drop to zero or below. While the area gets less than 10 inches of rainfall in an average year, fierce summer thunderstorms can quickly fill the arroyos and turn them into raging torrents. Sometimes during the winter months, heavy snows virtually stop all traffic on the dirt back roads.

KTNN radio, located at AM 660, provides periodic weather information. This station serves the Hopi and Navajo reservations from studios in Window Rock. Some of the programming is in Navajo, but there are news and weather reports in English. You might also telephone the Canyon de Chelley (tel. 602/674-5213) or the Navajo or Hopi tribal police (*see* Emergencies, *above*) for weather updates.

Time

The state of Arizona follows mountain standard time during the entire year; however, the Navajo reservation follows daylight saving time from May to October.

Banks

Citibank has branch offices in Window Rock and Tuba City on the Navajo reservation, but there are no automated teller machines at these locations. The Arizona communities of Flagstaff, Page, Winslow, and Holbrook, all adjacent to the reservation, have banks and automated teller machines.

The Hopi and the Navajo

No one knows where the ancestors of today's Hopi Indians came from, and archaeologists cannot pinpoint exactly when they arrived. However, the Hopi consider themselves to be the first people to arrive in the Americas, and their oral history has it that these ancestors came by sea, crossing on boats or rafts from one "stepping-stone" to the next. They may have island-hopped across the Pacific rather than crossed the frozen land of the Bering Straits. Many anthropologists think the Hopi are descended from the Anasazi people. Hopi stories suggest that they probably migrated widely for a very long time before being spiritually guided to the mesas that are their present home. It is believed that Oraibi, the earliest village, was established in about AD 1150. Over the years the Hopi have been an extremely peaceful people, taking a warlike posture only when Spanish priests came to the area around 1630, hoping to convert them to Christianity. In 1680, they joined the Indians of the New Mexico pueblos in a revolt that destroyed the Spanish missions and drove the intruders away.

The Navajo, a more warlike tribe believed to be related to the Athabascans of northeastern Canada, arrived in the Southwest sometime after the Hopi, probably around AD 1300. Thanks to the Pueblo Indians already established in the area, they learned the skills of pottery and weaving, and they also raised livestock and became expert horsemen after the arrival of the Spanish in the 17th century; the Navajo have continued farming and creating arts and crafts to this day. In the years 1863 and 1864, the U.S. Army descended on the Navajo with unjustified cruelty and forced them to make the infamous Long Walk to a virtual concentration camp in eastern New Mexico, releasing them four years later. In 1868, the U.S. government established the Navajo Indian reservation, today the largest in the country, occupying not only the entire northwestern portion of Arizona but also spilling over into Utah and New Mexico. The much smaller Hopi territory, smack in the middle of the Navajo holdings, was ceded to the tribe by the federal government in 1882. Border disputes between the two tribes continue, negotiated in court and before Congress. Differences are evident in their way of life, too: The Hopi tend to live together in villages, whereas the Navajo dwellings are usually dispersed.

Although the Navajo and Hopi peoples fall under certain federal laws, they are essentially self-governing. In earlier days, the Navajo were ruled largely by a complex clan system, but in 1923, they established a tribal government that consists of an elected tribal president, vice president, and more than 80 council members representing the various chapters throughout the Navajo Nation. In 1868, when the reservation was established, there were fewer than 8,000 Navajo, but now this democratically governed Native American entity has more than 185,000 people.

The Hopi live in 12 villages on their three primary mesas, with a population of about 10,000. Their government, like that of the Navajo, is solidly based on democratic principles. Although both the Navajo and Hopi peoples rely on their own tribal governments and adhere tenaciously to ancestral cultures, they are patriotic Americans as well; large numbers of Hopi and Navajo have served in the U.S. military with distinction.

Courtesy in Indian Country

Both the Hopi and Navajo peoples are friendly to tourists. However, their privacy, customs, and laws should be respected.

Do not wander across residential areas or disturb property. Always ask permission before taking photographs of the locals; you may have to pay to take the picture.

Littering is not allowed.

No open fires are allowed; fires are permitted only in grills and fireplaces. Bring your own wood or charcoal.

Observe quiet hours from 11 PM until 6 AM at all camping areas.

Animals, plants, rocks, or artifacts must not be disturbed or removed. They are protected by Tribal Antiquity and federal laws, which are strictly enforced.

The possession and consumption of alcoholic beverages or drugs is illegal.

No off-trail hiking or rock climbing is allowed.

A permit is required for fishing in lakes or streams or hunting for game; the use of firearms is otherwise prohibited.

Off-road travel by four-wheel-drive vehicles, dune buggies, Jeeps, and motorcycles is not allowed.

Bikinis or similar scanty clothing should not be worn in public.

Pets should be kept on a leash or in a confined area.

On the Hopi reservation making videos, tape recordings, and sketches of villages and ceremonies is strictly prohibited. At all sacred events, neat attire and respectful etiquette are requested. Camping is permitted for a maximum of two nights, but only in designated areas. All Hopi villages have separate rules about visitors; check with the individual village Community Development Offices (*see* Tour 2: The Hopi Mesas, *below*), or call the **Hopi Tribe Office of Public Relations** (tel. 602/734–2441) in advance for information.

Hopi Ceremonies

The Hopi are well known for their colorful ceremonial dances, many of which are supplications for rain, fertile crops, and harmony with nature. Most of these ceremonies take place in village plazas and kivas (underground ceremonial chambers) and last two days or longer; outsiders are permitted to watch only certain segments and are never allowed into the kivas. The dances may involve masks, beaded costumes, drums, and chanting. The best-known is the snake dance, in which participants carry live snakes, including poisonous rattlers.

The dances that visitors are allowed to watch usually take place on weekends, extending through the day until dusk. Each of the tribal clans has its own sacred rituals, and starting times and dates are determined by tribal elders. Visitors should show the proper respect while observing the dances. For more information, contact the **Hopi Tribe Office of Public Relations** (tel. 602/734–2441).

Exploring the Northeast

Excursions into northeastern Arizona can range from a brief, one-day tour to an extended sojourn of seven days or more. The tours that follow all begin at Flagstaff, the city from which most travelers set out. If you choose one of the other entry points (*see* Getting Around, *above*), you'll need to adjust the recommended tours accordingly.

Tour 1 of the Petrified Forest National Park and the Painted Desert may be included as part of Tour 3 of the southern Indian country if time permits. Tour 2 of the Hopi Mesas may be incorporated into both Tour 3 and Tour 4 of the northern Indian country.

Highlights for First-time Visitors

Canyon de Chelly (*see* Tour 3)

The Hopi Mesas (*see* Tour 2)

Lake Powell and Rainbow Bridge (*see* Tour 5)

Monument Valley (*see* Tour 4)

Navajo National Monument (*see* Tour 4)

Petrified Forest National Park and the Painted Desert (*see* Tour 1)

Tour 1: Petrified Forest National Park and the Painted Desert

Numbers in the margin correspond to points of interest on the Northeastern Arizona map.

1 From **Flagstaff,** drive east on I–40 for 115 miles to the north
2 entrance (25 miles east of Holbrook) of **Petrified Forest National Park,** a geological trip back in time. Fossils of plant and animal life here date from around 225 million years, to the Triassic period of the Mesozoic era.

In 1984, the fossil remains of one of the oldest dinosaurs ever unearthed were discovered in the Petrified Forest; this creature died more than 225 million years ago. Remnants of ancient human beings and their artifacts, dating from some 8,000 years, have been recovered at more than 500 sites in this national park. The grounds are also strewed with tree trunks whose wood cells were replaced over centuries by brightly hued mineral deposits—including silica, iron oxide, manganese, aluminum, copper, lithium, and carbon—and fossilized; in many places, the petrified logs scattered about the landscape resemble giant jackstraws. Most of the park's 94,000 acres include portions of the vast, lunarlike landscape known as the Painted Desert. In the northern area of the park, this colorful but essentially barren and waterless series of windswept plains, hills, and mesas is considered by geologists to be part of the Chinle formation, deposited at an early stage of the Triassic period. The most dramatic colors occur at dawn and sunset, when the oblique light causes shadows to deepen and makes the smaller chasms glow bright red.

If your schedule permits, you can easily spend most of a day in the park, which has 28 miles of paved roads with walking trails, parking areas, and spur roads. Along the way you can see some spectacular desert scenery and visit several petrified-wood sites. During the early years of this century, looters hauled away pieces of wood in large quantities. In 1906, President Theodore Roosevelt created a national monument in the area, and to this day, it is illegal to remove even a small sliver of petrified wood from the park.

The **Rainbow Forest Museum and visitor center,** located at the south entrance (off U.S. 180), features three skeletons from the Triassic period, including that of the ferocious phytosaur, a crocodilelike carnivore. The museum has numerous exhibits relating to the world of cycads (tropical plants), ferns, fish, and other early life, as well as artifacts and tools of ancient humans. The self-guided **Giant Logs Trail** starts at the Rainbow Forest Museum and visitor center and loops through a half-mile of huge fallen trees. The base of one specimen stands taller than 6 feet.

A movie entitled *The Stone Forest,* which traces the natural history of the area, is shown at regular periods each day in the **Painted Desert visitor center,** located at the north entrance of the park (off I–40). Within the park's boundaries, visitors also have access to gift shops, a restaurant, a soda fountain, and a service station.

Picnicking is allowed inside the park, but there are no overnight accommodations. You may hike into the nearby wilderness areas, but you must first obtain a park permit for an overnight stay. Free permits are issued at both visitor centers (*see* above).

North entrance: off I–40, 25 mi east of Holbrook. South entrance: off U.S. 180, 19 mi southeast of Holbrook. Tel. 602/524–6228. Admission: $5 per vehicle, free with Golden Eagle, Golden Age, or Golden Access pass. Open Oct.–Apr., daily 8–5; May and Sept., daily 7–6; June–Aug., daily 6:30 AM–7:30 PM. Park closed Christmas and New Year's Day.

Tour 2: The Hopi Mesas

From Flagstaff, drive east on I–40. AZ 99, 87, and 77 all go north into the Hopi reservation, but the best of these highways is AZ 87, the turnoff for which is 62 miles east of Flagstaff (4 miles past Winslow). From here, head north 58 miles to the Hopi's Second Mesa, where you will intersect AZ 264.

Northeastern Arizona

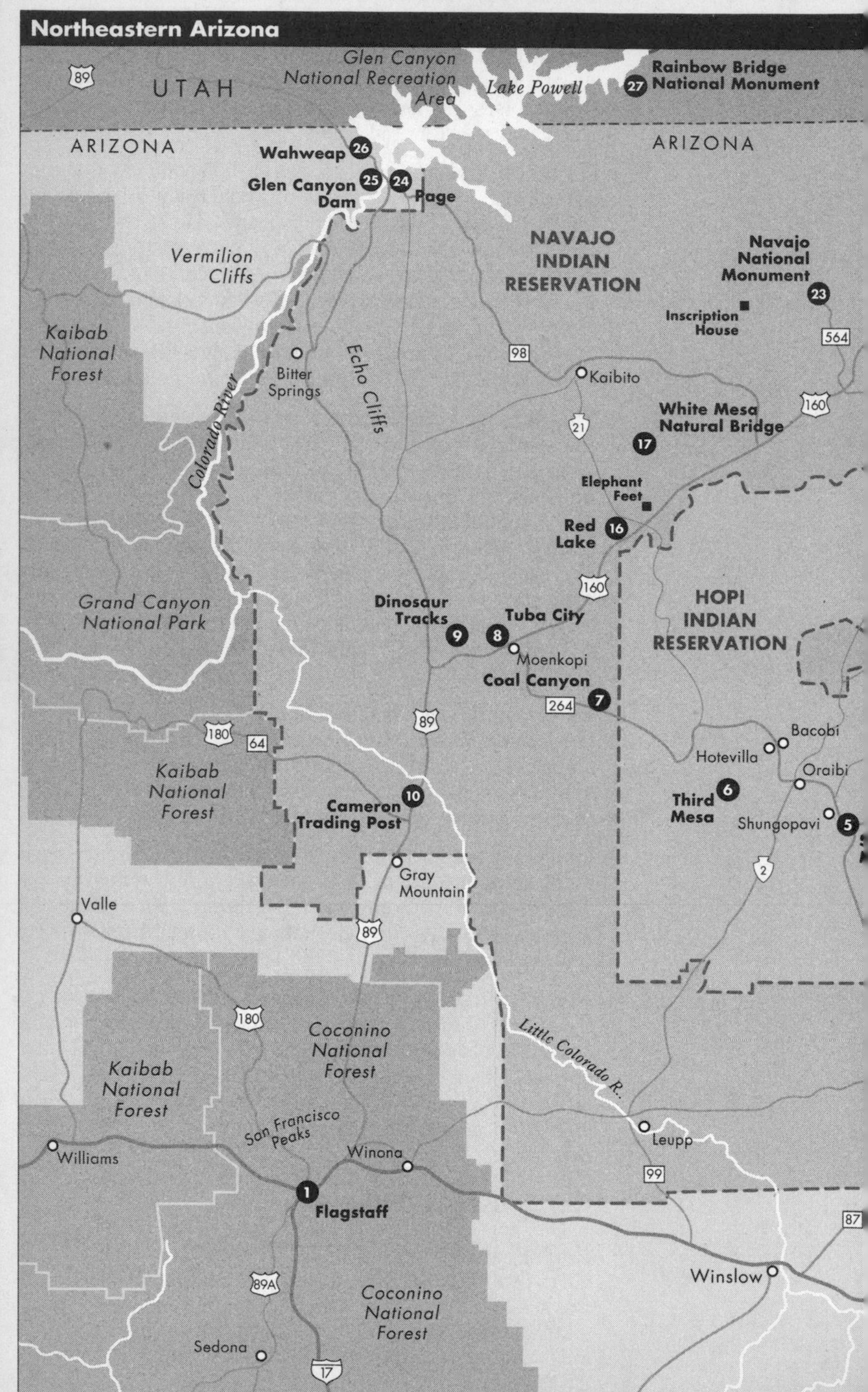

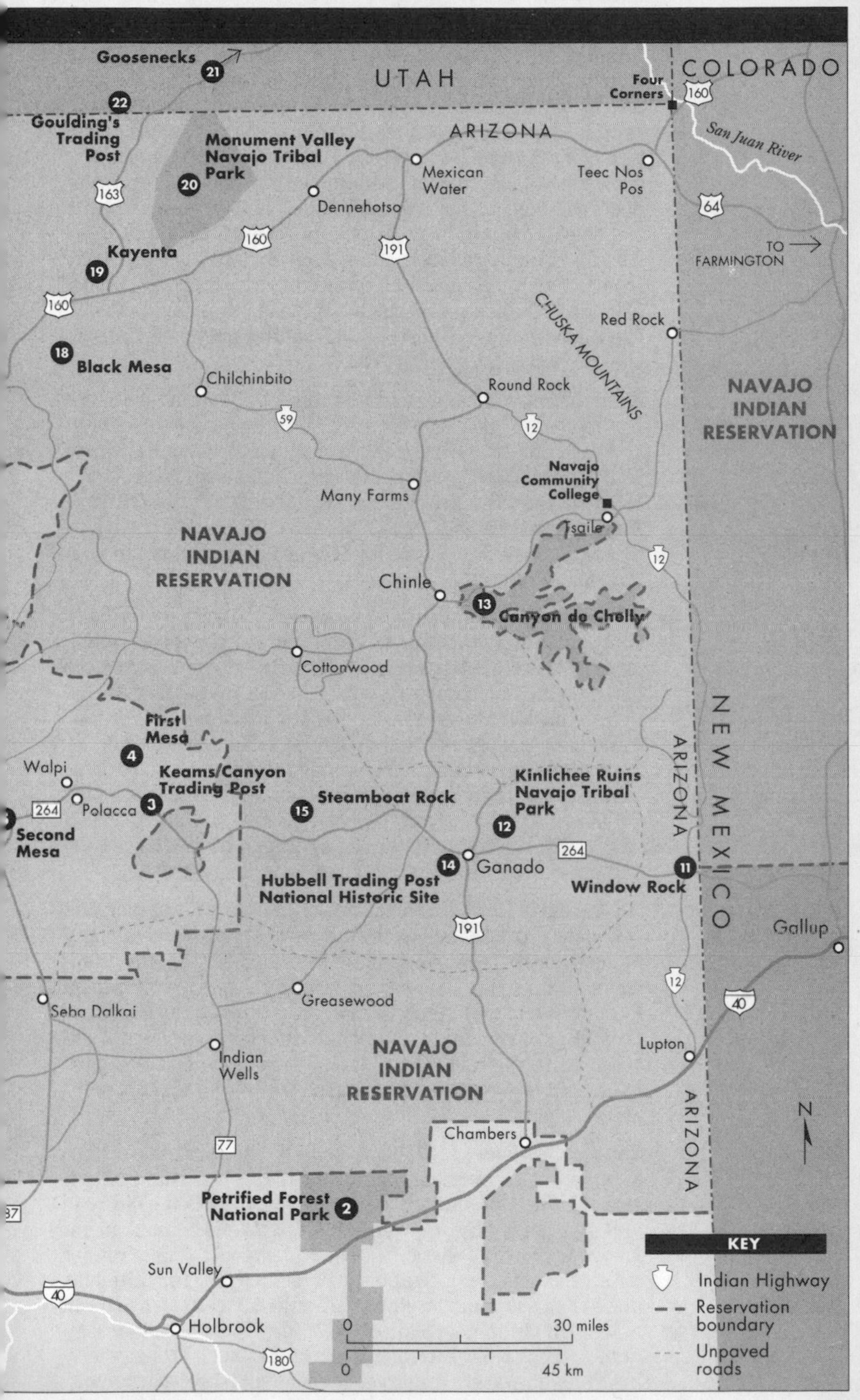

Goosenecks
21
UTAH
COLORADO
Four Corners
160
22
Goulding's Trading Post
Monument Valley Navajo Tribal Park
ARIZONA
San Juan River
20
Mexican Water
Teec Nos Pos
163
Dennehotso
64
160
191
Kayenta
19
TO FARMINGTON
160
CHUSKA MOUNTAINS
Red Rock
18
Black Mesa
Chilchinbito
Round Rock
NAVAJO INDIAN RESERVATION
59
12
Navajo Community College
Many Farms
Tsaile
NAVAJO INDIAN RESERVATION
12
Chinle
13
Canyon de Chelly
Cottonwood
NEW MEXICO
First Mesa
ARIZONA
4
Walpi
Keams/Canyon Trading Post
Kinlichee Ruins Navajo Tribal Park
264
Polacca
3
Steamboat Rock
15
12
Second Mesa
14
Ganado
264
11
Hubbell Trading Post National Historic Site
Window Rock
191
Gallup
12
40
Greasewood
Seba Dalkai
NAVAJO INDIAN RESERVATION
Lupton
Indian Wells
ARIZONA
N
Chambers
77
Petrified Forest National Park
2
KEY
Sun Valley
Indian Highway
40
Reservation boundary
Holbrook
0
30 miles
Unpaved roads
180
0
45 km

Drive 21 miles east on AZ 264 to start your tour at the 3 **Keams Canyon Trading Post,** established by Thomas Keam in 1875. Originally, it served only the Indians of the area, but today the trading post also includes a motel, a restaurant, a shopping center (*see* Shopping, *below*), and a primitive campground (*see* Lodging, *below*). An administrative center for the Bureau of Indian Affairs, Keams Canyon also hosts a number of government buildings. The first 3 miles of the canyon running toward the northeast can be seen by car. At Inscription Rock, about 2 miles down the road, early frontiersman Kit Carson engraved his name in stone. Though there are several picnic spots in the wooded canyon, the main attraction here is the trading post, offering authentic Indian arts and crafts.

From Keams Canyon, head west on AZ 264 for a tour of the Hopi villages, most of which are situated on the top of or at the base of a trio of mesas: First Mesa, Second Mesa, and Third Mesa. You'll need permission beforehand to visit the Hopi villages. For information, call the **Hopi Tribe Office of Public Relations** (tel. 602/734–2441), which also provides phone numbers for village leaders or village community development offices.

4 On **First Mesa,** 15 miles west of Keams Canyon, you will initially approach **Polacca;** the older and more impressive villages of **Hano, Sichomovi,** and **Walpi** are situated at the top of the mesa. From Polacca, a paved road (off AZ 264) angles up to a parking lot near the village of Sichomovi. For permission to visit Hano, Sichomovi, and Walpi, or to gain information regarding the free guided walking tours of these villages, call the **Community Development Office** (tel. 602/737–2670) or the **Visitor's Center at Ponsli Hall** (tel. 602/737–2262). Guided tours can be arranged between 9 AM and 5 PM; they are free, but a contribution is suggested.

All the older Hopi villages have structures built of rock and adobe mortar in a simple architectural style. **Hano** actually belongs to the Tewa, a Pueblo tribe that fled from the Spanish in 1696 and secured permission from the Hopi to build a new home on First Mesa. **Sichomovi** is built so close to Hano that only the residents know the actual boundary line. Constructed in the mid-1600s, this village is believed to have been built to ease overcrowding at Walpi, the highest point on the mesa.

For most outsiders, **Walpi** is usually the most impressive stop on the Hopi reservation, but it can be visited only if you are accompanied by a Hopi guide. Built on solid rock and surrounded by steep cliffs, Walpi stands against an immense expanse of distant earth and sky. At its narrowest point, the mesa measures only 15 feet across. Inhabited for more than 300 years, Walpi's cliff-edge houses seem to be an extension of the nearby terrain. Today, only about 30 residents occupy this settlement, which has neither electricity nor running water. Important ceremonial dances frequently take place here. You can purchase kachina dolls made by the local men and authentic Hopi pottery created by the local women.

5 **Second Mesa,** accessed by AZ 264, is 10 miles west of Polacca. The small villages of **Shipaulovi** and **Mishongnovi** are situated off a paved road that goes north from 264, about ⅕ mile east of the Hopi Cultural Center. Both communities lie on a projection of the Second Mesa; Mishongnovi, the easternmost settlement, was built in the late 1600s. Visitors can take guided tours ($6 per person) of Shipaulovi, the most recently established village. Call the Shipaulovi Village Community Center (tel. 602/737–2570) for tour times.

Shungopavi, the largest and oldest village on Second Mesa, may be reached by a paved road angling south off AZ 264 between the junction of AZ 87 and the Hopi Cultural Center. The famous Hopi snake dances (now closed to the public) are held here in August during even-numbered years. For permission to visit Shungopavi, call the village's **Community Development Office** (tel. 602/734–2262).

One of the livelier spots on Second Mesa is the **Hopi Cultural Center,** on the north side of AZ 264, west of the junction at AZ 87. In addition to its shops and pueblo-style museum, the center features a good restaurant serving American and native dishes and an immaculate motel (*see* Dining and Lodging, *below*). The cultural center is not only an excellent spot for an overnight stop, but it is also one of the best places on the reservation from which to obtain information. *Tel. 602/734-2401; museum tel. 602/734–6650. Museum admission: $3 adults, $1 children under 13. Open mid-May–Oct., weekdays 8–5, weekends 9–4; Nov.–mid-May, weekdays 8–5.*

If you drive 8 miles to the west of the Hopi Cultural Center on AZ 264, you'll approach **Kykotsmovi** at the eastern base
6 of **Third Mesa.** Indians from Oraibi (*see below*) descended from the mesa and built this village in a canyon with a perennial spring; the community is known for its greenery and peach orchards. The town also serves as the home of the **Hopi Tribal Headquarters** and the **Office of Public Relations** (tel. 602/734–2441), another good source of information regarding ceremonies and dances.

Oraibi, a few miles west and on top of Third Mesa, is widely believed to be the oldest continually inhabited community in the United States, dating from around AD 1150. It was also the site of a rare, bloodless conflict between two groups of the Hopi people; in 1906, a dispute, settled uniquely by a "pushing contest," sent the losers off to establish Hotevilla (*see below*). Oraibi is a dusty spot, and as an act of courtesy, tourists are asked to park their cars outside and approach the village on foot.

As you continue to drive west on AZ 264, you'll pass more crafts shops and art galleries. The Third Mesa villages are known for their baskets, kachina dolls, weaving, and jewelry.

Hotevilla and **Bacavi** are about 4 miles west of Oraibi, and their inhabitants are descended from the former residents of that village. The men of Hotevilla continue to plant crops along the mesa slopes, and in warmer months these gardens on the cliffs are lovely to behold.

Beyond Hotevilla, AZ 264 descends from Third Mesa, and
you will soon exit the Hopi reservation and cross Navajo
7 land. About 30 miles west of Hotevilla, you'll pass **Coal Can-**
yon, where Indians have long mined coal from the dark seam just below the rim. This canyon of colorful mudstone, dark lines of coal, and bleached white formations has an eerie, ghostlike appearance, especially by the light of the moon.

Another 20 miles to the west is **Moenkopi,** the last Hopi outpost, just before Tuba City at the junction of AZ 264 and U.S. 160. Established as a farming community, it was also
settled by the descendents of former Oraibi residents.
8 Across U.S. 160, **Tuba City** is the administrative center for the western portion of the Navajo Nation, with about 5,000 permanent residents. In addition to a motel and a few restaurants, this small town has a hospital, a bank, and a historic trading post. Founded in the early 1880s and recently restored, the octagon-shaped **Tuba City Trading Post** (Main St., tel. 602/283–5441) carries authentic Indian rugs, pottery, baskets, and jewelry; it also sells groceries.

From Tuba City, take U.S. 160 west. About 5½ miles from
the city, between mileposts 316 and 317, you'll see a small
9 sign for **Dinosaur Tracks.** More than 200 million years ago, carnivorous bipedal reptiles over 10 feet tall left their imprints in soft mud that subsequently turned to sandstone. There's no charge for a look.

Four miles west of Dinosaur Tracks on U.S. 160, turn left on
10 U.S. 89; 16 miles south, you will arrive at the **Cameron Trading Post** (tel. 602/679–2231). Established in 1916, this is one of the few remaining authentic trading posts in the Southwest. *See* Chapter 3, Grand Canyon Country and Lake Mead, for details.

After a stop at the Cameron Trading Post, continue south another 52 miles to Flagstaff. We recommend that you take at least one overnight on this tour, either at the Hopi Cultural Center on Second Mesa or at a motel in Keams Canyon (*see* Dining and Lodging, *below*). Another option is to sleep in Tuba City and head north into Navajo country (*see* Tour 4, *below*).

Tour 3: Indian Country—Southern Tour

To take the complete tour, allow at least three days and two nights. Begin your drive at **Petrified Forest National Park** and the **Painted Desert** (*see* Tour 1, *above*), if you haven't stopped here before.

From the Petrified Forest, continue east on I–40 to Lupton; turn north on Indian Highway 12, which will take you to
11 **Window Rock;** the total distance is 82 miles. Named for an immense hole in a massive sandstone ridge nearby, Window Rock is the capital of the Navajo Nation. With a population of less than 5,000, this small community serves as the shopping, business, and social center for countless Navajo families from the surrounding rural areas. It is also the home of the **Navajo Nation Council Chambers** (turn east off Indian Highway 12, about ½ mile from AZ 264), a handsome structure that resembles a large hogan—the traditional six-sided Navajo house with a domed roof. Near the Council Chambers lies Window Rock Navajo Tribal Park, a pleasant picnic area with juniper trees that provides a close-up view of the huge hole that gives the town its name.

A short drive south of Tribal Park is the **Navajo Tribal Museum,** a small space devoted to the art and culture of the region and the history of the Navajo people; there's an excellent selection of books on the Navajo Nation here. The adjoining **Navajo Arts and Crafts Enterprise** has local creative works on view, including pottery, jewelry, and blankets. *On AZ 264, next to Navajo Nation Inn, tel. 602/871-4090 or 602/871–4095 (Arts and Crafts Enterprise), 602/871–6673 (museum). Admission free. Open May–late Oct., Mon.–Sat. 8–5; late Oct.–Apr., weekdays 8–5.*

If you're curious about wildlife in northeastern Arizona, make a stop at the **Navajo Nation Zoological Park,** just east of the Navajo Tribal Museum. The small zoo—set amid sandstone monoliths—features golden eagles, hawks, elk, wolves, cougars, coyotes, and many other birds, reptiles, and mammals from the area. *East of Navajo Nation Inn and north of AZ 264, tel. 602/871–6573. Admission free. Open daily 8–5.*

Window Rock is a good place to stop for lunch, supplies, and gas. The local restaurants carry standard American fare, Navajo dishes, and fast food. Near the center of downtown is the **Navajo Tribal Fairgrounds,** the site of many all-Indian rodeos (in the Navajo Nation, many Indians are cowboys). The community hosts the annual July 4 Powwow, with a major rodeo, ceremonial dances, and a parade, and the Navajo Nation Tribal Fair (much like a traditional state fair, with a Navajo accent) in early September.

12 **Kinlichee Ruins Navajo Tribal Park** lies 22 miles west of Window Rock on AZ 264; a marked turnoff leads to this 640-acre park. A complex of ruins here dates from the early An-

asazi, a culture of prehistoric Native Americans who mysteriously abandoned their Southwest dwelling places prior to AD 1300. The park, which is always open, has a self-guided trail that takes you past the ruins and trailside exhibits (you are not permitted to descend into the pit, where the kiva is); it also offers picnic areas and a primitive campground. A camping fee of $1 per person may be collected.

Next, drive 6 miles west on AZ 264, passing through the community of **Ganado,** and continue for another 5 miles until you reach the intersection of U.S. 191 north; turn right and drive 30 miles to Chinle, a good place for an overnight stop before a visit Canyon de Chelly. In the vicinity, you'll find two motels, several restaurants, and a campground. Especially during the summer months, you should call ahead for motel reservations.

13 The nearly 84,000-acre **Canyon de Chelly** (pronounced deh-SHAY) near Chinle is one of the most spectacular of all national monuments in the Southwest. Its main gorges—the 26-mile-long **Canyon de Chelly** and the adjoining 35-mile-long **Canyon del Muerto**—have sheer, heavily eroded sandstone walls that reach up to 1,000 feet; ancient pictographs decorate some of the cliffs. Gigantic stone formations rise hundreds of feet above small streams, hogans, tilled fields, peach orchards, and grazing lands.

The first inhabitants in the canyons, the Anasazi people, arrived more than 2,000 years ago and built stone cliff dwellings between AD 300 and AD 1300. After the Anasazi disappeared around 1300, Hopi farmers settled here, followed by the Navajo, beginning around 1700. Centuries-old traditions have been passed down to the Navajo families now living here, who farm and raise sheep. Although the monument is administered by the National Park Service, the land itself belongs to the Navajo.

Canyon de Chelly and Canyon del Muerto each have a paved rim drive that offers marvelous views of the massive canyons, with prehistoric ruins that sometimes lie near the base of cliffs and at other times perch on high sheltering ledges. Occasionally you will also see the modern dwellings and cultivated fields of the present-day Navajo in the flatlands between the cliffs. Each canyon drive takes about two hours.

The **South Rim Drive** of Canyon de Chelly starts at the visitor center and ends at **Spider Rock Overlook,** where the cliffs drop 1,000 feet. Here you'll have a view of two pinnacles, Speaking Rock and Spider Rock; the latter rises about 800 feet from the canyon floor. Other highlights on the South Rim Drive are **Junction Overlook,** where Canyon del Muerto joins Canyon de Chelly; **White House Overlook,** which allows access to the canyon floor (*see below*); and **Sliding House Overlook,** where you can see ruins on a narrow, sloped ledge across the canyon.

The **North Rim Drive** of Canyon del Muerto also begins at the visitor center and continues northeast on Indian Highway 64 toward Tsaile, the site of Navajo Community College. Major stops on this drive include **Antelope House Overlook,** the site of a large ruin named for the animals painted on an adjacent cliff; the **Mummy Cave Overlook,** with the monument's largest cliff dwelling well preserved in two caves; and **Massacre Cave Overlook,** the last stop on the drive, which marks the spot where 115 Navajo were killed by the Spanish in 1805.

Within the monument, only one hike—the **White House Ruin Trail,** on the South Rim Drive—can be done without an authorized guide. The trail is easy to negotiate and starts near White House Overlook along the South Rim Drive of Canyon de Chelly, where sheer walls drop about 550 feet. The trail leads to the White House Ruin, with dwelling remains of nearly 60 rooms and several kivas. Bring your own water for this 2½-mile hike (round-trip).

Visitors can explore the area of Canyon de Chelly National Monument by taking truck and Jeep tours (*see* Guided Tours in Essential Information, *above*), by hiking with rangers and paid guides, and by horseback riding (*see* Sports and Outdoor Activities, *below*). The **visitor center** features exhibits on the history of the Anasazi cliff dwellers and provides information on scheduled hikes, tours, and other programs within the national monument. *Box 588, Chinle 86503, tel. 602/674–5436. Open May–Sept., daily 8–6; Oct.–Apr., daily 8–5.*

Retrace your steps after you depart Canyon de Chelly: head back south again for about 30 miles on U.S. 191, then turn east onto AZ 264 and continue on for several miles to

14 **Hubbell Trading Post National Historic Site.** This trading post was established in 1878 by John Lorenzo Hubbell, a native of the Southwest who was born in Pajarito, New Mexico. To the Navajo, Hubbell was not only a merchant but a good friend and teacher who translated letters, settled family quarrels, explained government policy, and helped the sick. During the 1886 smallpox epidemic in the area, he turned his home into a hospital and personally ministered to the sick and dying. Hubbell passed away in 1930 and is buried not far from the trading post.

Today the Hubbell Trading Post operates much as it did more than a century ago. At the **Visitor's Center,** National Park Service exhibits illustrate the post's history, and Navajo men and women frequently demonstrate the crafts of making jewelry and rugs. You may also take a guided tour of Hubbell's house, which contains one of the finest personal collections of Native American artistry anywhere, including rugs and paintings; six tours are given daily in summer, four in winter. *On AZ 264, 1 mi west of Ganado, tel. 602/755–3475. Admission free. Open June–Sept., daily*

8–6; Oct.–May, daily 8–5. Closed Thanksgiving, Christmas, and New Year's Day.

About 20 miles west of the trading post on the north side of
15 AZ 264 is **Steamboat Rock,** an immense, jutting peninsula of stone that resembles an early-day steamboat, complete with a geologically formed waterline.

At Steamboat Rock, you are only 5 miles from the eastern boundary line of the Hopi reservation, where you can visit the **Hopi Mesas** (*see* Tour 2, *above*). After driving through the mesas on AZ 264, you can join Tour 4 (*see below*) at Tuba City, 50 miles west of the Hopi village of Hotevilla.

Tour 4: Indian Country—Northern Tour

Twenty-two miles northeast of Tuba City on U.S. 160 is the
16 tiny community of **Red Lake.** Off to the left of the highway is a geological phenomenon known as **Elephant Feet.** These massive eroded sandstone buttes make a good photo stop.

If time permits, you might enjoy a short side trip to real
17 Navajo backcountry and a look at **White Mesa Natural Bridge,** about 17 miles north of Red Lake on Indian Highway 21, a graded dirt road. The payoff is a view of a massive arch of white sandstone that extends from the edge of White Mesa. Return by the same route to Red Lake.

About 30 miles north of Red Lake on U.S. 160, you'll come to the turnoff for Navajo National Monument (*see below*).

Continue north from this turnoff and take note of the pla-
18 teau to the right, the long **Black Mesa,** which will remain in view for about the next 15 miles. Above the prominent escarpments of this land formation, mining operations—a major source of revenue for the Navajo Nation—are busy delving into the more than 20 billion tons of coal deposited there.

Turn more directly north from U.S. 160 onto AZ 163; you'll
19 soon approach **Kayenta,** a small town with a few grocery stores, a motel, and a hospital. Kayenta is near the magnificent natural beauty of **Monument Valley,** which stretches to the northeast into Utah. At an altitude of approximately 5,500 feet, this sprawling expanse of land was originally populated by the ancient Anasazi and has also been home to generations of Navajo who have farmed and herded livestock in this arid country. With its soaring red buttes, eroded mesas, deep canyons, and naturally sculpted rock formations, Monument Valley is best enjoyed by simply driving through and pausing from time to time at roadside stops. Many westerns, including *Stagecoach, She Wore a Yellow Ribbon,* and *How the West Was Won,* have been filmed here.

20 Within this vast area lies the 30,000-acre **Monument Valley Navajo Tribal Park,** located 3½ miles off U.S. 163 and about

24 miles north of Kayenta. The park offers a scenic 17-mile self-guided tour, but the road is unpaved and rutted; if you don't want to wear out the shocks on your car, you might consider taking one of the many guided tours offered by operators in and around the visitor center; most take visitors around in enclosed vans and charge about $15 for 2½ hours. Also at the visitor center are an Indian crafts shop and exhibits devoted to both ancient and modern Indian history within the area. The park features a 100-site campground, which closes from early October through April. *Visitor center, tel. 801/727–3287. Park entrance fee: $2.50 adults, $1 senior citizens 60 and older, children under 7 free. Visitor center open May–Sept., daily 7–7; Oct.–Apr., daily 8–5.*

Monument Valley's scenic route, U.S. 163, continues from Arizona into Utah, where the land is crossed, east to west, by a stretch of the San Juan River known as the
21 **Goosenecks**—so named for the type of twists and curves it takes at the bottom of a wildly carved canyon. Set in a lonely, untrafficked domain, this barren, erosion-blasted gorge has a stark beauty that is nearly as awesome as that of the Grand Canyon. The scenic overlook for the Goosenecks is reached by turning west from U.S. 163 onto UT 261, 4 miles north of the small community of Mexican Hat, then proceeding on UT 261 for 1 mile to a directional sign and a 4-mile side road to the vista-point parking lot.

After a stop at the viewpoint for Goosenecks, retrace your route down U.S. 163 and then take Indian Highway 42 a
22 half-mile west to **Goulding's Trading Post.** Established in 1924 by Harry Goulding and his wife, this remote outlet was used as a headquarters by director John Ford when he was filming the western classic *Stagecoach*. Because of the numerous westerns that have been shot in the area, the trading post, motel, and restaurant have gained a measure of international fame. In the old trading post building, a museum showcases prehistoric and modern Indian artifacts as well as memorabilia of the Goulding family. The lodge here is an ideal place to stay overnight, but call in advance for reservations. (Note: the lodge is open all year, but the trading post and the restaurant are closed from November 15 to March 15.) Alternatively, you can overnight in Kayenta, which has two motels (*see* Lodging, *below*).

Take Indian Highway 42 back to the junction with U.S. 163, and proceed south until you reach U.S. 160; continue south, making a right turn on AZ 564 and traveling 9 miles to
23 **Navajo National Monument.** Here two unoccupied 13th-century cliff pueblos, **Keet Seel** and **Betatakin,** stand under the overhang of soaring orange and ocher cliffs. The largest Indian ruins in Arizona, these pueblos were built by the Anasazi people, whose reasons for abandoning the pueblos prior to AD 1300 are still disputed by scholars. The two large stone-and-mortar complexes were obviously built for permanent occupancy, yet the Anasazi had lived in them for

only about three decades when they disappeared. Betatakin (Navajo for "ledge house") consists of a well-preserved, 135-room ruin situated in a large alcove. Keet Seel (Navajo for "broken pottery") is also in good condition, with 160 rooms and five kivas in a serene setting.

For an impressive view of Betatakin, walk to the rim overlook about a half-mile from the visitor center. You can also hike to Betatakin (5 miles round-trip from the visitor center), but only on tours with ranger guides, offered between May 1 and September 30. The trips, generally held twice a day, are restricted to groups of 24. Only 20 people per day are allowed to visit the ruins of Keet Seel on ranger-supervised hikes, offered between Memorial Day and Labor Day. The distance to the ruins—which lie at an elevation of 7,000 feet—is 16 miles (round-trip) from the visitor center. A permit—which also allows campers to stay overnight near Keet Seel ruin—is required. If the idea of horseback riding appeals, you can arrange to rent a mount at the visitor center.

The visitor center houses a small museum, exhibits of prehistoric pottery, and a crafts shop. Free campground and picnic areas are nearby, and rangers present campfire programs in the summer. No food, gasoline, or lodging is available at the monument. *Navajo National Monument, HC71 Box 3, Tonalea 86044, tel. 602/672–2366. Admission free. Open daily 8–5. Closed Thanksgiving, Christmas, and New Year's Day.*

This tour may be followed by a visit to Page, Lake Powell, Glen Canyon Dam, and Rainbow Bridge (*see* Tour 5, *below*). To reach Page from the Navajo National Monument, return to U.S. 160 and travel south for 12 miles, then take AZ 98 for 66 miles.

Tour 5: Lake Powell and Rainbow Bridge

From Flagstaff, take U.S. 89 on a route almost directly north and drive 136 miles to Page and nearby Glen Canyon Dam and Lake Powell. For many miles of this trip, you'll pass an impressive stretch of the Painted Desert off to the right of the highway, with a multihued geography almost identical to that of the Painted Desert contained within the boundaries of Petrified Forest National Park (*see* Tour 1, *above*). Farther north, this landscape gives way to the immense Echo Cliffs, orange sandstone formations that rise well over 1,000 feet above the highway in some places. At Bitter Springs, the highway ascends the cliffs and provides a spectacular view of the 9,000-square-mile expanse of the Arizona Strip to the west and the sheer, 3,000-foot Vermilion Cliffs to the northwest.

Prior to 1957, the broad mesa on which the community of
24 **Page** is situated was essentially barren land, but when construction of Glen Canyon Dam commenced that year, Page

was born. Initially a construction camp, after the completion of the dam and the formation of Lake Powell, Page became a tourist stop and gradually grew to its present population of about 7,000—the largest community in far northern Arizona.

Page has two museums that are worth visiting. The **John Wesley Powell Memorial Museum** downtown honors the work of explorer John Wesley Powell, who, between 1869 and 1872, led the first expeditions down the Green River and the rapids-choked Colorado through the Grand Canyon. Powell mapped, explored, and kept detailed records of his trips, naming the Grand Canyon and many other geographic points of interest in northern Arizona.

Exhibits include expedition drawings and photographs, as well as fossil and minerals that cast light on the geological past of the Colorado River and the massive canyons it helped form across a span of millions of years. Others trace the cultural patterns of the Indians of the Southwest with examples of pottery, baskets, tools, and weapons. The museum also serves as an information center for river and lake trips and scenic flights. *6 N. Lake Powell Blvd. (corner N. Navajo Dr.), tel. 602/645–9496. Admission free. Open Mar.–Apr. and Oct.–Nov., weekdays 9–5; May–Sept., daily 8–7. Closed Dec.–Feb.*

If you drive 2 miles east of Page on AZ 98, you'll reach the **Big Lake Trading Post and Dinebekah Museum and Gallery,** which was funded by actor Chris Robinson of TV's *General Hospital.* Robinson has collected an array of modern and prehistoric Indian artifacts, with the newer pieces available for purchase. Besides crafts, groceries and fishing supplies are on offer, along with service for your car. *Tel. 602/645–2404. Admission free. Open daily 6 AM–9 PM.*

Drive northwest on Lake Powell Boulevard, which becomes U.S. 89 business route. Once you leave the Page business
75 district, the **Glen Canyon Dam** and Lake Powell behind it immediately become visible. Completed in September 1963, the construction of this concrete-arch dam and its power plant was an engineering feat rivaling the building of Hoover Dam. Nearly 5 million cubic feet of concrete were required. The dam's crest is 1,560 feet across and rises 710 feet from bedrock and 583 feet above the waters of the Colorado River. Lake Powell is 560 feet deep at the dam at full pool elevation.

Just off the highway at the north end of the bridge is the **Carl Hayden Visitor Center,** a museumlike facility dedicated to telling the story of the creation of Glen Canyon Dam and Lake Powell. Among the several exhibits is a giant, three-dimensional topographic map of Lake Powell country. The center's huge reception and observation room, with floor-to-ceiling glass, provides panoramic views of the dam, the wildly sculpted cliffs that border Lake Powell, and the immense sandstone buttes that protrude, islandlike, from the lake's emerald waters. Visitors also have the opportunity to take a 40-minute self-guided tour through the dam complex. *Glen Canyon Dam, tel. 602/645–2511. Admission free. Open daily 8–5. Closed Christmas and New Year's Day.*

Lake Powell, with more than 1,900 miles of shoreline, is the heart of the huge 1,255,400-acre Glen Canyon National Recreation Area. Created by the barrier of Glen Canyon Dam and fed by the mighty Colorado River, the jade-green lake extends through eroded canyon country that is nearly devoid of vegetation and so rugged that it was the last major area of the United States to be mapped. The waters of Lake Powell are confined by immense red cliffs that twist off from the main body of the lake into 96 major canyons and countless inlets and coves—so many, in fact, that no single person claims to have explored all of them. In a number of places, huge sandstone buttes jut from the water. Seeing the stark and stunning geography of Lake Powell often makes tourists feel they are visiting another planet.

The most popular destination on the lake, which stretches 120 miles through northern Arizona and southern Utah, is
26 **Wahweap,** a vacation village 5 miles north of the Glen Canyon Dam on U.S. 89. Most of the recreational activity in the region takes place around here, where everything needed for a water-oriented holiday is available. Visitors can easily rent boats and a wide variety of water-sports equipment (*see* Sports and Outdoor Activities, *below*). Stop at **Wahweap Lodge** (*see* Dining and Lodging, *below*) for an excellent view of the lake area.

Summer is a busy time in the Lake Powell area, and advance reservations are recommended. Travelers seeking a quieter vacation should plan a visit during late October through early May, when there are fewer people and lower prices. Skies in the Lake Powell area are blue nearly all year, and there is only about 8 inches of rainfall annually. Summer temperatures range from the 60s to the 90s (sometimes more than 100°F). Many fall and spring days are balmy, with daytime temperatures often in the 70s and 80s, but it is possible for chilly weather to set in. In winter the risk of a cold spell increases, but all-weather houseboats and tour boats make year-round cruising possible.

The best way to appreciate the beauty of Lake Powell is by boat. If you don't have access to one, the half-day excursion
27 cruise to **Rainbow Bridge National Monument** is the way to go; many people consider this to be among the highlights of a visit to Arizona's northeast. Along the 50-mile route (one-way from Wahweap Marina), you're treated to ever-changing scenery that is both beautiful and bizarre, including both huge monoliths that look like people turned into stone and a butte that resembles a dinosaur. You might also see eagles perched on ragged outcrops of rock. Finally, after

gliding through a deep and twisting canyon waterway, the boat docks near Rainbow Bridge, the massive 290-foot red sandstone arch that straddles a cove of the lake. The world's largest natural stone bridge, it can be reached only by water or by an arduous hike from a remote point on the Navajo reservation (*see* Sports and Outdoor Activities, *below*).

The excursion boats, which leave Wahweap daily, are two-tiered craft with upper sun decks, as well as interior seating with windows. Experienced pilots provide commentary throughout the trip. Pack a lunch or take snacks; no food is sold on the boats, though coffee and water are provided for passengers. And be sure to bring your camera.

Other cruises are offered at the Wahweap Marina, including an all-day trip that stops at Rainbow Bridge and then proceeds farther into the Utah portion of the lake. (*See* Boating and Cruises in Sports and Outdoor Activities, *below*, for information on prices and reservations)

Off the Beaten Track

Most of the 25,000 square miles of the Navajo reservation and other areas of northeastern Arizona are actually off the beaten track. Many visitors to the northeast generally stay on the paved roads, but this vast, sparsely populated region is crisscrossed with dirt roads. If you don't have the equipment for wilderness travel—including a four-wheel-drive vehicle, water, food, tools, and bedrolls—and do not have backcountry experience, we recommend that you stay off the dirt roads unless they are signed and graded, and the skies are clear.

Chuska Mountains. These impressive mountains in Navajo high country are covered with huge stands of ponderosa pine. To explore this part of the Navajo reservation, take Indian Highway 64 from the Canyon de Chelly visitor center to the community of Tsaile (23 miles). Here Navajo medicine men worked in conjunction with architects to design Tsaile's **Navajo Community College** (tel. 602/724–3311). Because all important Navajo activities traditionally take place in a circle (a hogan is essentially circular), the campus was laid out in the round with all of the buildings within its perimeter. The college's **Hatathli Museum** is devoted to Native American culture. *Tel. 602/724–6156. Donations accepted. Open weekdays 8:30–noon and 1–4:30; groups by appointment.*

Two miles northeast of Tsaile, turn left on Indian Highway 12 and continue 26 miles to Round Rock, where Indian Highway 12 meets U.S. 191. During your drive, the high country will rise off to the right. Dirt roads traverse the mountains, but they are often unsuitable for passenger cars. At U.S. 191, turn left and head back south to Chinle if you are following Tour 3, above.

Four Corners Monument. In the summer months, nearly 2,000 people a day wend their way to this simple concrete slab inlaid into the ground. The slab marks the only point in the United States where four states meet: Arizona, New Mexico, Colorado, and Utah. Most visitors stay only a few minutes to record the spot on film; you'll see many people posed awkwardly, with an arm or a leg in each state. *Off U.S. 160, 7 mi northwest of the U.S. 160–U.S. 164 junction (near Teec Nos Pos). The monument is a 75-mi drive from Kayenta, near Monument Valley.*

What to See and Do with Children

Although northeastern Arizona is an extremely popular area for families on vacation, the region has no attractions designed specifically for children. However, many youngsters will be fascinated by the area's scenic beauty and Indian culture. They will particularly enjoy the Navajo Nation Zoological Park in Window Rock (*see* Tour 3, *above*), and the Petrified Forest (*see* Tour 1, *above*), Canyon de Chelly (*see* Tour 3, *above*), and Navajo National Monument (*see* Tour 4, *above*), they'll have plenty of space for running around and exploring. In the Lake Powell region (*see* Tour 5, *above*), many motels have swimming pools, and there are numerous water-related recreational activities for children.

Younger children may get restless during some of the long and lonely driving stretches on the Indian reservations, so it's a good idea to bring along lots of toys and books for the car.

Shopping

Groceries, over-the-counter medicines, gasoline, and other supplies can be purchased in all of the major communities and trading posts on the Navajo and Hopi reservations, including Page, Window Rock, Fort Defiance, Ganado, Chinle, Hopi Second Mesa, Keams Canyon, Tuba City, Kayenta, Goulding's Trading Post, and Cameron Trading Post. Some of the smaller communities offer limited supplies; in general, don't count on a wide selection. Plan your gas stops for the locations cited.

Beyond the necessities for travel, most visitors to Indian country are looking for pottery, turquoise and sterling-silver jewelry, handwoven baskets, beautiful and often expensive Navajo wool rugs, and other examples of Native American crafts. In addition to the work of Hopi and Navajo artisans, many of the trading posts also carry the work of New Mexico's tribes, including exquisite Zuni jewelry and the world-acclaimed pottery of the Pueblo Indians. Many vendors have roadside stands that resemble Navajo shade arbors. Most products offered on the Hopi and Navajo reservations are authentic, but the possibility of imitations still exists. The trading posts are usually reliable.

Telephone lines—and thus connections with credit card verification sources—are often iffy at the Hopi Mesas. It's a good idea to carry cash or traveler's checks in order to make purchases here or anywhere else outside of the trading posts.

Outlets of the **Navajo Arts and Crafts Enterprise,** located in Window Rock (off AZ 264, next to Navajo Nation Inn, tel. 602/871–4095) and Cameron (near junction of U.S. 89 and AZ 64, tel. 602/679–2303), stock fine authentic Navajo products. The nearby **Cameron Trading Post** has a large selection of goods from a variety of tribes; *see* Chapter 3, Grand Canyon Country and Lake Mead, for details. The **Hopi Cultural Center** (off AZ 264, Hopi Second Mesa, tel. 602/734–2401) has a collection of shops featuring the work of local artists and craftsmen. The gift shop at **Navajo National Monument** (tel. 602/672–2366) has an excellent selection of jewelry. **Hubbell Trading Post** (off AZ 264, 1 mi west of Ganado, tel. 602/755–3475) is famous for its "Ganado red" Navajo rugs. **Keams Canyon Arts and Crafts** (Keams Canyon, tel. 602/738–2295) is another good outlet. But it's possible to find exactly what you want, at a good price, at a reservation roadside vendor. If you would like some tips on quality, the **Navajo Tourism Office** (Box 663, Window Rock 86515, tel. 602/871–6659 or 602/871–7371) has printed material on the subject.

Sports and Outdoor Activities

Bicycling For biking enthusiasts, the news is good and bad. If you carry a bike on your car, as many cyclists do these days, you will find endless miles of paved roads, and most of the time, traffic is very light. The bad news is that the mostly two-lane highways do not have paved shoulders, and local motorists and tourists alike are not accustomed to encountering cyclists. As a result, you should practice extreme caution when riding. For safe bike rides, the roads at Canyon de Chelly National Monument, Navajo National Monument, Monument Valley Navajo Tribal Park, and Kinlichee Navajo Tribal Park are your best bets. There are no bicycle rental companies in Indian country.

Boating **Lake Powell, Wahweap Marina.** The boating opportunities on Lake Powell are almost limitless. If you have your own boat, docks and launching ramps are available at State Line Marina, 1½ miles north of Wahweap Lodge. Rental boats, excursion boats, and water-sports equipment, including ski packages, water sleds, and motorized wave cutters, are available near Wahweap Lodge, 5 miles north of Page on U.S. 89. Houseboats range widely in size and price; one that sleeps six (in three double beds) costs $666 for three nights. Houseboats should be reserved well in advance. Small boats, too, vary in size and price. An 18-foot powerboat for eight passengers runs about $185 per day. Most of these prices drop after the summer months. For further information about Wahweap Marina, call 800/528–6154 (not accessible from Phoenix) or 602/278–8888.

Camping and RV Parks Although Indian country stretches thousands of square miles across an open and sparsely populated region, most visitors will want to camp in authorized areas. Most campgrounds are primitive, in many cases nothing more than open, level areas where sleeping bags can be laid out or RVs can be parked; only Monument Valley has developed camping facilities. If you plan to stay in national monument and park areas, camping permission can be obtained on-site; for other camping situations, contact the **Navajo Parks and Recreation Department** (Box 308, Window Rock, tel. 602/871–6645) to find out whether you need a permit. (*See* the Dining and Lodging section, *below*, for some of the recommended campsites in the area.)

Cruises **Lake Powell to Rainbow Bridge.** Both half- and full-day cruises leave from the dock at Wahweap Lodge to Rainbow Bridge National Monument. The 290-foot arch spans an isolated cove 50 miles from Wahweap. Experienced guides pilot the modern, double-decker scenic cruisers. *For advance reservations and information, call 800/528–6154. Half-day cruise, summer season: $49.95 adults, $26.50 children; full-day: about $63 adults, $33.50 children. Prices are lower Oct.–Apr.*

Lake Powell Sunset Dinner Cruise. *See* the Page/Lake Powell section in Dining and Lodging, below.

Wilderness River Adventures. These guided and piloted 4½-hour rafting excursions cover a portion of the Colorado River that is relatively calm, with no white-water rapids. The scenery through Glen Canyon Dam is spectacular as the rafts glide beneath multicolored sandstone cliffs that are frequently adorned with Indian petroglyphs (rock drawings). Transportation is furnished from Wahweap Lodge to the point of departure. *For advance reservations and information, call 800/528–6154. Cost: $37 adults, $29.95 children under 12. Prices are lower Oct.–Apr.*

Fishing Indian country has scattered lakes, most of them remote and small, that contain game fish. Two of the more popular and accessible lakes are located in the eastern portion of the Navajo reservation in the vicinity of Canyon de Chelly: **Wheatfields Lake,** on Indian Highway 12 about 11 miles south of the community of Tsaile, and **Many Farms Lake,** near the community of Many Farms, on U.S. 191. Permits are always required for fishing on the reservation. Contact **Navajo Fish and Wildlife Office** (Box 1480, Window Rock 86515, tel. 602/871–6451 or 602/871–6452).

Lake Powell and the area below Glen Canyon Dam are excellent fishing sites. Lake Powell features largemouth and striped bass, black crappie, catfish, bluegill, and walleye. The Colorado River below Glen Canyon Dam is known for its large trout. Keep in mind that Lake Powell stretches through both Arizona and Utah, and the appropriate permit is required depending on where you fish. (*See* Chapter 1, Essential Information, for more information on fishing permits.)

Hiking There are many excellent places to hike at the national monuments, tribal parks, and other points of interest in Indian Country, but the following merit special mention.

In **Canyon de Chelly,** some of the best hiking is up the streambed between the soaring, orange sandstone cliffs, with the ruins of the old Anasazi communities frequently in view. Guides, required for all but the White Horse Ruin Trail, currently charge about $10 per hour for day hikes. For overnights, there's a $10 surcharge for the guide and usually a $20 charge for permission to stay on private land in the area to which the guide will take you; groups of up to 15 people can be accommodated. The hikes aren't too strenuous, but you should wear hiking or running shoes. Contact the visitor center (*see* Tour 3, *above*).

In addition to casual hikes along the rim areas where the ruins of Betatakin can be viewed, in the spring and summer **Navajo National Monument** offers a guided 5-mile hike (round-trip) to Betatakin twice times a day, or a 16-mile hike (round-trip) to the more distant ruins of Keet Seel, both departing from the visitor center. It's advisable to make reservations in advance. For information, contact Navajo National Monument (*see* Tour 4, *above*).

Seasoned hikers in good physical condition might want to try either of the two trails leading to **Rainbow Bridge,** the 290-foot sandstone arch in a remote cove on Lake Powell; each runs about 26–28 miles round-trip. Take Indian Highway 16 north toward the Utah state border. When you come to a fork in the road, go down either "prong" for about 5 miles and you'll come to a trailhead leading to Rainbow Bridge. Excursion boats pull in at the dock at the arch, but no supplies are sold there. A topographical map of the area is strongly suggested: This is wilderness area, and trails are sometimes poorly marked and ill maintained. For a map and other information, contact **Rainbow Bridge National Monument** (Box 1507, Page 86040, tel. 602/645–2471).

Horseback Riding **Justin Horse Rentals** (tel. 602/674–5678), located near the South Rim Drive entrance of Canyon de Chelly, offers horseback trips into the canyon ranging from two hours to several days. The cost is $8 per hour for each horse and $8 per hour for a guide.

Native American guides conduct horseback tours to Keet Seel at Navajo National Monument daily from Memorial

Day weekend through Labor Day weekend; rates are approximately $55 per day. Reservations must be made in advance. Contact Virginia Austin (c/o Navajo National Monument, HC-71 Box 3, Tonalea, AZ 86044, tel. 602/672–2366 or 602/672–2367) for details.

If you've always wanted to ride off into the sunset at Monument Valley, get in touch with Edward Y. Black (Box 155, Mexican Hat, Utah 84531, tel. 800/551–4039). Prices for trail rides, which can be as short as 1½ hours or as long as five days, range from $20 to $65 (per overnight); rides leave from the corral, a half-mile north of the Monument Valley visitor center.

Dining and Lodging

Dining Northeastern Arizona offers no fancy restaurants for fine dining. Dress is casual, seating is on a first-come, first-served basis, and prices are reasonable. Only in the Page/Lake Powell area at the height of the summer season is it advisable to make reservations.

Because northeastern Arizona is a vast area and few communities offer eating establishments, visitors should keep in mind the following major locations that have restaurants and fast-food service: Page, Window Rock, Fort Defiance, Ganado, Chinle, Hopi Second Mesa, Keams Canyon, Tuba City, Kayenta, Goulding's Trading Post/Monument Valley, and Cameron. Most serve standard American fare, and some also feature Mexican and Native American dishes. In some of the smaller reservation communities, only fast food may be available.

Restaurants are open daily unless otherwise noted. Highly recommended restaurants are indicated by a star ★.

Category	Cost*
Very Expensive	over $25
Expensive	$15–$25
Moderate	$10–$15
Inexpensive	under $10

**per person, excluding drinks, service, and sales tax (6.7%), except on the Hopi and Navajo reservations, where no tax is charged*

Lodging Northeastern Arizona is a big land with few people and long distances between communities, and a top priority for travelers here is simply making sure that you have a place to lay your head at the end of the day. Half the battle is knowing in which of the scattered communities motels are located. During summer months, it is especially wise to make reservations in advance. Fortunately, all of the motels in Indian country are clean and comfortable, and the majority of the dozen motel and hotel locations in Page and at Lake Powell are also well maintained.

Unless otherwise indicated, all the establishments listed have air-conditioning, private baths, telephones, and TVs in their rooms. Highly recommended motels are indicated by a star ★.

Category	Cost*
Expensive	over $80
Moderate	$50–$80
Inexpensive	under $50

**All prices are for a standard double room, summer rates (rates may be lower at other times), excluding service charges and 8½% sales tax in the Page area. No tax is charged on the Hopi and Navajo reservations.*

Cameron

Dining and Lodging **Cameron Trading Post and Motel.** This is a good place for stop if you're driving from the Hopi Mesas to the Grand Canyon. (*See* Lodging section in Chapter 3, Grand Canyon Country and Lake Mead, for details.)

Camping **Cameron RV Park** (on U.S. 89, 26 mi southwest of Tuba City, tel. 602/679–2231) is adjacent to the Cameron Trading Post, with its restaurant, grocery store, and post office. The fee with hookup is $13.57 per day. The park is open all year.

Chinle/Canyon de Chelly

Dining and Lodging **Thunderbird Lodge.** Set in an ideal spot at the mouth of Canyon de Chelly, this pleasant establishment has stone and adobe units that match the architecture of the site's original 1896 trading post. Inviting rooms feature roughly hewn beamed ceilings, rustic wood furniture, and Navajo decor. You'll find the staff friendly and knowledgeable about the locale. The manicured lawns and large, sheltering cottonwood trees help create a resortlike atmosphere. A traditional cafeteria offers an inexpensive American menu that ranges from soup, salads, and sandwiches to complete meals, including charbroiled steaks, prepared by an all-Navajo staff. *Box 548 (½ mi south of Canyon de Chelly visitor center), Chinle 86503, tel. 602/674–5841. 72 rooms. Facilities: cafeteria, gift shop, Jeep tours. AE, D, DC, MC, V. Expensive.*

Canyon de Chelly Motel. This two-story, western-style motel, about a mile from Canyon de Chelly, has modern, cheerful rooms with light oak furnishings and American Indian–print bedspreads and drapes. *Box 295 (on Rte. 7, ¼ mi east of U.S. 191), Chinle 86503, tel. 602/674–5875 or 602/674–*

5288. 68 rooms. Facilities: restaurant, indoor pool, gift shop. AE, DC, MC, V. Moderate.

Camping **Cottonwood Campground** (Canyon de Chelly National Monument, near visitor center, Chinle, tel. 602/674–5436) has about 94 sites (including RV spaces but no hookups), available on a first-come, first-served basis, on grounds with cottonwood trees and a picnic area. Camping is free, and the campground is open all year, with water available April–September.

Hopi Reservation–Second Mesa

Dining **Tunosvongya Restaurant.** Also known as the Hopi Cultural Center Restaurant, this clean, comfortable establishment operated by Native Americans provides the opportunity to sample traditional dishes, including Indian tacos, Hopi blue-corn pancakes, fry bread, and a lamb stew that goes by the Hopi name *nok qui vi. On AZ 264 on Second Mesa, tel. 602/734–2401. DC, MC, V. Inexpensive.*

Lodging ★ **Hopi Cultural Center Motel.** This pleasant pueblo-style lodging set high atop a Hopi mesa offers immaculate rooms with mauve and white walls and charming Native American decor, including interesting artwork. *Box 67 (on AZ 264, at Hopi Cultural Center), Second Mesa 86043, tel. 602/734–2401. 33 units. Facilities: restaurant, museum, gift shop. DC, MC, V. Moderate.*

Kayenta

Dining and Lodging ★ **Anasazi Inn at Tsegi.** This unpretentious roadside motel, convenient to both Navajo National Monument and Monument Valley, offers clean, comfortable accommodations and striking views from its rear-facing rooms. Its restaurant, which features tasty Navajo fry bread sandwiches and tacos, is among the best in the area. *Box 1543 (on U.S. 160, 10 mi west of Kayenta), Kayenta 86033, tel. 602/697–3793. 56 units. Facilities: restaurant. AE, D, MC, V. Moderate.*

Lodging **Holiday Inn.** Except for the contemporary southwestern-style decor, this accommodation about a half-mile from Monument Valley provides what you would expect from the Holiday Inn chain. It's clean and comfortable, and has one of the few swimming pools in the western section of Indian country. *Box 307 (south of junction of U.S. 160 and U.S. 163), Kayenta 86033, tel. 602/697–3221. 160 rooms. Facilities: restaurant, gift shop, laundromat, swimming pool, Monument Valley tours. AE, D, DC, MC, V. Expensive.*

Wetherill Inn Motel. Named for John Wetherill, a frontier rancher, trader, and explorer who discovered many of the major prehistoric Native American ruins in Arizona, this clean and cheerful two-story motel without frills was recently renovated with orange-and-brown decor and carpeting. *Box 175 (on U.S. 163), Kayenta 86033, tel. 602/697–*

3231. 54 rooms. Facilities: gift shop, nearby café. AE, D, DC, MC, V. Moderate.

Keams Canyon

Dining **Keams Canyon Restaurant.** At this typical rural roadside dining spot, furnished functionally with Formica tabletops, you can choose from American dishes and a few Native American items, including Navajo tacos, made with Indian fry bread (not unlike a soft pizza crust) heaped with ground beef, chili, beans, lettuce, and grated cheese. *Keams Canyon Shopping Center (near AZ 264), tel. 602/738–2296. MC, V. Open weekdays 7 AM–8 PM. No dinner weekends. Inexpensive.*

Lodging **Keams Canyon Motel.** This clean motel in a rustic trading-post setting is conveniently located near the Hopi Mesas. The rooms are basic, with a hint of Native American decor, and some units have kitchenettes. *Box 188 (off AZ 264, adjacent to Keams Canyon Shopping Center), Keams Canyon 86034, tel. 602/738–2297. 20 units. Facilities: restaurant, grocery store, service station, post office all nearby. MC, V. Inexpensive.*

Camping **Keams Canyon Campground** (near Keams Canyon Trading Poston AZ 264, tel. 602/738–2297) offers free camping at two sites; there's no water or other facilities.

Monument Valley

Dining ★ **Stagecoach Restaurant.** Set deep in Monument Valley, this establishment is a part of the Goulding's Trading Post and motel complex. The restaurant stands in the lee of a massive red butte; large windows and the elevated vista provide a splendid view across the valley. The interior's southwestern decor features memorabilia from movies shot in the area. The mostly standard American dishes are well prepared, and the service is excellent. *2 mi west of U.S. 163, just north of Utah border, tel. 801/727–3231 or 800/874–0902. AE, D, DC, MC, V. Closed Nov. 15–Mar. 15. Moderate.*

Lodging ★ **Goulding's Lodge.** Built near the base of an immense red sandstone butte with spectacular views of Monument Valley from all the rooms, this comfortable motel often serves as headquarters for the location crews of filmmakers. The lodge has handsome pueblo-style buildings stuccoed in a deep reddish brown that makes them appear to be a part of the surrounding red-rock formations. The cozy rooms are furnished in contemporary style, with southwestern colors and Navajo-design bedspreads. *Box 1 (2 mi west of U.S. 163, just north of Utah border), Monument Valley, UT 84536, tel. 801/727–3231 or 800/874–0902. 62 rooms. Facilities: restaurant, trading post, museum (all closed Nov. 15–*

Mar. 15), laundromat, Monument Valley tours. AE, D, DC, MC, V. Expensive.

Camping **Good Sam Campground** (off U.S. 163, near Goulding's Trading Post, 27 mi north of Kayenta, tel. 801/727-3280) has tents and RV sites. The fee is $12 with no hookups, $14.50 with hookups. The site is open April–November.

Mitten View Campground (Monument Valley Navajo Tribal Park, near visitor center, off U.S. 163, 25 mi north of Kayenta, tel. 801/727-3287) has sites with a table, a grill, and a deck. Water is available; the fee is $10 per site; hot showers are extra. The campground is open March–October.

Navajo National Monument

Camping **Navajo National Monument** (reached by turnoff on U.S. 160, 21 mi south of Kayenta, tel. 602/672-2366) has two campgrounds with RV and tent sites, water, and rest rooms, but no hookups. Camping here is free and is available May–October.

Page/Lake Powell

Dining ★ ***Canyon King Paddlewheeler.*** Visitors embark this 95-foot boat, designed as an 1800s riverboat, for a 2½-hour sunset dinner cruise. Presented buffet style on the fully glassed lower deck, dinner includes one entrée—prime rib with fresh garden vegetables and a baked potato—and a salad and dessert. Cocktails are available at an extra charge. The cost of the dinner cruise is about $40 for both children and adults; adults who wish to take the cruise without eating pay $19, and it's $13 for children. *Board at Wahweap Lodge (off U.S. 89, 5 mi north of Page), tel. 602/645-2433 or 800/528-6154. Departure times vary seasonally, and the cruise has a 10-passenger minimum. AE, D, DC, MC, V. Very Expensive.*

★ **Rainbow Room in Wahweap Lodge.** You can't beat the beautiful setting of this attractive semicircular restaurant with panoramic views of Lake Powell and a colony of houseboats bobbing offshore. The dining room connects to a cocktail lounge, and live entertainment is offered during the summer months. An extensive menu features southwestern, standard American, and some Continental fare, accompanied by a good wine selection. Specialties include Southwest chicken breast, marinated in a sauce of honey and green jalapeño peppers, and coho salmon, panfried with a Dijon-mustard cream sauce. There is nightly salad-and-soup bar and a breakfast buffet. *Wahweap Lodge (on U.S. 89, 5 mi north of Page), tel. 602/645-2433 or 800/528-6154. AE, D, DC, MC, V. Moderate.*

Lodging ★ **Wahweap Lodge.** On a promontory above Lake Powell, Wahweap Lodge serves as the center for recreational activities in the area. This attractively landscaped property offers accommodations with oak furnishings and balconies or patios; many of the rooms have a lake view. The brightly colored, southwestern-style suites in the newest building are very attractive. Guests can enjoy two pools, a cocktail lounge, summer entertainment, a marina, and the excellent Rainbow Room (*see above*) for dining. *Box 1597 (on U.S. 89, 5 mi north of Page), Page 86040, tel. 602/645–2433 or 800/528–6154. 350 rooms. Facilities: gift shop, rental boats, cruises, fishing and water-skiing equipment, river-rafting excursions, houseboats. AE, D, DC, MC, V. Expensive.*

Inn at Lake Powell. Situated on a high bluff in the small community of Page, this motel has service and amenities you would expect from a good hotel. A number of the large rooms, with queen-size beds and southwestern-style decor, provide fine views of Glen Canyon Dam and Lake Powell. *Box C (716 Rim View Dr.) Page 86040, tel. 602/645–2466. 103 rooms. Facilities: restaurant, cocktail lounge, conference rooms, pool, hot tub. AE, D, DC, MC, V. Moderate–Expensive.*

Lake Powell Motel. This clean, reasonably priced, no-frills motel outside of Page provides a great panoramic view of Lake Powell and the beautiful surrounding countryside. *Box 1597 (on U.S. 89, 4 mi north of Glen Canyon Dam), Page 86040, tel. 602/645–2477 or 800/528–6154. 24 rooms. AE, D, DC, MC, V. Moderate.*

Camping

Wahweap Campground (5 mi north of Page on U.S. 89 near shore of Lake Powell, tel. 602/645–2511) is operated by the National Park Service and has 180 sites, some near the marina. The adjacent RV park, operated by Wahweap Lodge (tel. 602/645–2433 or 800/528–6154) and offering 120 full-service sites, has coin showers and a laundromat that campers may use. The fee with hookup is $19.60, and the fee for campsites with drinking water is $7.

Tuba City

Dining

Pancho's Family Restaurant. The main fare here is Mexican, but the menu also features American and Navajo dishes. Mexican entrées are copious and traditionally prepared, with chicken enchiladas and beef tamales as good as any you'll find south of the border. The large dining room looks like a western coffee shop but has beamed wood ceilings and incorporates such Native American touches as handmade pottery chandeliers and Navajo rugs on the walls. *Main St., adjacent to Tuba City Motel and Trading Post, tel. 602/283-5260. AE, D, DC, MC, V. Inexpensive.*

Lodging

Grey Hills Inn. Students at Grey Hills High School run this unusual lodging, a former dorm offering large, clean accommodations at excellent rates. The queen-size beds are comfortable, and pastel Native American print bedspreads and kitschy paintings add character to the otherwise plain rooms. Bathrooms and showers are down the hall, and it's hard to find your way to the inn's entrance in the large high-school complex at night, but you can't beat the prices: $10 for members of American Youth Hostel, $25 per room for nonmembers. *Box 160 (off U.S. 160, ½ mi north of junction with AZ 264), Tuba City 86045, tel. 602/283-6271. 32 rooms. No credit cards. Inexpensive.*

Tuba City Motel. In the largest community in the western part of Indian country, this property is conveniently situated near Pancho's Family Restaurant (*see* Dining, *above*), a trading post, and shops for essentials, gifts, and souvenirs. The well-maintained rooms are adequate for an overnight stopover before or after a visit to the Hopi Mesas. *Box 247 (at AZ 264–U.S. 160 junction), Tuba City 86045, tel. 602/283-4545. 80 rooms. Facilities: gift shop, nearby restaurants, post office, trading post. AE, D, DC, MC, V. Moderate.*

Window Rock

Dining and Lodging

Navajo Nation Inn. Indian officials in town on government business frequently stay in this motel in the Navajo Nation's tribal capital. The exterior is typical of contemporary roadside motels, but the rooms have been pleasantly decorated with Spanish Colonial furniture and Navajo art. The inexpensive restaurant serves standard American as well as Navajo entrées; the mutton stew is hearty, and the tasty taco on fry bread could easily feed two.*Box 2340 (on north side of AZ 264), Window Rock 86515, tel. 602/871-4108 or 800/662-6189 (reservations only). 56 units. Facilities: restaurant, conference rooms, nearby shopping and services. AE, D, MC, V. Moderate.*

Camping

Summit Campground (off AZ 264, 9 mi west of Window Rock, tel. 602/871-6645) has picnic tables but no water. A fee of $1 per person may be charged. The campground is open year-round.

Tse Bonito Tribal Park (near AZ 264, Window Rock, tel. 602/871-6645) is an essentially undeveloped site, with shaded picnic tables and nearby rest rooms but no water. A fee of $1 per person may be charged. The park is open all year.

Nightlife

Aside from sitting by a campfire, nightlife in northeastern Arizona is minimal. Wahweap Lodge (on U.S. 89, 5 mi north of Page, tel. 602/645-2433) on the shore of Lake Powell (*see* Lodging, *above*) and the sunset dinner cruise that departs from the dock at Wahweap Lodge (*see* Dining and Lodging, *above*) are about as close as you'll get to any nightlife. Wahweap Lodge has a cocktail lounge, as well as dancing and live entertainment in the Rainbow Room during the summer months. In addition, there's an inexpensive, first-run movie theater in Tuba City.

Keep in mind: No alcoholic beverages are sold on the Navajo and Hopi reservations, and possession or consumption of alcohol is against the law in these areas.

5 North-Central Arizona

Sedona and Flagstaff

By Trudy Thompson Rice

Updated by Edie Jarolim

Rich in history and natural attractions, north-central Arizona draws visitors to the striking red-rock formations of Sedona, the volcanic fields around Sunset Crater, the rolling, forested hills of Jerome, and Arizona's highest peaks, just north of Flagstaff. Several national and state parks hold well-preserved evidence of the architectural accomplishments of the many early Native American settlers who made their homes in this area.

Sedona sits at the southern end of Oak Creek Canyon, 125 miles north of Phoenix, where the Colorado Plateau meets the Sonora Desert to the south. Since about 1985, Sedona has developed a reputation as a center for New Age believers, who consider it one of the Earth's 11 most powerful energy centers. The city's full-time population of about 15,000 swells during the summer, when Arizona desert dwellers as well as out-of-state tourists come here to escape the heat. Throughout the year, travelers going to Flagstaff and on to the Grand Canyon choose scenic U.S. 89A, which traverses the town and Oak Creek Canyon. Just south of Sedona, funky old Jerome, a boomtown gone bust that has now been reclaimed by a few of the state's artsier residents, is also worth a visit. The forested mountain scenery is striking, and the drive is an adventure, with its many climbs, narrow curves, and switchbacks. Flagstaff, the largest city in north-central Arizona, is largely considered to be a jumping-off point for tours of the region, but despite its proliferation of fast-food eateries and chain motels, it has many of its own lures, especially for those interested in astronomy and Native American culture and crafts.

Essential Information

Important Addresses and Numbers

Tourist Information The **Flagstaff Chamber of Commerce** is located at 101 West Santa Fe Avenue (Flagstaff 86001, tel. 602/774–4505), as is the **Flagstaff Visitors Center** (tel. 602/774–9541 or 800/842–7293). The building is next to the Amtrak station, adjacent to the railroad tracks at the intersection of Beaver Street and Santa Fe Avenue.

For hiking maps and camping tips, contact the **U.S. Forest Service** (2323 E. Greenlaw La., tel. 602/527–7400).

The **Sedona–Oak Creek Canyon Chamber of Commerce,** at the corner of North U.S. 89A and Forest Road (Box 478, Sedona 86336, tel. 602/282–7722 or 800/288–7336), is staffed with knowledgeable residents who can help guide you to points of special interest.

Emergencies Call 911 to reach the **fire department, police,** and **emergency medical services.**

Hospitals and Doctors At an altitude of nearly 7,000 feet, Flagstaff has "thin" air; heart and respiratory patients may experience difficulty here, particularly upon exertion.

Flagstaff Medical Center, a full-service hospital, has a 24-hour emergency room downtown (1200 N. Beaver St., tel. 602/779–3366), about nine blocks north of Santa Fe Avenue (a main thoroughfare running east–west along the railroad tracks). The facility also provides referrals to local doctors and dentists.

The **Sedona Medical Center** has a doctor on call 24 hours. *75 Kallof Pl., tel. 602/282–1285. Open weekdays 8–6, weekends 10–6.*

Late-Night Pharmacies The pharmacy at the **Flagstaff Medical Center** (*see* Hospitals and Doctors, *above*) is open 24 hours. **Walgreen's** (1500 E. Cedar St., tel. 602/773–1011), a few blocks north of downtown off 4th Street, is open Monday–Saturday 9 AM–10 PM, Sunday 9 AM–8 PM; the pharmacy at **Smith's Food and Drug** (201 Switzer Canyon Rd., corner Santa Fe Ave., tel. 602/774–2719) is open Monday–Saturday 9 AM–9 PM, Sunday 10 AM–4 PM.

There are no late-night pharmacies in Sedona.

Arriving and Departing by Plane

Air travelers arrive in Flagstaff at **Flagstaff Pullium Airport** (tel. 602/774–1422), located 4 miles south of town off I-17 at Exit 337.

Those who want to fly directly into Flagstaff must travel by **America West** (tel. 800/247–5692). Flights to and from Phoenix, the Grand Canyon, Las Vegas, and Page, Arizona, are scheduled at least once a day.

If you plan to rent a car, the most cost-effective plan might be to fly into Phoenix, which has more flight options, and rent a car there. The drive from Phoenix to Flagstaff is a pretty one, climbing almost 5,000 feet in 134 miles.

Air Sedona (1225 Airport Rd., Suite 3, Sedona, tel. 602/282–7935 or 800/535–4448) has five daily round-trips between Phoenix and Sedona year-round; the cost is $90 round-trip.

Between the Airport and Downtown Flagstaff

By Taxi A taxi ride from the airport to the downtown area should cost about $10. Cabs are not regulated; some, but not all, have meters. It's wise to agree on a rate before you contract with a driver to take you to your destination. **Alpine Taxi Cab** (tel. 602/527–2400) and **Flagstaff Taxi & Limousine** (tel. 602/774–1374) are both known to be reliable and fair in their pricing.

By Bus There is no public bus from the airport to downtown. Some hotels offer a shuttle service; inquire when making reservations.

By Rental Car Rental-car agencies represented at the airport include **Budget** (tel. 800/527–0700) and **Hertz** (tel. 800/654–3131). Ask about a rate that allows you unlimited mileage, as you're likely to drive several hundred miles while you're in this part of the state.

To reach downtown from the airport, follow the signs out of the airport to I–17 (the airport is just off the highway). Turn right (north) on I–17, then exit at the downtown turnoff, less than 5 miles away.

Arriving and Departing by Car, Train, and Bus

By Car **Flagstaff** lies at the crossroads of I–40 (running east–west) and I–17 (running south from Flagstaff). It's 150 miles from Phoenix via I–17 (also known in Phoenix as Black Canyon Freeway) north. The road is a four-lane divided highway the entire way; there are several steep climbs and descents (you'll see a number of runaway-truck ramps—emergency stopping places for truckers who have lost their brakes on the steep declines). In summertime, make the trip with extra water for humans, pets, and radiators. In the winter, snowstorms can occasionally restrict travel to vehicles with snow chains.

To get to **Sedona** from Phoenix, take I–17 north for 113 miles, then drive another 15 miles on AZ 179; the trip should take about 2½ hours. From Flagstaff, it's a scenic 27-mile drive on U.S. 89A through Oak Creek Canyon.

By Train Flagstaff is a railroad town: The tracks that gave rise to the city's growth still run through the town today. **Amtrak** (tel. 602/774–8679 or 800/872–7245) comes into the downtown station at 1 Santa Fe Avenue twice daily.

There is no rail service into Sedona.

By Bus In **Flagstaff,** the **Greyhound/Trailways** station is downtown at 399 South Malpais Lane (tel. 602/774–4573). There are daily connections to Phoenix, but none to Sedona. Buses also serve travelers to San Francisco, Los Angeles, Las Vegas, and other cities. **Nava-Hopi** buses also depart daily to the Grand Canyon and offer sightseeing trips to Sedona (*see* Special-Interest Tours, *below*).

The **Sedona/Phoenix Shuttle Service** (Box 3342, Sedona 86340, tel. 602/282–2066 or 800/448–7988 in Arizona) makes four trips daily between those cities; the fare is $30 one-way, $50 round-trip. You can catch the bus in downtown Phoenix, and there is also a pickup at three terminals of Sky Harbor International Airport in Phoenix.

Getting Around

Flagstaff is a compact town, most of it situated along the railroad tracks. The street that parallels the tracks, **Santa Fe Avenue,** lined with motels and fast-food eateries, is the one that most locals use in giving directions. Going through Flagstaff, I–40 (east–west) and I–17 (north–south) cut the town into slightly skewed quarters. Restaurants and gas stations can be found along these highways or on Santa Fe Avenue.

Because Flagstaff is the gateway to the Grand Canyon, most people on the road here are from out of town; keep that in mind when you ask for directions!

Sedona is even more compact than Flagstaff, with U.S. 89A as its main commercial thoroughfare (known as Uptown), and a number of shopping centers and hotels off AZ 179. There is limited public transportation around town (*see* By Bus and Trolley, *below*); if you plan to spend some time in the area, it's best to rent a car (*see* By Car, *below*).

By Bus and Trolley The local bus company, **Pine Country Transit** (tel. 602/779–6624), offers clean and reliable service throughout the city of Flagstaff for 75¢. Senior citizens age 65 and older and children 7–17 pay only 60¢ a ride; children age 6 and under ride free. Buses run weekdays 6:15 AM–6:30 PM; there is no weekend service. Disabled passengers should check with the office to find out which buses are outfitted to accommodate wheelchairs.

The **Sedona Trolley** (tel. 602/282–6826) offers limited transportation around town every 20 minutes from 11 AM to 5 PM in winter and 10 AM–6 PM in summer (weather permitting); it runs weekends only February 14–March 17, and is closed December 1–21 and January 2–February 13. The trolley makes two stops Uptown and three on AZ 179; the cost is $1.

By Car It makes sense to rent a car at the airport if you fly into **Flagstaff** (*see* Between the Airport and Downtown Flagstaff, *above*). In **Sedona, Superstar Rent-A-Car** (2730 W. U.S. 89A, tel. 602/282–2897) and, at the airport, **Budget** (1225 Airport Rd., Suite 1, tel. 602/282–4602) are good bets for renting a vehicle.

Opening and Closing Times

Flagstaff is a traveler's and student's town, so restaurants tend to stay open late, some of them 24 hours. Sedona, on the other hand, is a resort that caters to many retirees, so restaurants tend to close earlier, many of them by 10 PM. In both places banking can be done at odd hours by way of automated teller machines (ATMs) located all over town. Some banks stay open until 6 PM on Friday. During the summer, shops and attractions are open longer: 9–9 during the week, 9–6 on Saturday, and noon–5 on Sunday.

Guided Tours

Orientation For self-guided tour maps of Flagstaff itself, stop at the **Flagstaff Visitors Center** (*see* Tourist Information, *above*); if you're going to spend any time in town, it's well worth taking the route outlined in the "Historic Downtown Walking Tour" pamphlet. If you're interested in a look at the **Northern Arizona University** campus (tel. 602/523–2491), from September through May tours are conducted Monday–Saturday at varying times. From June through August, tours are conducted weekdays at 11 AM.

Special-Interest Tours

Flagstaff

The Gray Line of Flagstaff, operated by **Nava-Hopi Tours** (Box 339, Flagstaff 86002, tel. 602/774–5003 or 800/892–8687), runs bus trips from the downtown Greyhound bus station to the **Grand Canyon** ($34 round-trip, including park entry fee). A tour of **Sedona** costs $32 per person; there are no drop-offs—that is, all passengers must return to Flagstaff on the same bus that evening. The company also offers a variety of package tours, such as the one to the **Hopi Indian Reservation** ($62 round-trip, including lunch). All require reservations, which are taken until two hours before departure. Free hotel and motel pickups are included in the price.

The Ventures program, run by the education department of the **Museum of Northern Arizona** (3001 N. Valley Rd. [Box 720], Flagstaff 86001, tel. 602/774–5211), offers tours of the area led by local scientists, artists, and historians. There are three types of trips, lasting from a weekend to eight days: expeditions, for those who want a rugged backpacking adventure; car camping, for those who like their outdoor stays supported by equipment and transportation; and bus and car tours, which provide hotel accommodations and restaurant meals. Trips might include rafting excursions down the San Juan and lower Verde rivers, hikes into the Grand Canyon or Arizona Strip Country, or bus tours into Albuquerque or Santa Fe. Prices start at $300 and go up to $1,300, with most tours in the $300 to $600 range.

Alpine Air Service (Box 252, Flagstaff 86002, tel. 602/779–5178) plane tours of the area's attractions leave from Flagstaff Pullium Airport. For reservations, call or write to the company. The cost for the plane, which carries three passengers, is $110 an hour plus tax; a typical trip to Monument Valley runs around $450 to $500. Recent changes in FAA regulations now prevent tour companies, including this one, from flying over the Grand Canyon.

Sedona

In the Sedona area, an option to consider is a **Jeep tour;** there are several operators headquartered along Sedona's main drag who offer a variety of excursions, some focusing on geology, some on vegetation, some on vortices, and some on all three. Some trips end with a western-style shoot-out; others are designed for more serious adventurers who like to head off the beaten track. **Pink Jeep Tours** (Box 1447, Sedona 86336, tel. 602/282–5000), **Sedona Red Rock Jeeps Tours** (Box 10305, Sedona 86336, tel. 602/282–6826 or 800/848–7728), and **Time Expeditions** (Box 2936,

Sedona 86336, tel. 602/282–2137) are all reliable operators. Prices start at about $25 per person for two hours; some tours include lunch or breakfast. Car seats are available for youngsters; if you need one, check with your operator before you buy. Although all the excursions are safe, those who dislike heights should choose one that's easy on the nerves.

A **hot-air-balloon tour** of Sedona provides a unique perspective of the magnificent red-rock landscape. Prices generally start at $125 per person for a 1½-hour tour. Plan to spend about three or four hours on this venture, including driving time to launch sites—most companies pick up their passengers at their hotels in Sedona and transport them in vans to the outskirts of town—inflating and deflating the balloon and, in some cases, offering a picnic along the way. Balloon companies here are very safety minded, flying only in clear, still weather and generally departing at sunrise, when winds are at their calmest. Children under the age of 4 aren't allowed. It can be chilly up in the air, even in the summertime, and downright cold in the winter, so dress warmly. Recommended companies include **Northern Light Balloon Expeditions** (Box 1695, Sedona 86336, tel. 602/282–2274) and **Red Rock Balloon Adventures** (Box 2759, Sedona 86336, tel. 602/284–0040).

It's the rare visitor who won't snap a roll or two of film in beautiful Sedona; those who need some guidance in their picture taking may want to call Sue Winters at **Photo Tours** (tel. 602/282–4320). For $15 for one hour, $28 for two hours, or $38 for three hours, she'll take you to all the prime spots and help you take your best shot.

Exploring North-Central Arizona

Highlights for First-time Visitors

Jerome (*see* Sedona and Environs)

Lowell Observatory (*see* Flagstaff and Environs)

Museum of Northern Arizona (*see* Flagstaff and Environs)

Oak Creek Canyon (*see* Sedona and Environs)

The red rocks of Sedona (*see* Sedona and Environs)

Snowbowl (*see* Flagstaff and Environs)

Sunset Crater Volcano National Monument (*see* Flagstaff and Environs)

Walnut Canyon National Monument (*see* Flagstaff and Environs)

Wupatki National Monument (*see* Flagstaff and Environs)

Sedona and Environs

Numbers in the margin correspond to points of interest on the North-Central Arizona map.

1 **Sedona,** 125 miles north of downtown Phoenix and 27 miles south of Flagstaff, is perhaps the most attractive stopover en route north to the Grand Canyon. With its numerous galleries, resorts, and restaurants, as well as a splendid setting in the midst of red-rock country, Sedona also makes a fine weekend destination in its own right.

The former artists colony is now home to some 15,000 residents, many retired, and many (alas) more interested in making money than in creating beauty. Expansion during the past 10 years has been rapid, and the lack of planning has taken its toll in increased traffic and congestion, especially on weekends and during the busy summer months, when Phoenix residents, overcome by heat, flee north to higher elevations.

That said, it's easy to see what draws so many visitors to Sedona. The deep-red rocks poke holes in what is almost always a clear blue sky—made to seem even bluer by the dark green of the forests. The wilderness—canyons, creeks, Indian ruins, and always a dreamscape of twisted red rock—is readily accessible on foot or on any number of Jeep tours. One of the state's finest restaurants is here, as are a tony tennis and health resort and at least an hour or two of interesting shopping. Sedona has also become a center of interest to New Age followers, who believe that the area contains some of the more important vortices of the Earth. Each vortex is said to give out energy that heightens creativity; thus the town has become somewhat of a haven for artists, the tofu set, and others in between. In the mid-1980s, Sedona was one of a handful of towns to host the Harmonic Convergence, celebrated to mark an unusual alignment of the planets that was believed to herald the dawn of a new, more peaceful age. Several entrepreneurs have set up crystal or New Age bookshops here, catering to the curious as well as to true devotees.

Exploring Sedona Visitors have a choice of Jeep tours (*see* Special-Interest Tours in Essential Information, *above*) and of a number of attractive hikes among the red rocks; the entire region is crisscrossed with trails. For free detailed maps and advice, speak to the rangers at the **Sedona Ranger District** office (250 Brewer Rd., tel. 602/282–4119), which is open Monday–Saturday 7:30–4:30. Ask here or at your hotel for directions to trailheads for Devil's Kitchen, Long Canyon, or the Indian ruins behind the Enchantment Resort. The most spectacular sunsets can be enjoyed at the top of Airport Mesa.

The main activity in Sedona itself is shopping, mostly for southwestern-style paintings, rugs, jewelry, and Native

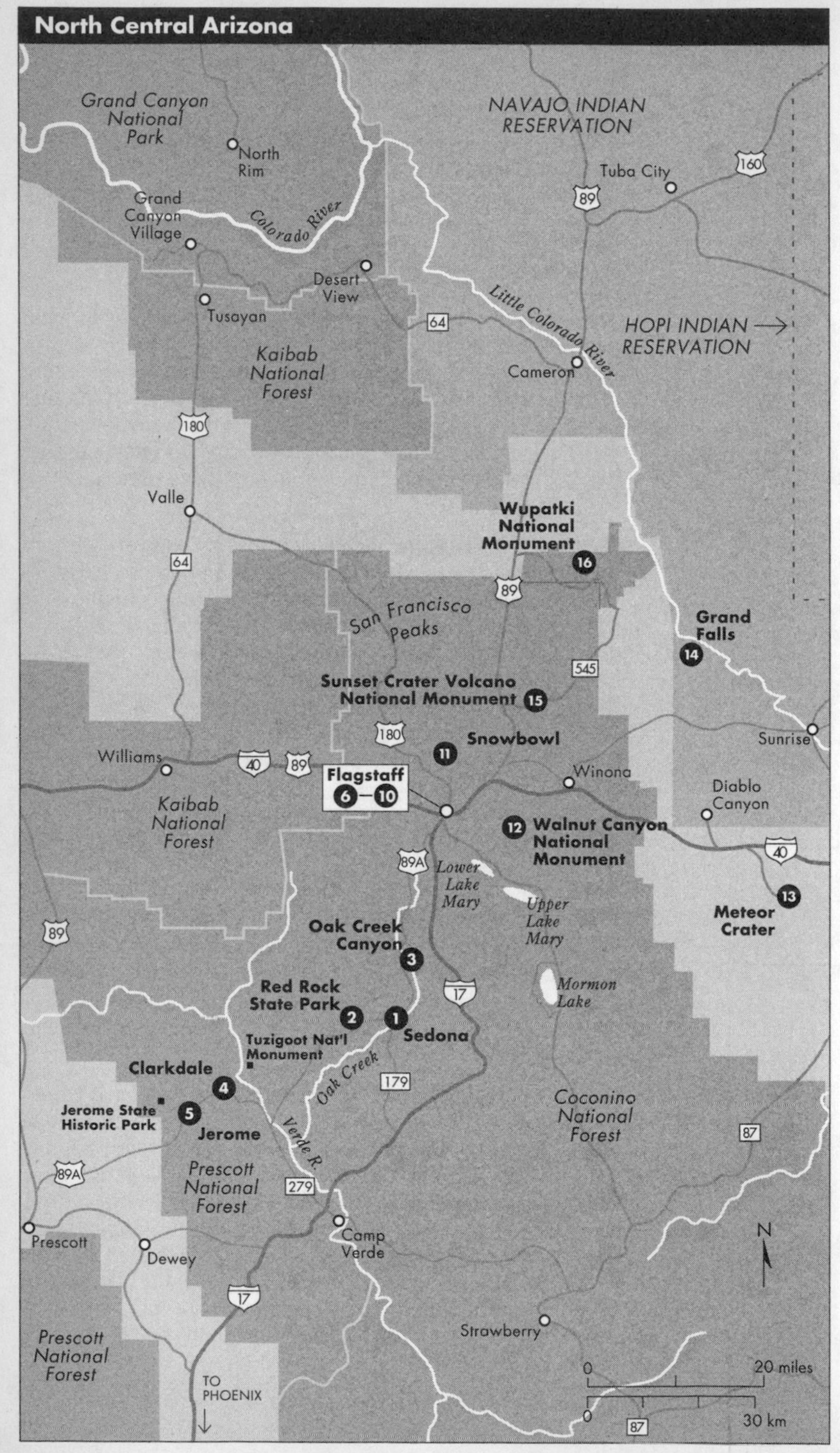

North Central Arizona
Grand Canyon National Park
North Rim
Grand Canyon Village
Colorado River
Desert View
Tusayan
Kaibab National Forest
NAVAJO INDIAN RESERVATION
Tuba City
160
89
64
Little Colorado River
HOPI INDIAN RESERVATION
Cameron
180
Valle
64
Wupatki National Monument
16
89
San Francisco Peaks
Grand Falls
14
545
Sunset Crater Volcano National Monument
15
180
Snowbowl
11
Sunrise
Williams
40
89
Flagstaff
6–10
Winona
Diablo Canyon
Kaibab National Forest
12
Walnut Canyon National Monument
40
89A
Lower Lake Mary
Upper Lake Mary
13
Meteor Crater
89
Oak Creek Canyon
3
17
Mormon Lake
Red Rock State Park
2
1
Sedona
Tuzigoot Nat'l Monument
Oak Creek
179
Clarkdale
4
Jerome State Historic Park
5
Jerome
Verde R.
Coconino National Forest
87
89A
Prescott National Forest
279
Camp Verde
Prescott
Dewey
N
17
Strawberry
Prescott National Forest
TO PHOENIX
0
20 miles
0
30 km
87

American artifacts. Duringthe warmer months it makes sense to visit the air-conditioned shops midday and save the hiking and Jeep tours for very early morning or late afternoon, when the light is softer and the heat less oppressive. The so-called **Uptown shopping area** is cut in half by U.S. 89A; even locals are upset by what they call the rubber-tomahawk quality of the shops here, which catering primarily to the tour-bus trade.

Time Out Chairs are molded plastic at the **Sedona Coffee House and Bakery** (293 N. U.S. 89A, tel. 602/282–2241), and everything comes in Styrofoam or paper, but for healthy sandwiches this is your best bet Uptown. A short walk away, on the north side of U.S. 89A, is the **Sedona Fudge Company** (tel. 602/282–1044). Some maintain that the mere act of watching the candy makers pour the fudge from giant copper kettles onto marble slabs can add bulk to your hips—so you may as well go all the way and indulge.

For more upscale shopping, drive less than a minute south to the attractive **Tlaquepaque** development (AZ 179, tel. 602/282–4348), where more than 100 artists, most of them painters and sculptors, sell their works. Prices tend to be high here; when asked how to pronounce the name of this shopping complex, locals joke that it's "to-lock-your-pocket." **Isadora** (tel. 602/282–6232) features contemporary silver and turquoise jewelry, and **Carusetta** (tel. 602/282–7793) showcases the more unusual combination of gold and turquoise. Some good bets for southwestern art are **El Prado Galleries** (tel. 602/282–7390), **Estaban's** (tel. 602/282–4686), and **Aguajito del Sol** (in the belltower, tel. 602/282–5258).

A half-mile south of Tlaquepaque (take a right out of the parking lot), at the junction of U.S. 179 and Schnebly Hill Road, a small strip of shops includes **Garland's Navajo Rugs** (tel. 602/282–4070), with its huge collection of new and antique carpets, as well as Native American kachina dolls, pottery, and baskets. Next door to Garland's, **Sedona Pottery** (tel. 602/282–1192) features unusual pottery, including life-size ceramic statues made by shop owner Mary Margaret.

Drive another minute or two south on AZ 179 and you'll come to the **Hillside Courtyard and Marketplace** (671 AZ 179, tel. 602/282–4500). Among the 23 shops and galleries, **Chula** (tel. 602/282–3899) carries a good selection of folk art from all over the world. **Wolfwalker Galleries** (tel. 602/282–7802, also at Tlaquepaque, tel. 602/282–1480) specializes in oils and watercolors of the Sedona area.

If it's bargains, not regional souvenirs, you're after, head for **Oak Creek Factory Stores** (6657 S. AZ 179, tel. 602/284–2150), just south of town, where Corning Revere, Mikasa,

Anne Klein, Van Heusen, and many other manufacturers have factory outlets.

Red Rock State Park

2

Two miles west of Sedona on U.S. 89A, the 286-acre **Red Rock State Park** is the newest state park in Arizona (opened in October 1991), and one of the most beautiful. An ideal place to enjoy both the red rock formations of the Sedona area as well as lovely Oak Creek, it's also a less crowded alternative to the popular Slide Rock State Park (*see below*). At press time, the visitor center, although open, was still under construction, and one of the five trails had not yet been completed; however, the four main trails already open (all fairly easy and less than 2½ miles long) are well-marked and provide beautiful vistas. Regular ranger-led hikes and bird-watching expeditions are planned; call ahead for the current schedule. Box 3863, West Sedona 86340, tel. 602/282–6907. Admission: $3 per car. Open daily 8–5.

Oak Creek Canyon

3

Whether you want to swim, hike, picnic, or enjoy beautiful scenery framed through a car window, head north on U.S. 89A, through the wooded **Oak Creek Canyon.** This is the most attractive route to Flagstaff and Grand Canyon. Although the forest is primarily evergreen, there are enough changing colors in the fall to make the view especially glorious at that time of year. The road winds through a steep-walled canyon, and visitors crane their necks for views of the dramatic rock formations above. Oak Creek, which runs along the bottom of the canyon, is lined with tent campgrounds, fishing camps, cabins, motels, and restaurants.

Look for **Slide Rock State Park** on your left, 7 miles north of Sedona. It's a good place for a picnic and a hike back into the forest. On a hot day, you can plunge down a natural rock slide into a swimming hole—a delightful experience. (Bring an extra pair of jeans to wear on the slide.) About 3 miles farther north is the popular West Fork Trail, which follows along a creek where you can cool off in summer. The only downside to this trip is the traffic and crowds, particularly on summer weekends.

Other Area Attractions

A short drive from town is the **Chapel of the Holy Cross** (Chapel Rd., tel. 602/282–4069), built by Marguerite Brunwig Staude, a disciple of Frank Lloyd Wright. This striking modern structure, with its huge cross on the facade, rises between two natural stone peaks. There are no regular services, but visitors are welcome to come in for peaceful meditation daily, April–October, 8–6; November–March, 9–5. Drive 3 miles south on AZ 179, turn left on Chapel Road, and drive 1 more mile.

South of Sedona, just east of Clarkdale, **Tuzigoot National Monument** is an impressive complex of ruins of the Sinagua Indians, who lived on this land overlooking the Verde Valley from about AD 1125 through 1400. Items used for food preparation, as well as jewelry, weapons, and farming tools excavated from the site, are displayed in the visitor center, where there is also a reconstructed room from the pueblo. *Box 68, Clarkdale 86324, tel. 602/634–5564. Admission: $1 adults, children under 17 and senior citizens free. Open Memorial Day–Labor Day, daily 8–7; Labor Day–Feb., daily 8–5; Mar.–May, daily 8–6 (hours may vary depending on the weather).*

4 **Clarkdale** draws train buffs who catch the **Verde River Canyon Excursion Train** (Arizona Central Railroad, Box 103, Clarkdale 86324, tel. 602/639–0010), just east of the business district, for a 22-mile ride that ends up in Perkinsville. A highlight of the trip is traversing a 680-foot-long stone tunnel barely 1 foot wider than the train itself. Round-trip rides cost $29.95 for adults, $26.95 for senior citizens 65 and older, and $17.95 for children under 12; trains depart every day at 1 PM and return at 5 PM. When you make your reservation, you can order a box lunch for $6; beer and snacks are also sold on the train. For $46.95, ride the comfy, living room–like club car, snacks included. Every Saturday, musical entertainment along the banks of the Verde River is part of the ride.

5 From Clarkdale, continue on U.S. 89A to **Jerome,** once known as the Billion Dollar Copper Camp. After the last mines closed in 1953, a booming population of 15,000 dwindled to a low of 50 determined souls. The town saw a slight revival during the mid-1960s, when hippies moved in and turned it into a funky art colony of sorts. Today some 450 people reside here full-time, but the tourists keep the place alive. Worth a visit for its historic interest as well as for its scenery, Jerome is literally built into the side of Cleopatra Hill, and from here you can see Sedona's red rocks, Flagstaff's San Francisco Peaks, and even eastern Arizona's Mogollon Rim country (*see* Chapter 6, Phoenix and Central Arizona).

Jerome sits about a mile above sea level, but structures within town vary in elevation by up to 1,500 feet, depending on whether they're perched on Cleopatra Hill or at its foot. Blasting at the mines regularly shook buildings off their foundations, and the town's jail slid across a road and down a hillside, where it can still be seen today. That's not all that was unsteady about Jerome. In 1903, a reporter from a New York newspaper called Jerome "the wickedest town in America" because of its abundance of drinking and gaming establishments; 1880 town records list 24 saloons. Whether due to divine retribution or drunken accidents, the town was burned down several times—some historians say five, others two or three.

Of the three mining museums in town, the most comprehensive is at **Jerome State Historic Park;** just south of town, signs on U.S. 89A will direct you to the turnoff for the park. The museum occupies the mansion of Jerome's mining king, Dr. James "Rawhide Jimmy" Douglas, Jr., who purchased Little Daisy Mine in 1912; the house was built in 1917 at the height of Little Daisy's success. On the grounds you'll see some of the tools and heavy equipment used to grind ore. A video details the history of Jerome; the bawdy parts have been left out, but you can read between the lines for some sense of the town's wild mining days. Views from the picnic grounds around the mansion are spectacular. *State Park Rd., tel. 602/634–5381. Admission: $2 adults, $1 children 12–17, under 12 free. Open daily 8–5.*

The other worthwhile mining museum, **The Mine Museum,** is downtown. Staffed by the Jerome Historical Society, the museum's collection of mining stock certificates alone is worth the (small) price of admission—the amount of money that changed hands in this town 100 years ago boggles the mind. *Main St., tel. 602/634–5477. Admission: 50¢. Open daily 9–4:30.*

Jerome, like Sedona on a smaller scale, is a scenic shopper's haven. Chic, artsy boutiques and galleries carrying local and imported goods line the streets in the tiny downtown area (*see* Shopping, *below*).

For those who plan to continue from Jerome to Prescott (*see* Chapter 6, Phoenix and Central Arizona), the 34-mile drive southwest down a mountainous section of U.S. 89A is gorgeous (if somewhat harrowing in bad weather), filled with twists and turns through the Prescott National Forest.

Flagstaff and Environs

Few visitors slow down long enough to explore Flagstaff, a town of 40,000, known locally as "Flag"; most stop only to spend the night at one of the town's many motels before making the last leg of the trip to the Grand Canyon, 80 miles north. But the city, set against a lovely backdrop of pine forests and the snowcapped San Francisco Peaks, retains a frontier flavor downtown and is home to several attractions, including the excellent Museum of Northern Arizona and the Lowell Observatory. Festivals celebrating the summer season often fill Flagstaff's streets with parades and its sidewalks with Native American art exhibits and crafts sales.

Flagstaff probably has more fast-food outlets per permanent resident than do most cities, no doubt because of the incredible demand for it: Two major interstate highways crisscross the town; thousands of tourists drive through on the way to the Grand Canyon; thousands of students attending Northern Arizona University reside here; and many Native Americans come from nearby reservations. The city is also packed with motels, although there are no major hotels or resorts. Traffic to the Grand Canyon is heavy all year, but in the summertime it skyrockets, increasing the number of overnight visitors. During that time of year, the streets are filled with Phoenix residents seeking relief from the desert heat.

Phoenicians also come to Flagstaff in winter to ski at the Snowbowl, a small ski resort about 15 miles northeast of town among the San Francisco Peaks. At any time of the year, temperatures in Flagstaff are approximately 20°F cooler than in Phoenix. It's generally wise to reserve a room ahead of time in Flagstaff, and during the summer months, it's almost mandatory.

Downtown Flagstaff

Numbers in the margin correspond to points of interest on the Flagstaff map.

This tour to the Lowell Observatory, Riordan State Park, and Northern Arizona University (where there's a second observatory), all fairly close to town, should appeal to amateur stargazers and history buffs alike.

6 To reach **Lowell Observatory,** less than 2 miles from downtown, drive northwest on Santa Fe Avenue. This scientific institution was founded in 1894 by Boston businessman, author, and scientist Percival Lowell, who studied the planet Mars from here. His predictions of the existence of a ninth planet led to the discovery of Pluto at Lowell in 1930 by Clyde Tombaugh. V. M. Slipher's observations made here between 1912 and 1920 led to the theory of the expanding universe.

Facilities for visitors are currently limited at the observatory (there are no public rest rooms, for example), but they are in the process of being expanded. During the day, the staff graciously welcomes guests and offers slide lectures and tours, including a look at the 24-inch Clark telescope. Hours change every month, so call when you're in town, or when you know on what date you plan to visit. There are several interactive exhibits (simple, but interesting) for children, who will especially enjoy the Pluto Walk, a scaled-down version of our solar system that is designed for exploring.

On different evenings each month, weather permitting, the public is invited to peer through the telescope. The greatest number of viewings are offered from June through August; again, call ahead for a current schedule. The observatory dome is open and unheated—any change in temperature would affect the telescope lens—so dress for an outdoor rather than an indoor activity. *1400 W. Mars Hill Rd., tel. 602/774–2096. Admission: suggested donations $1 per individual, $3 per family. Hours vary, so call ahead.*

7 The **Riordan mansion** (at the intersection of Milton and Riordan roads, about a half-mile south of downtown, behind Wendy's) is a 13,000-square-foot log house with volcanic-stone arches and hand-split wooden shingles, located on the grounds of Riordan Historical State Park. Two of Flagstaff's earliest influential citizens, brothers Timothy and Michael Riordan, married two sisters and raised their families here during the early 1900s. The mansion is furnished

Lowell Observatory, **6**
Museum of Northern Arizona, **10**
Northern Arizona University, **8**
Pioneer Historical Museum, **9**
Riordan Mansion, **7**

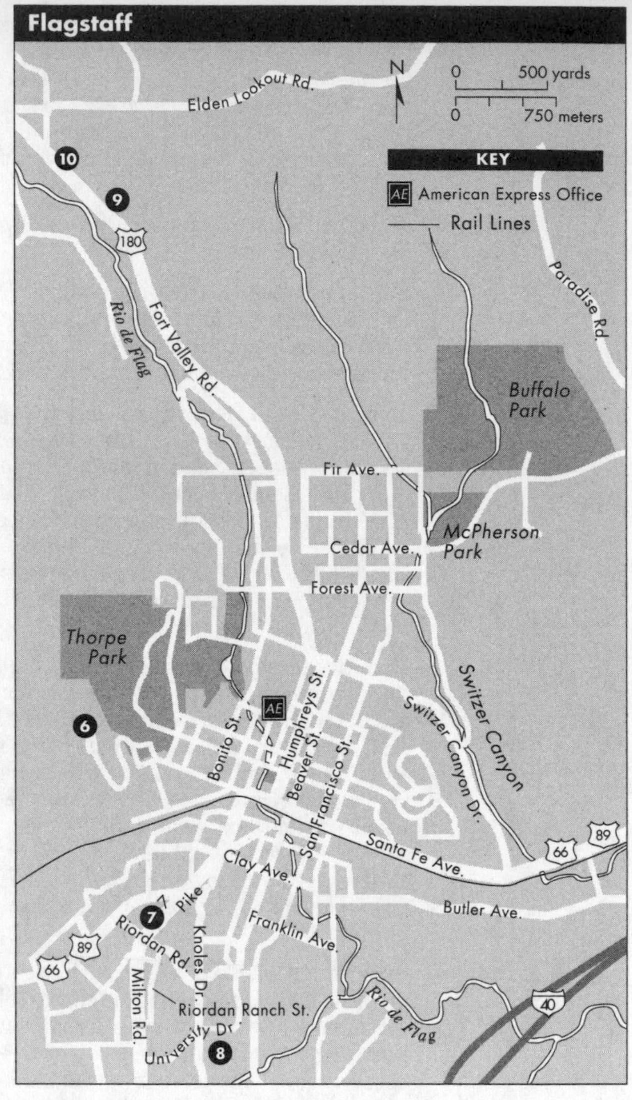

as it was then, complete with a grand piano in the elaborate parlor. A "touching table" for children includes a range of historical objects, from high-topped button shoes to a toy spinning top. Guided tours run from May 15 through September 14, hourly from 9 to 4 (except at noon), and from September 15 to May 14, from 1 to 4. There are picnic tables outside. *1300 Riordan Ranch Rd., tel. 602/779–4395. Admission: $2, children under 19 free. Open May 15–Sept. 14, daily 8–5; Sept. 15–May 14, daily 12:30–5. Closed Christmas.*

8 Riordan State Park is near **Northern Arizona University.** Go two blocks south on Milton Road, then make a left onto University Drive. After about a half-mile, turn right on San Francisco Street and continue to the university's **observatory.**

The observatory and 24-inch telescope were built in 1952 by Dr. Arthur Adel, who had been a scientist at Lowell Observatory until he joined the college faculty as a professor of mathematics. His work on infrared astronomy pioneered research into molecules that absorb light passing through Earth's atmosphere. Today's studies of our planet's shrinking ozone layer rely on some of Dr. Adel's early work. Visitors to the observatory—which houses one of the largest telescopes in the United States that the public is allowed to move and manipulate—are usually hosted by friendly students and faculty members of the university's Department of Physics and Astronomy.

Public viewings take place every clear Thursday night from 7:30 PM to 10 PM. Tours for individuals and small groups can be arranged any day except Thursday by calling at least 24 hours in advance. The staff requests a minimum of a week's notice for large tours. *Northern Arizona Campus Observatory, c/o Dept. of Physics and Astronomy, S. San Francisco St., tel. 602/523–7170. Admission free.*

Flagstaff Museums and Snowbowl

The Pioneer Historical Museum offers visitors a look at the area's recent history, while the Museum of Northern Arizona's broader scope gives insight into the archaeology, ethnology, geology, biology, and fine arts of the Flagstaff region. Although the Snowbowl is a ski slope, it's still worth taking the scenic 14-mile drive there in the summertime, when a ski lift will take you to the top of the San Francisco Peaks for a marvelous view of the area.

Head northwest of town on U.S. 180 from Santa Fe Avenue (there's a big sign directing drivers toward the Fairfield Snowbowl). Two miles from downtown Flagstaff, you'll see the Pioneer Historical Museum on your right. If you're short on time or interest, you might want to pass on this one in favor of the Museum of Northern Arizona.

9 The **Pioneer Historical Museum,** operated by the Arizona Historical Society, is in a building constructed in 1908 of volcanic rock—Coconino County's first hospital for the poor. Today the lives of the area's pioneer settlers may be imagined through reconstructions of buildings such as barns and cabins, furnished as they were 100 years ago, and through displays of western clothing and other changing exhibits. The museum hosts a folk-crafts festival on the Fourth of July, where you can watch traditional tradespeople, such as blacksmiths, weavers, spinners, quilters, and candle makers, at work. Their crafts, and those of other local artisans, are sold in the museum's gift shop, a tiny space filled with teddy bears, dolls, hand-dipped candles, and

hand-stitched quilts. *2340 N. Fort Valley Rd., tel. 602/774-6272. Admission: optional donation. Open Mon.–Sat. 9–5, Sun. 1:30–5.*

Turn right out of the museum's parking lot and drive 1 mile
10 northwest on U.S. 180; on your left you'll see the **Museum of Northern Arizona,** a large stone building shaded with trees. Founded in 1928, the museum is now respected worldwide for its research and for its collections centering on the natural and cultural history of the Colorado Plateau; only 1% of its vast holdings on the archaeology, ethnology, geology, biology, and fine arts of the region is on display at any given time. Among the permanent exhibitions are an extensive collection of Navajo rugs as well as an authentic Hopi kiva (men's ceremonial chamber). Every summer, the museum hosts exhibits and sales by Native American artists, whose wares are also sold in the museum gift shop (*see* The Arts in Arts and Nightlife, *below*). Two interesting outdoor features are a life-zone exhibit, which show the changing vegetation in the area from the bottom of the Grand Canyon to the highest peak in Flagstaff (the equivalent of a trip from Mexico to Canada), and a nature trail that heads down across a small stream into a canyon and up into an aspen grove.

Two new galleries—one devoted to the biology and the other to the geology of the area—opened in the fall of 1992. The latter includes a cast of the dilophosaurus; this medium-size carnivorous dinosaur, unique to northern Arizona, roamed the area back when much of it was swampland.

This is not a particularly child-oriented museum, but a new upstairs gallery geared toward youngsters offers hands-on biology displays. Docent-led tours are available for individuals or groups, but appointments must be made at least two weeks in advance. In addition, the museum's education department sponsors excellent tours of the area and some as far away as New Mexico and California (*see* Guided Tours in Essential Information, *above*). *3001 N. Valley Rd., tel. 602/774-5211. Admission: $4 adults, $3 senior citizens, $2 students and children under 19. Open daily 9–5. Closed Thanksgiving, Christmas, and New Year's Day.*

Five miles farther along the same road is the turnoff for the
11 **Snowbowl,** listed on some maps as the Arizona Snowbowl and on others as the Fairfield Snowbowl. The Fort Valley Lodge to the right is a good place to stop for groceries and clean rest rooms, as well as for information about skiing and other recreational opportunities at the Snowbowl; it's open in the daytime only. If there's a crowd visiting the ski area or a recent heavy snow that makes travel difficult, park here and ride the shuttle to the top; it runs continuously and costs $3 per person round-trip.

After you leave U.S. 180, it's another 7 paved miles on Snowbowl Road to the **Snowbowl Skyride** (tel. 602/779-

1951), which takes you through the Coconino National Forest to a height of 11,500 feet. From this vantage point, you can see up to 70 miles; views include the North Rim of the Grand Canyon. The Hart Prairie and Agassiz lodges closer to the lifts offer parking, food, and rest rooms year-round. Skyride tickets: $7 adults, $5 senior citizens age 65 and older, $3.50 children 6–12, free for children 5 and under. Group discounts are available. The ride, which takes 25 minutes each way, operates Memorial Day weekend–mid-October, weekends and holidays 10–4. Operating hours may change, so call before you go.

There is plenty of **hiking** here in Arizona's alpine tundra, where more than 80 species of plants grow on the upper elevations of the San Francisco Peaks. The habitat is fragile, so hikers are asked to stay on established trails (and there are lots of them). The Humphreys Peak Trail is 9 miles round-trip, with a vertical climb of 3,133 feet to the summit of Arizona's highest mountain (12,633 feet). Those who don't want a long hike will be well rewarded if they do just the first mile of the 8-mile-long Kachina Trail; completely flat, this route is surrounded by huge stands of aspen and offers fantastic vistas. It's particularly worthwhile in fall, when the changing leaves paint the landscape shades of yellow, russet, and amber. All trails are well marked and maintained by the **Coconino National Forest** (tel. 602/556–7400). Remember that the altitude here will make even the hardiest hikers breathe a little harder. Individuals with cardiac or respiratory problems should be cautious of over-exertion.

In winter, the Snowbowl offers an average of 250 inches of snow and 35 trails of varying difficulty (8 novice, 17 intermediate, and 10 advanced) for **skiing.** Enthusiasts who favor the challenging slopes of Colorado's Rockies might find the Snowbowl a bit disappointing, but it's just fine for skiers of beginning or moderate ability. Senior citizens age 65 years and older and children 6 and younger ski for free. Private instruction costs $35 an hour. Equipment rentals are also available for $14 a day. Weekend lift tickets cost $28. Many Flagstaff motels offer ski packages, including transportation to the Snowbowl. Write or call the Snowbowl Ski Area (Box 2430, Flagstaff 86003, tel. 602/779–1951) for more information. For the current snow report, phone 602/779–4577.

East of Flagstaff

Numbers in the margin correspond to points of interest on the North-Central Arizona map.

The area east of Flagstaff is often overlooked by visitors to the region because there's little, regardless of beauty or historical significance, that can compete with the Grand Canyon, west of Flagstaff. But if you have any extra time, traveling east has its unique rewards, including Walnut Canyon, once home to thousands of Sinagua Indians; Grand Falls, a part-time waterfall that flows only during the spring; and the 4,100-foot-wide Meteor Crater, created more than 49,000 years ago when a meteor slammed into the Earth. If you don't have enough time to do everything, opt for taking the quick drive to Walnut Canyon—only about 15 minutes out of town—and staying in this lovely spot for as long as you can; for many, Meteor Crater is worth neither the extra hour or so (round-trip) spent crossing a desolate landscape nor the high entrance fee.

12 **Walnut Canyon National Monument** is 7½ miles east of Flagstaff (exit 204 off I–40), then 3 miles south. Towering Douglas firs, pinion pines, and alligator juniper trees keep the area green—hundreds of shades of green—year-round; the canyon is especially beautiful on a snowy winter day.

The Sinagua Indians (possibly ancestors of today's Pueblo Indians) lived and farmed the area of Walnut Canyon starting in approximately AD 800. They vanished around 1250; archaeologists have speculated that they left because of a drought—the name Sinagua means "without water"—or because invaders chased them out. The canyon was unoccupied until 1883, when more than 300 cliff dwellings abandoned by the Sinagua were discovered by Mormon settlers from Utah, who regarded the ruins as curiosities but nothing more.

A national monument, maintained by the National Park Service, was established here in 1915. Today an informative visitor center is staffed by guides who conduct tours daily during the summer and on weekends in the winter. You can see many of the cliff dwellings at close range—a number of them in near-perfect condition—by descending 185 feet by way of the mile-long stepped Island Trail, which starts at the visitor center. The dwellings are in such good condition because visitors are restricted from entering them; they were also carefully constructed under the protection of overhanging cliffs, and the weather here is dry and temperate. The Island Trail, which closes one hour before the park closes, takes about an hour to complete. Those with health problems should opt for the easier Rim Trail (a half-mile route that most people can complete in about a half-hour), which takes visitors past several overlooks from which the dwellings can be viewed, as well as an excavated and reconstructed pit house.

No food or drinks are sold here (there are water fountains and rest rooms), but attractive picnic areas dot the grounds and line the road leading to the park. Although no fires are permitted, gas stoves are allowed in picnic areas. A store at the visitor center carries a nice range of books about the region's history and natural attractions. *Walnut Canyon Rd., tel. 602/526–3367. Admission: $1 per person, $3 per car; Open Labor Day–Memorial Day, daily 7–6; off-season, daily 8–5.*

13 To reach **Meteor Crater** from Walnut Canyon, drive about 33 miles farther east on I–40, get off at Exit 233, then go 6 miles south on Meteor Crater Road. This natural phenomenon, set in a privately owned and run park, is impressive if for no other reason than its sheer size. A hole in the ground 600 feet deep, nearly a mile across, and more than 3 miles in circumference, Meteor Crater is large enough to accommodate the Washington Monument or 20 football fields. It was created when a meteorite came hurtling through space at a speed of 43,000 miles per hour and crashed here some 49,000 years ago. The area looks so much like the surface of the moon that NASA made it one of the official training sites for the *Apollo* astronauts.

Meteor Crater was first discovered by non–Native American explorers in 1871; they believed it was an extinct volcano. A mining engineer from Philadelphia, Daniel Moreau Barringer, spent 25 years trying to convince others of the meteoric origin of the hole; he acquired the land surrounding the crater—still owned by his family today—to conduct research to confirm his theory, which was accepted by the time he died in 1929.

Visitors can't descend into the crater because of the efforts of its owners to maintain its present excellent condition—scientists consider this to be the best-preserved crater on Earth—but a 3-mile rim trail gives visitors a bird's-eye view of the hole. Two short, rather corny films, which play every half-hour, detail the history of the crater and of astronaut training here. A small snack bar sells soft drinks, coffee, and sandwiches. Rock hounds will enjoy the Lapidary Shop, filled with raw specimens from the area as well as with jewelry made from native stones. *Meteor Crater Rd., 40 mi east of Flagstaff, tel. 602/289–2362. For information, write or call administrative offices, 603 N. Beaver St., Suite C, Flagstaff 86001, tel. 602/774–8350. Admission: $6 adults, $5 senior citizens 65 and over, $2 children 13–17, $1 children 6–12, children 5 and under free. Open May 16–Sept. 14, daily 6–6; Sept. 15–May 15, daily 8–5.*

14 If you're touring this area in March or April, **Grand Falls** is a worthwhile detour on your way back to Flagstaff. Head toward town on I–40 and take the Winona exit (number 211), which will take you to Camp Townsend–Winona Road. Turn right and drive 2 miles, then turn right again onto Leupp Road. Signs will lead you to Grand Falls (you'll turn left onto 10 miles of dirt road). You're on Navajo land here, so tribal laws apply. For example, if you have an accident or hit any of the many free-roaming livestock, you'll be tried in a tribal court. Consuming or even possessing alcohol on Indian territory is prohibited. *See* Chapter 1, Essential Information, and Chapter 4, The Northeast, for details on reservation regulations.

The muddy 180-foot waterfall generally slows to a drip during the rest of the year, but in springtime, when the snow melts, there is often a raging cascade, impressive for its sheer power. The falls were created about 100,000 years ago by a lava flow from Merriam Crater, 10 miles southwest; today they plunge over a cliff into the Little Colorado River below. At peak strength, the roar of the rushing water greets you before you actually see the torrent. This is not a well-touristed site; no food or drinks are sold here. Dogs must be kept on a leash to prevent them from disturbing the area's livestock.

To return to Flagstaff, drive back to I–40, which is about 7 miles east of town.

San Francisco Volcanic Field

North of Flagstaff, the San Francisco Volcanic Field encompasses 2,000 square miles of fascinating geological phenomena—the San Francisco Peaks themselves, some of which soar to almost 13,000 feet; ancient volcanoes; cinder cones; and valleys carved by water and ice—as well as some of the most extensive Indian ruins in the Southwest. If you have any time at all, don't miss Sunset Crater and Wupatki; these national monuments are not only extremely interesting but can be explored in relative solitude during a large part of the year. The area is short on services, so fill up on gas and consider bringing along a picnic; there are plenty of lovely spots for lunch along the way. A good source for hiking and camping information in this area is the Peaks Ranger Station (5075 N. U.S. 89, tel. 602/526–0866).

15 To get to **Sunset Crater Volcano National Monument,** so designated in 1930, take Santa Fe Avenue east of town to U.S. 89, and drive north for about 20 miles. Turn right onto the road marked Sunset Crater—it's another 2 miles from here to the visitor center.

Sunset Crater, a cinder cone that rises some 1,000 feet into the air, was an active volcano 900 years ago. The final eruption contained iron and sulfur, which gives the rim of the crater its glow and thus its name, Sunset. You can walk around the edge, but you can't descend into the huge but fragile cone. If you take the Lava Flow Trail, a half-hour, 1-mile-long self-guided walk, you'll have a good view of the evidence of the volcano's fiery power: lava formations and holes in the rock where volcanic gases vented to the surface. The volcano is dormant and very unlikely to erupt again; nevertheless, gazing down into the crater, you can almost feel the earth's heat and rumbling beneath your feet. Even the bravest visitor can become a little weak in the knees while contemplating this site, which is remarkably well preserved.

If you're interested in hiking a volcano, head to **Lenox Crater,** about a mile east of the Sunset Crater visitor center. It's 280 feet to the top of the cinder cone. Wear closed, sturdy shoes if you plan to do this; the cinder is soft and crumbly, without vegetation.

From **O'Leary Peak,** 5 miles from the visitor center on Forest Route 545A (an unpaved but decent road), there are some great views of the San Francisco Peaks, the Painted Desert, and beyond.

The Sunset Crater visitor center is staffed by rangers who are knowledgeable about the area, as well as about volcanoes and geology in general. Films of Hawaii's active Kilauea volcano help visitors imagine the former fury of this site. Sunset Crater is open daily 8–5, and entry fees are $4 per car, which includes admission into Wupatki National Monument (*see below*). For more information, write or call the National Park Service business office (2717 N. Steves Blvd., Suite 3, Flagstaff 86004, tel. 602/556–7042).

Drive 20 miles north of the Sunset Crater visitor center
16 along AZ 545 to get to the entrance of **Wupatki National Monument.** En route, parts of the Painted Desert are visible in the distance; the immediately surrounding landscape is starkly beautiful, without much vegetation. Exhibits at the site's visitor center show how the area's earliest inhabitants lived—including examples of their pottery, baskets, and farm implements—and how the community evolved. During the summer months, rangers give interpretive lectures on the history of the region.

Some 2,700 identified sites contain archaeological evidence of Native American settlement in this area. Families from the Sinagua, Anasazi, and perhaps other cultures are believed to have lived together in harmony here, farming and trading with one another and with others who passed through their "city." The eruption of Sunset Crater, 20 miles away, may have caused migration to this area—and may have disrupted the settlement more than once around 1064. The earliest inhabitants are believed to have settled here around AD 600, and some anthropologists think the last of them had abandoned the land by about AD 1300 because of a drought; others conjecture that poor soil conservation or social unrest may have led to the desertion of the pueblo.

The site for which the national monument was named, the **Wupatki,** originally three stories high, was built above a system of unexplored natural caves. The structure had almost 100 rooms and a large, open ball court, that was probably the site of religious ceremonies. Next to the ball court is a blowhole, a geologic phenomenon in which air is forced upward by underground pressure; scientists speculate that early inhabitants may have attached some spiritual significance to the many blowholes found in the region.

Although there are extensive, easily viewed remnants of Native American settlements at Wupatki National Monument, most of them are closed to the casual visitor. Many are being studied by professional archaeologists (the park service can provide information on these research projects). Permits are available from the park service for limited access beyond the open areas, but rules regarding entering closed sites are strictly enforced.

If you are interested in an in-depth tour of the area, consider taking a ranger-led overnight hike to the **Crack-in-the-Rock Ruin.** The 14-mile trek (round-trip) covers areas marked by ancient petroglyphs and dotted with well-preserved ruins. The cost is $10; anyone who is interested should contact the rangers at the Wupatki National Monument (HC 33, Box 444A, Flagstaff 86004, tel. 602/556–7040) for details. There are a limited number of trips, conducted in April and October; it's best to call in February and August if you'd like to take part in the lottery for one of the 100 available places on these hikes.

The visitor center is open daily 8–5; entry fee to the monument is $3 per car. As noted earlier, one admission price gets you into both Wupatki and Sunset Crater. For more information, contact the business office at the National Park Service (*see* Sunset Crater, *above*).

The archaeological site in the park closest to U.S. 89 (the most direct route back to Flagstaff) is the **Citadel Ruin,** a pueblo that sits on a knoll above a limestone sink. It's 9 miles northwest of the visitor center on the main loop road.

What to See and Do with Children

Small children should enjoy the **Grand Canyon Deer Farm** in Williams, 25 miles west of Flagstaff on I–40, at Exit 171 (8 miles east of Williams). Visitors can pet and feed the deer, including the tiny fawns born every June and July. There are also pygmy goats, llamas, and other animals to pet. *100 Deer Farm Rd., Williams 86046, tel. 602/635–4073. Admission: $4.50 adults, $2.25 children 3–13, children under 3 free. Open Mar.–May, daily 9 AM–dusk; June–Aug., daily 8 AM–dusk; Sept.–Oct., daily 9 AM–dusk; Nov.–Feb., daily 10–5 if the weather is good.*

Anglers young and old will enjoy the sure catch at the **Rainbow Trout Farm.** For $1 you'll get a cane pole with a hook and bait. There's a charge for every fish you catch unless you can hook a really big one—fish 9 inches and under cost $1, a 10–11 incher costs $2.50, 11–12 inchers go for $3, and so on until you reach 20 inches; anything that size is yours for free. The real bargain is that the staff will clean your fish for 30¢ each and pack them in ice for you. *3 mi north of Sedona on U.S. 89A, tel. 602/282–5799. Open weekdays 9–5, weekends 8–6; summer, daily 8–7, weather permitting.*

Youngsters will love to plunge down the **natural rock slide** into the water at Slide Rock State Park in Oak Creek Canyon (*see* Sedona and Environs, *above*).

School-age children will be impressed by **Meteor Crater** (*see* Flagstaff and Environs, *above*). All ages enjoy **Jeep tours** in Sedona (*see* Special-Interest Tours in Essential Information, *above*). The **train from Clarkdale** (*see* Sedona and Environs, *above*) also keeps children entertained.

Shopping

Flagstaff

There aren't as many interesting shops in Flagstaff as there are in Sedona, but a few places are worth a browse, especially if you like antiques and vintage clothing. **The Carriage House** (413 N. San Francisco St., tel. 602/774–1337) is a collection of 19 antiques shops featuring old clothes, furniture, fine china, and jewelry. The **Old Highway Trading Post** (698 E. Santa Fe Ave., tel. 602/774–0035) also brings together a number of purveyors of advertising art, jewelry, clothing, and other collectibles. Rhoda Vihel's **Pine Country Quilts** (1 W. Riordan Rd., tel. 602/779–2194) is packed with fabrics, notions, and antique quilts, and there is likely to be a lesson going on in the shop when you visit.

Old Town Gallery (2 W. Santa Fe Ave., tel. 602/774–7770), owned by anthropologist Bruce Hudgens, features fine art and Native American jewelry. **Crystal Magic** (5 N. San Francisco St., tel. 602/779–2528) carries New Age books, records, tapes, and crystals.

Most shops are downtown; **Flagstaff Mall** (4650 N. U.S. 89, tel. 602/526–4827) is just east of town off Exit 201 of I–40. Small by most standards, this mall has the most department and specialty stores in the area, including Dillards, Sears, and J C Penney. It's a good place for travelers who need camping gear, car-repair items, or warm clothing to cope with the area's cool nights.

Jerome

Shoppers in Jerome will find a variety of boutiques located in houses precariously perched on the side of Cleopatra Hill. The town has its share of art galleries, but they're likely to be a bit more on the funky side than the ones you'll find in Sedona. An exception is the **Anderson-Mandette Art Studios** (Old Mingus High School, Bldg. C, tel. 602/634–3438). Robin Anderson and Margo Mandette made the building their workplace in 1978; at almost 20,000 square feet, it is considered by many to be the largest private art studio and gallery in the United States. The gallery is open daily 11–6; guided tours are available on request.

Shopping is easy in Jerome; all you need to do is stroll up and down Main Street. Your eyes may begin to glaze over after browsing one boutique after another with tasteful—

and generally pricey—southwestern goods. At the bottom of Main, **Aurum** (tel. 602/634–3330) carries lovely imported and locally made jewelry, much of it silver. Next door, you'll be drawn in by the bright-colored patterns and attractively styled women's clothing of **Designs on You** (tel. 602/634–7879). Farther up the hill, **Sky Fire** (tel. 602/634–8081) has two floors of items to adorn your person and your house, ranging from wrapping paper and confetti to a $1,000 fabric bench in the shape of an iguana. **Nellie Bly** (tel. 602/634–0255) offers a wide range of walking sticks in addition to a good selection of jewelry. Around the corner, the **Gift Shop of Jerome** (Jerome Ave., tel. 602/634–5105) is a good source for moccasins, hats, pottery, minerals, and other Jerome souvenirs ranging from tacky—plastic-encased scorpion or tarantula paperweights—to collectible.

Sedona

See Exploring Sedona, *above*.

Sports and Outdoor Activities

Camping There are more than 50 campgrounds in the Flagstaff, Sedona, and Jerome areas. The best way to learn about them is to consult the *Arizona Camping and Campgrounds Guide*, available from the **Arizona Office of Tourism** (*see* Chapter 1, Essential Information).

In **Coconino National Forest** near Flagstaff (ranger's tel. 602/527–7400), the campgrounds near Mormon Lake and Lake Mary—including Pinegrove, Lakeview, Forked Pine, Double Springs, and Dairy Springs—are usually less crowded than those closer to town.

Campgrounds close to **Sedona** often fill up in the summertime, especially those along Oak Creek in Oak Creek Canyon; two good places to try are Manzanita and Banjo Bill (ranger's tel. 602/282–4119).

Jerome's campgrounds are generally less crowded. A few good ones are Jerome State Historic Park (tel. 602/624–5381) and Mingus Mountain and Potato Patch (tel. 602/634–8851).

If you're camping in the wintertime, remember that this area gets quite cold, with frequent snowstorms. In summertime, night temperatures can dip to the 40s, while daytime temperatures can reach 90°F.

Golf In addition to the many private clubs in the Flagstaff–Sedona area, golfers will find semiprivate courses, which accept a limited number of nonmembers, as well as public courses. Among the recommended ones in the **Flagstaff vicinity** are the Fairfield Flagstaff resort's **Elden Hills Golf**

Club (2380 N. Oakmont Dr., Flagstaff, 602/527-7999), a public course, and **Pinewood Country Club** (Box 584, Munds Park, tel. 602/286-1110), which is semiprivate. In the **Sedona area,** the **Oak Creek Country Club** (690 Bell Rock Blvd., Sedona, tel. 602/284-1660) is a good semiprivate option. (*See* Sports and Outdoor Activities in Chapter 1, Essential Information, for other sources of golf information in the area.)

Hiking Hikers will find an abundance of trails all across the region. In **Sedona,** contact the **Sedona Ranger District** office (250 Brewer Rd., tel. 602/282-4119) for detailed hiking maps. Just **north of Flagstaff**, but still in town, the **Peaks Ranger Station** (5075 N. U.S. 89, tel. 602/526-0866) also has excellent hiking and recreational guides. Around Mormon Lake, **south of Flagstaff,** the **Happy Jack Ranger Station** (Forest Hwy. 3, Happy Jack, tel. 602/527-7371) provides information about treks in the area. The **Verde Ranger District** office of the **Prescott National Forest** (General Crook Trail, Camp Verde, tel. 602/567-4121) is a good resource for places to hike—as well as to fish and boat—along the Verde River. The **Coconino National Forest** north and east of Camp Verde is mapped by the **Beaver Creek Ranger District** (Forest Service Rd. 618, Rimrock, tel. 602/567-4501). (*See* Red Rock State Park and Snowbowl in the Exploring section, above, for other hiking options.)

Horseback Riding Spring, summer, and fall are the best times of the year to ride in this area. In **Flagstaff,** the wranglers at **Hitchin' Post Stables** (448 Lake Mary Rd., tel. 602/774-1719 or 602/774-7131) lead rides into Walnut Canyon as well as horseback or horsedrawn wagon rides with sunset barbecues. In **Sedona, Kachina Riding Stable** (West Sedona, tel. 602/282-7252) offers a package that includes an Oak Creek swim and picnic lunch. Weight limit for riders is 225 pounds.

Skiing The ski season usually starts in mid-November and ends in mid-April. A good option for **downhill** skiers is the nearby **Snowbowl** (*see* Flagstaff and Environs in Exploring North-Central Arizona, *above*). **Cross-country** skiers can find well-groomed trails in several places around Flagstaff, among them **Flagstaff Nordic Center** (15 mi northwest of town, tel. 602/774-6216); drive U.S. 180 to milepost 232, where you'll see the center. The trail fee is $7.50–$12 for adults, $3–$5 for children ages 5–12. **Mormon Lake Ski Center** (21 mi southeast of Flagstaff by way of Lake Mary Rd., Mormon Lake, tel. 602/354-2240) also offers cross-country skiing, as does **Montezuma Nordic Ski Center** (just north of Mormon Lake, tel. 602/354-2220.

Dining and Lodging

Dining Highly recommended restaurants are indicated by a star ★.

Category	Cost*
Very Expensive	over $35
Expensive	$25–$35
Moderate	$15–$25
Inexpensive	under $15

**per person, excluding drinks, service, and sales tax (6% in Flagstaff, 7% in Sedona)*

Lodging Highly recommended lodgings are indicated by a star ★.

Category	Cost*
Very Expensive	over $125
Expensive	$90–$125
Moderate	$50–$90
Inexpensive	under $50

**All prices are for a standard double room in high (summer) season, excluding room tax (8% in Flagstaff, 10½% in Sedona).*

Flagstaff

Dining **Black Bart's Steakhouse Saloon & Old West Theater.** Fans of the Old West—or a sanitized facsimile thereof—will enjoy the atmosphere in this rustic old barnlike structure, complete with beamed ceilings and lanternlike light fixtures. Aged prime beef is grilled over an open oak fire, and the barbecue chicken is tender and flavorful. Don't be surprised to see your waiter or waitress get up onstage and belt out a couple of show tunes; when there's no live entertainment, a player piano fills the restaurant with its tinny renditions of old favorites. *2760 E. Butler Ave., tel. 602/779–3142. Reservations advised during summer months. Dress: informal. MC, V. Closed for lunch. Moderate.*

Buster's Restaurant. This deservedly popular restaurant, located in a strip shopping center close to the university, is built to handle volume efficiently. Students and families tend to frequent the comfortable booths and tables. The menu is varied—fresh seafood, homemade soups, salads, giant burgers, and mesquite-grilled steaks. Try the pizza appetizer—a giant cracker heaped with a choice of toppings ranging from smoked salmon to mushrooms to fruits and vegetables—big enough for two to split as a meal. *1800 S. Milton Rd., tel. 602/774–5155. Reservations advised. Dress: informal. AE, D, DC, MC, V. Inexpensive–Moderate.*

Chez Mark Bistro. In late 1991, the Cannes-born head chef of L'Auberge de Sedona resort headed north to set up his own restaurant in a restored mansion, built in 1911 by the influential Babbit family. In three lovely French country–

style dining rooms one can enjoy such entrées as venison with cloudberries or seared salmon with glazed carrots. Don't expect the sophisticated service or attention to culinary detail you'd find in a major city; the salad dressing can be heavy and the French bread not very crusty. This is nevertheless a fine addition to Flagstaff's rather limited repertoire of upscale restaurants. *503 Humphreys St., tel. 602/774–1343. Reservations advised. Dress: neat but casual. MC, V. Closed Sun. Expensive.*

★ **Cottage Place.** Another unexpectedly elegant spot in a town known for hearty food and drive-through service, this restaurant is in a homey little cottage built more than 50 years ago. The dining area is candlelit, with lace curtains on tall, wood-frame windows; it's broken up into many tiny, intimate rooms. Service is friendly and professional. The menu focuses on classic Continental cuisine. The shrimp scampi and the veal Regina are both well prepared and beautifully presented. *126 W. Cottage Ave., tel. 602/774–8431. Reservations advised. Dress: neat but casual. AE, MC, V. Dinner only, closed Mon. Moderate.*

★ **Horsemen Lodge & Restaurant.** In a ranch-style stone building decorated with hunting trophies (the furry kind that stare at you during dinner), this restaurant is cozy and very "Flagstaff," reflecting the blend of Native American and frontier cultures that shaped the area. The knotty-pine beams and huge stone fireplace make this a perfect place to spend a snowy evening. Fresh trout and oak-grilled steaks are particularly good choices on the menu, which features traditional American fare, prepared without pretense for the hearty appetite. *3 mi north of Flagstaff Mall on U.S. 89, tel. 602/526–2655. Reservations advised. Dress: neat but casual. MC, V. Dinner only, closed Sun. Moderate.*

★ **Kachina Restaurant.** Tables in this family-style Mexican restaurant are Formica and chairs are vinyl, but the food is well prepared, spicy, and served in copious portions. The two cheerful dining rooms have pseudostucco walls with tiles and lantern-style chandeliers; one has a fireplace and the other a central fountain. The combination plates are a real bargain; you can get an enchilada, taco, and tostada with beans, rice, and a *sopapilla* (fried dough coated with powdered sugar), and coffee for $6. There are terrific breakfast specials too, and the selection of Mexican and American beers is unusually large. *2240 E. Santa Fe Ave., tel. 602/779–5790; and 522 E. Santa Fe Ave., tel. 602/779–1944. Reservations accepted. Dress: informal. MC, V. Inexpensive.*

Little America Coffee Shop. Part of the Little America motel, this is one of Flagstaff's busiest restaurants, offering both coffee-shop service and seating in a more upscale dining room. In both areas, the 70s-style decor is red and black, and furnishings are rather dark. As you might expect, the menu features American dishes, among them a tasty walnut-packed chicken salad. At breakfast the pancakes are light and fluffy, and are served with an efficiency that travelers who want to get an early start appreciate. A Sunday champagne brunch offers a nice assortment of omelets, waffles, fruit, and salads. *2515 E. Butler Ave., tel. 602/779–2741. Reservations accepted. Dress: informal. AE, D, DC, MC, V. Open daily 24 hrs. Inexpensive–Moderate.*

Sakura Restaurant. The oddness of finding of a good sushi bar in Flagstaff is compounded by the fact that the only other entrées available at Sakura are prepared *teppan* (Japanese grill) style. If your dining companion doesn't like raw fish, you'll be eating yours at a large table to the accompaniment of a grill chef's pyrotechnics. That said, the fish, flown in every other day from the West Coast, is excellent; the spicy sushi-style tuna salad will knock your socks off. And even if you haven't stepped foot in a Benihana's in years, you'll enjoy the well-seasoned, large portions of steak or seafood with vegetables being flipped around in front of you. *1175 W. Hwy. 66, tel. 602/773–9118. Reservations accepted. Dress: casual. No smoking. AE, D, DC, MC, V. Moderate.*

Lodging

Hotels and Motels

Best Western Woodlands Plaza Hotel. This upscale link in the Best Western chain is the glitziest accommodation in town—which isn't saying much in Flagstaff. The brass-and-marble lobby, although tasteful, is somewhat oddly eclectic in style. But the hotel is conveniently located near downtown and the main outbound roads; the rooms are large, comfortable, and nicely furnished in southwestern pastels; and there are two good restaurants on the premises, including Sakura (*see* Dining, *above*). *1175 W. Hwy. 66, Flagstaff 86001, tel. 602/773–8888 or 800/528–1234. 125 rooms with bath. Facilities: 2 restaurants, cocktail lounge, fitness center, outdoor pool, Jacuzzi, gift shop. AE, D, DC, MC, V. Expensive.*

Howard Johnson's. Just off I–40, this three-story motel is a convenient stop for travelers. It's a typical Howard Johnson's, with functional modern furniture, rooms that are built for sleeping and little else, and a 24-hour coffee shop instead of room service. Some suites have fireplaces, which make for cozy evenings in the winter and even during some of Flagstaff's chilly summer evenings. A courtesy van transports guests to the airport, train, or bus station. *2200 E. Butler Ave., 86004, tel. 602/779–6944 or 800/654–2000. 100 rooms with bath. Facilities: indoor pool, sauna, restaurant, lounge, free in-room movies. AE, D, DC, MC, V. Moderate.*

Little America of Flagstaff. The biggest motel in town, with 248 rooms, this is a popular place. It's far enough from the tracks (many of the town's motels are along Santa Fe Avenue, which runs parallel to the railroad) to allow visitors to sleep undisturbed as the trains roar through town. The grounds are surrounded by evergreen forests, and the motel's two-story buildings are spread out so that lodgers don't feel crowded. The rooms, furnished in plush reds and dark browns, all have little private patios. *2515 E. Butler*

Ave. (Box 850), 86002, tel. 602/779–2741 or 800/352–4386. 248 rooms with bath. Facilities: pool, kitchenettes, restaurant, cocktail lounge, gift shop, courtesy van, service station/garage. AE, D, MC, V. Moderate.

★ **Monte Vista Hotel.** Built in 1927, this appealing downtown hotel has been restored to its original Art Deco style: Each room features a claw-foot bathtub, upright candlestick telephone, and other period furnishings. Some rooms on the fourth (top) floor afford beautiful views of the San Francisco Peaks. The gift shop in the lobby carries some unusual and tasteful items; it's especially good for stocking stuffers at Christmas. *100 N. San Francisco St., 86001, tel. 602/779–6971. 35 rooms with bath. Facilities: restaurant, cocktail lounge. AE, MC, V. Inexpensive–Moderate.*

Bed-and-Breakfast

Birch Tree Inn. Set in a refurbished 1917 home, this little B&B largely furnished with antiques from the era features afternoon tea as well as a full breakfast. There is a game room with a pool table and a lovely porch where you can sit and while away the hours. Smoking is not permitted. *824 W. Birch Ave., 86001, tel. 602/774–1042. 5 rooms, 3 with bath. MC, V. Moderate.*

Jerome

Dining

House of Joy. Situated in a former bordello, left over from Jerome's mining days more than 100 years ago, this now respectable restaurant attracts patrons from all over the region—perhaps as much for its legendary setting as for its food. The decor is just what you'd expect: lots of heavy, dark furniture, red velvet—and even red lights. Book a table several weeks in advance as this popular restaurant is open only on weekends. Classic Continental dishes such as chicken Kiev and veal Marsala are well prepared. The hot muffins are excellent, as are the desserts, which vary from one day to the next. *Hull Ave., just off Main St., tel. 602/634–5339. Reservations required. Dress: neat but casual. No credit cards; personal checks accepted. Closed weekdays; dinner only weekends. Moderate.*

Jerome Inn. A throwback to the days of Woodstock and tie-dye, this funky Main Street restaurant serves good burgers, soups, and salads. Seating is in plush booths or coffee shop–style tables, and the decor is eclectic, to say the least—old ads, silly posters, Tiffany-style lamps, and lots of plants. The 1920s-era jukebox doesn't work, but never mind; on any given day you might dine to the impromptu accompaniment of live folk music by a local duo. *Main St., tel. 602/634–5094. No reservations. Dress: casual. MC, V. Inexpensive.*

Lodging

The Cottage Inn. Set in a 1917-era porch-fronted house off the main road (in a neighborhood known as Upper Hogback), this B&B offers beautiful views of Verde Valley. A pot of hot coffee greets early risers in a central sitting area, and a full breakfast is served upstairs in the dining room at

8 AM. The two bedrooms have a private bath and a private entrance; the sitting room, which can accommodate two on a pullout bed, is used when a party of six rents the entire house. Make your reservations in advance—the place is usually full. *747 East Ave., Box 823, 86331, tel. 602/634–0701. 2 rooms with bath. No credit cards; checks accepted. Moderate.*

Miner's Roost Hotel. The style is Victorian, and most of the rooms share baths in this creaky but characterful old hotel left over from Jerome's heyday almost 100 years ago. Reserve in advance, because it's one of only two hotels in town, and it's small (seven rooms). The bar and restaurant downstairs can be noisy, especially on Saturday night, and the walls in the rooms are thin. Try to book the Montana—it's one of the hotel's largest, and it offers a lovely view of the mountains and downtown as well as a firm mattress. *Main St., Box 36, 86331, tel. 602/634–5094. 7 rooms, 1 with private bath. Facilities: library, restaurant, MC, V. Moderate.*

Sedona–Oak Creek Canyon

Dining

★ **L'Auberge de Sedona.** Though a bit self-conscious, this formal French restaurant is one of the best in the state. The atmosphere is country French, with Pierre Deux–type fabrics. Ask for a table overlooking the stream, preferably in the smaller room near the entrance. The cuisine takes advantage of both classic and nouvelle styles, with light, subtle sauces, somewhat modest portions, and the freshest of ingredients. The six-course fixed-price menu ($45) may feature beef tenderloin with a Périgord sauce or venison with wild mushrooms Bordelaise; sometimes alligator or wild boar are among the choices. *301 Little La., tel. 602/282–1667. Reservations required. Jacket required. AE, D, DC, MC, V. Expensive.*

★ **Canyon Rose at Los Abrigados.** Canyon Rose brings together a lovely, romantic setting—plush booths or chairs upholstered in stylized floral patterns, rose-colored tablecloths, and dim lights from stylish brass wall sconces and chandeliers—and excellently prepared, beautifully presented food. This is the best of the Southwest, with local ingredients used in innovative combinations; the Oak Creek trout, for example, is sautéed in rolled oats and served with roasted corn relish and black-bean cakes. Service is impeccable, and the wine list is wide-ranging. *160 Portal La., tel. 602/282–ROSE. Reservations advised. Dress: neat but casual. AE, D, DC, MC, V. Expensive.*

Hitchin' Post Restaurant. The worn plastic booths and tile floor here have seen thousands of diners, both locals and tourists, who frequent this popular place. It's a family-style coffee shop staffed by friendly, efficient waitresses—a good bet for a comforting bowl of soup and a sandwich. The homemade pie can't be beat either. Blue-plate special lunches and burgers satisfy the heartier appetites. Breakfast choices are traditional and delicious. *269 W. U.S.*

89A, tel. 602/282–7761. No reservations. Dress: informal. No credit cards. Inexpensive.

Humphreys. A seafaring motif in a restaurant located in a desert mountain town may seem a bit odd, but this one works. The fish is fresh and well prepared, sans any fancy sauces whose names you can't pronounce. You can request that your selection be grilled over mesquite, fried, or poached. If you have a special dietary concern, call ahead; the friendly manager will do everything possible to accommodate you. For those who don't care for seafood, there are several steak, pasta, and chicken dishes on the menu. *1405 W. U.S. 89A, tel. 602/282–7745. Reservations advised on weekends. Dress: neat but casual. MC, V. Open daily for dinner. Moderate.*

Mandarin House. If you're going to do something as un-Arizonan as shop at the Oak Creek Factory Stores, you might as well go all the way and have a meal at this worthwhile Chinese restaurant just down the road from the outlet mall. Its name notwithstanding, the Mandarin House serves everything from standard Cantonese to Szechuan fare, with dishes ranging from the exotic (shark fin salad) to the old standbys (egg foo young). The large dining room is light and not overly kitschy. *6486 Hwy. 179, Suite 114, tel. 602/284–9088. Reservations accepted but not required. Dress: casual. AE, MC, V. Moderate.*

Oak Creek Owl Restaurant. In this pretty, cheerful restaurant with beamed ceilings, a fireplace, and stained-glass windows, you can enjoy a casual meal of Cobb salad or steak fajitas; the pasta dishes are particularly recommended. Service can be a bit loopy: During one visit the kitchen staff lost the chicken and the waitress passed around cards advertising her boyfriend's air-tour business. The wine list, which focuses on California vineyards, is extensive, but ask about the Arizona labels; nearby vineyards produce a limited supply, and sometimes the Owl has a bottle stashed for customers savvy enough to ask about it. Don't expect to get a table at this popular place without reservations. *329 AZ 179, tel. 602/282–3532. Reservations advised. Dress: neat but casual. DC, MC, V. Moderate.*

★ **Rincon del Tlaquepaque.** This lovely garden restaurant nestled in the upscale Spanish-style Tlaquepaque mall features Sonoran Mexican food and some Native American–inspired items such as Navajo tacos and pizzas. Towering sycamores shade the outdoor patio, where diners can watch shoppers stroll through the flower-filled and stone-sidewalked shopping area. Try the margaritas and *chimichangas*, deep-fried burritos filled with seasoned beef or chicken. *Tlaquepaque Arts and Crafts Village, AZ 179 at the bridge, tel. 602/282–4648. Reservations advised. Dress: informal. AE, MC, V. Closed Mon. Moderate.*

Lodging

Bell Rock Inn. Named after one of Sedona's red-rock landmarks, this motel is made of contemporary adobe, with well-furnished rooms in southwestern style. The scenery is typically Sedona—striking red-rock spires shooting into a clear blue sky. During the winter, the dusting of snow contrasts with the red rocks, making for an even more striking scene. Bargain hunters take note: Right across the highway is the Oak Creek Factory Stores (*see* Exploring Sedona, *above*). *6246 AZ 179, 86336, tel. 602/282–4161. 47 rooms with bath. Facilities: restaurant, pool, Jacuzzi, tennis courts. AE, MC, V. Inexpensive–Moderate.*

Garland's Oak Creek Lodge. In the heart of Oak Creek Canyon, this lodge was built in the 1930s and bought by its current owners, Gary and Mary Garland, in the 1960s. Fifteen comfortably furnished cabins, some including fireplaces and some pullout beds for extra guests, share 17 acres of beautiful land (at an elevation of 5,000 feet) with an organic apple orchard. Accommodations look out over the canyon itself or the rugged cliffs surrounding it. The lodge is operated on a modified American plan, with excellent, copious breakfasts and dinners included in the room price. Garland's is usually booked solid months in advance–it's open only from November through April–but it's worth a phone call to check. *U.S. 89A, 8 mi north of Sedona (Box 152), 86336, tel. 602/282–3343. 15 cabins with bath. Facilities: restaurant, volleyball court, croquet, tennis court, swimming hole. MC, V. Very Expensive.*

★ **Enchantment Resort.** This upscale resort in secluded Boynton Canyon features tennis, golf, croquet, a full health spa, and a six-hole golf course. Accommodations are in suites with private entrances and patios. The decor is tasteful southwestern, with adobe exteriors, muted colors inside, and high-quality contemporary art and sculpture throughout. In keeping with the theme, the dining room serves elegant Southwest cuisine as well as Continental fare. *525 Boynton Canyon Rd., 86336, tel. 800/826–4180. 162 rooms with bath. Facilities: 6 outdoor pools, 12 tennis courts, 6-hole golf course, fitness center, health center, kitchenettes, restaurant. AE, D, MC, V. Expensive.*

★ **L'Auberge de Sedona Resort.** This resort consists of a central building and—the major attraction—a number of sweet, secluded cabins in a wooded setting along a stream. Phoenix couples flock to those romantic, country-French hideaways and dine in the first-class French restaurant (*see* Dining, *above*). There's a small heated pool for summertime swimming. *L'Auberge La. (Box B), 86336, tel. 602/282–1661 or 800/272–6777. 96 rooms, 34 cottages, all with bath. Facilities: pool, spa.AE, D, DC, MC, V. Expensive.*

★ **Los Abrigados.** This is one of those "I-would-happily-move-out-out-of-my-home-and-live-here" resorts—and indeed, some of the lovely, fully equipped units at Los Abrigados are available on a time-share basis. All the spacious suite accommodations, attractively decorated in shades of plum and teal or rust and salmon, have microwaves, minibars stocked with microwavable items, and coffee-making facilities, as well as two TVs and two phones; in addition, some have private spas and fireplaces. A state-of-the-art health club, offering such extras as massages and facials, will help burn off the calories picked up at the excellent Canyon Rose restaurant (*see* Dining, *above*). Guests can also picnic at Oak Creek, which runs through the grounds of this tree-lined property, built on the site of the oldest (1879) patented land in the area. *160 Portal La., Sedona 86336, tel. 602/282–1777 or 800/521–3131. 175 suites. Facilities: 2 restaurants; jazz lounge; health club with sauna, steam, whirlpool, tanning, and fitness classes; heated outdoor pool; 3 tennis courts; volleyball court. AE, D, DC, MC, V. Very Expensive.*

Poco Diablo Resort. One of Sedona's original resort properties, Poco Diablo sits on 22 green and beautifully landscaped acres south of town. All the accommodations and public areas underwent a major refurbishment in 1991. Some rooms have fireplaces and private whirlpools; all have private patios—some with spectacular red-rock views—and all are tastefully decorated and furnished in southwestern style. *1752 AZ 179 (Box 1709), 86336, tel. 602/282–7333 or 800/352–5710 in AZ, 800/526–4275 outside AZ. 104 rooms with bath, 14 with kitchenette. Facilities: 2 pools, 9-hole golf course, 4 tennis courts, 2 racquetball courts, restaurant, AE, D, DC, MC, V. Moderate–Expensive.*

Sky Ranch Lodge. There may be no better vantage point in town from which to view Sedona's red-rock canyons than the private patios or balconies at Sky Ranch Lodge. Some rooms have stone fireplaces, some have kitchenettes; all are well decorated in the pastels of the Southwest. Paths on the grounds wind around fountains and, in summer, through colorful flower gardens. This is an excellent value choice. *Airport Rd. (Box 2579), 86336, tel. 602/282–6400. 92 rooms, 2 cottages, all with bath, 20 rooms with kitchenette. Facilities: pool, whirlpool. Accepts pets. MC, V. Inexpensive–Moderate.*

The Arts and Nightlife

The Arts

Tourists who wish to visit the symphony, ballet, or theater must drive to Phoenix or Tucson. However, some excellent local events offer out-of-towners a chance to enjoy the unique cultural contributions of the area.

Flagstaff Perhaps the most exciting happening in town is the Flagstaff **All Indian Powwow,** held downtown during the weekend before the Fourth of July. Representatives of tribes from all over the world gather for three days every year to give exhibitions of native dances and to compete for performance awards in a variety of categories: men's, women's, boys', girls'—and even tiny tots'. Concurrently, at the **Native Arts Fair,** an international array of tribal crafts are displayed and sold. For details, contact the Flagstaff Visitors

Center (*see* Important Addresses and Numbers in Essential Information, *above*).

Festival in the Pines, sponsored annually during the first weekend of August by the Mill Avenue Merchants' Association (tel. 602/967–4877), features an arts-and-crafts fair; 200 artists from all over the United States gather for this event in Flagstaff at Coconino County Fair Grounds at Fort Tuthill. Among the 20 categories of crafts shown here are watercolors, oil paintings, ceramics, and stained glass. In addition, food vendors compete with three entertainment stages—featuring musicians playing everything from country and western to rock—as well as carnival rides for the crowd's attention.

The **Coconino Center for the Arts** (2300 N. Fort Valley Rd., U.S. 180 north, tel. 602/779–6921) hosts a **Festival of Native American Arts** each summer from late June through early August. During this six-week period, artists from tribes of the Four Corners region are invited to exhibit jewelry, ceramics, weavings, and paintings. Special events include performances of Native American music and dance, crafts demonstrations, auctions, and a Native American banquet. Cowboy art is the featured attraction at the **Trappings of the American West** festival held here from mid-May to early June—everything from painting and sculpture to cowboy poetry readings.

Individual sales shows of artwork by Zuni, Hopi, and Navajo tribes are held in the galleries and on the patio of the **Museum of Northern Arizona** (3001 N. Fort Valley Rd., tel. 602/774–5211) from late May through early August. Items collected at the reservations for this event by staff members—including kachina dolls, jewelry, textiles, and ceramics—are judged, with cash prizes awarded to the winners in each category. Native American dances and crafts demonstrations are also scheduled throughout the period.

Jerome The **Jerome Music Festival** has been a popular annual event for a number of years and is expected to take place again in the fall of 1993. The type of music changes—one year it may be Creole; another, blues—but the venue stays the same: Bands play for one day in the town's old open mining pit. People come from all over the Southwest, so if you're planning to attend, you might need to book a room in one of the nearby towns; Jerome doesn't have many places to accommmodate guests. For information, contact the **Jerome Chamber of Commerce** (160 Main St., 86331, tel. 602/634–2900).

Sedona The Sedona **Jazz on the Rocks Festival** (tel. 602/282–1985), held every September, always attracts a sellout crowd that fills the town to capacity; it's even more important than usual to book ahead for rooms at jazz-festival time. Call for particulars. The **Sedona Heritage Day Festival,** sponsored by the Sedona Historical Society (tel. 602/282–7191 weekdays

9–5), is celebrated in late June; it includes such activities as cake- and pie-baking contests and the reenactment of horseback mail delivery. Pie lovers should also take note of the **Sedona Apple Festival** (tel. 602/282–5631) in October; phone for specific dates and events. The **Sedona Art Center** (tel. 602/282–3809) sponsors events ranging from classical concerts to plays; phone for information about upcoming programs.

Nightlife

A university town, **Flagstaff** has a number of places where the college crowd gathers after dark. The misleadingly named **Museum Club** (3404 E. Santa Fe Ave., tel. 602/526-9434) is a tourist-friendly cowboy honky-tonk, housed in an old barnlike structure with a dance floor; there's usually a country-swing band. For live entertainment nightly—everything from rock and roll to blues and jazz—try **Charly's Restaurant and Pub** (23 N. Leroux St., tel. 602/779–1919), in the lobby of the historic Weatherford Hotel. **Busters** (1800 S. Milton, tel. 602/774–5155) offers a large selection of domestic and imported beers, and **Main Street Bar and Grill** (4 S. San Francisco St., tel. 602/774–1519) stirs up the best margaritas in town.

The nightlife in Sedona geared more toward a resort crowd, tends to be a bit less rowdy. **On the Rocks,** the lounge at Canyon Rose at Los Abrigados (160 Portal La., tel. 602/281–1777), hosts bands nightly, mostly of the swing and jazz variety. **The Enchantment Resort** (525 Boynton Canyon Rd., tel. 602/282–2900) has an attractive bar where live piano and jazz keep the local and visiting beautiful people entertained. For a taste of old Sedona, try the **Oak Creek Tavern** (121 U.S. 89A, tel. 602/282–7921), an old western bar with a pool table, dark, private booths, and a giant stuffed polar bear. The **West 89th Street Club** (West U.S. 89A, tel. 602/282–1655) is the place to go if you feel like kicking up your heels on the dance floor.

6 Phoenix and Central Arizona

By Mark Hein

In central Arizona, one of the world's great deserts meets one of its great mountain ranges, providing a stunning variety of natural environments for the visitor to enjoy within easy touring distance. Central Arizona also combines some of the oldest human dwellings in the Western Hemisphere with the homes of contemporary Indian tribes and America's newest, fastest-growing major urban center, metropolitan Phoenix.

At the center of central Arizona lies the Valley of the Sun, named for its 330-plus days of sunshine each year. This 1,000-square-mile valley is the northern tip of the Sonoran Desert, a surprisingly fertile, rolling expanse of prehistoric seabed that stretches from central Arizona deep into northwestern Mexico.

The Valley, like the rest of the Sonora, is studded with cacti and creosote bushes, crusted with hard-baked clay and rock, and scorched by summer temperatures that can stay above 100° F for weeks at a time. But its dry skin responds magically to the touch of rainwater. Spring is a miracle of poppies strewn among the flower-crowned saguaros, of ruby, ivory, and gold blossoms bursting from the dry spikes of the ocotillo, and the thorny beaver-tail pads of the nopal. And, as the Hohokam discovered, this miracle can be augmented by human hands. From 300 BC to AD 1450, their tilled, rowed, and irrigated fields yielded cotton, corn, and beans. Then, for reasons neither archaeology nor Indian lore has yet revealed, these skillful, energetic people suddenly abandoned their homes.

From the time the Hohokam left until the American Civil War, the once-fertile Salt River valley lay forgotten, used only by occasional small bands of Pima and Maricopa peoples. Then in 1865, the U.S. Army established Fort McDowell in the mountains to the east, where the Verde River flows into the Salt. To feed the men and the horses stationed there, Jack Swilling, a former Confederate army officer, had the idea of reopening the Hohokam canals in 1867. Within a year fields bright with barley and pumpkins earned the area the name of Punkinsville. But by 1870, when the town site was plotted, the 300 inhabitants had decided that their new city would rise "like a phoenix" from the ashes of a vanished civilization.

Phoenix indeed grew steadily. Within 20 years, it had become large enough—at about 3,000 people—to wrest the title of territorial capital from Prescott. It got a high school in 1895, and at statehood, in 1912, the area, irrigated by the brand-new Roosevelt Dam and Salt River Project, had a burgeoning cotton industry. Copper and cattle were mined and raised elsewhere but were banked and traded in Phoenix, and the cattle were slaughtered and packed here, in the largest stockyards outside Chicago.

Meanwhile climate, so long a crippling liability, became an asset. Desert air was the prescribed therapy for respiratory ills rampant in the sooty, factory-filled East; Scottsdale began in 1901 as "30-odd tents and a half-dozen adobe houses" put up by health seekers. By 1930, visitors seeking warm winter recreation rather than a cure were filling the elegant San Marcos hotel in Chandler and the new Arizona Biltmore, first of the many luxury resorts for which the area is known worldwide today.

When low-cost air-conditioning made its summer heat manageable, the Sun Belt boom began. From 1950 to 1990, the Phoenix urban area more than quadrupled in population, catapulting real estate and home building into two of the state's biggest industries. Cities planted around Phoenix have become its suburbs, and fields that for decades grew cotton and citrus now grow microchips and homes. Glendale and Peoria on the west side, Tempe, Mesa, and Chandler on the east, make up the nation's third-largest Silicon Valley.

The Valley of the Sun is ringed by mountains. In Phoenix itself are Squaw Peak to the north of downtown, and the Papago Peaks between Phoenix and Scottsdale. East of Phoenix, past Tempe and Mesa, stand the barren peaks of the Superstition Mountains, named for their eerie habit of seeming just a few miles away and luring unwary prospectors to a dusty death. Beyond the Superstitions, central Arizona is mountains all the way into New Mexico. South of Phoenix, easily visible from the airport, rise the much less lofty peaks of South Mountain Park. Not 5 miles from downtown, this 12-mile-wide chain of dry mountains divides the Valley from the rest of the Sonora Desert. West of Phoenix, past Glendale and Tolleson, the formidable, barren-seeming White Tank Mountains separate the Valley from the empty lands that slope steadily downward toward the Colorado River and the Mojave Desert of California on the other side.

But north of Phoenix, behind the dusty Hieroglyphic Mountains (misnamed for Hohokam petroglyphs found there), rises the gigantic Mogollon Rim. This shelf of land, almost as wide as Arizona, was thrust 2,000 to 5,000 feet into the air back in the Mesozoic age; it got its name for posing an overwhelming *mogollon* (obstruction) to Spanish-speaking explorers probing northward. Here, the slopes are green with pine trees, and the alpine meadows lush with grasses and aspens. Here, after gold was found in the early 1860s, President Lincoln sent the Arizona Territory's first governor to found the capital at Prescott and secure the mineral riches for the Union.

Today, the northern mountains serve as a cool, green refuge for Valley dwellers. The bumpy wagon roads up the Black Canyon toward Prescott and Flagstaff were key summer escape routes 100 years ago, and their dramatically engineered successor, the four-lane split-level I–17, leads tens of thousands on exodus every weekend from May to September.

Phoenix and central Arizona are places in which to take it easy, go slow, and dress informally. As the old desert hands say, you don't begin to see the desert until you've looked at it long enough to see the colors; and you aren't ready to get up and move until you've seen the sun go down.

Essential Information

Arriving and Departing

By Plane Most air travelers visiting Arizona fly into **Sky Harbor International Airport** (tel. 602/273–3300). Just 3 miles east of downtown Phoenix, it is surrounded by freeways linking it to almost every part of the metro area. Although it is one of the nation's half-dozen busiest airports, it is also one of the most compact.

Sky Harbor has four commercial terminals, each with rental luggage carts, taxi stands, car-rental booths, ATM banking, and courtesy telephones. Terminals 3 and 4—the latter completed in late 1990—also have extensive shops (from Godber's Jewelry to a Bloomingdale's boutique) and restaurants, and their car-rental booths are open 24 hours.

Passenger service desks at terminals 3 and 4 (tel. 602/225–0773) offer fax, currency exchange, and notary and insurance services; the airport chaplain's office (tel. 602/244–1346) aids travelers in distress.

Airlines Sky Harbor is the home airport of **America West** (tel. 800/247–5692) and a hub for **Southwest** (tel. 800/531–5601). Other airlines with frequent flights to Sky Harbor are **Alaska** (tel. 800/426–0333), **American** (tel. 800/433–7300), **Continental** (tel. 800/525–0280), **Delta** (tel. 800/221–1212), **TWA** (tel. 800/221–2000), **United** (tel. 800/241–6522), and **USAir** (tel. 800/428–4322).

For flights to the Grand Canyon, Page, Lake Powell, Lake Havasu, and other Arizona points, try **America West** (tel. 800/247–5692) and commuters' **Mesa Airlines** (tel. 800/637–2247) and **SkyWest** (tel. 800/453–9417).

Between the Airport and Downtown Its easy access to downtown Phoenix and Tempe (3 miles away to the west and east, respectively) is one of Sky Harbor's strong points. It's also only 15 minutes by freeway from Glendale (to the west) and Mesa (to the east).

Unfortunately, two favorite tourist areas, Scottsdale (to the northeast) and Sun City (to the northwest) are harder to reach—each takes 30 to 45 minutes by car and requires using surface roads for all or part of the trip.

Sky Harbor has limited bus service, ample taxi service, and very good shuttle service to points throughout the metro area. Very few hotels offer a complimentary limo or shuttle, but most resorts do. You will probably want to rent a car, either at the airport or from wherever you are staying (most rental firms will deliver).

These companies have airport booths or free pickup from nearby lots: **Alamo** (tel. 800/327–9633), **Avis** (tel. 800/331–1212), **Budget** (tel. 800/527–0700), **Hertz** (tel. 800/654–3131), **Thrifty** (tel. 800/367–2277), and, if you care more about your wallet than appearances, **Rent-A-Wreck** (tel. 602/254–1000).

By Bus **Phoenix Transit** buses (tel. 602/253–5000) will get you directly from Terminal 2, 3, or 4 to downtown Phoenix's outdoor bus terminal (1st and Washington Sts.) or downtown Tempe (Mill and University Aves.) in about 20 minutes for less than $1. Senior citizens and children ages 6–12 pay half fare; children 5 and under ride free.

The No. 2 bus runs westbound to Phoenix every half hour from about 6 AM to 6 PM weekdays (Saturday, you take the No. 13 bus and transfer at Central Avenue to the No. 0 north; there is no Sunday service). The No. 2 runs eastbound to Tempe every half hour from 4 AM to 7 PM weekdays (no weekend service); in another 25 minutes, it takes you to downtown Mesa (Center and Main streets).

With free transfers, Phoenix Transit can take you from the airport to most other Valley cities (Glendale, Sun City, Scottsdale, etc.), but the trip is likely to be slow unless you manage to catch an express line.

By Taxi Only three firms—and one specializing in transporting handicapped travelers—are licensed to pick up at Sky Harbor's commercial terminals. All add a $1 surcharge for airport pickups, do not charge for luggage, and are available 24 hours a day. A trip to downtown Phoenix can range from $4 to $12, or $13.75 for a wheelchair-lift van. The fare to downtown Scottsdale averages around $13.

AAA Cab (tel. 602/253–8294), **Checker/Yellow Cab** (tel. 602/252–5071), and **Courier Cab** (tel. 602/232–2222) all charge around $2 for the first mile and $1.25 per mile thereafter. **American HTS** (tel. 602/272–7211) offers wheelchair and stretcher service, the former at a $10 pickup fee ($15 evenings and weekends) and $1.25 per mile. All expect tips.

The blue vans of **Supershuttle** (tel. 602/244–9000) also cruise Sky Harbor, each taking up to five passengers to their individual destinations, with no luggage fee or airport surcharge. Fares range from competitive with the cheapest taxi for a short run, such as downtown Phoenix or Tempe, to 25% or more below the best taxi fares on longer trips. You can reserve a Supershuttle back to the airport (call a day ahead and expect to be picked up two hours before your flight). Drivers expect tips.

By Limousine A few limousine firms are allowed to cruise Sky Harbor, and many more provide airport pickups by reservation. All of these are on 24-hour call. **La Limousine** (tel. 602/242-3094) can be hailed at the curb ($15 to $50, depending on distance) or reserved ($25 to $50). **Classic Limousine** (tel. 602/252-LIMO) will take up to five riders (by reservation only) for $30 to $50, depending on how far you're going. **All-American** (tel. 602/951-2188), by reservation only, needs just a couple of hours' notice and runs $65, tax and tip included, anywhere in the Valley. **Scottsdale Limousine** (tel. 602/946-8446) also requires reservations but offers a toll-free number (tel. 800/747-8234) and complimentary soft drinks; it costs from $55 to $85, plus tip.

By Car If you're coming to Phoenix from the west, you'll probably come on I-10—this transcontinental superhighway's last link was joined in 1990 in a tunnel under downtown Phoenix. The trip from the Los Angeles basin, via Palm Springs, takes five to eight hours, depending on where you start and how many rest stops you make. The older I-40 runs along old "Route 66," entering Arizona in the northwest, near Kingman; U.S. 93 traverses from there to Phoenix, for a total journey of 10 to 12 hours. From San Diego, I-8 slices across low desert to Yuma and on toward the Valley on what the Spanish called El Camino del Diablo (the Devil's Highway); at Gila Bend, take AZ 85 up to I-10. The trip takes a total of 8 to 10 hours.

From the east, **I-10** takes you from El Paso, across southern New Mexico, and through Chiricahua Apache country into Tucson, then north to Phoenix (a total of about 9 to 11 hours). The northeastern route, **I-40** from Albuquerque, crosses Hopi and Navajo historic lands to Flagstaff, where I-17 takes you south to Phoenix, also a 9- to 11-hour journey. For a scenic shortcut, take AZ 377 south at Holbrook, across Petrified Forest country to Heber, in the pines of the Mogollon Rim; then take AZ 260 down the 2,000-foot drop to Payson, and AZ 87 through saguaro cactus forests to Phoenix.

By Train **Amtrak** (tel. 800/USA-RAIL) has only one line, the former Southern Pacific line between New Orleans and Los Angeles, that passes through Phoenix; on Monday, Wednesday, and Saturday (8 AM eastbound, 11:30 PM westbound), it stops at the downtown terminal (4th Ave. and Harrison St., tel. 602/253-0121). It's in what is now the industrial part of town, and you may have to phone for a taxi. The much more heavily used former Santa Fe line between Los Angeles and Chicago runs through Flagstaff, 150 miles north of the Valley, stopping daily (8 AM eastbound, 10:30 PM westbound); it's a two- to three-hour ride by bus or car from there.

By Bus **Greyhound/Trailways** (tel. 602/248-4040) has statewide and nationwide routes from its main terminal in the heart of downtown (525 E. Washington St.), sandwiched between the Civic Plaza complex and the new America West Phoenix Suns Arena.

Important Addresses and Numbers

Tourist Information The **Phoenix and Valley of the Sun Convention and Visitors Bureau** (1 Arizona Ct., Suite 600, tel. 602/254-6500) has a satellite office in the Hyatt Regency Phoenix (2nd and Adams Sts., tel. 602/254-6500). The **Phoenix Chamber of Commerce** (34 W. Monroe St., tel. 602/254-5521) is in the heart of downtown.

Emergencies **Police, fire,** or **ambulance** (tel. 911).
Highway emergencies (tel. 800/525-5555).

Hospitals **Samaritan Health Service** (tel. 602/230-CARE) has four Valley hospitals—Good Samaritan (downtown), Desert Samaritan (east), Maryvale Samaritan (southwest), and Thunderbird Samaritan (northwest)—and a Deer Valley (north) urgent-care clinic; all share a 24-hour hotline. **Scottsdale Memorial Hospital** (tel. 602/481-4411) has three campuses in the northeastern Valley. **Maricopa County Medical Center** (tel. 602/267-5011) has been rated one of the nation's best public hospitals.

Doctors The **Maricopa County Medical Society** (tel. 602/252-2844) and the **Arizona Osteopathic Medical Association** (tel. 602/840-0460) offer referrals during business hours on weekdays.

Dentists The **American Dental Association Valley** chapter (tel. 602/957-4864) has a 24-hour referral hotline.

Late-Night Pharmacies **Walgreen's** has seven 24-hour locations throughout the Valley—in east Phoenix (38th St. and Thomas Rd., tel. 602/275-7507), north Phoenix (7th St. and Bell Rd., tel. 602/375-0093), and west Phoenix (5121 W. Indian School Rd., tel. 602/247-1014); in the eastern suburbs of Tempe (1719 E. Southern Ave., Tempe, tel. 602/838-3642), Chandler (1986 N. Alma School Rd., Chandler, tel. 602/899-6711), and Mesa (Main St. and Recker Rd., Mesa, tel. 602/985-0155); and in the western suburb of Peoria (6815 W. Peoria Rd., Peoria, tel. 602/878-7998). **Osco Drugs** has two 24-hour outlets, in central Phoenix (3320 N. 7th Ave., tel. 602/266-5501) and in Tempe (1836 W. Baseline Rd., tel. 602/831-0212).

Weather **Pressline** (tel. 602/271-5656, then press 3333) gives up-to-date Valley conditions and three-day forecasts, as does the **U.S. National Weather Service** (tel. 602/265-5550).

Getting Around

If you plan to see anything, *you will need a car.* The metro area developed in the automobile era, and only a few downtowns (Phoenix, Scottsdale, Tempe) are pedestrian-friendly. There is no mass transit beyond a bus system that does not even run seven days a week.

By Car Driving is easy in the Valley of the Sun: Rain is rare, fog makes headlines, and it never snows. Most metro-area streets are well marked and well lighted, and the freeway system (not funded until the late 1980s and still being built) has made dramatic strides in linking most of the Valley together. Arizona requires seat belts on front-seat passengers and children 16 and under. (For car-rental firms, *see* Between the Airport and Downtown, above.)

Around downtown Phoenix, I–17 (Black Canyon Freeway) and I–10 (Maricopa Freeway) make an elongated east-west loop, embracing the state capitol area on the west and the airport on the east. At midloop, AZ 51 (Squaw Peak Freeway) runs north into Paradise Valley. And from the loop's east end, I–10 runs south to Tucson, 100 miles away, while AZ 360 (Superstition Freeway) branches east to Tempe and Mesa.

Driving in the Valley presents one major challenge: Phoenix and all its suburbs are laid out on a single, 800-square-mile grid of horizontal and vertical streets. Even the freeways all run north–south and east–west. (Grand Avenue, running about 20 miles from downtown northwest to Sun City, is the *only* diagonal.) This makes places easy to find but means you must allow generous driving time to get from point A to point B, since you have to trace two legs of a right triangle to do it.

By Bus **Phoenix Transit** (tel. 602/253–5000) is a good rudimentary bus system, with 18 express lines and 33 regular routes that reach most of the Valley suburbs. But there are no 24-hour routes; only a skeletal few lines run between sundown and 10:30 PM or on Saturday; and there is no Sunday service. Fares are less than $1, with free transfers; senior citizens and children 6–18 pay half fare, and children 5 and under ride free. Phoenix Transit also runs a free **Downtown Area Shuttle** (DASH), with purple minibuses circling the area between the renovated east end of downtown and the state capitol, on the west end, at 10-minute intervals. Several suburbs have their own minibus systems that connect with Phoenix Transit buses: **Glendale Transit** (tel. 602/931–5432), **Scottsdale Connection** (tel. 602/253–5000), **Tempe Metro Trolley** (tel. 602/829–1226), and **Mesa Sunrunner** (tel. 602/461–1920). In addition, **Dial-A-Ride** services (tel. 602/253–7755) are available throughout the Valley.

By Taxi Taxi fares are unregulated in Phoenix, except at the airport. (For a listing of leading firms and their fares, *see* Between the Airport and Downtown, above.) The 800-square-mile metro area is so large that one-way fares of $30–$50 are not uncommon; you might want to ask what the damages will be before you get in. Except within a compact area, such as central Phoenix, travel by taxi is not recommended.

Opening and Closing Times

Generally, banks are open Monday–Thursday 9–4, Friday 9–6. Selected banks have Saturday morning hours, and a few large grocery stores have bank windows that stay open until 9 PM.

Most enclosed shopping malls are open weekdays 10–9, Saturday 10–6, and Sunday noon–5; some of the major centers (*see* Shopping, below) are open later on weekends.

Many grocery stores are open 7 AM–9 PM, but several stores within major chains throughout the Valley are open 24 hours.

Guided Tours

Reservations for tours are a must all year, with seats often filling up quickly in the busy season, October–April. All tours provide pickup services at area resorts, but some offer lower prices if you drive to the tour's point of origin.

Orientation Tours **Gray Line Tours** (3415 S. 36th St., Phoenix 85040, tel. 602/437–3701) offers a daily five-hour narrated drive through Phoenix and Scottsdale for $25, touring downtown Phoenix, the Arizona Biltmore hotel, Camelback Mountain, mansions in Paradise Valley, Arizona State University, Papago Park, and Scottsdale's 5th Avenue. For $28, **Vaughan's Southwest Custom Tours** (Box 31312, Phoenix 85046, tel. 602/971–1381) offers a four-hour trip for 11 or fewer passengers in custom vans, stopping at the Heard Museum, the Arizona Biltmore, and the state capitol building.

Both firms will also take visitors east of Phoenix on the Apache Trail, a scenic route that passes through old mining towns and includes a narrated boat ride on **Dolly's Steamboat Cruises** at Canyon Lake. Prices range from $39 to $50, with the tour available September through April.

Special-Interest Tours If you prefer to see the desert country from a four-wheel-drive vehicle, you'll find plenty of options. For example, **Carefree Jeep Adventures** (Box 5423, Carefree 85377, tel. 602/585–9755) travels into the Tonto National Forest on old stage and mining roads, where you can see petroglyphs and rock carvings, taste the fruit of cholla cactus, and hold target practice with tin cans and .22 rifles. That three-hour journey costs $50, as does a sunset tour; there's also a breakfast trip for $60. **Arizona Scenic Desert Tours** (2948 E. Shangri-La Rd., Phoenix 85028, tel. 602/971–3601) heads past Pinnacle Peak toward the Verde River on dirt desert roads. Two people can expect to pay $50 each for 3½ hours, but the price drops to $45 per person if more than two make the trip.

If you'd rather hike than ride, **The Open Road Tours** (1622 E. Gardenia Ave., Phoenix 85020, tel. 602/997–6474) takes hikers to the Squaw Peak Mountain Preserve or South Mountain Park for $35 per half day. Longer trips to the Superstition Mountains include lunch and cost $65. Three- to five-day hikes can be arranged.

Cimarron Adventures and River Co. (7714 E. Catalina Dr., Scottsdale 85251, tel. 602/994–1199) arranges half-day float trips and moonlight dinner cruises down the Salt, Verde, and Gila rivers. Day trips cost about $55 per person, with the night cruise about $70. Special-occasion evening trips for two can be reserved for about $100 apiece.

Want to tour Phoenix from above? Check out the many hot-air-balloon ascents. **Pegasus Hot Air Balloon Co.** (Box 50893, Phoenix 85076, tel. 602/224–6111) sells typical flights valleywide at $110 per person. The cost includes champagne at the end of the one-hour ride and a souvenir photo. *See also* Hot-Air Ballooning in Sports and Fitness, below.

At the Estrella Sailport, where **Arizona Soaring Inc.** (Box 858, Maricopa 85239, tel. 602/568–2318) offers sailplane rides in a basic trainer or high-performance plane for prices ranging from $45 to $90. The adventuresome can opt for a wild 15-minute acrobatic flight for $75, or a 20- to 45-minute spin in a World War II open-air biplane at $80 to $150.

If you prefer a less dizzying option, **Heritage Carriages** (7031 E. Camelback Rd., Suite 359, Scottsdale 85251, tel. 602/941–0369) leads 30-minute to 4-hour horse-drawn-carriage tours around Old Scottsdale for $30–$150. Their desert-adventure tour for six heads out to the wilderness for a half- or full-day journey that includes a catered cookout. The cost starts at $250.

One of the most interesting guided tours in town explores **Taliesin West** (13201 N. 108th St., Scottsdale 85259, tel. 602/860–2700), winter headquarters of the Frank Lloyd Wright Foundation. With its redwood-and-rock design set at the base of the McDowell Mountains, Wright's winter home typifies his concept of blending function with nature. Hour-long guided tours cost $10; a weekly three-hour tour goes behind the scenes and talks with architects working and studying at the site. The cost is $25.

Walking Tour

A 45-minute self-guided walking tour of **Old Scottsdale** takes visitors to 14 historic sites in the area. Maps showing the route can be picked up in the **Scottsdale Chamber of Commerce** office (743 E. Scottsdale Mall, Scottsdale 85251, tel. 602/945–8481) weekdays 8:30–5, Saturdays 10–5, and Sundays 11–5.

Exploring

Highlights for First-time Visitors

Casa Grande (*see* Tour 4)
Downtown Scottsdale (*see* Tour 3)
Heard Museum (*see* Tour 2)
Heritage Square, The Mercado, and **Arizona Center** (*see* Tour 1)

Tour 1: A Walking Tour of Downtown Phoenix

Numbers in the margin correspond to points of interest on the Phoenix: Tours 1 and 2 map.

A stroll through the renovated east end of downtown gives you a look at Phoenix's past and present, as well as a peek at its future. In moderate weather, it's a pleasant walking day; from late May to mid-October, it's best to break it up over two days. And be sure to take advantage of the free DASH (Downtown Area Shuttle)—*see* By Bus in Getting Around in Essential Information, above.

You'll notice a number of Time Out options in this and the tours that follow—in the warm months, it's best to allow a half hour of sitting indoors, sipping a tall, cool drink (not alcohol; it speeds dehydration) for every hour of walking or shopping.

1 Begin your tour at **Heritage Square,** from 6th to 7th streets between Monroe and Adams, a city-owned block of renovated turn-of-the-century homes in a parklike setting. (There's ample parking in adjacent lots, and it's free if you get your ticket stamped by a merchant along the walking tour.)

To the east, across 7th Street, you'll see the ornate brick bulk of Monroe School; built in 1914, it now houses part of the U.S. Department of Defense Analysis. Just south of it are the graceful modern copper-roofed condos of Renaissance Square, a pioneering urban project built on city-donated land.

The queen of Heritage Square itself is the **Rosson House,** an 1895 gingerbread Victorian in the Eastlake style (made famous in San Francisco). Built by a physician who served a brief term as mayor, it is the sole survivor of the fewer than two dozen Victorians erected in Phoenix. It was bought and restored by the city in 1974. A 30-minute tour of this classic is worth the modest price. *6th and Monroe Sts., tel. 602/262–5071. Admission: $3 adults, $2 senior citizens and students, $1 children 6–13. Open Wed.–Sat. 10–3:30, Sun. noon–4.*

On the south side of the square, along Adams Street, stand four houses built between 1899 and 1901 on sites bought

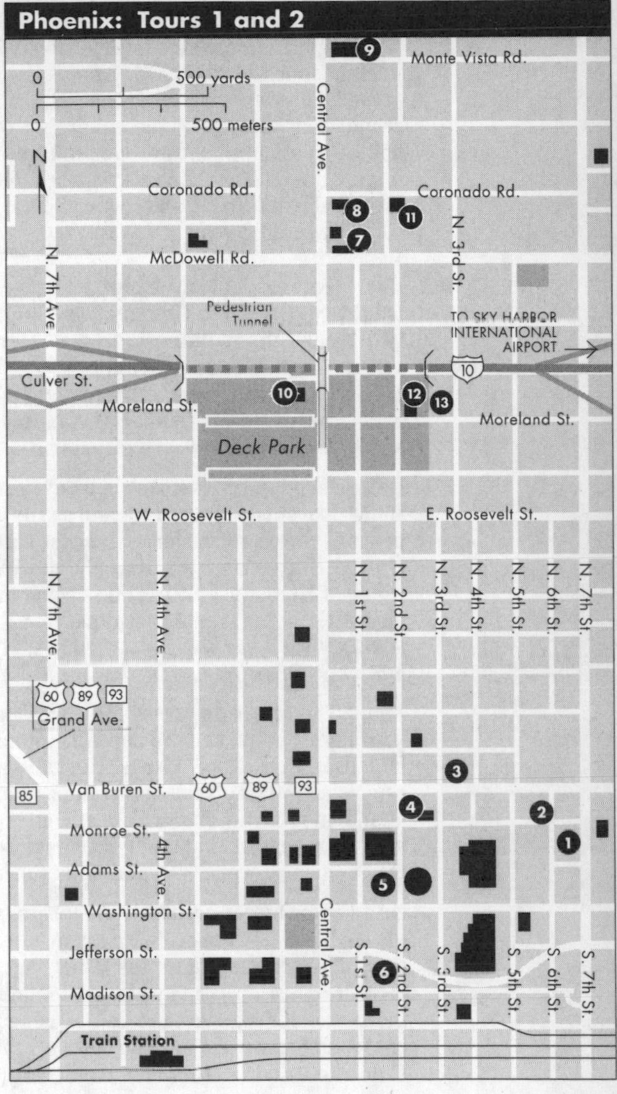

from the Rossons. The midwestern-style **Stevens House** holds the **Arizona Doll and Toy Museum** (602 E. Adams St., tel. 602/253–9337); next to it, in the California-style **Stevens-Haustgen House,** are the handworks of **Craftsmen's Gallery** (604 E. Adams St., tel. 602/253–7770). The fourth dwelling is the **Silva House,** a mail-order 1900 bungalow restored by the Salt River Project (one of the Valley's two major power companies and its largest irrigator) that includes a room devoted to Phoenix history and one with rotating displays on water and electricity in the Valley. Two houses on the south side of Adams Street are still being restored.

Time Out The third house in the row, the Bouvier-Teeter House, offers elegant refreshment—afternoon high teas at the **Heart in Hand Tea Room** (622 E. Adams St., tel. 602/256–7572), served Tuesday through Sunday from 2 to 5. Or, for more casual fare, in one of the square's two restored carriage houses, just north of the Heart in Hand Tea Room, the **Heritage Café** (618 E. Adams St., tel. 602/252–1634) makes sandwiches to order and has a wide array of fruit, juices, soft drinks, and sweets.

---

2 **The Mercado** (542 E. Monroe St., tel. 602/256–6322), a bright-colored, neo-Aztec fantasy built in 1990, occupies two blocks immediately north of Heritage Square, just across Monroe Street, from 5th to 7th streets. In it are shops with Latin American handicrafts, two fine local booteries, the Valley's only specialist in fine African handwork, and several boutiques and gift shops.

Before shopping, to attune your eye to Mexican art, spend some time at the **Museo Chicano** on the second story. It supports the work of modern Hispano-American artists in the United States and Mexico, and its exhibits portray the range of Hispanic culture, classic and modern. Its gift shop also offers some terrific bargains. *641 E. Van Buren St., tel. 602/257–5536. Admission: $2 adults, $1 senior citizens and students. Open Wed.–Sat. 10–5, Sun. noon–4.*

From The Mercado, cross 5th and Van Buren streets. On your right, you'll see the imposing buildings of old Phoenix Union High School, Greek Revival–style buildings that served as the city's first secondary school in 1900 and were abandoned three-quarters of a century later. With their shells preserved and their interiors remodeled, they are now home to several city and county offices.

On the northwest corner of the intersection, you'll see two glass-clad office towers with a lane of royal palms between
3 them. Follow the palm trees: They lead to the **Arizona Center's** dramatic sunken garden and fountains (see how many giant bronze frogs you can find). Opened in 1991, this multiuse complex provides downtown's premier spot for cool, shaded outdoor sitting and wandering, even in the heat of summer.

On the other side of the ponds stands the curved, double-deck open structure of the city's newest downtown shopping mall. There are a variety of chain and specialty stores, from men's and women's clothing to southwestern art and '50s collectibles, and a host of clever cart merchants. And there's usually live music (including top Valley jazz artists) in the courtyard. In addition to hosting several good eateries, Arizona Center is the home of the state's biggest sports bar—would you believe eight restaurant-size spaces spread over two stories, indoors and out?

Time Out The most restful refreshment spot in the center—perhaps in the city—is **Amalfi** (455 N. 3rd St., tel. 602/257-0605), a real Italian sidewalk café that does great Caesar salads, sandwiches, and desserts as well as the entire range of steamed coffees.

Leaving the Arizona Center at Amalfi, head south to 3rd
and Van Buren streets. You can catch the free DASH shuttle here, or you can stroll a block south to Monroe, with the
mission-style adobe of **St. Mary's Basilica** on your left, then
a block west between the dramatic modern facades of the
4 **Herberger Theater Center** (on your right) and **Symphony
Hall** (on your left), facing each other across the fountain-
and sculpture-dotted Phoenix Civic Plaza courtyard. One
more block, south along 2nd Street past the Hyatt Regency
Phoenix to Adams, takes you to the next stop.

Here, amid the splendor and dignity of downtown, is a
building with children's paintings all over its windows. It's
5 the **Arizona Museum of Science and Technology,** a hands-on
exploratorium for children of every age. Permanent displays include exercises in gravity, a trip inside a working
"eyeball" (actually a primitive camera big enough to sit in),
and a Third World village that challenges you to help plan
its development. *80 N. 2nd St., tel. 602/256-9388. Admission: $3.50 adults, $2.50 senior citizens and children 4–12.
Open Mon.–Sat. 9–5, Sun. noon–5.*

Finally, if you're really an indefatigable walker and an avid
sports fan, another two blocks down 2nd Street will take
6 you to the site of the **America West Phoenix Suns Arena** (2nd
and Jefferson Sts., tel. 602/222-5888). This multifacility
sports palace is almost a mall in itself, with cafés and an athletic club and shops, in addition to the basketball-and-hock-
ey stadium and team offices. It's an interesting tour even
when there's no game on.

From the arena (or from Symphony Hall, across from the science museum, if you skip the arena), you can catch the DASH northbound for The Mercado and walk back to your car.

Tour 2: Cultural Center Walking Tour

The heart of Phoenix's new downtown cultural center is the rolling greensward of **Deck Park.** Begun in 1991 atop the I-10 tunnel under Central Avenue, it spreads a mile from 3rd Avenue on the west to 3rd Street on the east, and a quarter mile from Portland Street north to Culver. When it is completed, in 1993, it will be the city's second-largest downtown park (the largest is half-century-old Encanto Park, 2 miles northwest).

Gathered around Deck Park, mostly to the north, are museums, theaters, an art center, and the central library. Seeing all of them makes a comfortable day tour in moderate weather; in the warm months, it is too much for one day. The No. 0 bus line runs up and down Central Avenue every 10 minutes on weekdays (at half fare from 9 to 3) and every 20 minutes on weekends.

7 Start at the **Phoenix Central Library** (12 E. McDowell Rd., tel. 602/262–4636), on the northeast corner of McDowell and Central. It's easy to find, and its palm-lined parking area has no time limit.

Immediately north of the library, in the same complex and
8 sharing a courtyard, is the **Phoenix Art Museum.** It is particularly noteworthy for its clothing and costume collection, fine Asian art, 19th-century European paintings and drawings, and the American West collection, featuring painters from Frederic Remington to Georgia O'Keeffe. *1625 N. Central Ave., tel. 602/257–1222. Admission: $4 adults, $3 senior citizens over 65, $1.50 students, children 5 and under free. Admission free on Wed. Tours free. Open Tues. and Thurs.–Sat. 10–5, Wed. 10–9, Sun. noon–5.*

At the next corner north, cross Monte Vista and turn right
9 100 yards to the **Heard Museum.** In 1928, Dwight and Maie Heard donated their classic Arizona adobe home and their impressive southwestern art collection to found what has become the nation's leading museum of Native American art and culture. Orient yourself with the multimedia show, then see the award-winning "Native Peoples of the Southwest" exhibit; don't miss the kachina doll room (anchored by the Barry Goldwater collection). Modern Indian arts, interactive art-making displays for children, and live demonstrations by artisans are always on hand. In the spring, you may catch the annual Native American Arts & Crafts Show; call and ask, because its dates vary. *22 E. Monte Vista Rd., tel. 602/252–8840. Admission: $4 adults, $3 students and senior citizens $1 children, Native Americans free. Open Mon.–Sat. 10–5, Sun. noon–5.*

If your day hasn't unaccountably disappeared in the museums, go back to Central, cross the street, and catch a No. 0 bus heading south. (Or walk, if it's below 90° F and you're hardy.)

At Culver Street, a long block south of McDowell, is the northern edge of Deck Park. The stately brick home with the gabled roof on the southwest corner is the
10 **Ellis-Shackelford House** (1242 N. Central Ave., tel. 602/255–4470). One of Phoenix's first mansions, it was long the home of the Arizona Historical Society Museum (now in Papago Park, near the Phoenix Zoo). It houses offices and, in back, the restored railcars of the **Phoenix Street Railway.**

Time Out Halfway back to McDowell Road are two places that offer both rest and nourishment. At the **Spaghetti Company** (1418 N. Central Ave., tel. 602/257–0380) you can have lunch, spinach salad and wine, any of countless pasta dishes (try the house mizithra cheese on top), or other dinners, any day of the week. Across the street at **The Blue Fin** (1401 N. Central Ave., tel. 602/254-3171), the atmosphere is quick and informal, the Japanese fast food light and delightful.

Now you have a choice: You can head back to the library
11 complex, where you haven't yet seen the **Phoenix Little Theatre** (25 E. Coronado Rd., tel. 602/254-2151), just east of the museum and north of the library. Here the city's leading community theater group and its adjunct, the PLT Cookie Company, present plays and musicals for adults and children; you might end your day by catching a show.

If you're not ready to head back, you can go into Deck Park at the Ellis-Shackelford House, through the pedestrian tunnel under Central (with I-10 roaring beneath your feet), and walk 2½ blocks east to the **City Arts Center** (3rd
12 and Moreland Sts., tel. 602/262-6583). In the **Phoenix Visual Arts Building,** Valley professional and amateur artists do class and studio work in graphics, ceramics, sculpture, photography, and other media; check for current exhibits and
13 sales. Adjacent is the **Phoenix Performing Arts Building,** a venue for small, experimental dance and theater groups (*see* The Arts, below). A performance here is a fine way to spend an evening after a day spent walking the city's cultural paths.

Tour 3: Scottsdale Walking Tour

Numbers in the margin correspond to points of interest on the Scottsdale map.

Historic sites, nationally known art galleries, and lots of clever boutiques fill downtown Scottsdale, easily turning a walking tour into several hours if you browse. Historic Old Scottsdale features the look of the Old West, while fashionable 5th Avenue is known for its shopping. Cross onto Main Street and enter a world frequented by the international art set; discover more galleries and interior design shops on Marshall Way and Craftsman Court. Looming over the neighborhood is the new **Scottsdale Galleria** (4343 N. Scottsdale Rd., tel. 602/949-3222) with its 80 stores, 7 restaurants, and 2 theaters. This tour offers an overview of the area; *see* the Shopping section, below, for some specific recommendations.

While your tour easily can be completed on foot, a trolley (cost: $2 in summer, free the rest of the year) runs through the 5th Avenue area; the Ollie Trolley tours all of Scottsdale and charges $2 for an all-day pass. For information for both, call 602/941-2957. Also look for the horse-drawn carriages that provide romantic transportation after dark on Heritage Carriages (tel. 602/941–0369), usually found where Brown Avenue intersects Main Street.

Begin your tour by parking in the free public lot on the northwest corner of 2nd Street and Wells Fargo Avenue east of Scottsdale Road. A portion of the garage is signed for a three-hour limit; go to upper levels that don't carry time restraints, as enforcement is strict.

Head north on the brick-paved sidewalks leading to
1 **Scottsdale Mall.** This tree-shaded setting has plenty of benches and grassy areas for restful contemplation. To your right, walks lead to a sculpture- and fountain-filled plaza around Scottsdale's **city hall, public library,** and **Center for the Arts** (7383 E. Scottsdale Mall, tel. 602/994–2301). The center presents a full schedule of concerts, and exhibits are changed frequently. Its gift shop, **The Artspot,** has unusual jewelry as well as posters and art books.

After circling the plaza, head west to the redbrick
2 **Scottsdale Chamber of Commerce** building (7343 Scottsdale Mall, tel. 602/945–8481), constructed in 1910 as Scottsdale's first schoolhouse. Inside, shopping maps and helpful tips are provided if you're looking for something special. Ask for the walking tour map of Old Scottsdale so you can note historic buildings as you go.

3 Continue west into **Old Scottsdale** on Main Street. Billed as "The West's Most Western Town," this area features rustic storefronts and wooden sidewalks; it's touristy, but it's also the genuine item, giving visitors a taste of life here 80 years ago. Stores carry kitschy souvenirs, but you'll also find some nicer jewelry, pots, and Mexican imports.

Head north on Brown Avenue and turn left on 1st Avenue to continue sightseeing in Old Scottsdale.

Time Out The southeast corner of 1st Avenue and Scottsdale Road
4 marks a landmark of sorts: the candy pink-and-white **Sugar Bowl Ice Cream Parlor** (4005 N. Scottsdale Rd., tel. 602/946–0051), run by a local family since 1958 and frequented from its beginning by Paradise Valley cartoonist Bil Keane (the menu carries his "Family Circus" work). Although sandwiches, soups, and salads are available, you're missing the point if you don't indulge in the gooey sundaes, floats, and parfaits.

For an entirely different milieu, walk south on Scottsdale
5 Road and turn right onto **Main Street.** This block is literally filled with art galleries on both sides of the street, featuring work that ranges from contemporary to western realism, Native American, and traditional. With very few exceptions, casual visitors are made welcome in the galleries, although children may be bored. Another option for viewing the galleries is the seasonal **Art Walk,** held from 7 to 9 PM each Thursday, October through May. The street

5th Avenue, **6**
Main Street (art galleries), **5**
Old Scottsdale, **3**
Scottsdale Chamber of Commerce, **2**
Scottsdale Mall, **1**
Sugar Bowl Ice Cream Parlor, **4**

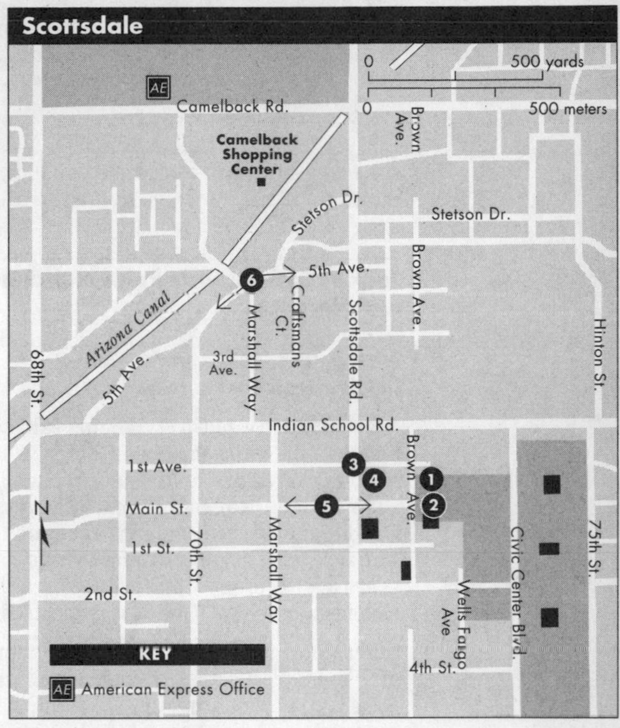

takes on a party atmosphere during the evening hours when everyone is browsing.

Continue on Main Street across Marshall Way for several antiques shops, where specialties include elegant porcelains and china, fine antique jewelry, and Oriental rugs.

Time Out For a cool drink or light meal after gallery-hopping, two alternatives are close by. At **Bistro La Chaumière** (6910 E. Main St., tel. 602/946–5115), guests are served casual French fare in a solarium out front. Or head one block north on 70th Street to 1st Avenue and turn right to **Arcadia Farms** (7014 E. 1st Ave., tel. 602/941–5665), where such eclectic sandwiches as rosemary-seasoned *focaccia* with chicken, roasted eggplant, and feta cheese are brought out to diners on a tree-shaded patio. Desserts at both restaurants are exceptional, so leave room.

If you walk north on 70th Street and cross Indian School Road, you'll discover another niche of galleries, upscale gift and jewelry stores, and several specialty boutiques. Farther north on Marshall Way across 3rd Avenue, the street is filled with more art galleries and creative stores with a southwestern flair.

When you reach the fountain with the prancing horses,
6 you're on **5th Avenue,** a 40-year-old stretch that is a shop-

ping tradition in Phoenix. Whether you're seeking cacti or casual clothing, fine art or handmade Indian jewelry, you'll find it here.

Off 5th Avenue, Stetson Drive has a few interesting stores carrying original Indian artifacts, as well as books on Arizona and the Southwest; here you'll find **O'Brien's Art Emporium** (7122 E. Stetson Dr., tel. 602/945–1082), the oldest art gallery in Scottsdale.

Tour 4: Casa Grande Ruins National Monument and Florence

Numbers in the margin correspond to points of interest on the Around Phoenix map.

An hour's drive south of Phoenix takes visitors back to prehistoric times and the site of Arizona's first known civilization, as well as one of its major pioneer western towns. The Casa Grande Ruins National Monument, 1 mile north of Coolidge, captures some vivid reminders of the Hohokam Indians, who began farming in this area more than 1,500 years ago. Florence, one of central Arizona's first cities, is rich in examples of Territorial architecture.

Start your tour by heading southeast on I–10 leaving Phoenix. You'll pass Exit 160, which leads to **Williams Air Force Base,** site of the largest pilot-training facility in NATO but recommended for closure by mid-1993. The same exit is the closest freeway access to **Compadre Stadium,** spring-training home of the Milwaukee Brewers each February and March.

1 Soon you'll see a sign noting that you've entered the **Gila River Indian Reservation.** On the right, Exit 162A indicates **Firebird International Raceway** (20000 S. Maricopa Rd., tel. 602/268–0200), site of the Arizona National drag-racing finals each February and local Friday night races; **Firebird Lake** (20000 S. Maricopa Rd., tel. 602/268–0200), a boat-racing site where the World Hydroplane Finals are held each November; and **Compton Terrace** (20000 S. Maricopa Rd., tel. 602/796–0511), one of the Valley's largest outdoor concert venues.

The landscape changes to desert scrub, and the sun can become intense, so make use of sunscreen, hats, and drinking water. Large, strangely shaped saguaro cacti next begin to dominate the landscape, covering a hillside as you cross the
2 dry **Gila River.**

Time Out Thirty-seven miles out of Phoenix off I–10 is a disabled-accessible **rest area** with covered picnic tables. It's the last available stop until you reach your destination 20 miles later.

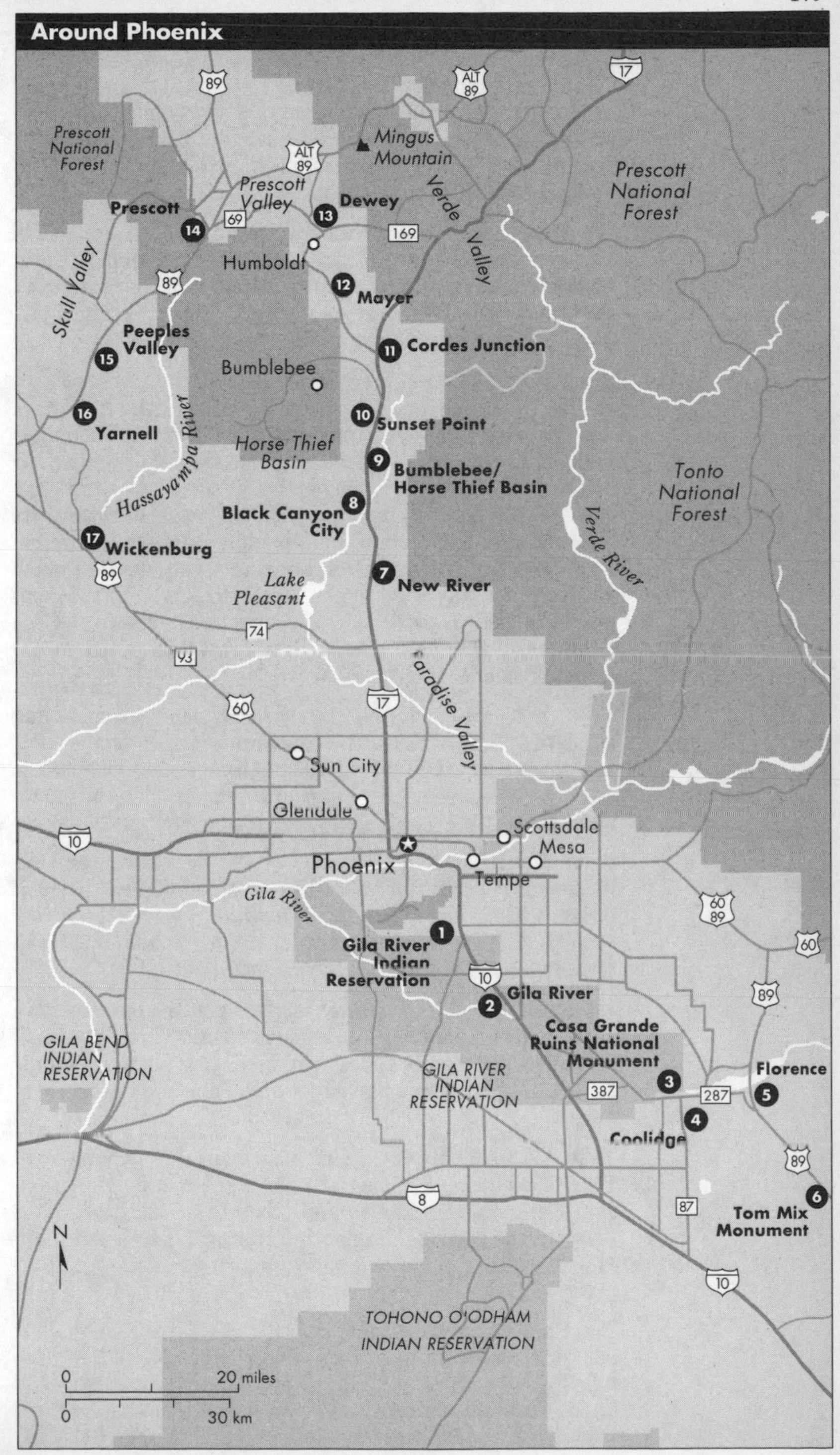
Around Phoenix
Prescott National Forest
Prescott
Prescott Valley
Dewey
Mingus Mountain
Verde Valley
Prescott National Forest
Humboldt
Skull Valley
Mayer
Peeples Valley
Cordes Junction
Bumblebee
Yarnell
Hassayampa River
Horse Thief Basin
Sunset Point
Bumblebee/ Horse Thief Basin
Tonto National Forest
Black Canyon City
Verde River
Wickenburg
Lake Pleasant
New River
Paradise Valley
Sun City
Glendale
Scottsdale
Mesa
Phoenix
Tempe
Gila River
Gila River Indian Reservation
Gila River
Casa Grande Ruins National Monument
GILA BEND INDIAN RESERVATION
GILA RIVER INDIAN RESERVATION
Florence
Coolidge
Tom Mix Monument
TOHONO O'ODHAM INDIAN RESERVATION
N
0
20 miles
0
30 km

Take Exit 185 east off I–10 and follow the signs a short way to AZ 387. It's a two-lane road flanked by saguaros, and the spring landscape features brilliant red-tipped ocotillo cacti and yellow and purple wildflowers. Halfway into this 7-mile stretch, you'll climb a rise and see the Gila River valley spread out below. Four miles later, turn right onto AZ 87 and head 7½ miles to the ruins.

3 The **Casa Grande Ruins National Monument,** established in 1918, provides a close look at a structure first seen by European explorers in the 17th century. Allow an hour to inspect the site, longer if park rangers are giving a talk at the interpretive ramada or leading a tour.

Start at the visitor center, where a small museum features artifacts and information on the Hohokam, who lived here and farmed irrigated cotton fields until they vanished mysteriously in about AD 1450. Step outside and begin your self-guided tour with an inspection of the 35-foot-tall Casa Grande (Big House), built around 1350 and still close to its original size. It's covered by a modern roof for protection from the sun and wind. Neighboring structures are much smaller, and only a bit of the 7-foot wall around the compound is still in evidence. The original purpose of Casa Grande still puzzles archaeologists; some think it was an ancient astronomical observatory.

Cross the parking lot by the covered picnic grounds and climb the platform for a view of an unexcavated ball court, said to date from the 1100s. Although only a few prehistoric sites can be viewed, more than 60 are included in the monument area.

A small gift shop in the lobby of the visitor center sells books about early Indian civilizations and other aspects of Arizona history. *1 mi north of Coolidge on AZ 87, tel. 602/723–3172. Admission: $1 adults, children under 16 and senior citizens over 62 free. Open daily 7–6.*

If traipsing among the ruins has given you an appetite, it's a
4 short trip to **Coolidge,** 1 mile south on AZ 87, where you'll find fast-food hamburgers, chicken, and pizza. A public park with a children's playground is at 4th and Central avenues.

Take AZ 287 another 9 miles east from the monument to
5 **Florence,** an old western town distinguished by an American Victorian courthouse and more than 125 other sites listed on the National Register of Historic Places. An annual walking tour of historic Florence is held on the first Saturday in February.

The **Pinal County Visitor Center** (912 N. Pinal St., tel. 602/868–4331) answers questions and provides brochures from 9 to 5 Monday through Friday September through May and 10 to 2 June through August. Two attractions are the **Pinal County Historical Museum** (715 S. Main St., tel. 602/868–

4382), which displays furnishings from early 1900s homes and Native American crafts and tools, and the **McFarland Historical State Park,** where the 1878-era Pinal County Courthouse (Main and Ruggles Sts., tel. 602/868–5216) houses memorabilia of former Governor and U.S. Senator Ernest W. McFarland.

Several attractive shops and restaurants are found on Florence's Main Street, including the turn-of-the-century **Florence General Store** (1218 N. Main St., tel. 602/868–5748) and **Old Pueblo Restaurant** (505 S. Main St., tel. 602/868–4784), serving good Mexican food.

Time Out At **Jim-Bob's Auld Tyme Ice Cream Parlor** (289 N. Main St., no phone) ice cream and hard-packed frozen yogurt are made on the circa 1886 adobe-walled premises.

Fans of western-movie hero Tom Mix may want to drive 18
6 miles south on AZ 89 to the **Tom Mix Monument,** at the site of his fatal automobile accident in 1940. Pack some soft drinks; it's low desert (in fact, a showplace of dry-land vegetation), and no refreshments are on hand.

From Florence, retrace your route to Phoenix via AZ 287, 87, and 387 to link up with I–10 north and the 40-minute drive back to the Valley of the Sun.

Tour 5: Prescott and Wickenburg

Just over two hours north of Phoenix, after one of the most scenic drives in a state renowned for breathtaking vistas, you disappear into the tall pine country of Arizona's territorial capital. A slight westward jog on the way back leads you through legendary gold country and past modern dude ranches.

Start your tour by getting on I–17 (Black Canyon Freeway) and heading north. The sunken freeway is accessible from most major east–west arteries from Washington Street north. Between Van Buren Street and McDowell Road, it also connects with I–10 in a tall "stack" interchange.

Traveling north, you'll pass off ramps for **Metrocenter,** the western Valley's giant shopping-mall complex (*see* Shopping, below), and **Turf Paradise** (at Bell Road), the Valley's popular Thoroughbred horse track.

Abruptly, the developed areas thin out, and within 5 miles, as you pass the dark volcanic rubble of Adobe Mountain on your left, you are in open desert. Another half-dozen miles, just past Carefree Road (AZ 74), and you start climbing into foothills, where you'll see huge, spiky saguaro cacti; thick-leaved creosote bushes; and thin, spiny cholla cacti.

7 **New River,** spread out in the dry valley under which the Fria River's south fork flows, has service stations and several modest eating places.

Another 10 miles up the road is your last chance to be sure you're ready for the 2,000-foot ascent of the Mogollon Rim. On the way, the scenery shifts to classic desert mountainscape: exposed granite jutting up, covered with broken rock and scrappy vegetation; saguaros and creosote; and tall, lacy, green-limbed paloverde trees standing in the dry, flat washes. You may spot hawks or even eagles circling on the thermal currents, watching for prey.

8 At **Black Canyon City,** you enter Yavapai County and begin the climb up the rim. It's a beautifully graded modern highway, four lanes and completely divided, but it's a challenge—and an unfair one to an undercooled engine—so be sure to top out your car's fluids (and your own, if you don't want a half-hour wait).

Time Out Almost out of town, Exit 244 offers you the choice of going west to the greyhound-racing track or east to the **Squaw Peak Buffalo Steakhouse** (Dog Track Rd., Black Canyon City, tel. 602/374–9247 or 602/395–9913). Choose the steak house: Besides big steaks, burgers, Maggie Mine sandwiches, and homemade pie, it has a pair of live buffalo in a half-acre pen. Also on the site are a large gas station and a small souvenir shop.

As you make the dramatic climb up the Mogollon Rim, you can see the geologic strata of the upthrust earth neatly laid out in the roadside rock—rust and pink, black and purple—and feel the air temperature drop rapidly. And in 6 miles,
9 almost at the summit, you'll see the exit for **Bumblebee** and the **Horse Thief Basin.** The former, about 10 miles away, is a mining ghost town in the cleft of the Black Canyon to your left; the latter, some 20 miles farther along, is a beautiful wilderness area high in the Bradshaw Mountains on the other side. But go only if you've got good shoes and tires: 100 yards from the freeway, the paved road turns to dirt.

Three more miles and you suddenly reach the top—a wide, flat, grass-covered mesa, like a huge chunk of Nebraska pastureland stuck in the middle of purple mountaintops (and dotted with the clustered beaver-tails of nopal cacti). In fact, this semidesert plateau at about 4,000 feet *is* cattle-grazing land; you'll probably see some of the herds. At
10 **Sunset Point Rest Area,** you can also see the spectacular view off the mesa and across the Black Canyon; the rest area is on the southbound side, but you can switch back at the next exit, in about a mile.

In 10 more miles, you come to the edge of the plateau, and for a moment you see the breathtaking sweep of the Verde Valley from above; then you swoop down a steep incline, at
11 the bottom of which is the **Cordes Junction** turnoff, AZ 69. Here, you leave I–17 and head northwest to Prescott.

But first, about a mile down a partly paved road northeast from the gas stations and cafés, is one of the world's architectural wonders—**Arcosanti.** This evolving community, masterminded by Italian architect Paolo Soleri, is being built by its residents as a totally energy-independent town. It looks almost like a huge playground or modern-art theme park, with its desert-rock retaining walls and festive forms in earth-cast concrete. But it's full of ideas for dramatic design and ecologically sensitive living; it's worth taking an hour out for a tour, eating at the café, and bringing home one of the hand-cast wind-bells. *I–17 at Cordes Junction, Mayer 86333, tel. 602/632–7135. Admission: $5. Open daily 9–5; tours hourly 10–4.*

Back on AZ 69, you're in the valley of Big Bug Creek (you can see its course by looking for the willows south of the road). In 7 miles, after crossing the Big Bug a couple of
12 times, you'll reach **Mayer,** a provisioning center for the gold hunters who scoured the area in the last century. The tall stack of its long-silent smelter peers over a hill, and some enchanting historic buildings still stand on Main Street, a mile or so off the road.

Another 12 miles through the rolling chaparral hills (highlighted by white datura blossoms and fiery Indian paintbrush in the fall), past Mayer's sister mining town of
13 Humboldt, is **Dewey.**

Time Out Right on the edge of town, take AZ 169 east toward the looming 7,000-foot shoulders of Mingus Mountain; after 100 yards, pull in at **Young's Farm** (AZ 169, tel. 602/632–7272). This family-run, 45-year-old farm with its 22-year-old store has become a beloved purveyor of potpies and pumpkins, sweet corn and cider, hayrides and honey, fresh bread, and wooden butterflies to folks from all over Arizona.

As you leave Dewey, the road widens to five lanes (the "Arizona lane" in the middle is for left turns only), and the landscape turns to scrub pines. In about 6 miles, you pass through **Prescott Valley,** a strip of mobile-home lots and fast-food stores that sprouted in the absence of zoning laws (watch your speed—they do have traffic laws), and then the pine trees and the hills suddenly grow taller.

14 Eight miles later, you enter **Prescott,** with the sandstone red Sheraton standing atop a butte in the foreground and Thumb Butte towering a few miles in the background. In a forested bowl at 5,300 feet above sea level, this lovely site was the first capital of the Arizona Territory and remains first choice for summer refuge among Phoenix-area desert dwellers.

As soon as you see the Sheraton, get into the left lane: For some reason, at the junction with U.S. 89, most lanes take you back out of town to the north. But the left lane becomes **Gurley Street,** the city's main drag. Immediately, you have a choice of motels, including the historic Mission Inn, now the **American Motel** (1211 E. Gurley St., 86301 tel. 602/778–

0787), and the venerable **Senator Inn,** famous for its themed rooms (1117 E. Gurley St., 86301, tel. 602/445–1440).

Heading into town, you'll notice the many Victorian frame houses. Prescott was proclaimed capital by President Lincoln and settled by Yankees to ensure that gold-rich northern Arizona would be a Union resource—Tucson and southern Arizona were strongly pro-Confederacy. Despite a devastating downtown fire in July 1900, Prescott remains the Southwest's richest store of late-19th-century New England–style architecture (some wags say that long before Scottsdale declared itself "The West's Most Western Town," Prescott was "The West's Most Eastern Town").

About 1½ miles along Gurley is **Courthouse Plaza,** between Cortez and Montezuma streets. This is the heart of the city, where the old Yavapai County Courthouse stands, guarded by an equestrian bronze of turn-of-the-century journalist and lawmaker Bucky O'Neill, who died while charging San Juan Hill with Teddy Roosevelt. A block east of Courthouse Plaza, the historic **Hassayampa Inn** (122 E. Gurley St., 86301, tel. 602/778–9434) was recently restored to its classic 1927 splendor; it's priced like a Phoenix hotel but delivers memorable southwestern elegance for the money.

The quickest way to get oriented is to find the south end of the plaza. There, across from the courthouse's rear entrance, stands the **Chamber of Commerce** (117 W. Goodwin St., tel. 602/445–2000). Among the many maps and brochures here are two gems—"Historic Downtown Prescott: Walking Tour Guide" and "Prescott's Driving Tour Guide." Either of these will have you feeling like an old Prescott hand in a half-hour.

Flanking the plaza's west side, Montezuma Street, is **Whiskey Row,** named for a string of brawling pioneer taverns; some still stand, though the social activity there is much subdued. Upgrading one end of Whiskey Row is the mahogany-paneled **Hotel St. Michael** (205 W. Gurley St., tel. 602/776–1999), reopened in 1988 as a very modestly priced hostelry with a café and a row of shops. Near the middle is **Maude's** (146 S. Montezuma St., tel. 602/778–3080), an always full, fresh-scrubbed breakfast and lunch spot that would be at home in Mendocino or Santa Fe. And at the row's south end, the **Galloping Goose** (162 S. Montezuma St., tel. 602/778–7600) is a former gas station filled with lots of kitschy cowboy and Indian crafts alongside stunning collections of kachina dolls and jewelry by some of the Southwest's best working Native American artists.

Farther south on Montezuma is a good place to look for more lodging options. Four blocks from Whiskey Row is the **Prescott Country Inn** (503 S. Montezuma St., 86303, tel. 602/445–7991), a 1940s motor court transformed into a cozy bed-and-breakfast; about 2 miles farther, after Montezuma changes names (to White Spar and then Copper Basin

Road), there is a mile-long stretch with seven hotels and motels in the pines, four restaurants strategically set among them.

Fun eating places are all over town. On the plaza's east side is the playful restored '50s experience of **Kendall's Burgers** (113 S. Cortez St., tel. 602/778–3658), complete with soda fountain; up the street a block or so is **Chris' New York Deli** (125 N. Cortez St., tel. 602/776–8677), a lively hole-in-the-wall with noshes that taste like Brooklyn's. Farther north is the classy fern-and-brass of **Murphy's** (201 N. Cortez St., tel. 602/445–4044), with a 60-beer pub and an award-winning kitchen that turns out prime rib and pasta, a dozen seafoods, and some sharp appetizers (how about bay shrimp nachos?). Back south to Gurley Street and west past Montezuma Street is **Nolaz** (216 W. Gurley St., tel. 602/445–3765), where Cajun dishes get tender treatment.

Time Out For unforgettable tortillas, go one block west of the plaza on Gurley Street, turn right on McCormick for half a block, and swing left into the curved driveway under the big apple tree. The little building beside the white house is **Angel's Food Products** (120½ S. McCormick, no phone). Try a tortilla hot from the oven.

Antiques and collectibles have become such an extensive part of the Prescott scene that the best bet is to stop at the first shop you see and ask for a brochure. The local dealers' group has put together a clear map of more than two dozen shops, noting their specialties and hours.

Lovers of the past also won't want to miss the **Sharlot Hall Museum,** a remarkable two-square-block re-creation of territorial Arizona, including the original log mansion of the governor, just two blocks west of Courthouse Square. Besides the mansion and museum, the parklike setting holds three other fully restored period homes, a working blacksmith shop, and the first territorial jail. It's easy to spend half or all of a day in this place. *415 W. Gurley St., tel. 602/445–3122. Admission free; donation requested. Open Apr.–Oct., Tues.–Sat. 10–5; Nov.–Mar., Tues.–Sat. 10–4, Sun. 1–5; closed Mon.*

Prescott also boasts the **Bead Museum** (140 S. Montezuma St., tel. 602/445–2431), an extensive historical collection; the respected **Phippen Museum of Western Art** (on U.S. 89 about 2 mi north of the entrance to town, tel. 602/778–1385); and the impressive **Smoki Museum** of Indian artifacts (100 N. Arizona, tel. 602/445–1230).

If you make Prescott a day trip, you'll probably find you've stayed a little longer than you expected. Your best bet is to end the day by retracing your route along Gurley Street, back onto AZ 69, and then south on I–17. The trip, from Courthouse Square to downtown Phoenix, can be done comfortably in 2½ to 3 hours, including a rest stop or two.

If you decide to spend a night or two in Prescott, you'll have some time to view another part of Arizona and its past on the way back to Phoenix. To do that, take Montezuma Street south out of town; in about 4 miles, it enters the **Prescott National Forest** and winds through the forested tops of the northern Bradshaw Mountain range (you saw the south end of these mountains across Black Canyon on the way up).

Then the road drops and winds about 15 miles to the lush
15 meadows of **Peeples Valley,** named for the rancher who
started a gold rush by finding nuggets in Antelope Creek.
16 Another 8 miles and you're at **Yarnell,** dropping below the
timberline and into the desert.

Here you'll enter the watershed of the elusive Hassayampa River, whose furtive habits (traveling below the surface most of the year, then bursting into flood in winter or spring) gave the reputation of liars to locals who swore they lived on a river.

17 About 25 miles along the way is **Wickenburg,** home of dude ranches and tall tales. This city is named for Henry Wickenberg, whose nearby Vulture Mine was the richest gold strike in the Arizona Territory. On the main drag are the **Hassayampa Bridge,** the nearby **Jail Tree** (where prisoners were chained, not hanged, the desert heat sometimes finishing them off before their sentences were served), and the Gold Nugget (222 E. Wickenburg Way, tel. 602/684–2858), a western-style eating place where you can refresh yourself. Half a block north on Valentine Street is Anita's Cocina (62 N. Valentine St., tel. 602/684–5777), which offers creditable Mexican food. If you have time, the **Desert Caballeros** (20 N. Frontier St., tel. 602/684–7075), a local charitable equestrian group, maintains a fine museum of Hassayampa lore. If you opt for a longer stay in Wickenburg, there are plenty of dude ranches to accommodate you (*see* Lodging, *below*).

About 10 miles out of Wickenburg, you can save yourself considerable time by taking AZ 74 east (it's the Carefree Road you passed going north). In just 30 miles, it reaches I–17, leaving you with a 15-minute trip into downtown, whereas if you stay on U.S. 89, you angle into the urban area through every suburb on the west side before reaching downtown.

What to See and Do with Children

Aimed at children of elementary-school age, the **Arizona Museum for Youth** displays fine arts in a manner attractive to youngsters. Hands-on exhibits allow them to make crafts or participate as they go through the museum. A tour takes about 1–1½ hours. *35 N. Robson St., Mesa, tel. 602/644–2468. Admission: $2. Open Tues.–Fri. 1–5, Sat. 10–5, Sun. 1–5.*

Arizona Museum of Science and Technology (*see* Tour 1, above).

About an hour east of Phoenix on U.S. 60, the **Boyce Thompson Southwestern Arboretum** is one of the treasures of the Sonoran desert. From the visitor center, well-marked self-guided trails traverse 35 acres, winding through all of the desert's varied habitats—from gravelly open desert to lush creekside glades—rich with native flora and wildlife. The **Smith Interpretive Center,** a National Historic Site, houses rotating displays on such topics as geology and mining plus two greenhouses with cacti and other succulents. The arboretum is a wonderful place to stop for a picnic on your way to the mining towns of Superior and Miami. *Box AB, Superior 85273, tel. 602/689–2811. Admission: $3 adults, $1.50 children 5–12. Open daily 8–5. Closed Christmas.*

Great Arizona Puppet Theatre (Box 7001, Phoenix 85011, tel. 602/277–1275) mounts a yearlong cycle of inventive puppet productions, mostly original, in a converted firehouse; it also offers classes in puppet-making and operation.

At the **Hall of Flame,** retired fire fighters lead tours past more than 100 restored fire engines and over 3,000 helmets, badges, and other fire-fighting-related articles. *6101 E. Van Buren St. (in Papago Park), tel. 602/275–3473. Admission: $4 adults, $1.50 children 6–17, children 6 and under free. Open Mon.–Sat. 9–5.*

Model-train displays, stores with railway memorabilia and items for the train hobbyist, and a restored Pullman car fill the popular **McCormick Railroad Park.** For 75¢, children can ride the miniature train or the 1929 merry-go-round. *7303 E. Indian Bend Rd., tel. 602/994–2408. Admission free. Open weekdays 10–7, weekends 11–7.*

At the foot of South Mountain, **Mystery Castle,** hand-built out of found desert rocks, is chock-full of oddities that will fascinate everyone in the family. There are 18 rooms with 13 fireplaces, 90 bottle-glass portholes, a downstairs grotto, and a rollaway bed with a mining railcar as its frame. *800 E. Mineral Rd., tel. 602/268–1581. Admission: $2.75 adults, 75¢ children 5–15. Open Tues.–Sun. 11–4.*

Phoenix Children's Theatre (1202 N. 3rd St., tel. 602/265–4142) stages a full season, usually adaptations of fairy tales and children's books, at the city's Performing Arts Building.

At the **Phoenix Zoo,** a new 21,000-square-foot Baboon Kingdom exhibit brings together more than 1,300 animals, grouped by continent of origin. Indian and African elephants (including one that produces artworks sold in galleries!) and a rare Sumatran tiger are among the attractions. A 30-minute narrated tour on the safari train costs $1 and gives a good overview of the park. *5810 E. Van Buren St. (in*

Papago Park), tel. 602/273–7771. Admission: $6 adults, $3 children 4–12. Open daily 9–5.

Original and reconstructed buildings from all over Arizona set the stage for the **Pioneer Arizona Museum.** Guides in the blacksmith shop, print shop, schoolhouse, and homes demonstrate daily activities from the past. *Pioneer Rd. exit off I-17, tel. 602/993–0212. Admission: $5.75 adults, $5.25 senior citizens and students, $4 children 4–12, children 3 and under free. Open Wed.–Sun. 9–5, closed July 4–Oct. 1.*

The false fronts on **Rawhide**'s dusty Main Street house "saloons," gift shops, old-time photo studios, and craftspeople as well as opportunities to take a stagecoach ride or to pan for gold. Hayrides travel a short distance into the desert for a cookout under the stars on weekends. *23023 N. Scottsdale Rd., Scottsdale, tel. 602/563–5111. Admission free; separate charges for shops, restaurants, attractions. Open weekdays 5–10 PM, weekends 11–10.*

Similar to Rawhide, but a better deal because the price of entry is all-inclusive, **Rockin' R Ranch** includes a petting zoo, a staged shoot-out, and—the main attraction—a nightly cookout and western stage show. Browse the shops until the chow—beef, beans, and biscuits—is served, followed by music and entertainment. Reservations are required. *6136 E. Baseline Rd., Mesa, tel. 602/832–1539. Admission (includes meal and show): $12.95 adults, $7.95 children 3–12. Open Sept.–May, Wed.–Sat. 5:30 PM; June–Aug., Fri.–Sat. 5:30 PM.*

The **Sunrise Preschool** (642 E. Monroe St., tel. 602/253–0381) at the east end of The Mercado (*see* Tour 1, above) offers high-quality child care at drop-in rates, 24 hours a day.

Shopping

Since its resorts began multiplying in the 1930s and 1940s, Phoenix has acquired a healthy share of high-style clothiers and leisure-wear boutiques. But well before that, western clothes were dominant here—jeans and boots, cotton shirts and dresses, 10-gallon hats and bola ties (the state's official neckwear). They still are. Plain or designer, cowboy or vaquero, with rivets or silver *conchos* or diamonds, western is always in style, and outfitters abound.

In the past decade, Sun Belt awareness has brought a tide of interest in southwestern furnishing styles as well, from the pastels of the desert mountains and skies to the handmade lodgepole furniture of the pueblo and rancho. These—as well as Mexican tiles and tinware, wrought iron and copper work, courtyard fountains and paper flowers—have never died out here. Always an essential part of the way southwesterners shape their homes, work spaces, and public places, these crafts have flourished in the current revival.

At the same time, the drivers of many a wagon train in the past century and many a U-Haul in this one have headed west and ended up unloading here. As a result, the shops and auctions of Phoenix and its suburbs contain an unexpectedly wide array of antiques and collectibles.

On the scene long before any of these, of course, were the fine and powerful arts of the Southwest's true natives—Navajo weavers, sand painters, and silversmiths; Hopi weavers and kachina-doll carvers; Pima and Papago basket makers and potters; and many more.

Inspired by the region's rich cultural traditions, contemporary artists have flourished here as well, making Phoenix—and in particular, Scottsdale, a city with more art galleries than gas stations—one of the Southwest's two great art centers (alongside Santa Fe, New Mexico).

Most of the Valley's power shopping is concentrated in central Phoenix and downtown Scottsdale. But auctions and antiques shops cluster in odd places—and as treasure hunters know, you've always got to have an eye open.

Malls and Department Stores

The open-air **Park Central Mall** (Central Ave. and Earll Dr., tel. 602/264–5575) is the oldest and closest to downtown, amid the high rises of Central Avenue. Anchored by a **Dillard's** department store (3033 N. 3rd Ave., tel. 602/277–0564), Park Central also has **Hanny's** (3100 N. Central Ave., tel. 602/264–5857) and **Switzer's** (44 Park Central Mall, tel. 602/264–4361), two traditional Phoenix clothiers; the ever-popular **Miracle Mile Deli** (9 Park Central Mall, tel. 602/277–4783); and **Leonard's Luggage** (Park Central Mall, tel. 602/264–3591), the Valley's oldest purveyor of luxury leather goods and accessories.

Metrocenter (I–17 and Peoria Ave., tel. 602/997–2641), on the west side of Phoenix, is an enclosed double-deck mall, the state's largest. The adjacent **Castles N Coasters** (9445 N. Metro Pkwy. E, tel. 602/997–7575), a miniature-golf park and video-game palace, and the in-mall **Discovery Zone** (13615 N. 35th Ave., tel. 602/993–2805), an exciting science-oriented exploratorium, make Metro the Valley's best mall for teens and younger children. Inside, its anchor department stores include **Robinson's** (9700 N. Metro Pkwy. E, tel. 602/943–2351). Metrocenter has nearly every store Park Central has (except the deli) and many more, but in a Muzak-filled, disinfected, deodorized environment that might as easily be in St. Louis or Seattle or Secaucus.

Fiesta Mall (AZ 360 and Alma School Rd., Mesa, tel. 602/833–5450) and the new **Superstition Springs Mall,** a dozen miles farther east (AZ 360 and Superstition Springs Rd., Mesa, tel. 602/832–0212), provide slightly smaller copies, without the youth attractions, for the eastern Valley—though the latter does boast a handsome indoor carousel and a pleasant outdoor cactus garden to stroll in. The somewhat older but just expanded **Paradise Valley Mall** (Cactus and Tatum Rds., tel. 602/996–8840) does likewise for northeastern Phoenix.

Scottsdale Fashion Square (Scottsdale and Camelback Rds., Scottsdale, tel. 602/990–7800) is a step upscale. Besides Robinson's and Dillard's, it is anchored by **Bullock's** (6900 E. Camelback Rd., Scottsdale, tel. 602/994–3111), and its mix of stores runs more to specialty shops; children will want everything in the **Disney Store** (7014 E. Camelback Rd., Scottsdale, tel. 602/423–5008).

Biltmore Fashion Park (24th St. and Camelback Rd., tel. 602/955–8400), about 8 miles west in Phoenix, is several more steps upscale. **I. Magnin** (2400 E. Camelback Rd., tel. 602/955–7200) and **Saks Fifth Avenue** (2500 E. Camelback Rd., tel. 602/955–8000) are its anchors, and designer boutiques are its stock-in-trade—**Alexander Julian** (2554 E. Camelback Rd., tel. 602/954–7005), **Beaton's** (2480 E. Camelback Rd., tel. 602/955–5061), **Bruno Magli** (2542 E. Camelback Rd., tel. 602/956–6661), **Gucci** (2504 E. Camelback Rd., tel. 602/957–8710), and **Polo by Ralph Lauren** (2580 E. Camelback Rd., tel. 602/952–0155) are among them. Adult toy shops include **The Sharper Image** (2596 E. Camelback Rd., tel. 602/956–8077) and **Williams-Sonoma** (2450 E. Camelback Rd., tel. 602/957–0430). Biltmore Fashion Park also has more fine eating in a small compass than anywhere else in Arizona; *see* the reviews of **Roxsand, Steamers, Oscar Taylor's,** and **Christopher's** in the Dining section, below.

The Borgata (6166 N. Scottsdale Rd., tel. 602/998–1822), a re-creation of a medieval Italian walled village, may not quite challenge Biltmore Fashion Park for class, but it goes far beyond it in providing an amusing, theme-park approach to shopping. It has several good designer boutiques and interior-design shops, a handful of galleries of uneven quality, a fine book and music store in **Shakespeare Beethoven & Co.** (tel. 602/945–2646), and the pleasant **Ciao Café** (tel. 602/948–2999).

Markets and Auctions

Guadalupe Farmer's Market (9210 S. Avenida del Yaqui, Guadalupe, tel. 602/730–1945) has all the fresh ingredients of Mexican cuisine, as you'd find them in a rural Mexican market—tomatillos, many varieties of chili peppers (fresh and dried), fresh-ground *masa* (cornmeal) for tortillas, cumin and cilantro, and on and on. **Mercado Mexico** (8212 S. Avenida del Yaqui, Guadalupe, tel. 602/831–5925), about six blocks north, sells childhood treats Mexican adults remember fondly, from *cajetas* (goat's milk candy) to cocoa blocks and sweet powders in paper tubes. But most of the shop consists of shelf after shelf of ceramic, paper, tin, and lacquer ware, at unbeatable prices.

John Brunk & Sons Auctions (4001 N. 7th St., tel. 602/264–3204) moves a barnful of cast-off furnishings, appliances, tools—and almost always several decent antiques or collectibles—twice each Wednesday, at 9AM and from 7 PM until the last lot is gone. **Ron Brunk Inc. Auction** has a warehouse in the western Valley, not far from Sun City (11001 N. 99th Ave., Peoria, tel. 602/933–7748). **Hudson & Associates** (3602 N. 35th Ave., tel. 602/269–8662) gavels off a diverse gathering of goods starting at 7 PM each Friday, as does **Ware's Auction** (38th Ave. at Indian School Rd., tel. 602/278–0489) at 7 PM Monday.

Barrett & Jackson Classic Car Auction (5552 E. Washington St., tel. 602/273–0791) is a nationally recognized dealer in rare and antique autos, and the annual megaauction draws collectors from around the world.

Southwestern Arts and Crafts

The **Heard Museum** (22 E. Monte Vista Rd., tel. 602/252–8848) sells the finest selection of southwestern Indian arts and crafts in the Valley—both traditional and modern—at its gift shop. The museum is also the ideal place for learning about whatever medium or art form interests you and to see Native American artists and artisans at work almost every day.

Herman Atkinson's Indian Trading Post (3957 N. Brown Ave., Scottsdale, tel. 602/949–9750) is another fine—but eclectic—source for Native American and especially Mexican work, from silver to lacquer goods to boots and paper flowers. Mixed in is a good deal of inexpensive (but often pretty good) tourist ware, and even an intriguing roomful of African carvings.

Godber's Jewelry (7542 E. Main St., Scottsdale, tel. 602/949–1133) is one of the oldest, most reliable Indian-jewelry outlets in central Arizona. Begun 60 years ago by a reservation trading-post family, it's a fine place for learning the many styles of southwestern jewelry and discovering your own preferences.

Gilbert Ortega (7229 E. Main St., Scottsdale, tel. 602/947–2805) began as a reliable trader, then mushroomed into an industry with nine Scottsdale locations (including two at The Borgata), four in Phoenix, and one each in Sun City and Carefree. Only a fairly experienced Indian-jewelry buyer should shop here.

Folklórico (7216 E. Main St., Scottsdale, tel. 602/947–0758) is a fine purveyor of southwestern folk arts and crafts.

Finally, the shops at **The Mercado** (542 E. Monroe St., tel. 602/256–6322) include some delightful selections of gifts and art from Mexico and Latin America—and don't forget the gift shop at the **Museo Chicano** (641 E. Van Buren St., tel. 602/257–5536), on The Mercado's second floor.

Sports and Fitness

Participant Sports

When participating in outdoor sports in Phoenix, be aware that the desert heat imposes its particular restraints on activities. From May 1 to October 1, do not jog or hike from one hour after sunrise until a half hour before sunset. During those times, the air is so hot and dry that your body will lose moisture—and burn calories—at a dangerous, potentially lethal rate. Don't head out to desert areas at night, however, to jog or hike in the summer; that's when rattlesnakes and scorpions are out hunting. Hikers and bicyclists should wear light but opaque clothes, strong sunscreen (rated 15 or higher), high UV-rated sunglasses, and a hat or visor and should carry a water supply of one quart per person for each hour of activity, even in winter.

Bicycling Although its relatively level terrain is great, the desert makes special demands on cyclists: *See* the advice on hours and clothing, above. Be sure to have a helmet and a mirror when riding in the streets: There are few adequate bike lanes in the Valley.

Scottsdale's Indian Bend Wash (along Hayden Rd., from Shea Blvd. south to Indian School Rd.) has bikeable paths winding among its golf courses and ponds. **Pinnacle Peak,** about 25 miles northeast of downtown Phoenix, is a popular place to carry bikes to for the ride north to Carefree and Cave Creek, or east and south over the mountain pass and down to the Verde River, toward Fountain Hills. **Cave Creek and Carefree,** in the foothills about 30 miles northeast of Phoenix, offer pleasant riding with a wide range of stopover options. **South Mountain Park** (*see* Hiking, below) is the prime site for mountain bikers, with its 40-plus miles of trails—some of them with challenging ascents, and all of them quiet and scenic.

For rentals, contact **Landis Cyclery** (712 W. Indian School Rd., tel. 602/264–5681; 2180 E. Southern Ave., Tempe, tel. 602/839–9383) or **Tempe Bicycle** (330 W. University Dr., Tempe, tel. 602/966–6896; 9180 E. Indian Bend Rd., Scottsdale, tel. 602/998–2219; 267 E. Bell Rd., tel. 602/375–1515).

To get in touch with fellow bike enthusiasts and find out about regular and special-event rides, contact the **Arizona Bicycle Club** (Gene or Sylvia Berlatsky, tel. 602/264–5478), the state's largest group, or the **Greater Arizona Bicycle Association** (Mary Walker, tel. 602/345–8747).

Golf The Valley of the Sun is the valley of year-round golf par excellence. More than 100 courses, from par-3 to PGA championship links, are available (some lighted at night), and the PGA's Southwest section headquarters here. For a detailed listing, contact the **Arizona Golf Association** (*see* Chapter 1, Essential Information).

One of the newer, upscale courses, **Ahwatukee Country Club** (12432 S. 48th St., tel. 602/893–1161), set along the edge of South Mountain Park, is semiprivate but also has a public driving range. The **Arizona Biltmore** (24th St. and Missouri Ave., tel. 602/955–9655), the granddaddy of Phoenix golf courses, offers two 18-hole PGA championship courses, lessons, and clinics. Two low-price public courses, both in scenic city settings, are **Encanto Park** (2705 N. 15th Ave., tel. 602/253–3963) and **Papago Golf Course** (5595 E. Moreland St., tel. 602/275–8428). If you're in the Superstition Mountains area, try the desert course at **Gold Canyon Golf Club** (6100 S. Kings Ranch Rd., Apache Junction, tel. 602/982–9449). The best course in the Sun Cities, **Hillcrest Golf Club** (20002 N. Star Ridge, Sun City West, tel. 602/975–1000), is a PGA Senior Tour site. Take the children along to **PGA Tour Family Golf Center** (8111 E. McDonald Dr., Scottsdale, tel. 602/991–0018), which combines goofy golf, a driving range, and beginners' lessons. For big, sweeping views of the city, **Thunderbird Country Club** (701 E. Thunderbird Trail, tel. 602/243–1262) has 18 holes of championship-rated play on the north slopes of South Mountain. **Tournament Players Club at Scottsdale** (17020 N. Hayden Rd., Scottsdale, tel. 602/585–3600), a 36-hole course created by Tom Weiskopf and Jay Morrish, is the site of the PGA Phoenix Open.

Health Clubs

The Arizona Athletic Club (1425 W. 14th St., Tempe, tel. 602/894–2281), near the airport at the border between Tempe and Scottsdale, is the Valley's largest facility. It offers nonmember visitors a day rate of less than $15.

Jazzercise (tel. 602/420–1006) has 36 franchised sites in the Valley, where people who are already on a program can keep on course while on vacation.

Life Centers of Arizona (4041 N. Central Ave., tel. 602/265–5472), in central Phoenix, is geared to the working man and woman, so it offers nonmembers both reasonable day rates ($5–$15) and a variety of quick workout options.

Naturally Women (3320 S. Price Rd., Tempe, tel. 602/838–8800) focuses on women, from its health profiles to its diet and exercise programs; it offers one free visitor's day, then a day rate of about $10 afterward.

Hiking

The Valley boasts the best desert mountain hiking in the world—the **Phoenix Mountain Preserve System,** in the mountains ringing the city, even has its own park rangers, who can help you select and plan your hikes. For information and group hiking reservations, call the South Mountain Rangers' Office (tel. 602/495–0222).

Squaw Peak (2701 E. Squaw Peak Dr., just north of Lincoln) is a favorite two-hour hike that ascends the landmark mountain from a well-equipped park in the North Mountains Preserve. Children can handle this one if the adults take it slow. The rangers also lead a fine, easy hike through the park, introducing desert geology, flora, and fauna.

Camelback Mountain (north of Camelback Rd. on 48th St.), another landmark hike, has no park, and the trails are noticeably more difficult. This is for intermediate to experienced hikers.

The soft sandstone **Papago Peaks** (Van Buren St. and Galvin Pkwy.) were sacred sites for the Tohonó O'odham tribe and probably the Hohokam before them; now they provide accessible caves, some petroglyphs, and splendid views all around the Valley. This is another good spot for family hikes. The Phoenix Zoo, the Desert Botanical Garden, and the new Arizona Historical Society Museum are on the site.

South Mountain Park (10919 S. Central Ave.) is the jewel of the South Mountain Park Preserves. At 16,000 acres, it is the nation's largest city park, and its mountains and arroyos contain more than 40 miles of marked and maintained trails—all multiuse, for hiking, horseback riding, and mountain biking. It also has three auto-accessible lookout points, with 65-mile sightlines. The rangers can help you plan hikes to see some of the 200 petroglyph sites located so far.

Horseback Riding

More than two dozen stables and equestrian tour outfitters in the Valley attest to the saddle's enduring importance in Arizona—even in this auto-dominated metropolis.

All Western Stables (10220 S. Central Ave., tel. 602/276–5862), one of several stables at the entrance to South Mountain Park, offers rentals, guided trail rides, steak fries, and hayrides.

Hole-in-the-Wall Stable (7677 N. 16th St., tel. 602/997–1466) and **Watering Hole Stable** (7777 Pointe Pkwy., tel. 602/431–0817) are both near large parts of the Phoenix Mountain Preserve System and have guided solo and group, hourly and overnight options.

Adjacent to the Phoenix North Mountains Preserve, **North Mountain Stables** (25251 N. 19th Ave., tel. 602/581–0103) offers everything from pony rides to pack trips—even stagecoach rentals.

Old MacDonald's Ranch (26540 N. Scottsdale Rd., Scottsdale, tel. 602/585–0239) provides guided trail rides, hayrides, and catered cookouts.

Superstition Stables (Windsong Rd., Apache Junction, tel. 602/982–6353) is licensed to lead tours throughout the entire Superstition Mountains area for more experienced riders; easier rides are also available.

Hot-Air Ballooning

Another unusual sport that has soared in the desert air is hot-air ballooning. The following are a few of the three dozen companies that offer uplifting experiences; all use FAA-certified pilots: **An Aeronautical Adventure** (tel. 602/992-2627) has daily flights and will sell you a balloon if the bug really bites. **Hot Air Promotions** (tel. 602/788-5555) features a champagne flight and free pickup and return at local resorts. **Naturally High** (tel. 602/252-6766) offers not only ascents with trained pilots but also training for aspiring crew members.

Jogging Phoenix's unique 200-mile network of canals provides a naturally cooled (and often landscaped) scenic track throughout the metro area. Two other popular jogging areas are Phoenix's **Encanto Park,** 3 miles northwest of Civic Plaza, and Scottsdale's **Indian Bend Wash,** which runs for more than 5 miles along Hayden Road—both have lagoons and tree-shaded greens.

Tennis **The Arizona Biltmore Racquet Club** (24th St. and Missouri Ave., tel. 602/954-2508) has 12 lighted hard or clay courts open to nonmembers as space is available. The cost is $14/hour. At **Hole-in-the-Wall Racquet Club** (7677 N. 16th St., Pointe Hilton at Squaw Peak Resort, tel. 602/997-2543), eight paved courts are available for same-day reservation for $15/hour; at the affiliated **Watering Hole Racquet Club** (11111 N. 7th St., Pointe Hilton at Tapatio Cliffs Resort, tel. 602/997-7237) the courts are hard and lighted for night games. **Mountain View Tennis Center** (1104 E. Grovers St., tel. 602/788-6088), just north of Bell Road, is a Phoenix city facility with 20 lighted courts that can be reserved for $2.50 for 90 minutes of singles. For the same price you can play at **Phoenix Tennis Center** (6330 N. 21st Ave., tel. 602/249-3712), another city facility with 22 lighted courts. **The Pointe Hilton at South Mountain Tennis Club** (7777 S. Pointe Pkwy., tel. 602/438-9000) has 10 lighted hard courts for $20/hour.

Tubing In a region not known for water, one indigenous aquatic sport has developed. Tubing—riding an inner tube down calm water and mild rapids—has become a very popular tradition on the Salt and Verde rivers. Outfitters that rent tubes include **Saguaro Lake Ranch Tube & Raft Rental** (13020 N. Bush Hwy., Mesa, tel. 602/984-2194), right on the way into the McDowell Mountains, where the river action is, from Phoenix, and **Salt River Recreation Tube Rental & Shuttle** (Bush St., Mesa, tel. 602/984-3305), conveniently located and offering transportation to and from your starting point.

Spectator Sports

Auto Racing **Phoenix International Raceway** (7602 S. 115th Ave., Tolleson, tel. 602/252-3833), the Valley's NASCAR track, is the site of a Winston Cup 500 each November and the Indy car Valvoline 200 each April.

Balloon Racing **The Thunderbird Hot-Air Balloon Classic** (tel. 602/978-7208) has grown into a schedule of festivities surrounding the national invitational balloon race, held each November.

Baseball *See* Chapter 1, Essential Information, for information on **Cactus League** spring training.

Basketball **The Phoenix Suns** (2nd and Jefferson Sts., tel. 602/263-7867) have been NBA playoff regulars for several years. Their new America West Phoenix Suns Arena is almost as exciting as their game.

Golf **The Phoenix Open** (tel. 602/585-4334), played each January at the Tournament Players Club in Scottsdale, is a $1 million event on the PGA Tour. In March, the women compete for the $550,000 purse in **Standard Register PING Tournament** (tel. 602/495-4483), held at the Moon Valley Country Club.

Rodeos **The Parada del Sol,** held each year by the Scottsdale Jaycees (3515 N. 75th St., Scottsdale, tel. 602/990-3179), includes a rodeo, a lavish parade famed for its silver-studded tack, and a 400-mile daredevil ride from Holbrook down the Mogollon Rim to Phoenix by the Hashknife Riders.

The Rodeo of Rodeos, sponsored by the Phoenix Jaycees (4133 N. 7th St., tel. 602/263-8671), boasts a parade and is one of the Southwest's oldest and best.

The World's Oldest Rodeo (117 W. Goodwin St., Prescott, tel. 602/445-2000), held each July as part of Frontier Days, gives the Phoenix rodeos a run for their money.

Dining

Phoenix's food traditions arose from a unique blend of Old West and New West cultures. In the mid-19th century, the north Mexican rancho cooking that had been in Arizona for 150 years was joined by the Anglo-European food of American settlers. Arizona Territory was also an outpost of the West's cattle-ranching boom, and railroads brought a significant early influx of Chinese settlers.

By the mid-20th century, the Valley was rich in Mexican food, mostly in the style of the adjoining Mexican state of Sonora; steak houses, from cowboy to fancy (Phoenix was a major stockyard center until the 1970s); and Chinese restaurants, mostly Cantonese. There was lots of good family eating, but not much haute cuisine; when Phoenicians wanted to get fancy, the men put on bola ties and the women donned silver-and-turquoise jewelry, and they paid someone to pour "Continental" sauces on their steaks.

Then, during the 1970s, things took off. Southeast Asian refugees brought peppery Oriental dishes that were instantly welcome in a city used to salsa and sweet-and-sour. Immigrants from Central America and the Middle East brought more variations on familiar themes, as well as new approaches. Soon, "southwestern international" was born—and by the late '80s, it had taken hold of America's culinary imagination. Today, as innovative chefs and restaurateurs create new offshoots, this lively, eclectic cuisine continues to thrive.

Few restaurants require men to wear a jacket and tie; in any of these, a bola tie (the official state ornament) will qualify. The *guayabera* (Mexican wedding shirt) is also an appropriate warm-weather option in all but the fanciest places. Similarly, slacks or a simple dress are welcome almost everywhere for women; the fanciest places expect a dress or pantsuit.

Restaurants are open daily, unless otherwise noted.

Highly recommended restaurants are indicated by a star ★.

Category	**Cost***
Very Expensive	over $40
Expensive	$20–$40
Moderate	$10–$20
Inexpensive	under $10

**per person, excluding drinks, service, and sales tax (6%–7%)*

American

American Grill. The decor is leather, brass, ferns, and etched glass; a large bar at the entry and a lounge with cozy tables and soft, live jazz add to the classic San Francisco pub ambience. But the action is in the glassed-in exhibition kitchen and the booths, where regional varieties of American cuisine (notably Cajun and southwestern) are prepared and consumed. The N'awlins Barbecued Shrimp is a fine appetizer; chowder in a bowl of sourdough bread can't be beat. Powerful desserts, too. *6113 N. Scottsdale Rd., Scottsdale, tel. 602/948–9907; 1223 S. Alma School Rd., Mesa, tel. 602/844–1918. Reservations advised. Dress: casual. AE, D, DC, MC, V. Moderate.*

★ **Bev's Kitchen.** Some folks call it country, some call it soul food, and some just call it home. Whatever you call it, you may have to wait in line a bit to enjoy it, 'cause nobody does it better than Bev's. This unpretentious diner beside an auto lot on the south side contains gracious (but often very busy) staff and great food—hand-pounded chicken-fried steak, crumbling moist catfish, lively hot links, and potatoes and greens and corn and cabbage and yams done by people who love their vegetables (boiled down some, of course). Then there are those pies! *4220 S. 16th St., tel. 602/*

Adrian's, **46**
American Grill, **28, 74**
Bahía San Carlos, **45**
Bev's Kitchen, **64**
La Bruschetta, **30**
Byblos, **66**
Char's, **57, 69**
Chianti, **33**
China Doll, **42**
China Gate, **5, 37, 49, 72**
Chopandaz, **50**
Christo's, **15**
Christopher's, **22**
Compass Room, **55**
Delhi Palace, **48**
Los Dos Molinos, **63, 75, 76**
DuMone's, **58**
Durant's, **43**
Ed Debevic's, **35**
Eddie's Grill, **38**
The Eggery (Good Egg), **2, 7, 11, 12, 19, 25, 27**
Eliana's, **47**
French Corner, **18**
Golden Moon Palace, **60**
Goldie's 1895 House, **59**
Gourmet of Hong Kong, **44**
Greekfest, **21**
Greektown, **14**
La Hacienda, **3**
Havana Café, **32**
Jasmine Café, **70**
Korean Garden, **68**
Landmark, **77**
Lone Star Steak House, **17**
Lucky Restaurant, **40**
Macayo, **4, 39, 41, 67**
Marquesa, **3**
Matador, **56**
Mint Thai, **79**
The Moroccan, **31**
Mrs. White's Golden Rule Café, **53**
The Olive Garden, **1, 6, 10, 73**
Oscar Taylor's, **23**
Roxsand, **23**
Rustler's Rooste, **65**
Ruth's Chris Steakhouse, **26, 36**
Shogun, **9**
Steamers, **23**
The Stockyards, **51**
T-Bone Steakhouse, **62**
Tapas Papa Frita, **34**

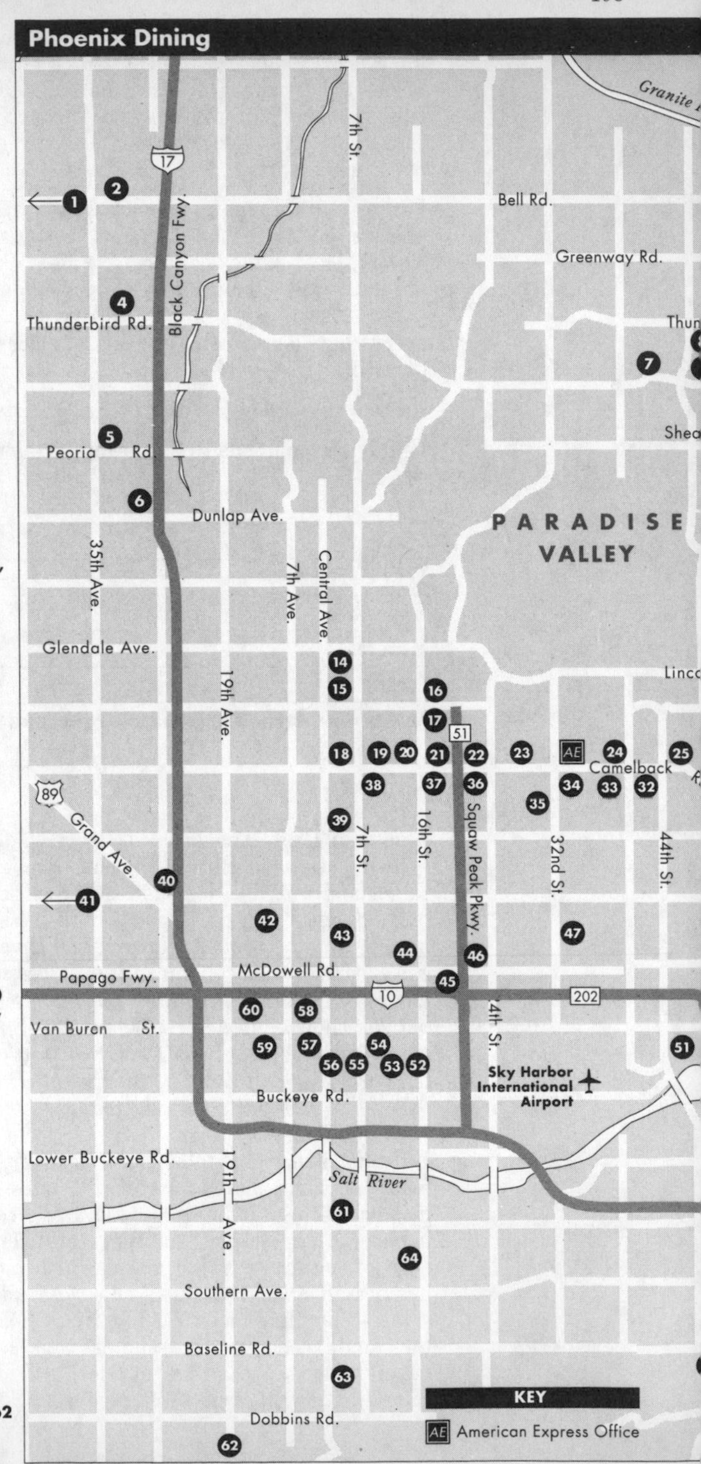

0
4 miles
0
6 km
N
ite Reef Aqueduct
Scottsdale Rd.
Pima Rd.
Scottsdale Municipal Airport
SCOTTSDALE
hunderbird Rd.
Cactus Rd.
hea Blvd.
Shea Blvd.
Indian Bend Rd.
ncoln Dr.
Rd.
Indian School Rd.
Thomas Rd.
Scottsdale Rd.
Hayden Rd.
Alma School Rd.
Beeline Hwy.
Country Club Rd.
Mesa Dr.
Salt River
Brown Rd.
MESA
Pries Dr.
University Dr.
Apache Blvd.
Main St.
Broadway Rd.
Dobson Rd.
TEMPE
Superstition Fwy.
360
10
60
89
Guadalupe Rd.
Price Rd.
McQueen Rd.
AE
3
12
8
9
10
11
13
26
27
28
29
5
30
31
48
49
50
67
69
68
66
65
70
71
72
73
74
75
76
77
79

268–8569. No reservations. Dress: casual. No credit cards. Inexpensive.

DuMone's. Comfortably elegant in blue and burgundy tones and conveniently located on the northern edge of downtown, the restaurant at the West Coast Executive Park hotel is a quiet, tony haven of American-Continental cuisine with some nice southwestern edges. The mushroom-and-walnut tortellini is a house specialty, as is the chicken quesadilla, and the chef has a nice hand with lamb. *1100 N. Central Ave., tel. 602/252–2100. Reservations required. Dress: informal. AE, D, DC, MC, V. Moderate.*

Durant's. This old downtown standby in black leather and red wallpaper hasn't changed since the '50s, and neither has its popularity (even its prices are charmingly out-of-date). It has a front door, but everyone enters through the kitchen from the parking lot. With its crowded bar and open booths, Durant's is one of Phoenix's prime see-and-be-seen places. On the menu, steaks and chops are prominent, of course, but check out the steamed clams or the chicken livers. *2611 N. Central Ave., tel. 602/264–5967. Reservations advised for dinner. Dress: informal. AE, D, DC, MC, V. Moderate.*

Ed Debevic's. This brash, noisy place adjacent to Marriott's Camelback Courtyard hotel is to restaurants what "Happy Days" was to TV—a nostalgic, half-accurate, but wholly entertaining revision of the '50s. It has red-leather dinettes, a working jukebox with Elvis and Tessy Brewer and dozens more, gum-snapping waitresses—and terrific burgers, malts, and fries. Blue plate specials, from chili to meatloaf and gravy, are a tasty hoot. With prodding, "Cookie" and the girls (and the waiters, led by a guest-kissing nerd) will provide tableside diversions. Forty-plus diners blush to remember, but children love it. *2102 E. Highland Ave., tel. 602/956–2760. Reservations advised on weekends. Dress: casual. MC, V. Inexpensive.*

The Eggery/The Good Egg. Cute decor (more airy and southwestern at Eggery outlets, more cluttered country at Good Eggs) and a lengthy menu mark this cheerful, comfy breakfast-brunch chain. Besides an array of cleverly named egg creations, from scrambler skillets to frittatas, as well as pancakes and waffles, there are welcome light options such as yogurt, granola, and fruit dishes. Service is brisk and friendly, children are welcome, and there's no rush despite the crowds. *5109 N. 44th St., tel. 602/840–5734; 4326 E. Cactus Rd. (at Paradise Valley Mall), tel. 602/953–2342; 2957 W. Bell Rd. (northwest), tel. 602/993–2797; 6149 N. Scottsdale Rd., Scottsdale, tel. 602/991–5416; 14046 N. Scottsdale Rd., Scottsdale, tel. 602/483–1090; 6990 E. Shea Blvd., Scottsdale, tel. 602/951–1123. No reservations. Dress: casual. AE, MC, V. Inexpensive.*

Unique Foods & Services. For snappy barbecue and soul classics done simply and with authority, this handsome little downtown café across the street from the restored Booker T. Washington School (now home of the *New Times* alternative newspaper) is the place to be. Hot links and ribs are memorable, and the delicate fried chicken reflects chef Wazir Karim's concern for healthful cooking. Greens and gumbo are cooked with love, and don't say you weren't warned about the bean pie. *1153 E. Jefferson St., tel. 602/257-0701. No reservations. Dress: casual. No credit cards. Inexpensive.*

★ **Landmark.** After 50 years as a Mormon church and a brief turn as a college, this massive brick Victorian became a restaurant. It's done in lush carpeting, rose-patterned wallpaper, and wall-to-wall antiques; expect to wait a half-hour downstairs in the small lounge, surrounded by historical photos. Upstairs, you start at the huge salad bar of well-made Americana, from garden marinade to seafood salad and thick, rich soups. A sauerbraten-sauced pot roast with heavenly mashed potatoes leads the entrées; the Landmark pie is a must for fudge lovers. *809 W. Main St., Mesa, tel. 602/962-4652. No reservations. Dress: casual. AE, DC, MC, V. Moderate.*

Lone Star Steak House. Tucked in an uptown corner mall, this noisy and crowded spot cluttered with Texas and country-western items does simple, effective things with steaks (including a classic chicken-fried) and serves up some of the best mashed potatoes you've had since you were a youngster. On the steaks, ask them to hold the lemon butter; the meat's better by itself. *6003 N. 16th St., tel. 602/248-STAR. Reservations accepted for groups of 5 or more. Dress: casual. AE, MC, V. Inexpensive.*

Mrs. White's Golden Rule Café. This little downtown, down-home lunch spot brings smiles to those who love liver and boiled cabbage, as well as to fanciers of such standard American fare as fried chicken and corn on the cob and yams. The food is cooked with a light, loving touch, service is friendly, prices are low, and the payin' is honor system. *808 E. Jefferson St., tel. 602/262-9256. No reservations. Dress: casual. No credit cards. Lunch only. Inexpensive.*

Oscar Taylor's. Another favorite with the meat-and-potatoes crowd, this Chicago-style '20s steak house combines a cozy atmosphere, brisk service, and beautiful cuts of meat. The prime rib is a house specialty; the ribs are, too. But the best-kept secret is a huge, delicately simple veal chop. *2420 E. Camelback Rd., tel. 602/956-5705. Reservations advised. Dress: informal. AE, DC, MC, V. Moderate.*

★ **Rustler's Rooste.** The Johnny-come-lately among the Valley's western restaurants is the biggest and nearest to town—and the most fun. It's at the east end of South Mountain Park just off I-10 (take the Baseline exit west), in the theme-park atmosphere of The Pointe Hilton on South Mountain, Arizona's largest resort. Decorated in a playful miner-cowpoke style, complete with a slide from the bar down to the dining rooms, it offers excellent steaks, juicy barbecued pork ribs and chicken, hefty Mexican-style shrimp, and homemade ice cream. The Cowboy Stuff Platter ($16) puts a sample of almost everything the restaurant serves (except rattlesnake) on your plate. *7777 S. Pointe*

Pkwy., tel. 602/231–9111. Reservations advised. Dress: casual or western. AE, D, DC, MC, V. Moderate.

★ **Ruth's Chris Steakhouse.** Most meat fanciers agree that steak gets no better handling than at this New Orleans–based chain. Amid brass, wood, and glass (and great views, in the Scottsdale location), you can get thick, juicy lamb or pork chops, but planks of beef are this restaurant's business. Calorie and cardiac watchers, beware: Portions are massive, and everything—even the broiled shrimp—comes swimming in the house butter bath. *2201 E. Camelback Rd., tel. 602/957–9600; 7001 N. Scottsdale Rd., Scottsdale, tel. 602/991–5988. Reservations required. Jacket suggested. AE, MC, V. Expensive.*

Steamers. Watching the chefs at work in the open kitchen is one of the main attractions of this spacious, brightly decorated seafood house. Another is the attentive, knowledgeable service staff; yet another is the wonderful array of New England–style standards, from chowders to halibut to lobster. (Don't stray into the fancy nouvelle part of the menu; simplicity is the strong point here.) *2576 E. Camelback Rd., tel. 602/956–3631. Reservations advised. Dress: informal. AE, MC, V. Expensive.*

The Stockyards. When Arizona had cattle barons, they cut their deals and steaks here. The feedlots and barons are gone, but the restaurant remains, a landmark just a half mile east of Sky Harbor Airport. Its ornate Victorian interior retains the original brass-trimmed bar and three salons—the black-leather Cattleman's Room, the gold-papered Gold Coast Room, and the mural-walled Rose Room. The menu features beef handled with respect, from massive prime rib and steaks to succulent calves' liver and calf fries (Rocky Mountain oysters). *5001 E. Washington St., tel. 602/273–7378. Reservations advised. Dress: informal. AE, DC, MC, V. Moderate.*

T-Bone Steakhouse. You drive south on 19th Avenue past the end of the pavement a ways, and there, on the slopes of South Mountain, is a big outdoor barbecue in a parking lot. Inside the rustic wooden building are wooden benches at oilcloth-covered tables; to the tables come steaks and chicken done to match the splendid, sweeping vistas of the desert sunset or the Valley lit up at night. Serve-yourself salad and beans, giant slices of toast, and fresh hot baked potatoes are always on hand, and sometimes an amateur western musician will take the microphone. *10037 S. 19th Ave., tel. 602/276–0945. No reservations. Dress: casual or western. AE, MC, V. Moderate.*

★ **Top of the Market.** This smaller, slightly costlier annex upstairs from the larger, noisier Fish Market (itself a popular place) has captured the atmosphere of a San Francisco wharf restaurant. Its menu would stand up well in the City by the Bay, too. Everything from charbroiled orange roughy to whole Dungeness crab is skillfully handled and imaginatively seasoned; the handmade pastas are terrific, too. (But go someplace else for dessert.) *1720 E. Camel-*

back Rd., tel. 602/277-3474. Reservations required. Dress: informal. AE, DC, MC, V. Expensive.

Asian
Chinese

China Doll. The venerable ancestor of Valley Cantonese restaurants still is *the* place for family and association banquets and Chinese New Year's feasts. Its dinners—including ginger fish, for which you select your own tilapia swimming in the lobby tank—are reliably executed classics. And its dim sum, a cart of exotic afternoon snacks, is one of the two best in town (*see* Ocean City, below). Annie White is a gracious, witty hostess. *3336 N. 7th Ave., tel. 602/264-0538. Reservations advised. Dress: informal. AE, DC, MC, V. Moderate.*

★ **China Gate.** Seldom do chain restaurants rise so high or remain so consistent in quality—not to mention the breadth of cuisines, from Mongolian to Cantonese, Beijing to spicy Szechuan. Mandarin ribs are a special experience, as is the combination of shrimp and sea cucumber. Decor is striking, and layout emphasizes privacy amid open space. *1815 E. Camelback Rd., tel. 602/264-2600; 3033 W. Peoria Ave., tel. 602/944-1982; 7820 E. McDowell Rd., Scottsdale, tel. 602/946-0720; 2050 W. Guadalupe Rd., Mesa, tel. 602/897-0607. Reservations advised for dinner. Dress: casual. AE, D, DC, MC, V. Moderate.*

Golden Moon Palace. A modest place in the somewhat seedy area just north of the state capitol mall, Golden Moon has been serving very fine food for a very long time. Half is simply decorated with red-leather booths and paper lanterns; half is a banquet room where local families celebrate and entertain guests. Service is gentle and attentive. The egg rolls are sweet and stuffed with fresh veggies, the garlic chicken is a masterpiece, and the fried rice is a meal in itself. *1408 W. Van Buren St., tel. 602/254-9229. Reservations advised for dinner. Dress: casual. AE, DC, MC, V. Closes 9 PM. Inexpensive.*

Gourmet of Hong Kong. Here are the bustling din and incomparable food of Hong Kong, in a tiny place near downtown. Staff and owners rush in and out of the narrow, steamy open kitchen to take your order and serve you; to-go diners stand between the tables, eagerly waiting. The house plate is a succulent, satisfying sampler; hot-sour chicken wings, Peking duck, lobster, and garlic pork are delightful. *1438 E. McDowell Rd., tel. 602/253-4859. Reservations advised. Dress: casual. MC, V. Inexpensive.*

Lucky Restaurant. Lucky you, if you look past the unpromising exterior, skip the buffet, and try something from the menu or the chalkboard. A little nerve and you'll have a rewarding adventure. If beef with bitter melons is available, don't miss it. The soft-shell crabs in black-bean sauce are unforgettable, too. *3317 N. 19th Ave., tel. 602/274-9477. No reservations. Dress: casual. No credit cards. Inexpensive.*

Indian

Delhi Palace. Midway between downtown and Tempe, right across from Motorola's semiconductor plant, you'll step through the door of a double storefront and into India. Attentive service and delightful flavors enhance the illusion. Sip tea and nibble home-baked *naan* and *kalcha* breads while perusing the long menu. The tandoori chicken and the yogurt lamb are two of many wonderful dishes, but the best bet is the inclusive dinner, a tour of the subcontinent's varied and subtle cuisine. The lunch buffet is another fun way to tour India's kitchens. *5050 E. McDowell Rd., tel. 602/244–8181. No reservations. Dress: informal. MC, V. Moderate.*

Japanese
★ **Shogun.** In this small converted tavern, the cheerful staff offers the best all-around Japanese experience in the Valley, starting with an outstanding sushi bar. At the tables, there are both finely turned standards such as teriyaki and tempura, and adventures into such unfamiliar areas as fish marinated in rice wine. Children are welcome here, too. *12615 N. Tatum Blvd., tel. 602/953–3264. Reservations advised. Dress: informal. DC, MC, V. Moderate.*

Yamakasa. Simple and serene in decor and service, this family-run restaurant offers excellent sushi and a menu that has been focused on the basics of tempura- and teriyaki-style cooking. No dazzle, but calm consistency makes this a refreshing place to enjoy an unhurried evening in the shadow of Fuji. *9301 E. Shea Blvd., Scottsdale, tel. 602/860–5605. Reservations advised. Dress: informal. AE, DC, MC, V. Moderate.*

Korean
Korean Garden. Simple in decor and menu, this well-staffed, friendly place provides both familiar fare, such as *bulgoki* (grilled, marinated beef strips), and exotic treats such as *bibim bab* (a bowl of assorted vegetables and beef, with hot sauce, topped with a fried egg) and *jap chae* (panfried clear noodles with vegetables and beef). And the many kinds of *kimchi* (hot, marinated chopped cabbage) are a fiery treat. *1324 S. Rural Rd., Tempe, tel. 602/967–1133. No reservations. Dress: casual. MC, V. Inexpensive.*

Thai
Char's. This austerely simple pair of restaurants gave birth to Phoenix's brood of Thai houses, and Grandpa Char still oversees things here. Meals are carefully prepared and courteously served, from the snappy skewered-chicken *satay* appetizer to the *tom yum gai* (hot-sour soup) and *yum yai* salad (chicken and shrimp salad with peanut dressing) to a noodle-rich *pad Thai* or a belly-warming curry. Tell your server if you want the pepper meter set on low; Thai like it hot. *130 N. Central Ave., tel. 602/252–6053, closed Sun.; 927 E. University Dr., Tempe, tel. 602/967–6013. Reservations advised for large groups. Dress: casual. AE, MC, V. Inexpensive.*

★ **Mint Thai.** A tiny, graceful place that started out remarkable and has never wavered, Mint Thai offers the broadest menu of the Valley's Thai restaurants—and if you find a dish not prepared with delicacy and power, it'll be a first. Soups range from the subtly simple *tom ka gai* (hot-sour in coconut milk) to the spectacular *Thai suki* (a beef-pork-chicken-squid-shrimp extravaganza); curries are gentler than those of north India, with deep flavors; the *rama* beef in peanut sauce is amazing. And you've never had sweet-and-sour like this before. Even the tea is unusually good. *1111 N. Gilbert Rd., Gilbert, tel. 602/497–5366. Reservations advised on weekends. Dress: casual. AE, MC, V. Moderate.*

Trans-Asian **Jasmine Café.** This bright eastern Valley spot, done in a California clutter of neon and ferns and collectibles, allows you to tour virtually all the Far East's cuisines at one sitting. The trans-Asian menu embraces Chinese, Japanese, Thai, Korean, and a little poetic license in a fun, endlessly varied array that's served in small portions—you can fill your table with experiments and share. The service is a bit uneven, but the food is worth it. *1805 E. Elliott Rd., Tempe, tel. 602/491–0797. No reservations. Dress: casual. DC, MC, V. Inexpensive.*

Deli ★ **Tradition.** A north Phoenix corner not far from Paradise Valley Mall hides a gem—a true New York deli. Pickles and other delicacies are flown in from Manhattan's finest purveyors; the brown, seed-rich Tradition mustard is concocted fresh, as is a host of wonderful meals and snacks, from creamy breakfast blintzes to a heavenly thick sweet-sour cabbage soup (chicken soup with the woiks will cure any ill) to heavenly chopped liver and piled wafers of corned beef on fresh marble rye, flaky sweet brisket, or fall-off-the-bone fricassee. And oh, the killer kugel and the double-chocolate pudding! You can't finish it all; take plenty home. *13637 N. Tatum Blvd., tel. 602/996–2202. No reservations. Dress: casual. AE, D, MC, V. Inexpensive.*

European *French* ★ **Christopher's.** Christopher Gross, one of the Valley's leading chef-entrepreneurs, has re-created a bistro worthy of the Champs-Elysées and, adjacent to it, an elegant, monogrammed linen-and-silver modern restaurant. They share an open kitchen (which competes with the bistro musicians for attention). Classic fish, veal, and chicken are flawlessly cooked, sauced, and presented—with delightful southwestern surprise touches. *2398 E. Camelback Rd., tel. 602/957–3214. Reservations required. Jacket and tie suggested. AE, DC, MC, V. Very Expensive.*

★ **French Corner.** At Camelback and Central, this Parisian-style restaurant packs a long, gleaming bar, crisp-linened tables and booths, a bakery, and a jazz stage all into one. Breakfast—from coffee and croissants to omelets—runs from 7 to 11 AM. Always pleasant and intimate, even in the after-work crush hour, this is a wonderful place for a quiet dinner for two. Dramatic salads (including tableside Caesar) and creative appetizers make a lovely light meal, leaving room for selections from the tempting dessert book. *50 E. Camelback Rd., tel. 602/234–0245. Reservations advised for dinner. Dress: informal. AE, DC, MC, V. Moderate.*

Voltaire. The Valley's most consistent classical French cuisine makes its home in a residential Scottsdale neighborhood. Nothing nouvelle here; there may not be a recipe that's less than 100 years old. But when you want to savor escargots, onion soup *gratinée,* and perfectly handled rack of lamb, this is the place. Then there's the hard work: crêpes suzette, cherries jubilee, or the exquisite crème caramel? *8340 E. McDonald Dr., Scottsdale, tel. 602/948–1005. Reservations required. Jacket and tie suggested. AE, MC, V. Closed Sun. and Mon. Expensive.*

German **Zur Kate.** Outside, you're in a corner mall on a busy Mesa thoroughfare; inside, you're in a friendly family inn in Bavaria. Steins and Tyrolean caps belonging to regulars line the walls; the soups are hearty and good, the sauerbraten, *kassler ripchen* (smoked pork loin), dumplings, and tiny *spätzle* noodles are wonderful. Not to mention the wursts. And the fresh apple strudel. Music and gemütlich service complete the pleasures. *4815 E. Main St., Mesa, tel. 602/830–1244. Reservations accepted. Dress: casual. MC, V. Closed Sun. Moderate.*

Greek ★ **Greekfest.** Here, Greek cooking meets haute cuisine. In a tasteful Athenian taberna, with painted vines and racked wines on the whitewashed walls, classic dishes are handled exquisitely. The feather-light *spanakopites* (spinach pie) appetizers; the sweet and succulent lamb; fresh, tart *dolmades* (grape leaves) stuffed to bursting and sour-light *avgolemono* as both soup and sauce—it's a quietly festive meal you won't soon forget. *1940 E. Camelback Rd., tel. 602/265–2990. Reservations advised. Dress: casual. DC, MC, V. Moderate.*

Greektown. At this warm family operation cheered by posters and murals, Papa greets, Mama cooks, and Son seats. The combo appetizer offers a tour of the Greek islands; lamb stew and seafood are good bets. When it's time for dessert, there is honey, nuts, and filo dough aplenty—and Mama's rice pudding. Wash it down with good, thick coffee. *539 E. Glendale Ave., tel. 602/279–9677. Reservations advised. Dress: casual. AE, MC, V. Moderate.*

Italian ★ **La Bruschetta.** In a tiny space between a comedy club and a gas station, Gianni and Linda Scorza have tucked a tasty bit of Tuscany with 14 linen-draped tables, a mural of Florence, and palms in huge antique olive jars. The complimentary *bruschetta* (tangy bread topped with dried tomato and olive oil) comes first. For an appetizer, don't miss the colors and flavors of the marinated and cooked vegetables; for an entrée, consider light Gorgonzola-sauced pasta, roast Cornish hen dusted in herbs, or delicately tender squid. *4515 N. Scottsdale Rd., tel. 602/946–7236. Reservations required. Jacket suggested. AE, MC, V. Closed Sun. Expensive.*

Chianti. This charming little poster-hung restaurant stays crowded, but the unusually alert service neither forgets nor flusters you. The antipasto salad is a crisp overture of clear, tangy flavors, the pastas are well handled and sauced. Espresso or cappuccino, with perhaps a gelato or spumoni, ends a delightful meal. *3943 E. Camelback Rd., tel. 602/957–9840. Reservations advised. Dress: informal. AE, MC, V. Inexpensive.*

The Olive Garden. Plant-filled rooms, cleverly chopped into private nooks on varied levels, create a pleasing atmosphere. The food does more justice to the range of Italian cuisine than you would expect from a chain, from the garlicky bread sticks to a fine pesto and very creditable sauces (Alfredo and marinara are both consistently successful). A good place to explore beyond spaghetti and pizza, and a nonthreatening "grown-up" setting for the young. *10223 N. Metro Pkwy. E (at Metrocenter mall), tel. 602/943–4573; 9805 W. Bell Rd., Sun City, tel. 602/977–8378; 1261 W. Southern Ave. (at Fiesta Mall), Mesa, tel. 602/890–0440; 4868 E. Cactus Rd., Scottsdale, tel. 602/494–4327. No reservations. Dress: casual. DC, MC, V. Inexpensive.*

Spanish

★ **Marquesa.** Two soft-hued, intimate rooms at the Scottsdale Princess are accented with huge glass jars of jewellike vegetables and fruits and graceful giant clay olive-oil urns. Here, Catalan food gets an exciting southwestern interpretation. The stunning presentations match the flavors—duck-breast fillets in fruit sauce; pimientos stuffed with crab; a rich chowder of mussels, scallops, and spicy chorizo sausage; and huge shrimp in almond sauce, to name a few. Service is gracious, wines well chosen, desserts inspired. *7575 E. Princess Dr., Scottsdale, tel. 602/585–4848. Reservations required. Jacket and tie suggested. AE, DC, MC, V. Very Expensive.*

Tapas Papa Frita. Master chef Joseph Gutiérrez (the genius who created Marquesa) opened his own place here, in honor of his Spanish parents. The traditional *tapas* (tavern snacks of Madrid) are the basis of the menu—such exotic nibbles as fried squid in garlic mayonnaise, mushroom- and herb-stuffed little turnovers, countless escargot treatments. But magnificent Spanish entrées, such as sweet, spit-roasted pig and tender, heartily sauced oxtails, are not to be missed. *3213 E. Camelback Rd., tel. 602/381–0474. Reservations advised. Dress: informal. AE, DC, MC, V. Expensive.*

Mexican and Latin American

Adrian's. This modest, creek-rock building with the wrought-iron grilles and tiny outdoor patio transports you in food and decor a little farther south than Sonora, to the coastal towns of Sinaloa on the Sea of Cortés (Anglos call it the Gulf of California). Many dishes are similar to Sonoran rancho fare, and Adrian does them well, especially pork with *nopalitos* (sliced cactus pads); but local Hispanic families keep coming for such treats as *Vuelve a la Vida* (Return to Life)—a cocktail of shrimp, abalone, oyster, and crab—or garlicky broiled whole pike over which you squeeze tiny, sweet Mexican limes. *2234 E. McDowell Rd., tel. 602/273–*

7957. No reservations. Dress: casual. No credit cards. Inexpensive.

Bahía San Carlos. In the shadow of the Squaw Peak Parkway, just down the street from Adrian's, is its best competitor in the *mariscos* (seafood) category. This popular, noisy little place is hung with huge posters of Mexico's palm-shaded beaches and serves almost nothing but seafood. Tostadas piled with sweet-tangy *salpicón* (lime-soaked, seasoned, shredded crab) make a splendid appetizer; the *Caldo Siete Mares* (Seven Seas Soup) is a wonderful sampler of fish, squid, shrimp, crab, and more. *19th St. and McDowell Rd., tel. 602/340-0892. No reservations. Dress: casual. No credit cards. Inexpensive.*

★ **Los Dos Molinos.** One is an A-frame with a former life as a pseudo-Tyrolean hot dog outlet; another is a more standard storefront; and the third is a large white hostelry in south Phoenix. All three house pure, hot New Mexico–style cooking—Victoria Chávez and her daughters turn out delicious *barbacoa* (spicy rancho barbecue), multitextured *chilaquiles* (layered tortillas, cheeses, and homemade chili sauce), and other delights with a humor as lively as the seasonings. It keeps the handful of tables and booths full. Beware: The hot sauce can rip your lips off. *1156 W. Main St., Mesa, tel. 602/835-5356; 260 S. Alma School Rd., Mesa, tel. 602/835-5356, both closed Sun.; 8646 S. Central Ave., tel. 602/243-9113, closed Mon. No reservations. Dress: casual. No credit cards. Inexpensive.*

Eliana's. Salvadoran food is an interesting variation on the staple themes of Latin American fare, and this tiny converted pizzeria has plenty of heart and hearty food. You know tacos and burritos; now meet *papusas*, crisp crosses between tortillas and puffy pita pockets, stuffed with meat, cheese, and sauces. From tamales, it's a short but tasty leap to these veggie-filled varieties with their soft, creamy *masa* (cornmeal) wrappings. And the *sopas* (soups) are an adventure. *2401 N. 32nd St., tel. 602/957-9442. No reservations. Dress: casual. No credit cards. Inexpensive.*

★ **La Hacienda.** About 20 miles northeast of downtown in the chichi Scottsdale Princess Resort, this tile-roofed hacienda filled with carved tables and chairs and huge clay *ollas* (water jars) shows what happens when Sonoran food goes haute cuisine. It ranges from a quesadilla stuffed with crab to the tableside drama of *cochinillo asado* (roast stuffed suckling pig), from a chili relleno filled with pork loin and nuts to the sea-sweet *cabrilla rellena de salpicón* (crab-stuffed bass in lime mayonnaise). It doesn't get any better, amigo! *7575 E. Princess Dr. (1 mi north of Bell Rd.), Scottsdale, tel. 602/585-4848. Reservations required. Dress: informal. AE, DC, MC, V. Expensive–Very Expensive.*

★ **Havana Café.** At this clean, cozy café in black and gray, you'll likely have to wait; try Arriba, the tapas bar upstairs, for Spanish-style snacks and sherry. Cuban cuisine is farther from Latin America's mainland than the island is, showing European influence. Pork becomes a moist, marinated, garlic-laden roast; tamales are moist and sweet, with meat mixed throughout the masa, not wrapped in it. Hot sauces are unheard of, and *papas fritas* (we call 'em french fries) are much in evidence. Talk about a sweet tooth—try the desserts, but have a cup of espresso at hand (don't put three teaspoons of sugar in that tiny cup, like Habaneros do). *4225 E. Camelback Rd., tel. 602/952–1991. No reservations. Dress: informal. AE, MC, V. Closed Sun. Moderate.*

Macayo. This family-run chain has been a Valley standby for half a century, and its six colorful outlets provide well-prepared Sonoran dishes in a romantic setting of folk-art decor: tacos, tostadas, tamales (especially the sweet green corn), chili relleno, *huevos rancheros* (fried eggs rancho style, atop corn tortillas and slathered with fresh salsa), refried beans—and creamy flan or honey-filled *sopapillas* (puffy tortillas) for dessert. It's a great place for introducing children to Mexican food. *4001 N. Central Ave., tel. 602/264–6141; 7829 W. Thomas Rd., tel. 602/873–0313; 1909 W. Thunderbird Rd., tel. 602/866–7034; 7005 E. Camelback Rd., Scottsdale, tel. 602/947–7641; 300 S. Ash Ave., Tempe, tel. 602/966–6677; 1920 S. Dobson Rd., Mesa, tel. 602/820–0237. Reservations advised for dinner. Dress: casual. AE, D, DC, MC, V. Moderate.*

Matador. This downtown tradition, across from the Hyatt Regency Phoenix in a tastefully Mayan-modern setting, is a fine way to meet Mexican food in general and Sonoran cuisine in particular. Dishes are reliable, authentic, and well spiced without burning and range from the familiar (tacos, enchiladas, quesadillas) to the adventurous (*menudo*, or tripe soup; *burros de lengua*, or beef-tongue burritos). It's also a perennially popular breakfast spot where civic leaders and groups gather before the workday hits high gear. *125 E. Adams St., tel. 602/254–7563. Reservations advised for large parties. Dress: casual. AE, D, DC, MC, V. Inexpensive.*

La Tasca. Past this comfortable indoor-outdoor café that blends Mexican and Art Deco, shoppers stroll the cobbled lanes and pastel shop fronts of The Mercado center. *Canciones* play on the radio as black-vested waiters bring sherry or Mexican beer for you to sip while awaiting your meal in the unhurried air of Mexico City or Madrid. Appetizers include artfully presented *sopes* (hot minitortillas piled with shredded chicken, lettuce, Monterey Jack cheese, black beans, and a smart but gentle salsa). The soups, enchiladas, and especially the *barbacoa torta* (tender pork or chicken with light green barbecue sauce in fresh split rolls) make a lovely lunch or early dinner. *541 E. Van Buren St., tel. 602/340–8797. Reservations accepted. Dress: casual. AE, MC, V. Closed Sun. Moderate.*

Toño's. Few Americans have tried goat or have drunk *horchata* (cinnamon-sugared rice water). But these are just two of the simple pleasures from rural Mexico awaiting you at this modest, clean storefront in south Phoenix. The service is so warm and personal that good-faith efforts at Spanish on your part and English on theirs somehow suffice. Toño handles goat the way Julia Child treats filet mignon; his *caldos* (soups) and *caldillos* (stews) are heartwarming. And there's nothing like a tall, cold glass of *horchata* on a warm desert evening. *24 E. Broadway Rd., tel. 602/243-9684. No reservations. Dress: casual. No credit cards. Inexpensive.*

Middle Eastern and North African

Byblos. This Lebanese standby in Tempe is not heavy on ambience, but care is taken with the food, and the staff usually dines at one of the tables, inquiring regularly as to how you're doing. The appetizers are a good introduction, from the nutty *hummus* (garbanzo paste) to the complex flavors of *falafel* (herbed, deep-fried hummus in pita bread). But save room for the main courses, well sampled via the mixed grill, which includes three kinds of shish kebab. *3332 S. Mill Ave., Tempe, tel. 602/894-1945. No reservations. Dress: casual. AE, MC, V. Inexpensive.*

Chopandaz. Afghanistan's gift to the Valley is "The Horseman," where you can canter comfortably through crisp, moist shish kebabs, nutty rice, and a wonderful sweet-spicy mash of lentils. The atmosphere in this converted pizzeria is friendly (and the rug collection authentic); the owner-host takes pride in escorting guests through his homeland's hearty, often subtle cuisine. *1849 N. Scottsdale Rd., Tempe, tel. 602/947-4396. Reservations accepted. Dress: casual. MC, V. Closed Mon. Moderate.*

★ **The Moroccan.** Seated on tooled leather cushions, rinse your hands in warm rose water poured from a brass ewer, pull apart nutty hot pita and dip it in garbanzo-eggplant paste, then plow your way—fork free, if you dare—through a *fassi* (chicken in cilantro curry), a *m'rouzia* (honeyed lamb with raisins and almonds), or a good old couscous. Try some Moroccan red wine—and try ignoring the belly dancer. *4228 N. Scottsdale Rd., Scottsdale, tel. 602/947-9590. Reservations advised. Dress: informal. AE, MC, V. Moderate.*

Southwestern International

Christo's. The sign says "Ristorante," and the northern Italian food is finely done. But Christo and Connie Panagiotakapoulos have reached throughout the Mediterranean for their cuisine, offering pastas, lamb dishes, calamari, and other regional specialties in a variety of accents. The decor and ambience are crisply contemporary, the service adroit. That's why everybody keeps coming back to this north-of-Camelback favorite. *6327 N. 7th St., tel. 602/264-1784. Reservations advised. Dress: informal. AE, MC, V. Closed Sun. Moderate–Expensive.*

★ **Compass Room.** Spectacular views have always made the Hyatt Regency Phoenix's rotating crown room an attraction. Since 1989, chef Mark Ching has given it food to match. In fact, it's become one of the most exciting galleries for southwestern culinary art. Consider this dinner: smoky eggplant soup, a salad of peppered lamb slivers and greens, a choice of fiery southwestern cioppino or beef tenderloin in jalapeño-jus reduction and cilantro-lime hollandaise. Whatever you have, try the "Cajun croutons," crusty fried oysters in a red-pepper mayonnaise, as a side or in the Caesar salad. After the room rotates another 90 degrees, try one of Ching's cobblers or his chocolate pâté. *122 N. 2nd St., tel. 602/252-1234. Reservations required. Jacket and tie suggested. AE, D, DC, MC, V. Expensive.*

★ **Eddie's Grill.** Its look and location are upscale—a new office complex 4 miles north of downtown, black-trimmed Art Deco furniture, fine handmade ceramics on the tables. Its cuisine, as eclectic as the decor, makes this one of Phoenix's hottest half dozen. Chef-owner Eddie Matney's "Ameriterranean" is a playful, shifting blend of southwestern and North African. Try succulent Mo' Rockin' Shrimp in *chermoula* sauce (lime juice, olive oil, four kinds of pepper, coriander, cilantro, and mustard) or baked goat cheese with black beans and pita chips for starters. There's a Southwestern Tower (mixed greens and marjarita chicken with peppers and jack cheese dressing, layered in corn tortillas); and steak wrapped in herbed mashed potatoes—and Eddie loves to feed you. *4747 N. 7th St., tel. 602/241-1188. Reservations advised. Dress: informal. AE, MC, V. No dinner weekdays. Expensive.*

Goldie's 1895 House. This charmingly restored downtown Victorian would fit right in on California's Mendocino coast. There's always soft music (live jazz, classical guitar) and an art gallery and museum that change shows regularly. Intimacy and understatement are the themes. Standards get subtle extra touches—a hot turkey sandwich on sourdough under a light dill sauce, or baked orange roughy in parmesan-scallion butter—and there are surprises, such as roast duck in pomegranate sauce. Plan ahead: The hours are as compact as the rooms (lunch weekdays 11:30-2:30, dinner 5-9:30 (dinner theater Thursday through Sunday). *362 N. 2nd Ave., tel. 602/254-0338. Reservations advised. Dress: casual. AE, DC, MC, V. Moderate.*

★ **Roxsand.** Chef-owners Roxsand and Spyros Scocos have woven together Greek, Asian, Continental, and Caribbean influences (among others) to create a unique trans-Continental cuisine. Eclectic is the word in this trendy but very friendly café-restaurant, where a solo snacker is as welcome as a hungry foursome. Be on the lookout for such surprises as sea-scallop salad, salmon with piroshki and cabbage roll, Jamaican jerked rabbit, and an ever-changing array of handmade desserts. This is a meal for adventurers. Roxsand shares Biltmore Fashion Park mall's casual elegance, adding its own lively energy. *2594 E. Camelback Rd., tel. 602/381-0444. Reservations advised. Dress: casual. AE, DC, MC, V. Expensive.*

Timothy's. In this cozy cottage north of Camelback Road, chef-owner Tim Johnson offers a triple treat—Continental and Cajun cuisines and live jazz. He does jambalaya, steak au poivre, and veal Genovese; like the music, the food gets hottest when the voices blend, as in Cajun prime rib, or salmon in filo dough with chili hollandaise. It's not always quiet, but service is brisk and dinner is served until midnight. Grab a chair, cher! *6335 N. 16th St., tel. 602/277-7634. Reservations advised. Dress: casual. AE, DC, D, MC, V. Moderate.*

★ **Vincent Guerithault's on Camelback.** Guerithault is acknowledged to be among the West's master chefs extraordinaire; this is the place to experience his art. One of the handful of southwestern cuisine's originators, he joined his classical country-French training with Mexican traditions to create duck tacos, crab cakes in avocado salsa, lobster with smoky *chipotle* chili pasta, and so on. Racks of lamb and symphonic pâtés are here, too, as are a heart-smart menu and an intelligent wine list. Desserts aren't heart-smart, but they are luscious. *3930 E. Camelback Rd., tel. 602/224-0225. Reservations advised. Dress: casual but neat. AE, DC, MC, V. Very Expensive.*

Lodging

Metro Phoenix has a considerable array of lodging options, from world-class resorts and dude ranches to roadside motels, from luxury and executive hotels to no-frills business suites and family-style operations where you can do your own cooking.

Resorts are usually far from the heart of town—too far to be convenient if your interests are in Phoenix proper. The exceptions: the historic Arizona Biltmore, unthinkably far out when it was built and now handily close in; the gigantic Pointe Hilton on South Mountain, less than 3 miles from the airport; and its two sister Pointe resorts, each within 7 miles of downtown. Most of the others are in Scottsdale, a self-contained, very tourist-friendly suburb; a few are scattered 20 to 30 miles out of town. And the dude ranches cluster around Wickenburg, 60 miles northwest.

Business and family hotels are closer to town—and to the average vacation budget. Until 20 years ago, families drove in from the west on Grand Avenue or from the east on Van Buren Street and pulled into any of dozens of courtyard motels with mission-style adobe facades. That is no longer a safe option, as the neighborhood is seedy; but aside from the airport, no single hotel district has emerged, so offerings are scattered throughout Phoenix and its suburbs.

Travelers flee snow and ice to bask in the Valley of the Sun. As a result, winter is the high season, peaking in January through March, and summer is giveaway time, when weekend packages at the fanciest resorts cost less than a winter night at a midrange hotel.

The rise of suite hotels in recent years—with kitchenettes for in-room meal preparation—is rapidly making room service obsolete in all but luxury or resort-class hotels. In its place, such complimentary services as a made-to-order breakfast, poolside or lounge happy hour, and a morning newspaper are becoming standard. Where room service is not noted below, expect some combination of these.

Highly recommended lodgings are indicated by a star ★.

Category	Cost*
Very Expensive	over $160
Expensive	$110–$160
Moderate	$60–$110
Inexpensive	under $60

**All prices are for a standard double room, excluding 6½% state tax, 1% city tax, and 15% service charge.*

Central Phoenix
Expensive

Embassy Suites. Just 5 miles from downtown, this 19-year-old, four-story open courtyard hotel was overhauled in 1990. Lush palms and olive trees hide bubbling fountains and a huge sunken pool, while four glass-walled elevators lift you to your floor. Free breakfast and evening social hour are shared in the spacious clubhouse at café tables, by a large sunken fireplace-conversation pit, and in front of a wide-screen TV off in a corner. Suites are compact but dramatic, with emerald carpets and drapes, Santa Fe geometric wallpaper and bedspreads. The tiny kitchenette has a microwave, sink, and bar refrigerator. Sunset Grill, opened in late 1990, offers steaks and sandwiches in a bright tearoom atmosphere with wonderful views. *2333 E. Thomas Rd., Phoenix 85016, tel. 602/957–1910 or 800/EMBASSY, fax 602/955–2861. 187 suites. Facilities: pool, sauna, shop, restaurant, meeting rooms, free airport limo, parking. AE, D, DC, MC, V.*

★ **Hilton Suites.** A model of excellent design within tight limits, this 11-story atrium opened in 1990. A more luxurious version of the frequent-traveler suites concept, it sits off Central Avenue, 2 miles north of downtown amid the Phoenix plaza cluster of office towers. The marble-floored, pillared lobby with giant urns opens into the atrium, with fountains, palms, and the lantern-lighted New Orleans–style restaurant. Modern fauvist art hangs on the walls; thematic colors are sand and bright teal blue, and Navajo-inspired motifs mark carpets and borders. Suites continue the bold design, with bleached wood furniture and rough-cut custom metal chandeliers. Each large bathroom opens to both living room and bedroom, which have two windows apiece (one that opens), and every couch is a sofa bed. Each room has a microwave (the gift shop provides snacks, as well as free VCR movies). This property is likely to become a classic. *10 E. Thomas Rd., Phoenix 85012, tel. 602/222–*

Ambassador Inn, **16**
Arizona Biltmore, **6**
The Boulders, **13**
Camelback Courtyard by Marriott, **9**
City Square, **7**
Comfort Inn Airport, **24**
Crescent Hotel, **5**
Doubletree Suites, **26**
Embassy Suites, **18**
Flying E Ranch, **1**
Hilton Pavilion, **31**
Hilton Suites, **19**
Hotel Westcourt, **4**
Hyatt Regency Phoenix, **23**
Hyatt Regency Scottsdale at Gainey Ranch, **11**
InnSuites Phoenix/Central, **17**
Kay El Bar Ranch, **2**
Marriott's Camelback Inn, **10**
Mesa Travelodge, **30**
Motel 6 Scottsdale, **14**
Omni Adams, **21**
The Phoenician, **15**
The Pointe Hilton on South Mountain, **29**
Quality Inn Desert Sky, **25**
Rancho de los Caballeros, **3**
Ritz-Carlton, **8**
San Carlos, **22**
Scottsdale Princess, **12**
Sheraton Tempe Mission Palms, **27**
West Coast Executive Park, **20**
Westcourt in the Buttes, **28**

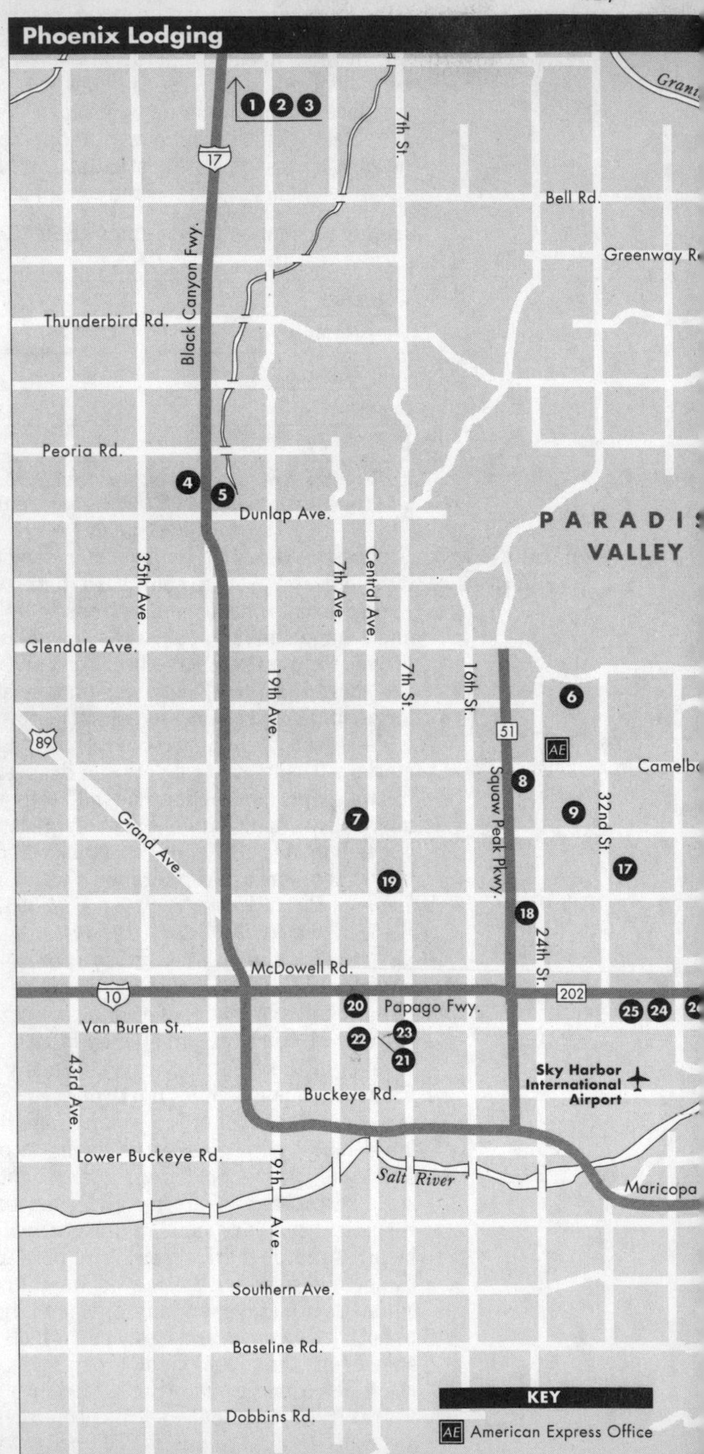

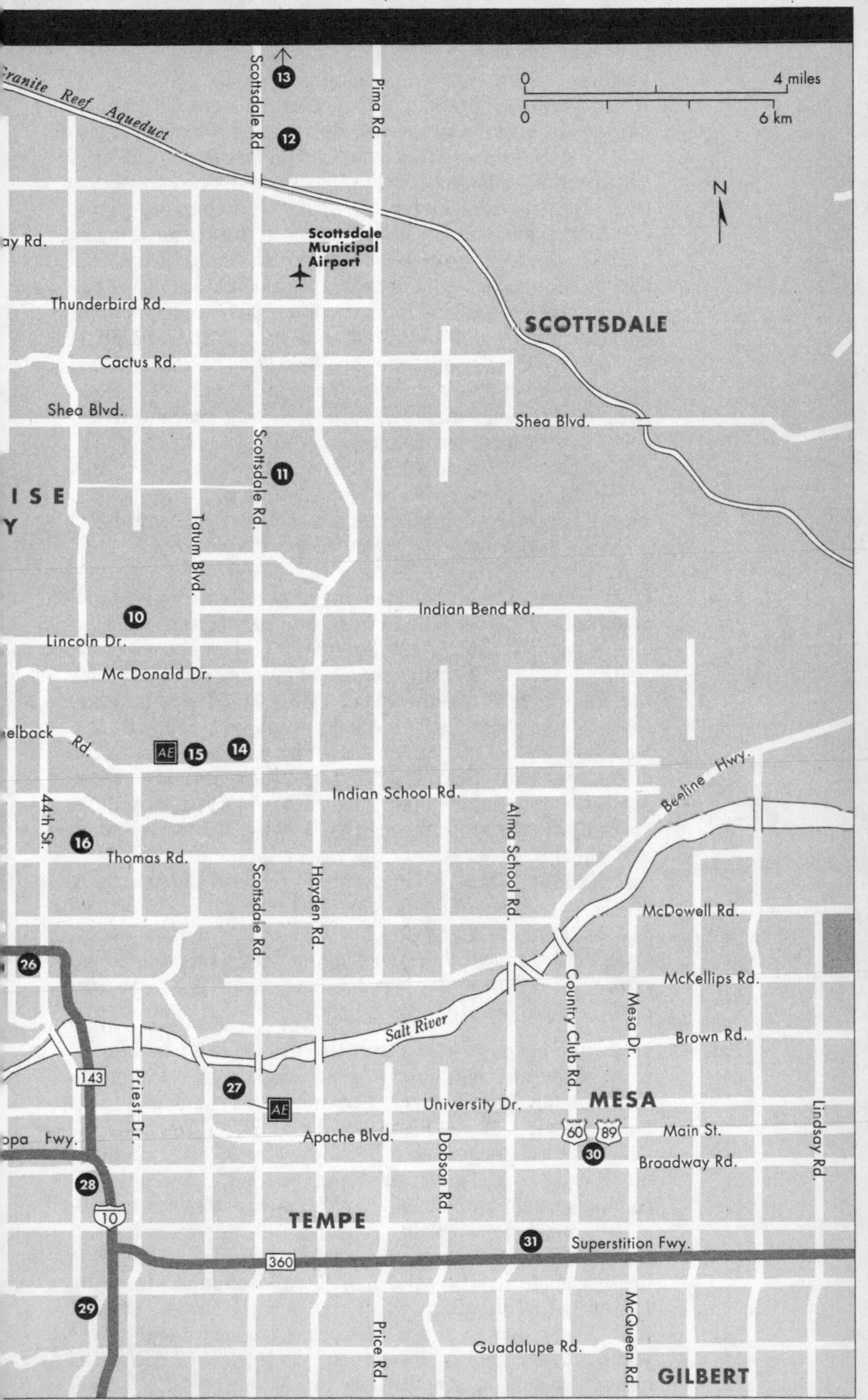

0
4 miles
0
6 km
N
Granite Reef Aqueduct
Scottsdale Rd
Pima Rd.
13
12
ay Rd.
Scottsdale Municipal Airport
Thunderbird Rd.
SCOTTSDALE
Cactus Rd.
Shea Blvd.
Shea Blvd.
Scottsdale Rd.
11
ISE
Y
Tatum Blvd.
10
Indian Bend Rd.
Lincoln Dr.
Mc Donald Dr.
elback Rd.
AE
15
14
Beeline Hwy.
Indian School Rd.
44th St.
Alma School Rd.
16
Thomas Rd.
Scottsdale Rd.
Hayden Rd.
McDowell Rd.
26
McKellips Rd.
Country Club Rd.
Mesa Dr.
Salt River
Brown Rd.
143
Priest Dr.
27
AE
University Dr.
MESA
Lindsay Rd.
opa Fwy.
Apache Blvd.
Dobson Rd.
60
89
Main St.
30
Broadway Rd.
28
10
TEMPE
31
Superstition Fwy.
360
29
Price Rd.
Guadalupe Rd.
McQueen Rd.
GILBERT

1111 or 800/HILTONS, fax 602/265–4841. 226 rooms. Facilities: pool, exercise room, sauna, shop, restaurant, bar, business center, covered parking. AE, D, DC, MC, V.

Hyatt Regency Phoenix. This landmark faces Civic Plaza like a giant kachina figure, its disk-shaped rotating restaurant atop 24 floors of dark sandstone. Renovated in 1990, it has Hyatt's trademark atrium design and sky-view elevators. Desert- and Indian-style decor dominate; shops, meeting rooms, and an on-site branch of the visitors bureau attest to the focus on conventions, which crowd the hotel in spring. Rooms are comfortable, utilitarian, and modestly sized; there are balcony rooms on floors 3–7, poolside rooms on 3 (the atrium roof blocks east views on 8–10). The Theater Terrace Café's southwestern food and themed seasonal menus are a cut above standard hotel fare; the rooftop Compass Room's meals match its splendid views (*see* Southwestern International in Dining, above). *122 N. 2nd St., Phoenix 85004, tel. 602/252–1234 or 800/233–1234, fax 602/254–9472. 711 rooms. Facilities: pool, health club, shops, meeting rooms, 2 restaurants, bar-lounge, "gold passport" floors (6–8), concierge, covered parking. AE, D, DC, MC, V.*

OmniAdams. The city's oldest major hotel is its biggest disappointment. After a huge fire, total rebuilding, and a series of owners, the historic Adams Hotel is just a memory; in its place is a 19-story modern shell cleverly crafted for the desert, with sand-colored walls, arcaded sidewalks, and scooped arches shading each window. But inside is a worn-looking hostelry that scrapes by on overflow from the next-door Hyatt. Staff is willing, and the scale and services are those of a major hotel, but vacant shop spaces and deservedly empty restaurants give it away. Rooms are small and cheaply decorated—tiny desks, minibars that don't match the furniture, thin towels. Not worth the price. *111 N. Central Ave., Phoenix 85004, tel. 602/257–1525 or 800/843–6664, fax 602/253–9755. 534 rooms. Facilities: pool, health club, sauna, outdoor jogging track, shops, meeting rooms, 2 restaurants, bar-lounge, concierge, limo-tour desk, covered parking. AE, D, DC, MC, V.*

Moderate

City Square. Only 3 miles from downtown, in a nest of midtown corporate-headquarters buildings, this is Phoenix's best bet for sports lovers. Carved out of the conference-poolside wing of the 25-year-old Del Webb TowneHouse (the old hotel became an office tower) in 1987, City Square now houses a sports bar (noisy and crowded), 12 racquetball courts (a national tournament site), an aerobics room, a 40-station machine workout center, a full indoor basketball court, and a large outdoor waterfall pool. The ambience is bright, modern, and informal. Rooms range in size from moderate (in the cabana wing, where baths have bidets and first-floor rooms have poolside patios) to very small (tower wing) and are sparsely decorated. In the locker rooms, no amenity is spared. And the restaurant serves hefty, home-cooked meals. This is where visiting pro teams—and fans—like to stay. *100 W. Clarendon Ave., Phoenix 85013, tel. 602/279–9811 or 800/272–2439; fax 602/631–9358. 167 rooms. Facilities: pool, health club, sauna, shops, restaurant, 2 bars, covered parking. AE, D, DC, MC, V.*

InnSuites Phoenix/Central. A mile east of the Embassy Suites is an older, cozier, and cheaper version of the open-courtyard suite hotel. Under its red tile roofs are apartment-style suites dating from the mid-1960s, with orange and brown outside trim and simple but stylish furnishings (rose carpet and a Japanese floral motif in wall art, drapes, and bedspreads) and half kitchen, complete with refrigerator, utensils, and dishes. Front suites hear 32nd Street's traffic; 24 second-story suites have balconies overlooking the pool and densely landscaped garden. An 8-by-10 nook serves daily breakfast, a second dispenses poolside happy hour, and a third houses the four-station exercise room. *3101 N. 32nd St., Phoenix 85018, tel. 602/956–4900 or 800/842–4242, fax 602/957–6122. 76 suites. Facilities: pool, exercise room, meeting rooms, free airport limo, parking. AE, D, DC, MC, V.*

San Carlos Hotel. Phoenix's second-oldest hotel is being reborn. Built in 1927, it was a popular downtown hub and landmark for decades; now, its seven stories are dwarfed by the Valley Bank Center and other skyscrapers. A 1990 refurbishment put deep blue carpeting in the halls and added new wallpaper, drapes, and spreads in the 120 snug rooms and suites (whose 3-inch concrete walls ensure quiet). Fixtures—from the pedestal sinks and old-fashioned toilets to Austrian crystal chandeliers in the lobby—echo '30s and '40s high style. *202 N. Central Ave., Phoenix 85004, tel. 602/253–4121 or 800/528–5446; fax 602/253–4121, ext. 209. 120 rooms. Facilities: pool, shops, restaurant, 2 delicatessens, bar, meeting rooms, covered parking. AE, D, DC, MC, V.*

★ **West Coast Executive Park.** One of downtown's hidden jewels, this small eight-story facility sits on Central Avenue at the new Deck Park (beneath which I–10 passes under the heart of the city). Finished in 1983 and renovated by new owners in early 1991, it's simply but elegantly decorated—peach and sand walls, prints by southwestern masters, unfinished antique reproductions. Moderate-size rooms have comfortable beds and large, well-lighted desks, compact brass-trimmed baths with coffee makers, and (above the second floor) commanding city views. The eighth-floor suites are dramatic, with ample balconies and sitting rooms; off the drape-swathed bedroom is a vast dressing room with Roman tub, plus a standard bathroom with shower. DuMone's restaurant does a nice array of American-Continental dishes, with southwestern accents. The Heard Museum, Phoenix Art Museum, and main library are within walking distance. This hotel has great charm, a great location—and great prices. *1100 N. Central Ave., Phoenix 85004, tel. 602/252–2100 or 800/426–0670, fax 602/*

340–1989. 107 rooms. Facilities: pool, health club, sauna, meeting rooms, restaurant, bar, parking. AE, D, DC, MC, V. Moderate.

Airport
Moderate–Very Expensive

Doubletree Suites. In the Gateway Center, just a mile north of the airport, this seven-year-old hotel is the best of a dozen choices for the traveler who wants to get off the plane and into a comfortable room. Past the lobby full of modernist regional art lies a honeycomb of six-story towers, linked by mazes of walkways and richly landscaped gardens. The modest-size rooms are rose, blue-gray, and Navajo white with plain but comfy furniture. The kitchenettes have microwaves. Topper's, a pleasantly intimate restaurant, offers a relaxed wine bar. Business and sports facilities are extensive; the casual elegance and easy access attract visiting celebrities. *320 N. 44th St., Phoenix 85008, tel. 602/225–0500 or 800/528–0444, fax 602/225–0957. 242 suites. Facilities: pool, health club, sauna, 2 tennis courts, shops, restaurant, bar-lounge, meeting rooms, free airport shuttle, parking. AE, D, DC, MC, V.*

★ **The Pointe Hilton on South Mountain.** The Southwest's largest resort (950 suites on 1,000 acres), this Mexican-Mediterranean extravaganza opened in 1987 alongside the nation's largest city park (South Mountain, a 16,000-acre desert preserve). Of all the Valley's luxury resorts, this is the most convenient—3 miles from the airport, about 7 miles from downtown Phoenix or the eastern Valley. Three lavishly designed and decorated suite hotels (one set on winding hillside streets like a coastal village), a four-story sports center, and four separate restaurants are linked by landscaped walkways and roads; carts and drivers are on 24-hour call. Spacious, high-ceilinged suites combine undyed fabrics, whitewashed timbers, and lodge fireplaces with dark-wood accent furniture, cinnamon carpets, and Mexican handicrafts. Golf, tennis, riding, and several pools are among the amenities. *7777 S. Pointe Pkwy., Phoenix 85044, tel. 602/438–9000 or 800/876–4683, fax 602/438–0577. 950 suites. Facilities: lake, 3 pools, health center, saunas, 100-horse stable, 10 tennis courts, 18-hole golf course, jogging and hiking trails, shops, 4 restaurants, 3 lounges, meeting rooms, parking. AE, D, DC, MC, V.*

★ **Westcourt in the Buttes.** Two miles east of Sky Harbor, nestled in desert buttes at I–10 and AZ 360, is Phoenix's best hotel buy. Built in 1986, it joins dramatic architecture (the lobby's back wall is the volcanic rock itself), classic Southwest design (pine and saguaro-rib furniture, original works by major regional artists), and stunning Valley views. Rooms are moderate in size and comfortable, with a compact bath and half closet; decor includes desert colors and live cactus. "Radial" rooms are largest, with the widest views; inside rooms face the huge free-form pool in its rock amphitheater, with waterfall, Jacuzzis, and cantina. Concierge-floor amenities are well worth the nominal added fee. The elegant Top of the Rock restaurant, the adjacent lively Chuckawalla's lounge, and the quiet elegance of the dawn-to-midnight Market Café all are definite pluses. *2000 Westcourt Way, Tempe 85282, tel. 602/225–9000 or 800/843–1986, fax 602/438–8622. 353 rooms. Facilities: pool, health club, saunas, 5 tennis courts, jogging and hiking trails, shops, 2 restaurants, 3 bars, business center, meeting rooms, concierge floor, parking (with lot shuttle), AE, D, DC, MC, V.*

Inexpensive
★ **Ambassador Inn.** The scenic enclosed courtyard with flowers, fountain, and bubbling stream sets the tone for this 170-room property 4 miles north of Sky Harbor International Airport. The blue-and-brown traditionally styled rooms have refrigerators and electric stove tops. A small, newly added weight room with exercise bikes as well as a cheerful pink coffee shop and brass-trimmed bar are on the premises. Less than a mile away are shopping, golf, tennis, and an indoor ice rink. Rates are adjusted for room location, with those nearest the pool costing more than those on the street side, but all are bargains. *4727 E. Thomas Rd., Phoenix 85018, tel. 602/840–7500 or 800/624–6759, fax 602/840–5078. 170 rooms. Facilities: exercise room, pool, whirlpool spa, restaurant, bar, banquet and meeting room, free airport shuttle, parking. AE, D, DC, MC, V. Inexpensive.*

Comfort Inn Airport. The location isn't scenic but it's convenient: This Spanish-style motel is 4 miles from downtown Phoenix and 2 miles north of Sky Harbor International Airport. A red-tile roof and Mexican-tile accents give character to the premises, where lush greenery surrounds the pool. The 49 traditional-style rooms are dark and small but include a table and two chairs. There's no restaurant, but Bill Johnson's Big Apple three blocks west has good biscuits, grits, and barbecue. *4120 E. Van Buren St., Phoenix 85008, tel. 602/275–5746 or 800/228–5150, fax 602/231–0973. 49 rooms. Facilities: pool, parking. AE, D, DC, MC, V.*

Quality Inn Desert Sky. Even though downtown Phoenix and the airport are only five minutes away, guests can retreat to a quiet garden at this modest two-story motel. Thick oleander hedges separate the parking lot from the well-tended courtyard and pool, which are surrounded on three sides by 90 rooms. First-floor accommodations open to the tropical greenery and flower beds from sliding patio doors. The orange-carpeted and dark-wood rooms are plain but large; the tiled bath has a separate dressing area. *3541 E. Van Buren St., Phoenix 85008, tel. 602/273–7121 or 800/221–2222, fax 602/231–0973. 90 rooms, 2 suites. Facilities: pool, coffee shop, lounge, parking. AE, D, DC, MC, V.*

Biltmore–Scottsdale
Very Expensive

The Boulders. A dozen miles north of The Princess on Scottsdale Road, in the foothills town of Carefree, the Valley's most dramatic luxury resort hides among hill-size granite boulders. Opened in 1984, The Boulders offers adobe casitas (and patio homes for long-term rental) in a graceful desert landscape; golf courses stretch like carpeting between the giant stones, and a stunning main lodge by the architect Robert Bacon blends beautifully with its surroundings. Remodeled in the summer of 1992, the casitas are compact but comfortable, with curving, pueblo-style half-walls and shelves; each has a view patio, mini-kiva fireplace, stocked wet bar, and a spacious bath and dressing area with a deep tub and adobe vanity. The modified American plan features breakfast at The Latilla (the lodge's main restaurant) or at The Club on the green, and dinner at either The Latilla or the Palo Verde. The Latilla is Californian in style, the Palo Verde Southwest international. The nearby el Pedregal center, a dramatic twin to the resort, has shopping and more eating options; and Carefree multiplies these many times over. *34631 N. Tom Darlington Dr., Carefree 85377, tel. 602/488–9009 or 800/553–1717, fax 602/488–4118. 136 casitas, 22 patio homes. Facilities: fitness center, 2 pools, 6 tennis courts, 2 18-hole golf courses, jogging and hiking paths, horseback riding, Jeep and balloon rides, llama treks, room service, meeting rooms, parking. AE, D, DC, MC, V.*

Marriott's Camelback Inn. Begun in the mid-'30s as a posh "by invitation only" resort, the Camelback Inn was bought and expanded in the late '60s by Jack Marriott, who recouped his investment by selling the 423 casitas and suites as condos in 1970–72. (Owners are guaranteed two weeks a year.) The inn "Where Time Stands Still," as its adobe clock-tower entrance still proclaims, is an oasis of comfortable predictability in the gorgeous valley between Camelback and Mummy Mountains. The lobby, a classic of early southwestern design, is a high point; so is the young, helpful staff and the airy, calm, and clean 25,000-square-foot spa. The pentagonal casita rooms are big on windows and amenities but small in size, and their architecture and decor are dull and embarrassingly motellike. The Chaparral Room serves standard Continental fare, and the Navajo Room offers American and southwestern dishes, neither shows much imagination. The Camelback is content to rest on its laurels, and a steady stream of guests are, too. *5402 E. Lincoln Dr., Scottsdale 85253, tel. 602/948–1700 or 800/24CAMEL, fax 602/951–8469. 400 rooms, 23 suites. Facilities: spa, 3 pools, 10 tennis courts, 2 18-hole golf courses, hiking paths, horseback riding, Jeep and balloon rides, 5 restaurants, 2 lounges, room service, meeting rooms, parking. AE, D, DC, MC, V.*

The Phoenician. Before the Arizona financier Charles Keating was otherwise distracted, he and his wife devoted a lot of time to this resort, now Kuwaiti owned. You may question the suitability of the lobby's French provincial decor and its authentic Dutch master paintings to a desert locale, but there's no question that a great deal of attention was paid to details. It's the highest priced property in town, and you wouldn't want to stay here if you didn't have lots of money (or were not on an expense account)—for example, unless you shell out for valet parking each time, you have to wander around a labyrinthine underground garage to fetch your car. But if this type of petty concern never crosses your mind, relax and enjoy the superb service and luxurious facilities, which include a pool fully inlaid with mother-of-pearl. *6000 E. Camelback Rd., Scottsdale 85251, tel. 602/941–8200 or 800/888–8234. 442 rooms, 107 casitas, 31 suites. Facilities: 4 restaurants, boutiques, golf course, 11 tennis courts, 7 swimming pools, health club, sauna, steam, beauty salon, barbershop, archery, badminton, croquet, volleyball, basketball, jogging trails, supervised children's programs. AE, D, DC, MC, V.*

★ **Scottsdale Princess.** The most tasteful of the Scottsdale resorts, the Princess can accommodate large groups—such as those who come to play in the PGA TOUR Phoenix Open, held here every year—without seeming crowded. Rooms in the red-tile-roofed main building and the casitas, spread out over 450 beautifully landscaped acres, are furnished in Spanish style, with large, carved pieces, but sand-colored rugs and bedspreads contribute to an overall airy effect; each has three telephones, an oversize tub, and such extras as an iron and an ironing board. The Marquesa Restaurant (*see* Dining, above) has been consistently rated one of the best in the state. *7575 E. Princess Dr., Scottsdale 85255, tel. 602/585–4848. 400 rooms in main building, 125 casitas, 75 villas. Facilities: 5 restaurants, bar, nightclub, horseback riding, 2 18-hole golf courses, 9 tennis courts, 3 pools, health club, spa, racquetball, squash, steam bath, saunas, boutiques and pro shops, hairdresser. AE, D, DC, MC, V.*

Arizona Biltmore. After a summer '91 face-lift, the 64-year-old grande dame of Arizona resorts is as lively and lovely as ever. Designed by Frank Lloyd Wright's colleague Albert Chase McArthur, it has been a masterpiece among world-class resorts since it opened. The lobby has stained-glass skylights and wrought-iron pilasters. Rooms feature gold-foil ceilings, handmade teak furnishings, and brown-and-pink marble baths. Outdoors there are lush flower gardens and stunning views. Restaurants—all very good—range from casual to late-night elegant, with a soda fountain open till 10. *24th St. and Missouri Ave., Phoenix 85016, tel. 602/955–5600 or 800/528–3696, fax 602/954–0469. 502 rooms. Facilities: 3 pools, 17 lighted tennis courts, 2 PGA golf courses, health club, jogging paths, bike rental, 3 restaurants, 3 lounges, concierge, airport and shopping limo, parking. AE, D, DC, MC, V.*

Expensive–Very Expensive

★ **Hyatt Regency Scottsdale at Gainey Ranch.** A fun place for families, with its complex of pools, fountains, waterslides, and lagoons plied by gondolas, this resort has a bit of a Disneyland ambience. At night the palm trees are lit up in bright shades of green and orange, and the public areas tend to be crowded. Rooms, which are comfortably if predictably furnished in contemporary style, offer all the expected amenities. A standout is The Golden Swan Restaurant, serving southwestern cooking at its best—

light and wonderfully tasty. Three 9-hole courses offer golfers a choice of terrains—dunes, arroyo, or lakes—depending on whether you fancy sand or water traps. *7500 E. Doubletree Ranch Rd., Scottsdale 85258, tel. 602/991-3388 or 800/233-1234, fax 602/483-5550. 493 rooms. Facilities: 10 pools, lagoons, 9 tennis courts, 3 9-hole golf courses, health club, 3 restaurants, 2 lounges, concierge floor, parking. AE, D, DC, MC, V.*

★ **Ritz-Carlton.** Like an 11-story false front, this sand-colored neo-Federal midrise facing Biltmore Fashion Square mall hides a graceful, well-appointed luxury hotel that pampers the traveler. Built in 1988, it has large public rooms decorated with 18th- and 19th-century European paintings and handsomely displayed china collections. Rooms are moderately spacious with an armoire closeting a TV and refrigerator (stocked), a small closet with a safe, and a marble bath well supplied with amenities. Rooms on floors 2–4 go for about 70% of the price of those on floors 8–10. The compact, elegant health club and the daily high tea are highlights, and the modestly named The Restaurant is among the Valley's best at Southwest-flavored Continental. *2401 E. Camelback Rd., Phoenix 85016, tel. 602/468-0700 or 800/241-3333, fax 602/468-0793. 267 rooms, 14 suites. Facilities: health club, pool, 2 saunas, tennis court, concierge, concierge floor, business center, outdoor meeting pavilion, shop, covered valet parking, 2 restaurants, 2 bars. AE, D, DC, MC, V.*

Moderate **Camelback Courtyard by Marriott.** This new (opened August 1990) four-story hostelry delivers compact elegance in its public areas and no-frills comfort in its rooms and suites. A medium-size lap pool and whirlpool fill the courtyard, landscaped with granite boulders and palms. Standard doubles are handsomely carpeted and draped while suites are done in gray with rose accents. The considerable savings are achieved by dropping such "hotel" features as 24-hour room service (it's available from 5 to 10 PM) and relying on the attached Town and Country mall for gift and grooming shops, travel services, and the like. *2101 E. Camelback Rd., Phoenix 85016, tel. 602/955-5200 or 800/321-2211, fax 602/955-1101. 143 rooms, 12 suites. Facilities: health club, pool, whirlpool, spa, restaurant, bar, parking. AE, D, DC, MC, V.*

Inexpensive **Motel 6 Scottsdale.** The best bargain in Scottsdale lodging is easy to miss, but it's worth hunting for the sign along Camelback Road. Just steps away from the newly renovated Scottsdale Fashion Square and Camelview Plaza, this motel is also close to the specialty shops of 5th Avenue and Scottsdale's Civic Plaza. Amenities aren't a priority here, but the price is remarkable considering the stylish and much more expensive resorts found close by. Rooms are small and plain with brown carpets and print bedspreads, but the well-landscaped pool offers a pleasant outdoor respite under the palms. *6848 E. Camelback Rd., Scottsdale*

85251, tel. 602/946–2280. 122 rooms. Facilities: pool, hot tub, parking. AE, D, DC, MC, V.

East Valley
Moderate

Hilton Pavilion. This eight-floor atrium hotel, built in 1985 and redone in mid-1989, is in the heart of the East Valley, just off its main artery, the Superstition Freeway (AZ 360). The East Valley's largest shopping mall, Fiesta Mall, is almost next door, and downtown Phoenix is 18 miles away. The Pavilion's ambience is defined by etched glass and brass, tropical greenery, and Art Deco furniture; the staff is young and eager to help. Rooms are moderately spacious and darkly earth-toned, with small baths and closets and a large lighted table; corner suites and the top two floors have unstocked minibars and the best views. *1011 W. Holmes Ave., Mesa 85210, tel. 602/833–5555 or 800/HILTONS, fax 602/649–1886. 263 rooms, 57 suites. Facilities: pool, whirlpool spa, weight room, restaurant, 2 bars, gift shop, parking. AE, D, DC, MC, V.*

Sheraton Tempe Mission Palms. Set snugly between the Arizona State University campus and Old Town Tempe, this informal courtyard hotel is handy to the East Valley and downtown Phoenix. The tone is set by the spacious adobe-and-verdigris lobby and the young, polo-shirted staff. Many visitors come for ASU sports and the pro football Cardinals (the stadium is virtually next door); Tempe's Chamber of Commerce and visitor's bureau both headquarter here. Rooms are bright, simple southwestern and comfortable. The hotel has a pleasant, quiet sports bar, and a creditable restaurant (The Arches); guests also have Old Town Tempe's wide array of restaurants, shops, and clubs at their feet. *60 E. 5th St., Tempe 85281, tel. 602/894–1400 or 800/325–3535; fax 602/968–7677. 303 rooms. Facilities: pool, exercise club, sauna, 3 tennis courts, shops, 2 restaurants, bar-lounge, meeting rooms, parking. AE, D, DC, MC, V.*

Inexpensive

Mesa Travelodge. Rooms are newly refurbished at this small, plain motel three blocks west of Mesa's downtown center: New blue carpet, cream wallpaper, and bedspreads and art prints in southwestern motifs brighten the 39 rooms overlooking a small pool. The motel's busy corner spot can mean continual street noise, but low prices help compensate. *22 S. Country Club Dr., Mesa 85202, tel. 602/964–5694 or 800/255–3050, fax 602/964–5697. 39 rooms. Facilities: pool, parking. AE, D, DC, MC, V.*

West Valley and Metrocenter
Expensive

Crescent Hotel. This eight-story, terraced white concrete hostelry across I–17 from Metrocenter, the state's largest shopping mall, was built in 1987 by now-troubled financier Charles Keating. In 1989, it was taken over by the federal government, and it was purchased in 1991 by Kuwaiti investors. They appear to have made the Crescent a viable upper-end hotel. Mrs. Keating's "southwestern imperial" decor remains—vast public rooms with massive stone arches and concrete columns, terra-cotta tile floors and bleached-wood wall paneling, with rose carpets in the hallways. The sizable rooms continue the look with deep rose carpet, mauve bedspreads and drapes, and pale-toned furnishings. The full-size pool and tennis courts are well kept; the health club is small but well appointed. Charlie's restaurant is pricey and uneven, but there are ample eating options nearby. *2620 W. Dunlap Ave., Phoenix 85021, tel. 602/943–8200 or 800/423–4126, fax 602/371–2856. 332 rooms, 12 suites. Facilities: health club, pool, 2 saunas, whirlpool spa, tennis court, squash courts, putting green, volleyball court, concierge, concierge floor, business center, shop, restaurant, bar, parking. AE, D, DC, MC, V.*

Hotel Westcourt. This undistinguished-looking brown block sits on the outer circle of the huge Metrocenter shopping mall, but in a small space it packs 284 rooms around a large central pool. Modest-size rooms (identical to those in the stunning sister hotel, Westcourt in the Buttes) are done in muted southwestern colors, with bentwood chairs, minirefrigerators, and compact baths. The small concierge floor costs a minimal fee; lobby-suite sitting rooms overlook the atrium; poolside junior suites (carved from regular-size rooms) are like elegant little cabanas. Breakfast and luncheon buffets are available in Trumps Bar and Grill, as is menu service through the evening. Other dining options abound within a short walk. *10220 N. Metro Pkwy. E, Phoenix 85051, tel. 602/997–5900 or 800/858–1033, fax 602/997–1034. 269 rooms, 15 suites. Facilities: health club, pool, sauna, whirlpool spa, tennis court, concierge, concierge floor, business center, shop, 2 restaurants, bar, parking. AE, D, DC, MC, V.*

Wickenburg
Very Expensive

Rancho de los Caballeros. Now more of a luxury resort than a dusty dude ranch, this 20,000-acre spread began with 320 acres in 1947 and gradually evolved to include an exclusive housing development, a championship golf course, and a 5,000-square-foot conference center. Trail rides are still a popular feature here, and the annual weeklong Los Caballeros Trail Ride, starting at the ranch, is a major event among southwestern horse folk. In the huge main lodge, the original *sala* (living room) has been remodeled; surrounding the copper fireplace now is bright, neo-Mexican decor, and adjacent are game rooms. The American Plan (15% tips included) meals are provided in the bright dining room (breakfast and dinner, restaurant style) and poolside from a half-dozen buffet carts. Rooms—from the original brick Sun Terrace duplexes to the five-year-old Bradshaw Suites (with optional kitchenette and sitting room)—are spacious and done in low-key southwestern decor; TVs are available on request only, and the baths do not have amenities. *Box 1148, Wickenburg 85358, tel. 602/684–5484, fax 602/684–2267. 73 rooms. Facilities: pool, horseback riding, cookouts, 4 tennis courts, 18-hole golf course, skeet and trap shooting range, parking. Closed June–Sept. No credit cards.*

Expensive **Kay El Bar Ranch.** Tucked into a hollow beside the Hassayampa River just 3 miles north of town, this is what dude ranches used to be—homey, comfy, and away from it all, with more horses than people, but not too many of either. This National Historic Site, opened as a dude ranch in 1925, was revived in 1980 by two sisters from the East, Jane Nash and Jan Martin. Immense old salt cedars tower over fat saguaros and some of the biggest mesquite trees in Arizona, all shading the 10-room adobe bunkhouse with its family-style lodge room; the two-bedroom, two-bath cottage (built in 1914); and the brightly decorated cookhouse, where eating is family style. Rooms are compact and clean, with small, modern bathrooms, and decor is down-home western. The American Plan rates include three hearty meals a day (some outdoors by the corral) and one two-hour ride; other rides cost $15 each. *Box 2480, Wickenburg 85358, tel. 602/684–7593. 10 rooms, 1 cottage. Facilities: pool, library, horseback riding, cookouts, volleyball, golf privileges, lodge room, parking. Closed May–mid-Oct. D, MC, V.*

Flying E Ranch. This spacious spread, on a breeze-swept rise with a 400-square-mile view, typifies the modern dude ranch. About 4 miles west of town to the site of the Wickenburg Massacre and then a mile back from the highway, the 21,000-acre ranch was built in 1946. Most of the rooms have wide views and the original knotty pine walls and white-washed pine and leather furniture; bathrooms are clean and modern. Minirefrigerators and wet bars are unstocked, as is the lounge (which does have mixers for the sundown cocktail hour); bring your own spirits. But the staff's spirits are high and infectious; city slickers adore the morning, lunch, and evening cookout rides and the occasional "dudeos," in which Flying E green-horns ride and rope against dudes from other spreads; and the weekly barn dance is not to be missed. American Plan meals are family style on gingham-checked oilcloth over trestle tables, with western music playing in the background. Rides cost extra. *Box EEE, Wickenburg 85358, tel. 602/684–2690 or 602/684–2713, fax 602/684–5304. 16 rooms. Facilities: pool and whirlpool, horseback riding, cookouts, weight room, tennis court, basketball court, outdoor chess, lounge, parking. Closed May–Oct. 31. No credit cards.*

The Arts and Nightlife

The Arts

Phoenix performing-arts groups have grown rapidly in number and sophistication, especially in the past two decades. Completion of the downtown **Symphony Hall** (225 E. Adams St., tel. 602/262–7272) and **Herberger Theater Center** (222 E. Monroe St., tel. 602/252–TIXS), which face each other across the Civic Plaza mall, has given many groups a state-of-the-art permanent home in elegant surroundings;

the developing "cultural district" just 2 miles north, around Deck Park, houses several more.

The most comprehensive ticket agencies are **Dillard's** (13 locations including all Dillard's department stores and Phoenix Civic Plaza, tel. 602/678–2222) and the **Arizona State University ticket office** (Gammage Center, Tempe, tel. 602/965–3434).

Theater

Actors Theatre of Phoenix (320 N. Central Ave., Suite 104, tel. 602/254–3475) is the resident theater troupe at the Herberger. Besides a full season of drama, comedy, and musical theater, it presents original one-act plays in its lunchtime Brown Bag series Tuesday through Thursday.

Arizona Theatre Company (Herberger Theater Center, 222 E. Monroe St., tel. 602/279–0534), Arizona's only full Equity company, splits its season between Tucson and Phoenix, where it performs at the Herberger. Its playbill usually includes four popular plays and two lesser-known works.

Black Theater Troupe (333 E. Portland St., tel. 602/258–8128) performs at the Herberger and at its own house, a half-block from the city's Performing Arts Building on Deck Park. It presents original and contemporary dramas and musical revues, as well as adventurous adaptations, such as its recent version of *Steel Magnolias*.

Mill Avenue Theatre (520 S. Mill Ave., Tempe, tel. 602/921–7777), a relative newcomer, established itself with *Guv: The Musical*, a long-running original satire (with constantly updated lyrics) on Arizona's politics. It regularly brings alternative-theater experiences to the Valley.

Teatro del Valle (817 N. 1st St., tel. 602/274–8814), a bilingual company, puts on contemporary and original works in a variety of forms, reflecting and interpreting Hispanic life and culture.

Dinner Theater

Copper State Players (6727 N. 47th Ave., Glendale, tel. 602/937–1671), the Valley's oldest dinner troupe, stages light comedy at Max's, a West Valley sports bar and steak house.

Murder Ink (7000 E. Indian School Rd., Scottsdale, tel. 602/423–8737) presents audience-participation whodunits at the Impeccable Pig restaurant and antiques/crafts shop in Scottsdale and other Valley locations.

Classical Music

Arizona Opera (Symphony Hall, 225 E. Adams St., tel. 602/266–7464), one of the nation's most highly respected regional companies, stages a four-opera season, primarily classical, in Tucson and Phoenix.

Phoenix Symphony Orchestra (3707 N. 7th St., tel. 602/264–6363), the resident company at Symphony Hall, has reached the first rank of American regional symphonies. Its rich season includes orchestral works from the classical and contemporary literature, a chamber series, composer festivals, and outdoor pops concerts.

Dance **a ludwig co.** (tel. 602/965–3914), the Valley's foremost modern dance troupe, includes the choreography of founder-director Ann Ludwig of the Arizona State University faculty in its repertoire of contemporary works.

Ballet Arizona (3645 E. Indian School Rd., tel. 602/381–0184), the state's professional ballet company, presents full seasons of classical and contemporary works (including commissioned pieces for the company) in both Tucson and Phoenix, where it is the resident dance company at the Herberger Theater Center.

Film Harkins Theaters, a locally owned chain, is the only one in the valley that shows anything but mass-market movies. Its **Cine Capri** (2323 E. Camelback Rd., tel. 602/956–4200), a classic wide-screen, superstereo theater from the '60s, occasionally offers a giant-screen revival such as *Dr. Zhivago* or *Spartacus*. At **Camelview 5** (70th St. and Camelback Rd., tel. 602/433–9900), one screen usually shows a major foreign release or domestic art film.

Galleries The gallery scene in Phoenix and Scottsdale is so extensive that your best bet is to consult the Friday and Sunday listings in *The Arizona Republic* or the Marquee section in Saturday's *Phoenix Gazette*. Southwestern art—from traditional to avant-garde Native American, from the Cowboy Artists of America to performance art—is varied and abundant. Photography also enjoys a strong tradition in Arizona.

Nightlife

Downtown Phoenix used to close up at sunset—until the advent of the Mercado and the Arizona Center. The heart of town at last has nightclubs, restaurants, and upscale bars that compete with livelier resorts and clubs in Scottsdale, along Camelback Road in north-central Phoenix, and elsewhere around the Valley.

Among music and dancing styles, country and western have the longest tradition here; jazz, surprisingly, runs a close second. Rock clubs also are numerous and varied, as are hotel lounges. At its major and minor venues, the Valley attracts a steady stream of pop and rock acts; for concert tickets, try **Trails** (5 Valley locations, tel. 602/265–6653).

The best listings and reviews are in the weekly *New Times* tabloid newspaper, distributed Wednesday; the Friday and Sunday Life & Leisure sections of *The Arizona Republic;* and the Marquee section of Saturday's *Phoenix Gazette*.

Bars and Lounges You can listen to the ivories tinkling at **The Plaza Bar** on the mezzanine of the Hyatt Regency Phoenix (122 N. 2nd St., tel. 602/252–1234), a quiet getaway with a sparkling downtown view.

A lively (during happy hour, noisy) upscale crowd takes advantage of the city's most spectacular view at **Chuckawalla's,** the lounge in Top of the Rock restaurant (2000 W. Westcourt Way, Tempe, tel. 602/225–9000) at Westcourt in the Buttes.

An elegant uptown spot, **Top of Central** (8525 N. Central Ave., tel. 602/861–2437) has soft music and room for larger groups.

Comedy

Fun Seekers (4519 N. Scottsdale Rd., tel. 602/949–1100), across from Scottsdale Fashion Square, is a stand-up comedy club headlining rising comics.

The Improv (930 E. University Dr., Tempe, tel. 602/921–9877), part of a national chain, books better-known talent.

Country and Western

Cheyenne Cattle Co. (455 N. 3rd St., tel. 602/253–6225), in the Arizona Center downtown, is the newest country and western dance spot in town.

LuLuBelle's (7212 E. Main St., Scottsdale, tel. 602/994–9800) looks like what it is—a tourist spot that's also one of the oldest and best sawdust dancin', easy listenin', and barbecue eatin' places around.

At **Mr. Lucky's** (3660 W. Grand Ave., tel. 602/246–0686), the granddaddy of Phoenix western clubs, you can dance the two-step all night (or learn it, if you haven't before).

Toolie's Country (4231 W. Thomas Rd., tel. 602/272–3100) books the best national acts, from Sweethearts of the Rodeo to Eddie Raven and Juice Newton.

Jazz

American Bar & Grill (6113 N. Scottsdale Rd., Scottsdale, tel. 602/948–9907; 1233 S. Alma School Rd., Mesa, tel. 602/844–1918) books solo artists for long-term soft jazz gigs that fit its San Francisco–style lounges. (Good neo–New Orleans and southwestern food are featured, too.)

At **The French Corner** (50 E. Camelback Rd., tel. 602/234–0245), a top local jazz venue, you can enjoy fine French cuisine (or pastries and coffee) while listening.

Timothy's (6335 N. 16th St., tel. 602/277–7634) is yet one more venerated venue that joins top jazz performances with fine French-influenced Continental and Cajun cuisine.

Rock and Blues

A small club, **Anderson's Fifth Estate** (6820 E. 5th Ave., Scottsdale, tel. 602/994–4168) mixes DJ nights, local bands, and occasional touring rock and country/folk acts.

Chuy's (310 S. Mill Ave., Tempe, tel. 602/968–5586; 410 S. Mill Ave., Tempe, tel. 602/967–2489), geared to the ASU crowd, books blues, rhythm and blues, alternative rock, and sometimes a little jazz.

Mason Jar (2303 E. Indian School Rd., tel. 602/956–6271) hosts regular alternative rock nights and occasional blues and rock oldies.

Warsaw Wally's (2547 E. Indian School Rd., tel. 602/955-0881) is the top Valley blues club, but its poolroom draws rough trade.

Singles Always crowded with young professional and business types, **Acapulco Bay Beach Club** (3837 E. Thomas Rd., tel. 602/273–0234) is often cheerfully boisterous.

With 36 TVs and five giant screens, as well as an outdoor volleyball court, **America's Original Sports Bar** (455 N. 3rd St., tel. 602/252–2112) in The Arizona Center is big and boisterous.

At the popular **Denim & Diamonds** (3905 E. Thomas Rd., tel. 602/225–0182), folks turn up in anything from jeans to glitzy jewelry for dancing and socializing.

In the Arizona Center, **Hooters** (455 N. 3rd St., tel. 602/257–0000) draws crowds with its T-shirted, short-shorted waitresses, its beer and burgers and potato skins menu, and its indoor-outdoor visibility.

Macayo's Depot Cantina (300 Ash Ave., Tempe, tel. 602/966–6677) combines a lively "meet market," frequented by students from the nearby ASU campus, with a very creditable Mexican restaurant.

Studebaker's (705 S. Rural Rd., Tempe, tel. 602/829–8495) joins bar, buffet, and dancing with live DJs for a noisy place to meet friends.

7 Tucson and Southern Arizona

By Trudy Thompson Rice

Updated by Edie Jarolim

A treasure of mountains, deserts, canyons, and dusty little cowboy towns, southern Arizona remains undiscovered, for the most part, by visitors; the vast majority of the state's tourists head north for the Grand Canyon, often neglecting the southern half of the state. But it would be a pity to miss southern Arizona. It's uncrowded, the weather is usually mild, and there is plenty to see and do. Among the area's myriad attractions are historic Tombstone and Bisbee, where you can indulge in Old West fantasies galore; the huge, oddly shaped cacti of Saguaro National Monument; the cool Huachuca Mountains; the lively shops and restaurants in Nogales, across the Mexican border; and, of course, Tucson. A gateway to southern Arizona, Tucson offers the traveler everything from culture to sports, from ballet, symphony, and the University of Arizona's photography museum, boasting one of the largest modern collection in the country, to golf, tennis, and Hi-Corbett Field, where the Cleveland Indians compete with seven other major-league baseball teams during spring training.

Although it is Arizona's second-largest city, Tucson feels like a small town, albeit one enriched by its deep Hispanic and Old West roots. It is at once a bustling center of business and a kicked-back university and resort town. Metropolitan Tucson has some 665,000 year-round residents—second in population to the state's capital, Phoenix—but the population swells in the winter, when "snowbirds" come to the area to enjoy the warm sun that shines on the city more than 300 days every year. Winter temperatures hover around 65°F during the day and 38°F at night. Summers are unquestionably hot—with July averaging 101°F during the day and 73°F at night—but not as hot as in Phoenix: Although it is 100 miles to the south and both cities lie in desert valleys created by surrounding mountains, Tucson is cooler in the summer because it's higher in altitude (2,400 feet, compared with Phoenix's 1,100 feet). And because Tucson averages only 11 inches of rain a year (more than half of which falls from July to September), the low humidity makes even July's heat feel far more comfortable than one would expect.

In a part of the world where everything seems new and buildings more than 50 years old are known as historical places, Tucson is an exception. Historians have dated Tucson's earliest citizens to AD 100, when the Hohokam Indians made their home in the fertile farming valley. During the 1500s, Spanish explorers arrived to find Pima Indians enjoying the mild weather and growing crops.

The name Tucson came from the Indian word *stjukshon* (pronounced "STOOK-shahn"), meaning "spring at the foot of a black mountain." (The springs at the foot of Sentinel Peak, made of black volcanic rock, are now dry.) The name became Tucson (originally pronounced "TUK-son") in the mouths of the Spanish explorers who built the *presidio* (walled city) of San Augustín del Tuguison in 1776 to keep Native Americans from reclaiming the city. The walled city was affectionately called the Old Pueblo by its early settlers, and the nickname has stuck till this day.

Father Eusebio Francisco Kino, a Jesuit missionary, first visited the village in 1687 and returned a few years later to build missions in the area. His influence is still strongly felt throughout the region; especially noteworthy is the Mission San Xavier del Bac, just south of Tucson.

Four flags have flown over Tucson—those of Spain, Mexico, the U.S. Confederacy, and the Union. Arizona didn't become a state until 1912, so its colorful days as a territory are still very much a part of the area's lore. The Butterfield stage line was extended to Tucson in the 1850s, bringing in adventurers, a few settlers, and more than a handful of outlaws. Much of the city's growth was shaped by the University of Arizona, opened in 1891 on land "donated" by two gamblers and a saloon keeper (their benevolence was reputed to have been inspired by a bad hand of cards).

Tucson's growth really took off during World War II, thanks to Davis-Monthan Air Force Base. It was also around this time that air-conditioning made the desert hospitable to visitors and residents alike. Today the city's economy relies heavily on tourism, the university, and some high-tech industries. The resident population is now almost one-quarter Hispanic, and some of the best Mexican food north of the border can be found in restaurants here. The influence of Spanish and Mexican settlers is also strongly felt in the city's architecture and culture.

Tucson is a good jumping-off point for a visit to southern Arizona. Several day trips can be coordinated from the city, but for excursions to such towns as Bisbee, Douglas, and Nogales it's best to find lodging along the way. This isn't difficult, although it does take some advance planning: In some of the sparsely settled parts of southern Arizona, accommodations aren't always plentiful. As you might expect, the desert areas are popular in winter, and the cooler mountain areas are more heavily visited in summer months.

Check plane fares carefully when you're planning your trip. Though you may not want to spend time in Phoenix, sometimes it's cheaper to fly into that city and then take a scenic two-hour drive down the Pinal Pioneer Parkway (U.S. 89) to Tucson.

Essential Information

Arriving and Departing by Plane

Tucson International Airport (tel. 602/573–8000) is 8½ miles south of downtown, west of I–10 off the Valencia exit. The city is served by 10 domestic and international airlines, providing 100 daily arrivals and departures.

U.S. carriers serving Tucson include **Alaska** (tel. 800/426–0333), **American** (tel. 800/433–7300), **America West** (tel. 800/247–5692), **Continental** (tel. 800/525–0280), **Delta** (tel. 800/221–1212), **Northwest** (tel. 800/225–2525), **United** (tel. 800/241–6522), and **USAir** (tel. 800/428–4322). International carriers include **Aero Mexico** (tel. 800/237–6639) and **TWA** (tel. 800/221–2000).

Between the Airport and Downtown

In addition to the modes of transportation listed below, many hotels provide courtesy airport shuttle service; inquire when making reservations.

By Car

If you plan to tour Tucson and southern Arizona by car, it makes sense to rent one at the airport. Parking is not a problem, even downtown. Rental-car agencies at the airport include **Budget** (tel. 602/889–8800) and **National** (tel. 602/573–8050). The driving time from the airport to downtown varies, but it's usually less than half an hour, 20 minutes extra during rush hours (7:30–9 AM and 4:30–6 PM).

By Taxi

Taxi rates vary widely; they are unregulated in Arizona. It's always wise to inquire about the cost of a trip before getting into a cab. You shouldn't pay much more than $15 from the airport to the heart of downtown. A few of the more reliable cab companies are **Yellow Cab** (tel. 602/624–6611), **Checker Cab** (tel. 602/623–1133; smoke-free cabs available on request), and **Fiesta Taxi** (tel. 602/622–7777), which features drivers who speak both English and Spanish.

By Van or Bus

Arizona Stagecoach (tel. 602/889–1000), with an office at the airport, takes groups and individuals to all parts of Tucson for $8.50 to $26, depending on the location.

If you're traveling light and aren't in a hurry, you can take a city **Sun Tran** (tel. 602/792–9222) bus downtown for only 60¢. Catch the Bus 25 (you'll see it to the left of the lower level as you come out of the terminal) and take it to the Roy Laos Transit Center at Sussex and Irvington, and then transfer to the Bus 8 downtown from there. Bus 11, which leaves from the same place, goes north on Alvernon Way, and you can transfer to most of the east–west bus lines from this main north–south road; ask the bus driver (they're all friendly and helpful) which one would take you closest to the location you need. You must have exact change, but transfers are free.

Arriving and Departing by Car, Bus, and Train

By Car From Phoenix, 111 miles northwest, I–10 east is the road that will take you to Tucson. Also the main traffic artery through town, I–10 has well-marked exits all along the route. At Casa Grande, 70 miles north of Tucson, I–8 connects with I–10, bringing travelers into the area from the west. From Nogales, 63 miles south on the Mexican border, take I–19 into Tucson.

By Bus Buses to Los Angeles, El Paso, Phoenix, Flagstaff, Douglas, and Nogales depart and arrive regularly from Tucson's **Greyhound** terminal (2 S. 4th Ave. at E. Broadway, tel. 602/792–0972). For information about travel from other cities, call the number listed for Greyhound/Trailways in your local yellow pages. For travel to Phoenix, **Air Coach** (tel. 602/882–7661) has express service from Park Mall or the University of Arizona for $19 one-way. Call 24 hours ahead for reservations. **Arizona Shuttle Service Inc.** (tel. 602/795–6771) is another Phoenix–Tucson service, transporting riders between Tucson's El Con Mall or the University of Arizona and Sky Harbor Airport in Phoenix for $18 one-way. All bus trips between the cities take approximately two hours.

By Train **Amtrak** serves the city with several westbound and eastbound trains weekly; the station is downtown at 400 East Toole Avenue (tel. 800/USA–RAIL).

Important Addresses and Numbers

Tourist Information The **Metropolitan Tucson Convention and Visitors Bureau** (130 S. Scott Ave., 85701, tel. 602/624–1817 or 800/638–8350) is downtown; the office is generally open weekdays 8–5, and phone inquiries are answered weekdays 8:30–5, weekends 9–4.

Emergencies For the **police, ambulance, fire department,** dial 911, a free call from public pay phones.

Doctors and Dentists **Community Information and Referral Services** (tel. 602/881–1794) will provide you with names of doctors or dentists who can assist you.

Hospitals **El Dorado Hospital and Medical Center** (1400 N. Wilmot Rd., tel. 602/886–6361), **Northwest Hospital** (6200 N. La Cholla Blvd., tel. 602/742–9000), **St. Joseph's Hospital** (350 N. Wilmot Rd., tel. 602/296–3211), **Tucson General Hospital** (3838 N. Campbell Ave., tel. 602/327–5431), **Tucson Medical Center** (5301 E. Grant Rd., tel. 602/327–5461), **University Medical Center** (1501 N. Campbell Ave., tel. 602/694–0111).

Late-Night Pharmacies Four **Walgreen** drugstores in the city (4730 E. Grant Rd., tel. 602/326–4341; 2560 S. Kolb Rd., tel. 602/790–7734; 4080 N. Oracle Rd., tel. 602/887–6975; and 3781 S. 12th Ave., tel. 602/623–2567) are open 24 hours.

Other Useful Numbers **Chamber of Commerce** (tel. 602/792–2250).
Local road conditions (tel. 602/294–3113).
State road report (tel. 602/573–7623).
Tucson Parks and Recreation Department (tel. 602/791–4873).
Weather (tel. 602/881–3333 or 602/623–4000).

Getting Around

A car is almost a requirement if you're really going to explore Tucson and southern Arizona. You can get around downtown on foot and by bus or taxi, but getting to know the area requires a road trip or two.

By Car Traffic isn't especially heavy in Tucson, except for the traditional rush hours in the morning and late afternoon. There's a seat-belt law in the state, as well as one that requires children under the age of four to ride in a secure child-restraint seat. Don't even think of drinking and driving; if you do, you'll spend your vacation in jail. Arizona's strict laws against drinking and driving are strongly enforced.

If you haven't rented a car at the airport (*see* Between the Airport and Downtown, *above*), you might try **U-Save Auto Rental** (tel. 602/790–8847), **Enterprise** (tel. 602/747–9700) or **Rent-A-Ride** (tel. 602/750–1900) downtown. In addition, **Carefree Rent-A-Car** (tel. 602/790–2655) offers reliable used cars at good rates.

By Bus and Trolley Within the city limits, public transportation is available through **Sun Tran** (tel. 602/792–9222), Tucson's bus system. On weekdays, some buses run until 10 PM, but most run only until 7 PM, and service is more limited on weekends. A one-way ride costs 60¢ (transfers are free); those with valid Medicare cards can ride for 25¢. The **Sun Tran Trolley** runs between downtown and the University of Arizona, Monday–Saturday, for 25¢ each way. Call for information on Sun Tran bus and trolley routes and costs.

Sun Tran's **Special Needs Department** (tel. 602/791–3211) offers details about specially outfitted buses and vans for physically challenged riders.

Opening and Closing Times

Downtown businesses, including shops and some restaurants, close at the end of the office workday, sometimes as early as 6 PM. In suburban malls, most stores are open weekdays 10–9, Saturday 10–6, and Sunday noon–5. Banking hours vary widely; most Tucson banks are open weekdays 9–4 (inside lobby services) and 9–5 (drive-in service); on Saturday some lobbies are open 8–noon. Many banks have automated teller machines (ATMs), so customers with a banking network card can get cash when the banks are closed.

Guided Tours

Orientation **Gray Line Tours** (tel. 602/622–8811) offers a basic city tour in a bus. **Arizona Stagecoach Company** (tel. 602/881–4111) offers excursions to local sites for groups or individuals. **Off the Beaten Path Tours** (tel. 602/296–0909) has excellent customized excursions year-round. (Note: Many tour operators are on limited schedules during the summer).

Special-Interest Tours The same tour operators noted above offer tours to museums, shopping areas, historical sites, and nature reserves. In addition, photography buffs will enjoy the various excursions scheduled by **Arizona Shutterbug Adventures** (tel. 602/296–8854).

Walking Tours For an easy-to-follow self-guided tour of historic downtown Tucson, head for the **Visitors Bureau** (130 S. Scott Ave., tel. 602/624–1889 or 800/638–8350). If you want guidance, call to check whether the friendly and knowledgeable docents of the **Arizona Historical Society** (tel. 602/628–5774) are conducting any walking tours of the city during your stay; their schedule varies with the season and the day of the week.

Out-of-Town Tours Several tour companies offer bus or van excursions to points throughout southern Arizona. **Gray Line Tours** (Box 1991, Tucson 85702, tel. 602/622–8811) and **Great Western Tours** (Box 31831, Tucson 85751, tel. 602/721–0980) take groups or individuals to destinations such as Bisbee, Thompson Canyon, and Mt. Lemmon. The photography experts of **Arizona Shutterbug Adventures** (*see* Special-Interest Tours, *above*) lead tours to many out-of-town scenic locations.

Exploring Tucson

Tucson covers more than 500 square miles in a valley ringed by mountains; for tours of the area it's necessary to have a car. Downtown, accessible just east of I–10 off the Broadway–Congress exit, is much smaller and easy to navigate on foot. (Streets there don't run true to any sort of grid, however, so it's best to get a good, detailed map.) If you're out walking at any time, stop for frequent breaks to drink fluids: Tucson's dryness can dehydrate visitors quickly, especially if they are accustomed to living in a high-humidity area. Avoid alcohol because it aggravates dehydration, and wear sunscreen and a hat (even in the winter months if you're sun-sensitive).

Highlights for First-time Visitors

Arizona–Sonora Desert Museum (*see* Tour 3)
El Presidio District (*see* Tour 1)
Kitt Peak National Observatory (*see* Tour 5)
Mission San Xavier del Bac (*see* Tour 5)
Mt. Lemmon (*see* Tour 4)

Old Town Artisans (*see* Tour 1)
Old Tucson Studios (*see* Tour 3)
Sabino Canyon (*see* Off the Beaten Track)
Saguaro National Monument (*see* Tour 3)
University of Arizona (*see* Tour 2)

Tour 1: El Presidio District

Numbers in the margin correspond to points of interest on the Tucson: Tours 1 and 2 map.

If you're on foot and enjoy historical buildings—as well as a bit of art and shopping—this is the tour for you.

The area bounded by Franklin and Pennington streets on the north and south and by Church and Main streets on the east and west encompasses more than 130 years of the city's architectural history, and dates from the original walled El Presidio del Tucson, a Spanish fortress built in 1776 when Arizona was still part of New Spain. The largest plaza in this historical area is now called **El Presidio Park;** it's bordered on the south side by several modern high-rise government buildings and on the east side by the mosaic-domed **Pima County Courthouse.** This Spanish Colonial–style structure, perhaps Tucson's most beautiful historical building, was built in 1927 on the site of the original single-story adobe court of 1869; a portion of the original Presidio wall can be seen on the courthouse's second floor. The park itself, an attractive open area with a large modern sculpture in the center, is shared by a combination of city workers and homeless people.

Head north and cross Alameda Street to the Tucson Museum of Art and Historic Block. You can walk around the area on your own, but it's worth catching one of the free tours given by the museum every Wednesday and Thursday at 2 PM from October 1 through May 31. The five historic buildings on this block are listed in the National Register of Historic Places and include La Casa Cordoba, the Fish House, and the Stevens Home (*see below*). The other two residences, the **Romero House,** believed to incorporate another section of the Presidio wall, and the **Corbett House,** occupied for 56 years by the influential Tucson family for whom Hi-Corbett Field is named, are not open to the public. In the center of the museum complex is the **Plaza of the Pioneers,** honoring Tucson's early citizens.

1 If you're ready to go inside, the **Tucson Museum of Art** houses an impressive collection of pre-Columbian art. There is also a permanent display of 20th-century art depicting the West—some wonderful, some less than inspiring. The museum's gift shop features a fine variety of works—jewelry, silk scarves, weavings, ceramics—by local artisans. *140 N. Main Ave., tel. 602/624–2333. Admission: $2 adults, $1 senior citizens and students, children under 12 free; Tues. free. Open Tues.–Sat. 10–4, Sun.*

Tucson: Tours 1 and 2

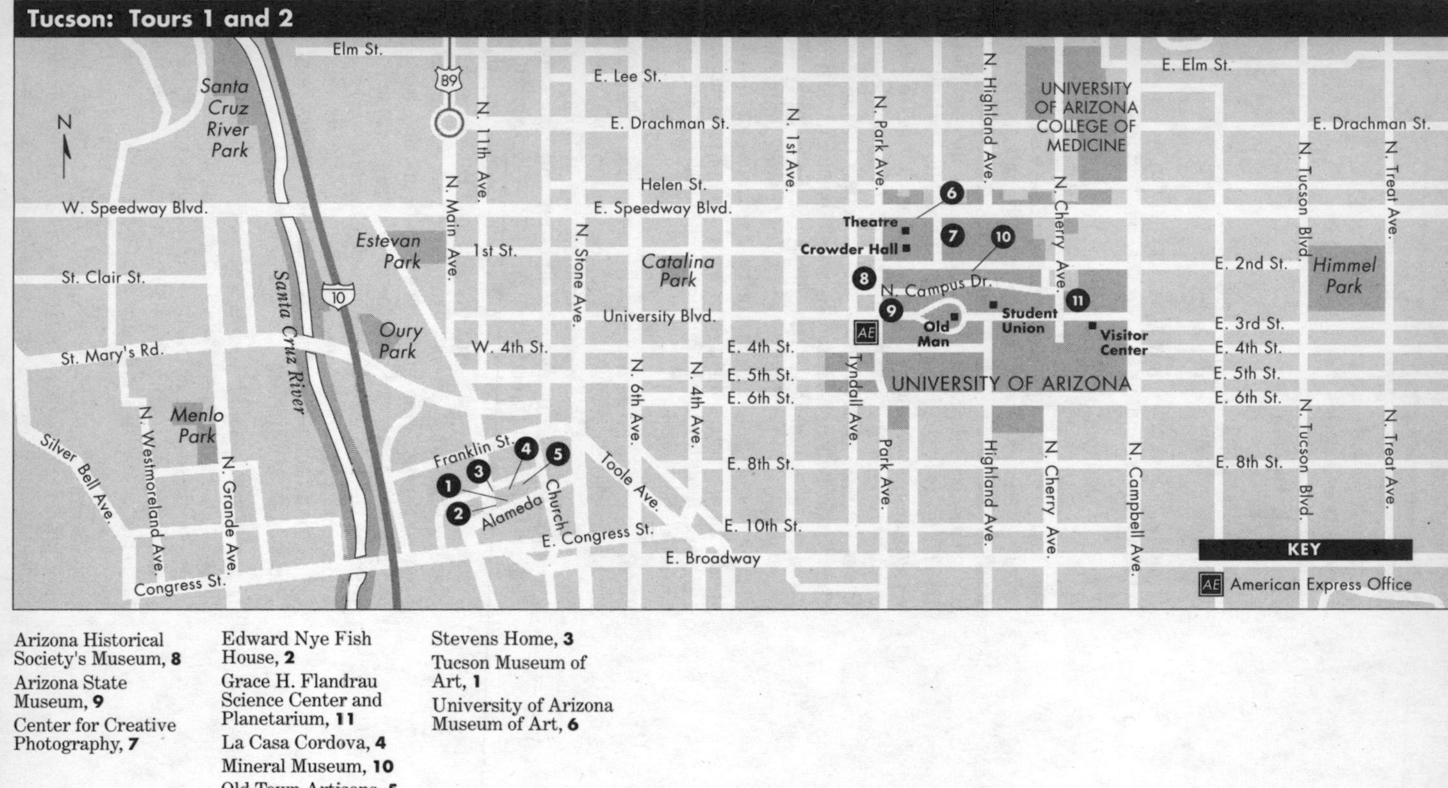

Arizona Historical Society's Museum, **8**

Arizona State Museum, **9**

Center for Creative Photography, **7**

Edward Nye Fish House, **2**

Grace H. Flandrau Science Center and Planetarium, **11**

La Casa Cordova, **4**

Mineral Museum, **10**

Old Town Artisans, **5**

Stevens Home, **3**

Tucson Museum of Art, **1**

University of Arizona Museum of Art, **6**

noon–4. Free docent tours are available Oct.–May, Tues.–Fri. 11 AM and 2 PM, weekends 2 PM. Closed national holidays.

When you leave the museum, walk down Main Avenue to the corner of Alameda (less than a block away) to the
2 **Edward Nye Fish House,** built in 1868 of adobe by the early Tucson merchant for whom it is named. Fish, a merchant, entrepreneur, and politician, and his wife, Maria Wakefield Fish, a prominent educator, shaped much of early Tucson history; they hosted such visitors as President and Mrs. Rutherford B. Hayes here. Their residence, notable for its 15-foot beamed ceilings and saguaro-cactus rib supports, now houses the El Presidio art gallery, which sells contemporary and traditional Southwest oils, watercolors, bronzes, and ceramics. *120 N. Main Ave., tel. 602/884-7379. Admission free. Open Mon.–Sat. 10–5, Sun. 1–4; other hours by appointment.*

Also on Main Avenue, just north of the Fish House and ar-
3 chitecturally similar, is the 1865 **Stevens Home.** Here wealthy politician and cattle rancher Hiram Stevens and his Mexican wife, Petra Santa Cruz, entertained many of Tucson's leaders—including Edward and Maria Fish—during the 1880s. A drought brought the Stevenses' cattle ranching to a halt in 1893, and Stevens killed himself—having unsuccessfully attempted to kill his wife—in despair. The house was restored in 1980 and now hosts one of Tucson's best restaurants, Janos (*see* Dining, *below*).

For one of the best examples of simple but elegant adobe ar-
4 chitecture, head across the Plaza of the Pioneers to **La Casa Cordova.** One of the oldest buildings in Tucson, with the original part built in about 1848, it is now home to the Mexican Heritage Museum. When you enter La Casa Cordova through the double doors on Meyer Avenue, the room on your right has an exhibit of the history of the Presidio; three rooms off the patio display furnishings of the Indian and pioneer settlers of the period. If you are lucky enough to be here from November through March, don't miss the Naciemento, a traditional Christmas display filling an entire room with miniatures arranged in elaborate scenes from the Old and New Testaments and from Mexican rural life. When you visit the museum, you'll understand why adobe—brick made of mud and straw, cured in the hot sun—was so widely used in early Tucson. It offers a natural insulation from the heat and cold, and it is durable in Tucson's dry climate. In some cases the woody cactus ribs built into the walls and ceilings for extra support poke through the hard-packed adobe. *175 N. Meyer Ave., tel. 602/624-2333. Admission free. Open Tues.–Sat. 10–4, Sun. noon–4. Closed national holidays.*

Retrace your steps through the double doors of Casa Cordo-
5 va, cross Meyer Avenue, and you'll see **Old Town Artisans** across the street. Another 19th-century adobe building, re-

stored as a 13-room marketplace, it features the wares of more than 175 craftspeople, most of them local. It's a wonderful place to buy gifts, everything from wind chimes, glass art, pottery, and jewelry to homemade salsa. *186 N. Meyer Ave., tel. 602/623–6024 (recording) or 602/623–8276. Open Mon.–Sat. 9:30–5:30, Sun. noon–5; summer hours are shorter.*

Time Out Those seeking either a snack or a full meal can sit out on the pretty patio of the **Courtyard Café** (tel. 602/622–0351) at the Old Town Artisans Patio. The menu includes tasty soups, salads, sandwiches, and nachos.

Tour 2: University of Arizona Neighborhood

A university—especially in the Southwest—might not seem to be the most likely spot for a vacation, but this one is unusual. Not only is the institution itself of historical importance, but it also hosts museums for special interests ranging from photography to mineralogy. Parking in the university area is a hassle, so it's best either to leave your rental car elsewhere or take extra care to park it legally in a university lot. Although there are several lots throughout the campus, they're often crowded, so it's a good idea to park in the first legal spot you find. Read and heed all the signs: They mean business.

The U of A, as the University of Arizona is known locally (versus ASU, its rival state university in Phoenix), covers 325 acres and is a major economic influence for the city. More than 35,000 students attend graduate and undergraduate classes here. The original land for the university was "donated" by a couple of gamblers and a saloon owner, and $25,000 of territorial money was used to build Old Main (the original building) and hire six faculty members. The money ran out before the Old Main's roof was placed, but a few enlightened local citizens pitched in with the funds to finish it. Most of the city's populace was less enthusiastic about the institution: They were disgruntled when the 13th Territorial Legislature granted the University of Arizona to Tucson and awarded rival Phoenix with what they considered to be the real prize—an insane asylum and a prison.

Note: For all of the university's institutions, it's best to call ahead and verify opening and closing hours; budget cuts in 1992 have caused schedule changes in a number of cases.

Start your tour on the northwestern corner of campus, at the junction of Speedway and Olive roads. Here you'll find
6 the **University of Arizona Museum of Art,** with a wide-ranging collection of European paintings from the Renaissance through the 17th century. A collection of bronze and plaster sculptures by Jacques Lipschitz is a highlight of the museum. *Tel. 602/621–7567. Admission free. Open Sept.–May,*

weekdays 9–5, Sun. noon–4; June, weekdays 10–3:30; July–Aug., weekdays 10–3:30, Sun. noon–4. Closed Sat., national and state holidays. Call ahead to verify hours.

Those interested in a more contemporary art form should
7 head for the **Center for Creative Photography,** just southeast of and across the street (Olive Road) from the University of Arizona Museum of Art. Set up to house the university's extensive Ansel Adams holdings, this is one of the world's largest collections of 20th-century photography, including works by such artists as Paul Strand, W. Eugene Smith, and Edward Weston. Changing exhibits in the main gallery highlight various holdings of the collection, but if you'd like to spend an hour looking at the pictures of a particular photographer in the center's archives, call to arrange an appointment. *1030 N. Olive Rd., tel. 602/621–7968. Admission free. Open Sept.–May, weekdays 11–5, Sun. noon–5; June–Aug., Sun.–Fri. noon–5. Closed Sat., national and state holidays.*

Head directly south one block on Park Avenue to the
8 **Arizona Historical Society's Museum.** If you're driving and this is your first stop, park your car in the lot at the corner of 2nd and Euclid streets and then inquire at the museum about the token system. Well-displayed exhibits transport the visitor through Arizona history, starting with the Hohokam Indians and Spanish explorers and highlighting important influences such as mining and cattle ranching. Children are welcome, and several exhibits are geared to the interests of older young people. The museum's gift shop focuses on items from the late 1800s; many are reproductions, but there are a number of antiques as well. Unusual souvenirs are also available at the library, which houses an extensive collection of historical Arizona photographs and sells reprints of most of them for a small fee. *949 E. 2nd St., tel. 602/628–5774. Admission free. Open Mon.–Sat. 10–4, Sun. noon–4. Closed national and state holidays.*

If you're interested in learning more about the original inhabitants of the state, head farther south for about three blocks, staying on Park Avenue. On University Boulevard,
9 just inside the main gate of the university, is the **Arizona State Museum,** the oldest in the state, dating from territorial days (1893). Dioramas highlight wildlife native to the area, and extensive displays contrast the different lifestyles of Arizona's Native American tribes. One of the more unlikely exhibits is the world's largest collection of tree rings. *Park Ave. (at University Blvd., just inside the main gate), tel. 602/621–6302. Admission free. Open Mon.–Sat. 9–5, Sun. 2–5. Closed national holidays.*

Walk directly east from the Arizona State Museum about three blocks to Old Main and head straight north (left) for three blocks to the Geology, Mines, and Metallurgy Build-
10 ing. Here you'll find the **Mineral Museum,** which houses an extensive, well-displayed collection of fossils and minerals.

Children will enjoy the huge dinosaur footprint and the fossil that shows the flying reptile from millions of years ago. *Old Geology Bldg., N. Campus Dr. (2nd bldg. west of parking garage at 2nd St. and Mountain Ave.), tel. 602/621-4227. Admission free. Open weekdays 8–3. Closed university holidays.*

Time Out When you leave this museum, you'll be across the street (North Campus Drive) from the **Student Union,** where there are places to graze or eat a full meal. All eateries in the building are casual, ranging from snack bars offering sandwiches and burgers to an informal sit-down Mexican restaurant. There is also a post office, a small variety store, a bookstore, and even a movie theater.

11 After you recharge your batteries at the Student Union, head directly east two blocks to the **Grace H. Flandrau Science Center and Planetarium** on Cherry Avenue at the Mall, an open grassy area. Tucson is a major center for astronomy; lighting ordinances have been designed here to allow viewing of the usually clear desert skies at night, even in the center city. Planetarium attractions include a 16-inch public telescope, the impressive Star Theatre, where a multimedia show brings astronomy to life, and an interactive meteor exhibit. Laser light shows are held here at night. Take your camera; special adapters allow you to take pictures through the telescopes. *Cherry Ave. and University Blvd., tel. 602/621-4515. Theater admission: $3.75 adults, $3 senior citizens, students, and children 3–18, children under 3 not admitted; laser light shows: $5; family laser shows on weekends: $3.75. Open Mon. 9–5, Tues.–Thurs. 9–5 and 7–9:30, Fri. 9–5 and 7–midnight, Sat. 1–5 and 7–midnight, Sun. 1–5. Showtimes vary; call 602/621-7827 for recorded message. Telescope hours during the summer are Tues.–Sat. 8–10 PM; in winter, Tues.–Sat. 7–10 PM.*

Tour 3: Tucson Mountain Park and Saguaro National Monument West

Numbers in the margin correspond to points of interest on the Tucson: Tours 3–5 map.

If you have a car at your disposal and are interested in getting to know the flora and fauna of the Sonora Desert—as well as some of its depictions in the cinema—this is an ideal trip for you. If you don't drive, at least consider taking one of the many tours to the Arizona–Sonora Desert Museum (*see* Guided Tours in Essential Information, *above*) in the 17,000-acre **Tucson Mountain Park.** Also within the boundaries of the park, which is just south of Saguaro National Monument West, is Old Tucson theme park. Your best plan is to head out early in the morning to Saguaro National Monument, the farthest of the three and the one without shaded areas for you to duck into. Then spend the rest of the morning at the Arizona–Sonora Desert Museum, and at lunchtime go over to Old Tucson, which offers the best choice of eateries. Most of the shows featured in Old Tucson do not start until noon, in any case.

From Tucson, take Speedway Boulevard west to where it joins Anklam Road and becomes Gates Pass Road; here you will see signs for Old Tucson Studios. At this juncture Gates Pass Road becomes Kinney Road; continue on for
about 12 miles (passing signs for the Arizona–Sonora De-
12 sert Museum) until you come to **Saguaro National Monu-
ment West.** The two portions of the Saguaro National Monument are separated by the city of Tucson: The eastern portion covers more than 62,000 acres and climbs through five climate zones; the smaller western portion, the one explored on this tour, has more than 21,000 acres, all approximately at the same elevation. Both sections of the park are forested by the huge saguaro (pronounced "suh-WAR-oh") cactus, which is native to the Sonora Desert and known for its towering height (often 50 feet) and arms that reach out in weird configurations. The cactus is ribbed vertically with accordionlike pleats that expand to store water gathered through its shallow roots during the infrequent desert rain showers. In the springtime (usually April or May), the giant succulent sports a tiny party hat of brightly colored blooms. At any time of year, the sight of these kings of the desert ruling over their quiet domain is awe-inspiring.

These slow-growing cacti (they can take up to 15 years to grow 1 foot) are protected by state and federal laws, so enjoy but don't disturb them. In recent years, they have suffered a decline because a decrease in the coyote population has led to an abundant rabbit population. Rabbits and other small animals nibble at the base of the young saguaro, gathering nutrients and water for survival and thereby hindering or halting the cactus's slow growth.

You'll see the most wildlife if you go through the park early in the morning, when the animals are at their liveliest. Desert critters such as snakes and scorpions aren't necessarily hostile unless you crowd them, so just watch your step and respect their habitat.

The visitor center at the Saguaro National Monument West is worth a stop in to peruse the assortment of books and brochures on desert flora and fauna. In addition, there's often an exhibit showcasing photography of the area, and you can get information here on the various hiking trails in the park. Rangers are knowledgeable and friendly and can also advise you on the best places to see a sunrise or, in season, desert flowers. *Tel. 602/883–6366. Admission free. Open daily 8–5.*

About another half-mile south of the visitor center, on
13 Kinney Road, the **Arizona–Sonora Desert Museum** is not to
be missed; it's the second most popular tourist attraction—

Tucson: Tours 3–5
0
2 miles
0
3 km
N
Marana
Silverbell Rd.
Silverbell Rd.
Silver Bell
Avra Valley Rd.
Avra Valley Rd.
Trico Rd.
Tangerine Rd.
Rillito
Santa Cruz River
Oro Valley
Mt. Lemmon Ski Valley
Summerhaven
Bear Wallow
Mt. Bigelow
CORONADO NATIONAL FOREST
Ina Rd.
Orange Grove Rd.
Sandario Rd.
Manville Rd.
El Camino de Cerro
Roger Rd.
River Rd.
Saguaro National Monument (West)
Tanque Verde
Grant Rd.
Speedway
Tanque Verde Creek
Broadway
22nd St.
University of Arizona
Campbell Ave.
6th Ave.
TUCSON
Arizona-Sonora Desert Museum
Gates Pass Rd.
Tucson Mountain County Park
Old Tucson Studios
Kinney Rd.
TOHONO O'ODHAM INDIAN RESERVATION (PAPAGO)
Brawley Wash
Hill Rd.
South Tucson
Escalante Rd.
Wilmot Rd.
Saguaro National Monument (East)
Valencia Rd.
Ajo Highway
Mission Rd.
Tucson International Airport
Houghton Rd.
Old Spanish Tr.
CORONADO NATIONAL FOREST
Three Points
SAN XAVIER INDIAN RESERVATION
Mission San Xavier Del Bac
Sasabe Rd.
Kitt Peak National Observatory
Mountain View
10
89
86
19
12
13
14
15
16
17
18

after the Grand Canyon—in the state. The name "museum" is misleading for this site, which is more like a beautifully planned zoo. In this microcosm of a desert environment, hummingbirds, cactus wrens, rattlesnakes, scorpions, bighorn sheep, and even beavers all busy themselves in a natural habitat ingeniously planned to allow the visitor to look on without disturbing them. Besides the wildlife exhibits, there is also the Earth Sciences Center, which features a damp limestone cave and meteor and mineral displays that encourage visitors to feel the texture of the stones and inspect them under magnifying glasses. Exhibits and interactive programs change with the season. For example, during the spring visitors are invited to help identify local wildflowers.

Allow at least two hours for your visit to the museum, longer if you have some real nature lovers with you. You'll be outdoors most of the time, so take a jacket if you're visiting in winter and take frequent water breaks if you're visiting in summer; it can get really hot and dry here. Wheelchairs and strollers are available; no pets allowed. *2021 N. Kinney Rd., tel. 602/883–2702. Admission: $7.95 adults, $1.50 children 6–12, children 5 and under free. Open Mar.–Sept., daily 7:30–6; Oct.–Feb., daily 8:30–5. Ticket sales stop 1 hr before closing time.*

14 Go another 2 miles south on Kinney Road to get to **Old Tucson Studios.** Signs all along the way from town will direct you to this film set cum theme park, which will look familiar to you if you've seen even one old western flick. More than 250 westerns have been shot here duirng the last 50 years, including *Gunfight at the OK Corral*, *Rio Lobo*, and *The Last Outpost*, starring Ronald Reagan. The TV series "High Chaparral," "Little House on the Prairie," and, more recently, "The Young Riders" have all used the set of frontier and adobe buildings of Old Tucson as a backdrop.

Time Out Enjoy Ruby's Red Garter Revue, a corny but fun honkytonk show, while having a burger or ribs at the **Red Dog Palace Saloon** at Old Tucson. There are also a half-dozen other places in the complex where you can have a snack or a drink.

Young children may be frightened by the loud gunfights staged in the streets, but the older ones will love them. Sheriff's deputies constantly run after bad guys (all local actors), and willing visitors are enlisted to take part in the chase through the park. Less energetic guests can sit down to view some of the films shot on location here. Other attractions include magic shows, stunt shows, a petting farm, stagecoach rides—and, as you might imagine, souvenir shops galore. Snacks can be purchased at food shops, and the Royal Oak Saloon offers full meals. *201 S. Kinney Rd. (inside Tucson Mountain Park), tel. 602/883–6457. Admission: $10.95 adults, $6.95 children 4–11, children 3 and un-*

der free; after 5 PM $6.95 adults, $6.20 children. Open daily 9–9.

Tour 4: Mt. Lemmon

This tour takes you to the southernmost ski slope of the continental United States, but you don't have to be a skier to visit; during the warm months, you can enjoy hiking and picnicking in this lovely area. In summertime, the mountain's 9,157-foot elevation brings welcome relief from the heat, and in the winter, the craggy old mountain often sports a cap of snow that draws all levels of slope enthusiasts.

Mt. Lemmon is one of the Santa Catalina Mountains, which stand guard over the southern rim of the valley that is Tucson. Every 1,000 feet of elevation in these mountains is equivalent to traveling 300 miles north—thus the vegetation at the top of Mt. Lemmon is similar to that found in southern Canada. Standing in a forest of pines blanketed by snow, you might have trouble remembering that there's a desert with cacti and wildflowers less than 35 miles away.

If you're making the trip in the winter, check road conditions with the **Pima County Sheriff's Department** (tel. 602/741–4900). For temperate days, consider packing a picnic lunch. Wear layers of clothing so you can cool or warm yourself as you change elevation. And be sure to fill up the tank before you leave town because there are no gas stations on Mt. Lemmon Highway.

If all's clear, take I–10, Speedway Road exit, and head east 10 miles to Pantano Road; then turn north, drive 1½ miles, and turn east onto Tanque Verde Road. Go another 1½ miles and turn north onto Catalina Highway, which becomes Mt. Lemmon Highway. Drive this road for 30 twisting, climbing miles until you come to Mt. Lemmon Ski Valley—unless the heat inspires you to turn off a little side road to the cool, charming village of Summerhaven. It's not a good idea to take trailers and recreational vehicles on this mountain road, and it's best for all drivers to travel during daylight hours. Safety aside, it would be a pity to miss seeing the rock formations along the way; they look as though they were carefully balanced against one another by architects from another planet.

Hikers can take any number of side trips on this tour; information on routes and weather conditions is available from the Pima County Sheriff's Department. There are some 150 miles of well-marked and well-maintained trails in the Mt. Lemmon area, for all levels of expertise. Of the several trails around Rose Canyon Lake, a good one for beginners is the **Green Mountain Trail,** which starts a half mile past the Rose Canyon turnoff from Mt. Lemmon Highway. The route takes you 4 miles (one-way) from San Pedro Vista—with lovely mountain views to the east—to General

Hitchcock Campground. More experienced hikers will enjoy the half-mile trek, ascending more than 600 feet, to the top of **Mt. Bigelow** from the Palisades ranger station. It's coming down that's the hard part. For guided walks, *see* Hiking, *below*.

15 If you brought your lunch, watch for **Bear Wallow** just after milepost 22 on Mt. Lemmon Highway. There are picnic areas and plenty of room to stretch out under a tree for a siesta. You probably won't see any bears, but the variety of birds is astounding. Watch for electric-blue Steller's jays and hummingbirds of many varieties.

16 Mt. Lemmon Highway ends at **Mt. Lemmon Ski Valley** (tel. 602/576–1321 or 602/576–1400 [recorded snow report]). Skiing here depends on natural conditions—that is, there's no artificial snow—so call ahead for information; some winters there's plenty of powder, and others it's rather scarce. There are 16 runs, open daily, ranging from beginner's to advanced. Lift tickets cost $25 for an all-day pass and $20 for a half day (starting at 1 PM); children 12 and under ski for $10. Ski equipment can be rented, and private instructions start at $16 an hour. Summertime (late May through September) visitors will enjoy a ride on the double-chair lift that whisks them to the top of the slope—some 9,100 feet. The cost is $4 for adults and $2 for children under 12. Many hikers ride the lift and then head out on one of several trails that crisscross the summit.

Time Out The **Iron Door** (tel. 602/576–1321) in Mt. Lemmon Ski Valley is open for breakfast on weekends from 9:30 AM, with all the hearty American standards and plenty of hot coffee. On weekdays, sandwiches and other lunch foods are served beginning at 10 AM. During the winter, the focus is on burgers, chili, corn bread, and soups; in warmer weather, lots of salads turn up on the menu. This place is popular on the weekends, and parking is limited.

Tour 5: Mission San Xavier del Bac and Kitt Peak National Observatory

Head to the second-largest Indian reservation in the country, that of the Tohonó O'odham tribe, for a mountain drive and a tour of a national observatory, with a stop at a historical mission. It's at least 10°F cooler on Kitt Peak than it is in Tucson, so in winter take along a jacket. There are few stations along the road, so fill the car with gas before you leave town.

Drive southwest of Tucson 9 miles on San Xavier Road, off I–19, and you'll see the shining White Dove of the Desert,
17 or **Mission San Xavier del Bac** (tel. 602/294–2624), miles before you actually reach the turnoff road. San Xavier del Bac, the oldest Catholic church in the United States still

serving the community for which it was built, was founded in 1692 by the Jesuits and built of native materials by Franciscan missionaries between 1777 and 1797. Today it is owned by the Tohonó O'odham Indian tribe (the name means "Desert People Who Have Come from the Earth"). Legends surround the mission. The bell tower remains unfinished, it is said, because a workman fell to his death from there; no one dared to go up afterward because his ghost haunted it. (In fact, the unfinished bell tower was probably a ploy to fool the Spanish IRS, which could not levy its heavy taxes on buildings until they were completed.) Daily mass is celebrated at 8:30 AM, and at 8 AM, 9:30 AM, 11 AM, and 12:30 PM on Sunday. On Sundays and religious holidays, there's often a mariachi band—one of the many Mexican influences in evidence here. Call for information about special celebrations.

The beauty of the mission, with elements of Spanish, Baroque, and *mudejar* (Spanish Islamic) architectural styles, is highlighted by the stark desert landscape against which it is set. Among the ornate carvings above the entrance is one of a cat chasing a mouse. Legend has it that the church will belong to the people for whom it was built, the Tohonó O'odham Indians, until the cat catches the mouse; another holds that the capture of the mouse will mark the end of the world. Inside, there's a wealth of painted statues, carvings, and frescoes; the mission has been called the Sistine Chapel of the United States by Paul Schwartzbaum, who worked on restoring Michelangelo's masterwork in Rome and is helping to supervise the restoration of the mission's artwork that began in 1992. A visitors center in the front part of San Xavier del Bac offers displays of the history and architecture of the church; it's adjoined by a gift shop, open from 9 to 5.

Across the parking lot from the mission, San Xavier Plaza has a number of shops that sell fine Native American crafts. Much of the work is by the Tohonó O'odham Indians (look especially for jewelry, pottery, and baskets featuring the man-in-the-maze designs, and for friendship bowls, both particular to the tribe), but works of the northern Arizona Hopi and Navajo are also represented.

Time Out For wonderful Indian fry bread—large, round pieces of dough brought up fresh from the hot oil and topped with all sorts of delicious possibilities—stop in **The Wa:k Snack Shop** (tel. 602/573–9923) at the back of the plaza. You can also have breakfast or a Mexican lunch here.

When you leave the mission, drive 9 miles back to I–19. Take Exit 99 (Ajo Way) west onto AZ 86, then drive 36 miles to the junction with AZ 286. Turn left and start your 13-mile ascent up the winding road to Kitt Peak (elevation 6,882 feet), part of the Quinlan Mountain range.

At the visitor center, orientation films are shown daily at 10:30 AM and 1:30 PM; free guided tours lasting about an hour are given after the 1:30 film during the week and after both films on weekends and holidays. Complimentary brochures enable you to take self-guided tours. A gift shop sells excellent examples of Tohonó O'odham handiwork as well as astronomy-related items.

18 Funded by the National Science Foundation and managed by a group of more than 20 universities, **Kitt Peak National Observatory** is part of the Tohonó O'odham reservation. After much discussion back in the late 1950s, tribal leaders agreed to share their 2.8 million acres—only the Navajo have more land—with the observatory's 19 telescopes. Among these is the McMath, the world's largest solar telescope, which is cooled by piped-in coolant. From a visitors' gallery, you can see into the telescope's light-path tunnel, which goes down hundreds of feet into the mountain. In addition to the vital research into aspects of the sun carried out here, Kitt Peak scientists have also observed distant galaxies. The scientists and staff are friendly and knowledgeable and keen to share their enthusiasm for astronomy; you never get the sense here, as you do at other serious scientific installations, that you are intruding. A picnic area is about 1½ miles below the observatory; aside from vending machines in the observatory buildings, there is no place to get food within 20 miles of Kitt Peak. *National Optical Astronomy Observatories (Kitt Peak), tel. 602/620–5350 or 602/325–9200 for recorded message. Admission free. Open daily 10–4. Closed Thanksgiving, Christmas Eve and Day, New Year's Day.*

What to See and Do with Children

There are plenty of things to occupy children in Tucson and southern Arizona. Besides the activities listed here, a number are cited in Participant Sports and Outdoor Activities, below. (Remember, however, that when you take children outdoors, their skin is especially prone to sunburn and windburn. Protect them with hats and sunscreen, and offer liquids frequently to prevent dehydration.) Many resorts also have activities designed to entertain children while their parents sightsee without them. Inquire when you make reservations.

Arizona–Sonora Desert Museum (*see* Tour 3, *above*).

Biosphere 2. This is a trip for school-aged children; little ones will enjoy being outdoors but won't really appreciate the tour. (*See* Off the Beaten Track, *below.*)

The dry limestone **Colossal Cave,** 20 miles east of Tucson and 6 miles north of I–10, is filled with stalagmites and stalactites. The cave has never been fully explored, and legend has it that gold is hidden in the dark recesses. *Old Spanish Trail Rd., tel. 602/791–7677. Admission: $5.50* *adults, $4 children 11–16, $2.50 children 6–10, children 5 and under free. Open Oct.–Mar., Mon.–Sat. 9–5, Sun. and holidays 9–6; Apr.–Sept., Mon.–Sat. 8–6, Sun. and holidays 8–7.*

Children love the old-fashioned melodramas at the **Gaslight Theatre** (7010 E. Broadway, tel. 602/886–9428), where hissing the villain and cheering the hero are part of the audience's duty. Tickets are $12 for adults, $10 for students and senior citizens, and $6 for children 12 and under. There is free popcorn, and beer and soft drinks are available.

At **Golf 'n' Stuff Family Fun Centers,** children can play video games and miniature golf, ride bumper boats, and drive little race cars. *6503 E. Tanque Verde Rd., tel. 602/296–2366. No admission fee; each attraction priced separately. Open Sun.–Thurs. 10 AM–10 PM, Fri.–Sat. 10 AM–1 AM.*

International Wildlife Museum allows youngsters to touch and feel different animal skins, and teaches them many other things about more than 200 species of birds and mammals from all over the world. There's a theater that shows wildlife films, a gift shop, and a small restaurant that features buffalo burgers. *4800 W. Gates Pass Rd., tel. 602/624–4024. Admission: $4 adults, $3.50 senior citizens, students, and military, $1.50 children 6–12, children under 6 free. Open Wed.–Sun. 9–5:30. Closed Thanksgiving, Christmas, and New Year's Day.*

The small but well-designed **Reid Park Zoo** won't tax the children's—or your—patience. If you're visiting in the summertime, go early while the animals are active. *1100 S. Randolph Way, tel. 602/881–4753. Admission: $2 adults, $1.50 senior citizens, 50¢ children 5–14, children 4 and under free. Open Sept. 15–Mar. 14, daily 9:30–4:30; Mar. 15–Sept. 14, weekdays 8:30–3:30, weekends 8:30–5:30.*

At **Tucson Children's Museum,** kids are encouraged to touch and explore the exhibits, which are oriented toward science, language, and history. There are fun things to do—and learn—for children of all ages. *200 S. 6th Ave., tel. 602/884–7511. Admission: $3 adults, $1.50 senior citizens and children 3–14. Open Tues.–Fri. 9–4, Sat. 10–5, Sun. 1–5.*

Off the Beaten Track

It sounds a bit like the stuff of science fiction: In order to study how human beings can live in harmony with their environment, eight persons set up housekeeping for two years in an enclosed three-acre environment. But this exercise in recycling on a grand scale is going on now at **Biosphere 2.**

To get to Biosphere 2, drive north on Oracle Road (U.S. 89), a major north–south road through Tucson, to Oracle Junction, where the road turns into AZ 77. Drive 5½ miles northeast to milepost 96.5, follow the signs for a half mile to SunSpace Ranch Conference Center Road, make a right turn, and drive 2 miles to the guard gate. You'll be required to sign in here before you proceed the final half mile to Biosphere 2. No pets, tape recorders, or cameras are allowed inside, and no picknicking is permitted on the site.

The miniature world created within Biosphere includes a tropical rain forest, savanna, desert, thorn scrub, marsh, ocean, and agricultural area as well as a living area for the humans who inhabit the sphere—along with 3,800 plant and animal species. The privately funded project is being watched with interest—as well as some skepticism—by scientists all over the world; there has been a good deal of controversy regarding the credentials of the project's participants and certain equipment being used to help control the environment. Walking tours—given continually and lasting about two hours—don't enter the sphere, of course, which was sealed in late 1991, but a film explains the project, and visitors are able to look at the human and animal residents through observation areas. Much of the tour is outdoors: Wear a hat, walking shoes, and sunscreen. The Canyon del Oro Dining Room, overlooking the Santa Catalina Mountains, offers meals and snacks. Attractive, reasonably priced hotel rooms, also with excellent views, are available on Biosphere's premises. *Hwy. 77, mile marker 96.5, tel. 602/825-6200. Admission: $11.95 adults, $10.95 senior citizens, $6 children 5–16, children 4 and under free. Open daily 9–4.*

On the way back into town from Biosphere, you might want to stop off at **Tohono Chul Park,** which is making its own effort to preserve our environment—specifically the desert region. On its 35 acres, a demonstration garden, greenhouse, geology wall, and other exhibits educate visitors about the unique area, while shady nooks and nature trails allow for leisurely sitting or strolling. Two gift shops, a small art gallery, a tearoom (*see* Dining, *below*), and the Haunted Bookshop (*see* Shopping, *below*) are additional reasons to visit this lovely landscaped setting. *7366 Paseo del Norte, tel. 602/742-6455. Admission: $2 donation suggested. Park open daily 7 AM–sunset; building open Mon.–Sat. 9:30–5, Sun. 11–5.*

All year round, but especially during summer, locals flock to **Sabino Canyon** in the northeast corner of town. Part of the Coronado National Forest but filled with saguaros and other desert flora and fauna, this is a good spot for hiking, picnicking, or enjoying the waterfalls, streams, natural swimming holes, and shade trees that provide a respite from the heat. No cars are allowed; a narrated tram ride (45 minutes round-trip) takes you to the top of the canyon and another takes you to adjacent Bear Canyon. When there's a full moon, nighttime tram tours are offered. *Sabino Canyon Rd. in the Santa Catalina foothills, tel. 602/749-2861* *or 602/749–8700. Tram fare: $5 adults, $2 children 3–12, children 2 and under free; Bear Canyon tram fare: $3 adults, $1.25 children. Call for tram schedules, which change throughout the year. Visitor center open weekdays 8–4:30, weekends 8:30–4:30.*

Tucson for Free

De Grazia's Gallery in the Sun is the museum, gallery, workshop, former home, and gravesite of Arizona's best-known, most-loved artist, Ted DeGrazia, who depicted Southwest Indian and Mexican life. From the metal mineshaft doors at the entranceway to the polished saguaro tiles in the floor, the museum is as appealing as the paintings on the wall. Built by the artist himself with the help of Native American friends, the sprawling, spacious single-story museum utilizes only natural material from the surrounding desert. Adjacent to the museum is the Mission in the Sun, a hand-built adobe chapel covered with De Grazia murals; it was completed in 1952 and dedicated to Our Lady of Guadalupe, patron saint of the Yaqui Indians and of Mexico. Close to the chapel is the artist's grave, frontier style, covered by a mound of rocks. None of DeGrazia's original oil paintings, sculptures, or watercolors are for sale, but the museum's gift shop offers a wide selection of cards, prints, lithographs, ceramics, and books by and about the colorful artist. *6300 N. Swan Rd., tel. 602/299–9191. Admission free. Open daily 10–4.*

Shopping

There are a lot of special gifts and souvenirs to be found in the Tucson area. **Native American crafts** range from exquisite jewelry and basketry to the more pedestrian (but still authentic) tourist items. You'll see an abundance of both varieties in shops and even in some department stores. **Locally produced food items** can be fun to give to friends at home: orange-blossom honey, cactus honey, cactus candy, and pepper salsa are a few treats to consider. Desert Rose Salsa is a popular item among both natives and visitors. If you call many of Tucson's Mexican restaurants a couple of days ahead, they will freeze some fresh tamales for you to transport in a special package with dry ice. (If you plan to try this, call your airline to make arrangements.) And if you're in Tucson during citrus season, consider stopping at one of the many roadside stands whose signs proclaim "We ship!" and investigate sending a box of grapefruit or oranges back home.

Hard-core bargain hunters usually head for **Nogales,** the Mexican border town south of Tucson. To get there, drive south on I–19 for 63 miles. Prices are low (be sure to bargain for the best deal), and you'll find some well-crafted items as well as plenty of schlock (Nogales probably has the most onyx chess sets east of Tijuana).

Those looking for work by regional artists should head for **Tubac,** an artist's community 45 miles south of Tucson, just off I–19 at Exit 34. The more than 70 shops—mostly staffed by the artists who make the goods sold in them—range from carved wooden furniture and hand-thrown pottery to delicately painted tiles and silk-screened fabrics. The Annual Tubac Festival of the Arts has been held in February for more than 30 years; for exact dates, contact the Tubac Chamber of Commerce (tel. 602/398–2704).

If you want to get the real flavor of Tucson, peek into its many shops, stores, and boutiques downtown, a few of the more distinctive of which are noted below. The **Fourth Avenue Merchants Association** (509½ N. 4th Ave., tel. 602/624–5004) represents the many artsy boutiques and restaurants on 4th Avenue between 2nd and 9th streets, near the University of Arizona. If you need a serious shopping fix—but one not particularly unique to Tucson—there is no shortage of malls in town.

Malls

Tucson Mall (4500 N. Oracle Rd. at Wetmore Rd., tel. 602/293–7330) is probably the most heavily shopped mall in town, serving both the sophisticated and the family shopper with two floors of stores, including Dillard's, Broadway Southwest, Sears, J C Penney, and almost 200 other smaller specialty shops. For tasteful southwestern T-shirts, belts, jewelry, and posters, try Señor Coyote, on the second floor of the mall.

El Con Mall (3601 E. Broadway at Alvernon Way, tel. 602/327–8767) is Tucson's oldest mall and has more than 130 stores, including J C Penney, Foley's, and Montgomery Ward. Possibly its most popular store is a huge House of Fabrics, headquarters for crafters as well as needleworkers of all persuasions. Quilters, home garment sewers, and decoupage artists all come here for supplies and inspiration.

Park Mall (5870 E. Broadway at Wilmot Rd., tel. 602/748–1222) is the suburban family shopping mecca, one of those utilitarian places where you can get all that practical stuff checked off your list in one trip. It has more than 120 stores, including Sears, Dillard's, and Broadway Southwest.

Foothills Mall (7401 N. La Cholla Blvd. at Ina Rd., tel. 602/297–1999) is a bit more upscale. For a break from shopping at such department stores as Dillard's and Foley's and a variety of tony boutiques, you can visit the Old Pueblo Museum, which offers media shows of southwestern history, among other exhibits.

Specialty Shops

Art Galleries

Check the **Cabat Studio** (627 N. 4th Ave., tel. 602/622–6362) for exceptional southwestern paintings and ceramics by Erni and Rose Cabat. **Impressions II, Ltd.** (2990 N. Swan

Rd., tel. 602/323–3320) features work by R. C. Gorman and many other internationally known artists, as well as art by several talented but well-kept local secrets.

Books **Tohono Chul Park** (*see* Off the Beaten Track, *above*) is home to the **Haunted Bookshop** (tel. 602/297–4843), designed for book lovers of all ages. There's a coffeepot on the porch in the wintertime, plenty of nooks for a quiet read, and a tunnel for children to crawl through. The selection is outstanding—the shop's shelves are packed with books that "haunt" readers until they are read, say the owners—and the staff is extremely helpful.

Settlers West Books & Prints (6420 N. Campbell Ave., tel. 602/577–8749) focuses on books about the Southwest, and offers a large collection of Western and wildlife prints, some of which are limited editions.

Gifts **Old Town Artisans** (*see* Tour 1, *above*) is one place to shop for uniquely Arizonan items, ranging from wind chimes to salsa and cactus candy.

Casas Adobe Shopping Center, at Oracle and Ina roads, is a collection of small shops, many of them specializing in handmade items; among them, **By Hand Gifts** (tel. 602/297–0071) is an excellent artists' cooperative featuring textile arts, paintings, pottery, and jewelry. Don't miss Sally Ann Hall's felt hats. The center has a comfortable courtyard for the nonshoppers in your crowd.

Desert House Crafts (2837 N. Campbell Ave., tel. 602/323–2132) has been part of the Tucson art scene for more than 40 years. Designs are inspired, and execution is flawless.

Native American Arts and Crafts **Bahti Indian Arts** (St. Philip's Plaza, 4300 N. Campbell Ave., tel. 602/577–0290) specializes in Native American art, including high-quality jewelry, pottery, baskets, and more. **Huntington Trading Co.** (111 E. Congress, tel. 602/628–8578) carries masks and pottery made by the Yaqui and Tarahumara Indians. The **Kaibab Shops** (2841 N. Campbell Ave. tel. 602/795–6905) have been selling a wide variety of Native American crafts in Tucson for more than 40 years.

Needlework Supplies Needle artists will enjoy **The West** (5615 E. River Rd., tel. 602/299–1044). Staffed by volunteers who donate profits to local charities, this shop has one of the best selections of needlework supplies in the area.

Western Wear **Corral Western Wear** (5870 E. Broadway Blvd., tel. 602/747–2117), with a large array of shirts, hats, belts, jewelry, and boots, caters to both urban and authentic cowboys and -girls. **The Bootery** (2511 S. Craycroft Rd., tel. 790–1212) has the largest selection of western footwear in town.

Sports and Fitness

Participant Sports

Ballooning What better way to take advantage of Arizona's mild winter months than to take a quiet balloon ride in the early morning hours and get a bird's-eye view of the frisky desert wildlife down below? Many operators offer balloon rides over the Tucson area. When you call or write ahead to make reservations, it makes sense to inquire about the experience of operators (all pilots should have Federal Aviation Administration licenses) and the safety record of the company. Three reputable companies in the region are **Balloon America** (Box 64600, Tucson 85740, tel. 602/299–7744), **A Balloon Experience** (7730 E. Lakeside Dr., Tucson 85730, tel. 602/747–3866), and **A Southern Arizona Balloon Excursion** (Box 5265, Tucson 85703, tel. 602/624–3599). All welcome individuals and groups and offer champagne celebrations and daily flights by FAA-licensed pilots. Prices range from $100 to $200 per person, depending on the company, season, and length of the flight.

Bicycling Tucson has designated bikeways, routes, lanes, and paths for bikers all over the city. You can cycle through rugged terrain, up and down winding roads, or even along frequently used byways in the Tucson area. There are many sights to see while pedaling on the outskirts of Tucson, where you will be likely to encounter less traffic. If you want even more isolated and scenic locations, try some of the mapped biking tours for the southern part of Arizona; contact the **Metropolitan Tucson Convention and Visitors Bureau** (130 S. Scott Ave., tel. 602/624–1817 or 800/638–8350) for additional information.

Reliable and centrally located places for bike rentals include **Broadway Bicycles** (140 S. Sarnoff Dr., tel. 602/296–7819), **Southwest Cycle and Sport** (818 E. University Blvd. tel. 602/791-0818) and **The Bike Shack** (835 N. Park Ave., tel. 602/624–3663; 6970 E. 22nd St., tel. 602/750–0800). Two tour operators, **Arizona Community Bicycle Tours** (tel. 602/322–9867) and **Desert Pedals** (tel. 602/323–8003), also offer rentals.

There are a number of cyclists' clubs in Tucson, and many of them offer tours throughout southern Arizona. Write ahead to **La Touristas** (3450 N. Stone Ave., No. 171, Tucson 85705) and **Tucson Wheelmen** (1016 Chauncey St., Tucson 85719)—neither has an official telephone number—for information about upcoming tours.

Camping There are at least 100 camping areas scattered throughout the southern region of Arizona; the weather's usually good enough year-round—though it can get very chilly at night in the desert—to make sleeping out under the vast, starry night sky an appealing option. Summertime is the time to camp in the state's cooler higher-altitude campgrounds.

The closest public campground to Tucson is probably at **Catalina State Park,** about 9 miles north of town on U.S. 89 (11570 N. Oracle Rd., tel. 602/628–5798). Located in the desert foothills of the Santa Catalinas, the campground accommodates tenters as well as recreational vehiclers. It fills up quickly in good weather because it's close to town; unfortunately, there is no reservation system.

Recreational vehicles can park in any number of facilities around town; the **Metropolitan Tucson Convention and Visitors Bureau** (130 S. Scott Ave., tel. 602/624–1889 or 800/638–8350) can provide information about specific locations.

The *Arizona Campground Directory* lists all the campgrounds in the state. For a copy—and for additional information on camping in southern Arizona—contact the Arizona Office of Tourism (1100 W. Washington, Phoenix 85007, tel. 602/542–8687).

Golfing There are five **municipal golf courses** within the city of Tucson (Randolph North, Randolph South, El Rio, Fred Enke, and Silverbell); call one week in advance (tel. 602/791–4336) for weekday reservations at any of them. For further details about these courses, contact Tucson Parks and Recreation Department (tel. 602/791–4873).

If you want to explore some of the golf courses to the south of Tucson, try **Meadow Hills Country Club** (3425 Country Club Rd., Nogales 85621, tel. 602/281–0011) in Nogales or **Rio Rico Resort and Country Club** (1550 Camino a la Posada, Rio Rico 85621, tel. 602/281–8567). In Sierra Vista, there's **Pueblo del Sol Golf Club** (2770 St. Andrews Dr., Sierra Vista 85635, tel. 602/378–6444). In Pearce, 20 miles south of I–10 on U.S. 666, **Arizona Sunsites Country Club** (Box 384, Pearce 85625, tel. 602/826–3412) and **Twin Lakes Golf Club** (Rex Allen Jr. Rd., Willcox 85643, tel. 602/384–2720) are both good choices. All the courses listed above are open to visitors.

Many of the resorts have their own full-size golf course or access to one; check when making reservations. Those interested in a golfing vacation might want to contact the **Arizona Golf Association** (*see* Chapter 1, Essential Information).

Hiking Tucson is a wonderful place for hiking; there are many desert trails to explore in the winter, and in summer the nearby mountain ranges offer cooler trekking options. The Exploring section (*see* Tours 3, 4, and 5, *above*) offers some options for day trips that include good hiking opportunities: **Tucson Mountain Park, Mt. Lemmon,** and **Kitt Peak. Sabino Canyon** (*see* Off the Beaten Track, *above*) has a variety of trails closer to town. In addition, for hiking inside Tucson city limits, you might test your skills climbing trails up Sentinel Peak, generally called **"A" Mountain** (it sports a huge *A* first painted on it by fans of a victorious university football team in 1915). State and city parks in the area also offer a variety of hiking experiences; there are literally hundreds of trails within the immediate Tucson area. **Catalina State Park** (11570 N. Oracle Rd. [U.S. 89], tel. 602/628-5798), less than 10 miles north of town, is crisscrossed by hiking trails.

If you want to go a bit farther afield, directly south of Tucson are the Huachuca Mountains, home of **Ramsey Canyon,** a bird-watcher's paradise. The Santa Ritas, closer to the metropolis of Tucson, host another bird lovers' haven, **Madera Canyon,** plus many other enjoyable hiking trails around the area. Farther south, past the Huachuca Mountain range, you can wander in and out of old **ghost towns** such as Fort Duquesne, Pearce, and Washington Camp in the Patagonia Mountains. To the east of Tucson, beyond the Rincons and the Whetstone Mountains, the Dragoon Mountains are both beautiful and of historical interest; located here is **Cochise's Stronghold,** where the Apache chief hid out with his people during 11 years of battle with U. S. troops. Farther east, **Chiricahua National Monument** (*see* Southeastern Arizona, *below*) offers a number of well-marked trails in a striking setting.

For more information on trails, mountain ranges, and hiking, contact the **Metropolitan Tucson Convention and Visitors Bureau** (130 S. Scott Ave., tel. 602/624-1817 or 800/638-8350). Another good source of information is **Summit Hut** (5045 E. Speedway, tel. 602/325-2554), which has an excellent collection of hiking reference materials and a friendly staff who will help you plan and outfit your trip; packs, tents, bags, shoes, and skis can be rented here.

Horseback Riding What's a trip to the Southwest without at least one bout on the back of a horse? **Desert-High Country Stables** (6501 W. Ina Rd., tel. 602/744-3789) offers a variety of trail rides; haywagon rides and cookouts are available, too. **Pantano Stables** (4450 S. Houghton Rd., tel. 602/298-9076) features special holiday and birthday rides—and even western weddings—in addition to regular trail rides. **Pusch Ridge Stables** (11220 N. Oracle Rd., tel. 602/297-6908) is adjacent to Catalina State Park, and its riders often see bighorn sheep in the Santa Catalina foothills.

Rockhounding If rockhounding interests you, before you plan your trip write to the Arizona Office of Tourism (1100 W. Washington, Phoenix 85007, tel. 602/542-8687) and ask for brochure RG/150M/8-89, which offers information about the best places in the area to visit. Amateur traders and buyers might consider joining the thousands of professionals who come to town in February for the huge **Tucson Gem and Mineral Show** (Box 42543, Tucson 85733, tel. 602/322-5773), the largest of its kind in the world. Many precious stones as well as affordable samples are displayed and sold here, and even if you don't buy a thing, it's fun to look at all the fascinating rocks and gems. If you do plan to attend, make reservations far in advance; every hotel and car-rental agency in town is likely to be booked up from February 11 through February 14, 1993.

When you're in the Huachuca City area, you might stop by the **Opal Art Gallery** (junction AZ 82 and Evans Rd., Huachuca City 85616, tel. 602/456–9202), run by Mike Anderson and Cheri Saunders. They discovered Arizona's precious blue opal in the area about 15 years ago and still mine for the pale-blue-and-white stones used in the lovely jewelry they sell in their shop.

Spectator Sports

Cactus League Baseball

Tucson's **Hi-Corbett Field** (900 S. Randolph Way, tel. 602/791–4266 or 602/791–4836) is where the Cleveland Indians compete with other Cactus League teams off-season (*see* Chapter 1, Essential Information). It's top-rated in the *Arizona Republic/Phoenix Gazette* "Spring Training Guide" for 1991 as the most enjoyable ballpark in the state.

Located adjacent to Randolph Park, Hi-Corbett Field is home to the Tucson Toros, a minor-league team, as well as spring-training home to the Indians. Many picnickers and squirrels sit side by side in the nearby park to enjoy the games. Inside the stadium, during the training games, beer is sold behind first and third bases. Parking isn't as easy to come by in the area, so park in any of the Randolph Park lots west of Hi-Corbett Field and take a short, pleasant walk through the park to get to the stadium. Call for ticket prices and schedules.

Greyhound Racing

It's fun to watch the sleek racing dogs compete at **Tucson Greyhound Park** (2601 S. 3rd Ave., corner of S. 4th Ave. and 36th St., tel. 602/884–7576), but parimutuel wagering is the real attraction. There are two betting areas, the concession and bar area on the main floor and the clubhouse restaurant and bar upstairs. From January through April, doors open nightly (except Monday) at 6 PM, and the first race starts promptly at 7:30 PM; doors open at 12:30 PM for matinees on Wednesday, Saturday, and Sunday, and the first race starts at 2 PM. From May to December, there's no race on Tuesday night. Admission to the clubhouse is $3, $1.25 for the concession area. Only persons 18 or older can bet; no children under the age of 12 are allowed in the clubhouse during evening hours.

Dining

Tucson's culinary reputation is growing, and there are restaurants in town to satisfy every appetite. Southwestern cuisine, naturally featured here, ranges from barbecue and cowboy steaks to light nouvelle recipes that use such innovative ingredients as cactus and blue corn.

Tucson's residents have long boasted about their city's Mexican food, some rather grandly proclaiming their town "Mexican Food Capital of the World" (a title regularly challenged by San Antonians and Phoenicians). Most of the Mexican food in Tucson is Sonoran style—that is, derived from the cooking native to the adjoining Mexican state of Sonora. It's the type that's familiar to most Americans, featuring cheese, mild peppers, corn tortillas, and beef or chicken. Although Sonoran Mexican food has a well-earned reputation for being high in calories and saturated fats, many restaurants in Tucson now feature *pescado* (authentically prepared fish) or *pollo* (chicken) dishes that are flavorful yet lower in cholesterol. (Note that the salsa, or hot sauce, served with baskets of tortilla chips may be spicier than what you are used to. Proceed with caution. Similarly, when you ask waiters whether a dish is "hot," remember that their definition of that term may be quite different from yours.)

Dress is more casual in Tucson than in many cities its size. A few restaurants request that men wear jackets to dinner. The issue of whether to wear a tie takes on a new slant here—there's at least one cowboy steak house where anyone caught wearing such formal neckwear will have it snipped off and added to the restaurant's collection of city-slicker garb.

Most restaurants in Tucson offer no-smoking areas, some prohibit cigarette smoking entirely, and many prohibit pipe and cigar smoking. Credit cards are generally accepted at the larger restaurants, but small, family-run establishments may accept only cash or local checks (with a bank-issued check-guarantee card). Sometimes alcohol is not served at the little neighborhood restaurants, but you may be permitted to bring your own.

Fall, winter, and spring make up the high season for travel here; it's a good idea to call ahead for reservations during these busy months. Some restaurants close for a portion of the summer, taking advantage of the slow time to make repairs or give staff vacations. Again, it's wise to call ahead, this time to ensure that your intended destination is open and hasn't altered its hours. Don't assume, incidentally, that you'll have to dine indoors in summer—many Tucson restaurants cool their outdoor patios with a system in which the temperature is lowered by a very fine mist emitted from unobtrusive pipes overhead, allowing patrons to dine comfortably.

While Tucson's variety of restaurants is akin to that of its big-city cousins, the city doesn't offer much in the way of after-hours dining. Hungry late-nighters had best head for I-10, where there is a large array of all-night fast-food places and coffee shops that cater to travelers, or for the University of Arizona neighborhood, where students pulling all-nighters can always find some brain food.

Category	Cost*
Very Expensive	over $35
Expensive	$25–$35
Moderate	$15–$25
Inexpensive	under $15

**per person, excluding drinks, service, and 7% sales tax (5% state plus 2% city)*

Highly recommended restaurants are indicated by a star ★.

American
Expensive

Solarium. This striking, plant-filled restaurant was created by artists with an eye to the environment: The dining room, with its inlaid tile mosaics, abundant wood and glass, and metal sculptured door, blends in well with its sylvan surroundings. The food is not really the main draw, though the heart-healthy entrées, which range from a charbroiled halibut fillet to poached sea scallops to pasta primavera, are tasty. The wine list is impressive, offering a full range of California bottles, and the fresh-ground coffee is great. *6444 E. Tanque Verde Rd., tel. 602/886–8186. Reservations advised. Dress: casual. AE, DC, MC, V. No lunch weekends.*

Moderate
★

Rancher's Club. The two wood grills on which most of the foods are prepared are the key to the success of this upscale western-style restaurant—with lots of dark wood, mounted animal heads, and sidesaddles—but you have to come here ready to make some decisions. As the friendly staff explains, different woods impart different flavors to foods, so diners are offered a choice of grills. The lobster is especially good, and the steaks are excellent, too (a note on the menu advises "Our steaks are copious and we encourage you to share"). An array of sauces, butters, and condiments provide diners with interesting ways to flavor their food. And—yet another choice to make—there's an incredible variety of beer offered. *5151 E. Grant Rd., tel. 602/797–2624. Reservations advised. Dress: casual. AE, DC, MC, V. Closed Sun. No lunch weekends.*

Inexpensive

Café Melange. Known for its breakfasts (frittatas, pancakes, omelets), this bright little spot is a good stop for lunch or dinner as well. Enjoy such specialties as homemade soups, chili, croissant sandwiches, or a plate of barbecued baby-back pork ribs on the plant-filled outdoor patio. *6761 E. Tanque Verde Rd., tel. 602/298–2233. Reservations advised for groups of 8 or more. Dress: casual. AE, MC, V. No dinner Sun. and Mon.*

Millie's Pancake Haus. Millie's place looks like a little European café, with lace curtains and cheerful waitresses in frilly aprons. Pancakes and waffles are the specialty here, with varieties ranging from Russian blintzes and rolled French pancakes with Cointreau sauce to buttermilk or potato pancakes. Lunch includes a nice array of sandwiches, blue plate specials, and, on Sunday, chicken and dumplings. Reservations are accepted every day except Sunday, when you can expect to wait for a table on the comfortable patio. *6530 E. Tanque Verde Rd., tel. 602/298–4250. Reservations advised for 6 or more; no reservations on Sun. Dress: casual. No credit cards. No dinner; closed Mon.*

Cajun
Moderate

Jerome's. It may seem strange to think of New Orleans specialties in the desert, but at Jerome's the menu goes beyond the usual jambalaya and etouffé. This casual, comfortable eatery serves some of the best fresh fish in town. There's a raw bar complete with chilled Gulf oysters, cherrystone clams, Gulf shrimp cocktail, and calamari ceviche. Buttermilk biscuits and bread pudding with bourbon sauce supply any calories saved by eating the excellent mesquite-grilled mahimahi. Sunday champagne brunch is a bargain at $14.95. *6958 E. Tanque Verde Rd., tel. 602/721–0311. Reservations advised. Dress: casual. No lunch Sat.; closed Mon.*

Continental
Expensive

Arizona Inn Restaurant. This confident, friendly establishment, a Tucson classic, welcomes old friends and new visitors alike. Sit out on the patio for a lovely view of the grounds of this 60-year-old adobe inn, or enjoy the view through huge windows in the dining room, a light, airy place with many 1930s southwestern details. On chilly evenings there's a fire. Steamed fish of the day served with ginger and leeks is a specialty, and the excellent grilled venison rib is also popular. For dessert, try a slice of the terrific apple or pecan pie. Breakfast here is also a treat. *2200 E. Elm St., tel. 602/325–1541. Reservations advised. Jacket suggested for dinner. AE, MC, V.*

The Gold Room. Located at the beautiful Westward Look Resort in the Santa Catalina foothills north of town, this rather upscale restaurant offers a panoramic view of Tucson sparkling in the sun (or twinkling at night) through its glassed-in dining room—as well as excellent food. A new chef was hired in 1992, so it's difficult to tell what direction the menu will take, but popular dishes such as the chateaubriand for two or veal Oscar are likely to remain staples. *245 E. Ina Rd., tel. 602/297–1151. Reservations advised. Jacket advised. AE, D, DC, MC, V.*

Dining

Anthony's, **9**

Arizona Inn Restaurant, **34**

Boccata, **12**

Café Melange, **44**

Café Poca Cosa, **26**

Café Terra Cotta, **13**

Caruso's, **20**

El Charro Café, **21**

The Gold Room, **5**

Guillermo's Double L, **27**

Jack's Original Bar-B-Q, **39**

Janos, **24**

Jerome's, **46**

La Hacienda, **29**

La Parilla Suiza, **15**

Le Bistro, **14**

Li'l Abner's, **3**

Mi Nidito Restaurant, **27**

Micha's, **28**

Millie's Pancake Haus, **42**

New Delhi Palace, **40**

Olson's, **32**

Olympic Flame, **50**

Pinnacle Peak Steakhouse, **43**

Presidio Grill, **35**

Rancher's Club, **37**

Solarium, **41**

The Tack Room, **47**

Tanque Verde Ranch, **51**

Tohono Chul Tea Room, **4**

Lodging
Arizona Inn, **34**
Best Western Royal Sun Inn and Suites, **19**
Canyon Ranch, **48**
Casa Tierra, **17**
Cliff Manor Inn, **6**
Copper Bell, **23**
Doubletree Hotel, **36**
El Presidio Bed and Breakfast Inn, **22**
Embassy Suites Tucson-Broadway, **38**
Frontier Motel, **18**
Holiday Inn Tucson Airport Hotel and Convention Center, **31**
Hotel Congress, **25**
Lazy K Bar Guest Ranch, **1**
The Lodge on the Desert, **33**
Loews Ventana Canyon Resort, **8**
Motel Six East, **30**
Park Inn/ Santa Rita, **26**
Ramada Inn Foothills, **45**
Rodeway Inn Tucson North, **16**
Sheraton Tucson El Conquistador, **10**
Tanque Verde Ranch, **51**
Triangle L Ranch, **7**
Tucson Hilton East, **49**
Westin La Paloma, **11**
Westward Look Resort, **5**
White Stallion Ranch, **2**

Moderate **Anthony's.** This is an elegant yet comfortable place for a tasty meal and a lovely view of the city. Pink linen, stemmed crystal, and pink-rimmed china lend a light, festive look to the dining room. On a nice day, ask for a patio table. Lamb Wellington, Norwegian salmon sautéed lightly in a tomato-basil sauce, and bananas Foster are all good dinnertime choices; for lunch you might try the crisp-baked lemon chicken with potato pancakes. The wine list is extensive. *6440 N. Campbell Ave., tel. 602/299–1771. Reservations advised. Dress: neat but casual. AE, DC, MC, V. Closed Sun. lunch.*

French
Moderate–Expensive
★

Le Bistro. Set in a nondescript building on a busy road near the university, Le Bistro is one of the prettiest restaurants in town: Towering palms preside over pink lace–covered tables, burgundy chairs, and Art Nouveau–style etched mirrors. The setting is matched by the creations of young chef/owner Laurent Reux; born in Brittany, he offers many fish and shellfish dishes inspired by the seascape of his native region, such as supreme of salmon in a ginger crust with lime butter. Another popular specialty is Long Island duck in a raspberry vinaigrette. A revolving glass dessert display at the entrance will leave you pondering throughout the meal whether to opt for the triple chocolate mousse cake, say, or the Key-lime tart. You can't hope for a more reasonably priced French lunch, and seasonal dinner specials for $12.95 include soup or salad, a choice of two entrées, and dessert. *2574 N. Campbell, tel. 502/327–3086. Reservations advised on weekends. Dress: casual but neat. No lunch on weekends. D, MC, V.*

Greek
Moderate

Olympic Flame. This clean, pleasant, light-filled restaurant serves such traditional Greek favorites as moussaka, but also offers well-prepared Continental selections for the unadventurous, including broiled pork chops and filet mignon. A specialty worth trying is the *horiatiki,* a salad with feta cheese, oregano, and a tasty oil-and-vinegar dressing. Olympic Flame has won several awards—including one from the Pima County Health Department. *7970 E. Broadway, tel. 602/296–3399. Reservations advised. Dress: neat but casual. AE, D, DC, MC, V. Closed Sun. lunch.*

Indian
Inexpensive–Moderate

New Delhi Palace. Vegetarians, carnivores, and seafood lovers will all find something to enjoy at this elegant Indian restaurant. The congenial staff is helpful in explaining the menu, which features a wide variety of tandoori dishes, curries, rice, and breads. The "heat" of each dish can be adjusted to individual preference by the chef. If you're undecided, a lunch buffet and complete dinners offer nice samplings of several dishes. The atmosphere is quiet, with Indian music played softly, and tasteful displays of Indian objets d'art. *6751 E. Broadway, tel. 602/296–8585. Reservations advised. Dress: casual. DC, MC, V.*

Italian
Moderate–Expensive

Boccata. Set in a tasteful mall in the foothills of the Santa Catalina Mountains, this pretty restaurant serves excellent northern Italian cuisine, with some southern French dishes for good measure. The flowered tablecloths match the delicate aubergine and Tuscan yellow walls, and the artwork ranges from contemporary to Victorian whimsy. A good wine list complements such pasta entrées as penne *ciao bella* (with grilled chicken and a delicate white-wine and Gorgonzola sauce) and sea-bass ravioli; the steamed mussel appetizer is plentiful. Save some room for the cannoli *carnevale,* filled with light ricotta and served on a portberry coulis. *5605 E. River Rd., tel. 602/577–9309. Reservations advised. Dress: casual but neat. AE, DC, MC, V. Closed Mon.; lunch served Fri. only. Open for Sun. brunch.*

Moderate

Olson's. Although the name and the southwestern decor suggest otherwise, this is an Italian restaurant, owned by University of Arizona men's basketball coach Lute Olson and his son, Greg. Don't worry—the original owner, Joe Scordato, a bona fide Italian, still expertly oversees operations. There are a few American and Continental dishes on the menu, but the focus is southern Italian, with such specialties as *pesce alla griglia* (salmon or swordfish grilled in a lemon-and-white-wine butter) and *braciole con fettuccine* (beefsteak with stuffing served over pasta with tomato sauce). *3048 E. Broadway, tel. 602/323–3701. Reservations advised. Dress: casual. AE, D, DC, MC, V. Closed Sun.*

Inexpensive

Caruso's. The crowds that sometimes gather outside this homey Italian restaurant might lead you to think they were giving something away inside—and you wouldn't be entirely wrong. Portions of the tasty lasagna, eggplant parmigiana, shrimp marinara, and other southern Italian standards are so large that it's the rare person who doesn't leave here with a free lunch for the next day. Prices are extremely reasonable and combination dishes are available, so for once you won't have to covet whatever your dining companion has ordered; you can have it all. The decor is of the candle-in-the-Chianti-bottle type, and haute cuisine this ain't. But if you need a pasta fix in a cheerful environment, you can't go wrong at Caruso's. *434 N. 4th Ave., tel. 602/624–5765. Reservations accepted for 6 or more. Dress: casual. MC, V. Dinner only.*

Mexican
Inexpensive
★

Café Poca Cosa. This is a marvelously colorful—hot pink, bright green, and tropical orange—and lively restaurant in an unlikely place: the downtown Park Inn, across from the visitor center. Locals caught onto this place before the tourists did—it's tucked into a corner of the hotel lobby, cheerful, and thoroughly Mexican. The dishes (which change daily) are creative, made with fresh ingredients, and aren't unduly saturated with cheese. Consider a breakfast of green chili tamales on the outdoor patio when the weather is fine. The tiny original restaurant across the street (20 S. Scott Ave.) is open for breakfast and lunch during the week. *88 E. Broadway, tel. 602/622–6400. Reservations advised for large parties. Dress: informal. MC, V. No dinner Sun.*

El Charro Café. Started by Monica Flin in 1922, and run by her grandniece and her grandniece's husband today, El Charro still serves excellent versions of the American-Mexican staples Flin claims to have originated—chimichangas (flour tortillas rolled around seasoned beef or chicken and deep-fried) and cheese crisps, most notably. Daily "fitness-fare" specials such as seafood enchiladas are delicious as well as healthful. You can dine outside on the front porch or inside in one of the bright, cheerful dining rooms. A gift shop next door sells mementoes of this Tucson classic. *311 N. Court Ave., tel. 602/622–5465. Reservations advised. Dress: casual (but no tank tops). AE, DC, MC, V.*

Guillermo's Double L. Many locals claim that no self-respecting Mexican food aficionado eats anywhere but at a restaurant located in this neighborhood, known simply as "Fourth Avenue." Guillermo's has great food, efficient service, prices straight out of another decade—and few tourists. Combination dinners and such à la carte items as tacos and tostados are excellent. Consider coming for a tasty Mexican breakfast. There's also an American menu for the "sissies". *1830 S. 4th Ave., tel. 602/792–1585. Reservations advised for large parties. Dress: informal. MC, V. Closed Sun.*

La Hacienda. South Tucson, technically a separate city, has a large Mexican population and, as a result, many authentic Mexican restaurants. La Hacienda, typical of them, is short on decor, low in price, and high in quality and portion size. Try any of the dishes made with *machaca* (sun-dried shredded beef). The *camerones fantasia* (shrimp wrapped in bacon) and the mixed-seafood ceviche appetizer are also excellent. But then again you'd be hard pressed to find anything here that's not tasty and freshly made. *4207 S. 6th Ave., tel. 602/889–6613. No reservations. Dress: casual. No credit cards.*

La Parilla Suiza (The Swiss Grill). This is one of those places that take a little while to figure out, but it's worth the effort. The mixed signals start with the name and continue with the architecture—the place looks like a Swiss chalet with cactus out front. But the food is typical of Mexico City, which is very different from the cuisine of Sonora, or northern Mexico. There is an emphasis on charcoal grilling (even the dishes prepared with cheese are often grilled). *Platon del alambre de pollo con chilequiles* (chopped breast of chicken, charcoal cooked with bacon, onions, and peppers and served with *chilequiles* and a smoky-flavored bean soup) is excellent, and a bargain at less than $7. *2720 N. Oracle Rd., tel. 602/624–4300, or 5602 E. Speedway Blvd., tel. 602/747–4838. Reservations advised for 6 or more. Dress: casual. AE, DC, MC, V.*

Micha's. This pretty little plant-filled place, with good service and well-prepared Sonoran-style Mexican food, is made even more enjoyable on Friday and Saturday evenings, when mariachi bands play. Have you tried a Mexican breakfast? You owe it to yourself—and this is a good place to start, perhaps with some spicy *huevos rancheros* (eggs with hot sauce and tortillas). This restaurant is another well-kept local secret. *2908 S. 4th Ave., tel. 602/623–5307. Reservations advised on weekends. Dress: informal. AE, MC, V.*

Mi Nidito Restaurant. Another fine establishment frequented by the locals, Mi Nidito ("My Little Nest") has been here since 1954 and serves some of the best chimichangas in town. If you haven't tried *nopalitos*, tender cactus cooked in a spicy sauce and served with rice and beans, this is a good place to go for it. The restaurant is small, dark, and cheerfully funky, with neon cactus, booths with plastic-covered serape seats, and bright Mexican murals. You can expect a crowd, but the wait is worth it. *1813 S. 4th Ave., tel. 602/622–5081. No reservations. Dress: informal. MC, V. Closed Mon. and Tues.*

Southwestern
Expensive–Very Expensive

★ **Janos.** Comfortably situated in the Hiram Stevens House, an adobe home built in 1855, this downtown restaurant—in the El Presidio neighborhood, adjacent to the Tucson Museum of Art—offers innovative and eclectic Southwest menus that will please nouvelle cuisine fans (if not less adventurous and heartier eaters). A series of small, flower-filled dining rooms create an intimate, elegant atmosphere. Typical offerings include sweetbread sauté, golden squash puree, and candied pecans, as well as black-bean-and-sweet-corn chowder. *150 N. Main Ave., tel. 602/884–9426. Reservations advised. Dress: neat but casual. AE, D, MC, V. Closed Sun. Nov.–mid-May;Sun. and Mon. late May–Oct.*

★ **The Tack Room.** This award-winning restaurant has been known for years for its exemplary food, outstanding service, and beautiful setting in a rustic but elegant old adobe house; the name is rather unfortunate for a place so gracious and romantic. Dark wood beams and furnishings and a blue-and-maroon color scheme are complemented by the lighter dusty-rose linen; walls are hung with southwestern landscapes by local artists. Arizona steak flavored with four types of mild peppercorns is a favorite, as is the rack of lamb Sonora, prepared with mesquite honey, cilantro, and southwestern limes. *2800 N. Sabino Canyon Rd., tel. 602/722–2800. Reservations advised. Jacket suggested. AE, D, DC, MC, V. Closed Mon. mid-May–mid-Dec., closed first 2 weeks of July.*

Moderate–Expensive

★ **Café Terra Cotta.** Everything about this restaurant says Southwest—from the decor, with its bright pastels and bleached woods, to the food, which features such contemporary Southwest specialties as prawns stuffed with herbed goat cheese, pork tenderloin with black beans, scallops sautéed in adobo with green chilis, corn, and tomatoes, and pizzas with sun-dried tomatoes; the garlic custard appetizer is superb. The place for native yupsters as well as their out-of-town guests, Café Terra Cotta offers an impressive by-the-glass California wine list. Come here, too, for a tasty Sunday brunch. *4310 N. Campbell Ave. (at St. Philip's Plaza, southeastern corner of River and Campbell), tel. 602/577–8100. Reservations strongly advised for dinner. Dress: casual. AE, D, DC, MC, V.*

Presidio Grill. If it weren't for the saguaro cactus flanking the cash register, you might at first think you were in one of New York's chic SoHo haunts: This large, noisy room has beamed tinwork ceilings, trompe l'oeil pillars, and plush booths. But the menu is southwestern all the way. Blue-corn pancakes with prickly-pear syrup appear on the breakfast menu; lunch and dinner entrées include lamb chops pan-seared with brown garlic and fresh rosemary, as well as eggplant, onion, sun-dried tomato, and mozzarella pizza. In the University of Arizona area, this place is open unusually late (for Tucson) on weekends and attracts a mix of students, professionals, and out-of-towners. *3352 E. Speedway Blvd., tel. 602/327–4667. Reservations required for 5 or more. Dress: casual. MC, V.*

Moderate

Li'l Abner's. Located in the old Butterfield Express stagecoach rest stop, dating from the early 1800s, this Old West institution draws locals, who go straight for the mesquite-broiled 2-pound porterhouse steaks. There's nothing here for vegetarians, except for the unlimited salad bar that comes with all the entrées. When the weather is fine on weekends (as it usually is), there's dancing under the stars and plenty of country music. It's about a 15-minute drive from downtown. *8501 N. Silverbell Rd., tel. 602/744–2800. Reservations advised. Dress: informal. MC, V. Dinner only.*

Pinnacle Peak Steakhouse. No nouvelle-cuisine fans welcome here: Anybody caught eating fish tacos or cactus jelly would probably be hanged from the rafters—along with all the ties snipped from loco city slickers. This is a cowboy steak house that the tourists love. It's fun, it's Tucson, and the food ain't half bad, either, pardner. The excellent mesquite-broiled steaks come with salad, baked potatoes, and pinto beans; if you can handle it after all that, try the hot apple cobbler with vanilla ice cream. The restaurant is part of Trail Dust Town, a re-creation of a turn-of-the-century town, complete with an "opera" house featuring cancan girls and a barbershop quartet, souvenir shops, and an old-time photographer's studio, where you can have your picture taken in western garb. *6541 E. Tanque Verde Rd., tel. 602/296–0911. No reservations. Dress: casual. D, DC, MC, V.*

Tanque Verde Ranch. For the total southwestern experience, drive 12 miles east of Tucson into the foothills of the Rincon Mountains to this dude ranch that caters to tourists and locals alike. Call ahead to find out what's on the menu, which changes daily: Entrées range from roast duck à l'orange to lobster sautéed with guacamole sauce. Meals are followed by such entertainment as square dancing or informative slide shows on the area's wildlife. Sometimes the dining room is abandoned in favor of Cottonwood Grove, where there's a steak fry or a barbecue. *14301 E. Speedway Blvd., tel. 602/296–6275. Reservations required. Dress: informal. AE, MC, V.*

Tohono Chul Tea Room. This is a good choice for anybody seeking a quiet cup of tea or glass of wine, a satisfying sandwich, a crunchy salad, or a particularly toothsome dessert. The setting is unique—the tearoom is nestled in a wildlife sanctuary and surrounded by a fantastic cactus garden. Although the tearoom is typically southwestern, with lots of light wood and glass, the menu covers southwestern, Mexican, and American dishes. House favorites include chicken enchiladas made with Monterey Jack cheese, corn, and green chilies, and a sliced-tomato-and-basil sandwich served on French sourdough bread. Sunday brunch is especially good. *7366 N. Paseo del Norte, tel. 602/797–1711. Reservations accepted for 8 or more. Dress: informal. AE, MC, V. Open for breakfast and lunch only.*

Inexpensive

Jack's Original Bar-B-Q. For those who like their Southwest cuisine messy and in big portions, this is the place to come. Jack's ribs are smoky, meaty, and without equal in these parts; the sauce is rich and subtly flavored. The beans are also a real treat. Jack's impresses through good, honest food, not atmosphere—the floor is linoleum; the chairs and flowers are plastic. *5250 E. 22nd St., tel. 602/750–1280. No reservations. Dress: informal. No credit cards.*

Lodging

In Tucson you can enjoy the luxury of a desert resort or the more basic accommodations offered by small motels. A number of guest ranches, some of them from the 1800s when they were real working cattle ranches, can be found on the outskirts of town. The mountains surrounding Tucson host a bountiful array of campsites and parks for recreational vehicles, offering a cool respite from the desert heat in summer (*see* Camping in Participant Sports, *above*).

There is also a variety of bed-and-breakfast establishments in the area, ranging from bedrooms in modest homes to private cottages nestled on wildlife preserves. The **Arizona Association of Bed and Breakfast Inns** (3661 N. Campbell Ave., Box 237, Tucson 85719, tel. 602/231–6777) can provide referrals to member inns. In addition, reservation services for Arizona bed-and-breakfast establishments include **Bed and Breakfast in Arizona** (Box 8628, Scottsdale 85252, tel. 602/995–2831), **B&B Scottsdale and the West** (Box 3999, Prescott 86302, tel. 602/776–1102), **Mi Casa Su Casa Bed and Breakfast** (Box 950, Tempe 85281, tel. 602/

990–0682 or 800/456–0682), and **Old Pueblo HomeStays** (Box 13603, Tucson 85732, tel. 602/790–2399).

Many lodging establishments set aside rooms for nonsmokers; inquire when you make your reservation.

Prices vary widely between seasons. Room rates in summer—generally defined as April 15 through October 1—are much lower than those in the winter, and visitors who don't mind warm weather can get some real deals at resorts that are quite pricey during the busy time. Locals often take advantage of weekend packages offered during summer months, spending the weekends resort hopping and enjoying their town in a way usually reserved for visitors.

Category	Cost*
Very Expensive	over $130
Expensive	$100–$130
Moderate	$60–$100
Inexpensive	under $60

**All prices are for a standard double room, excluding room tax (9.5% in Tucson and 6.5% in Pima County). Prices given here are winter, or high-season, rates.*

Highly recommended hotels are indicated by a star ★.

Hotels

Expensive ★

Arizona Inn. Although this landmark '30s-era inn is close to the university and downtown, you feel as though you're away from it all on its 14 acres of lushly landscaped grounds. All rooms have patios and lovely period furnishings; many have fireplaces. Service is excellent—friendly but unobtrusive. The staff hosts small conferences beautifully, attending to the details without fuss. Locals as well as guests frequent the hotel's restaurant (*see* Dining, *above*). *2200 E. Elm St., 85719, tel. 602/325–1541. 80 rooms with bath. Facilities: pool, 2 tennis courts, library, gift shop, cocktail lounge, restaurant. AE, MC, V.*

Tucson Hilton East. With its full conference facilities, this hotel draws lots of business travelers, but pleasure seekers will find it comfortable as well. It's just east of downtown, a few minutes from the airport and Davis-Monthan Air Force Base. An airy glass-atrium lobby takes full advantage of the view of the Santa Catalina Mountains. Rooms are nicely furnished, with modern light wood fittings, pastel carpeting, and subtly patterned pastel bedspreads. The Wine Bar features one of the most extensive selections in town. The VIP level offers extra service and luxuries such as complimentary hors d'oeuvres, deluxe Continental breakfast, and a library. *7600 E. Broadway, 85710, tel. 602/721–5600. 226 rooms with bath. Facilities: pool, golf course, restaurant. AE, D, DC, MC, V.*

Doubletree Hotel. Convenient to the airport and to the center of town, this comfortable, contemporary-style property is also across the road from the municipal golf course at Randolph Park, which hosts the LPGA tournament every year; most of the participants stay at the Doubletree. Rooms are large, and done in salmon or turquoise with southwestern-style furnishings. The pretty Cactus Rose Restaurant serves excellent nouvelle Southwestern cuisine and the Javelina Cantina in the lobby is a fun place in which to have a beer. *445 S. Alvernon Way, tel. 602/881–4200 or 800/528–0444. 295 rooms with bath. Facilities: restaurant, bar, pool, tennis courts. AE, D, DC, MC, V.*

Moderate

Best Western Royal Sun Inn and Suites. Convenient to both the University of Arizona and downtown, this white-brick motel is decorated in pleasing southwestern-style pastels. All the rooms have whirlpool baths, hair dryers, and refrigerators; suites have VCRs. Don't expect the unexpected—this is a typical member of the Best Western chain—but if you're looking for spacious, clean lodging at a good price, this is a reasonable choice. *1015 N. Stone Ave., 85705, tel. 602/622–8871. 58 rooms, 20 suites, all with bath. Facilities: pool, exercise room, dry saunas, dining room, cocktail lounge. AE, D, DC, MC, V.*

Embassy Suites Tucson–Broadway. This centrally located hotel is 10 miles from Tucson International Airport, 5 miles from downtown, and a bit less than 5 miles from the University of Arizona. Accommodations are two-room suites (with a kitchenette) opening onto an atrium full of plants. Furnishings are tasteful if not exciting. Among the extras are a free cooked-to-order breakfast every morning and complimentary happy hour every evening; transportation to the airport and parking are also on the house. *5335 E. Broadway, 85711, tel. 602/745–2700. 142 suites with bath. Facilities: outdoor heated pool, whirlpool, microwaves in rooms, washer and dryer for guest use on premises. AE, D, DC, MC, V.*

Holiday Inn Tucson Airport Hotel and Convention Center. Favored by businesspeople, this property is five minutes from the airport and adjacent to I–10. The decor is a mix of Mexican and Spanish, with the usual dark print bedspreads and carpets throughout. In contrast, the light, cheerful lobby has a plant-filled atrium with a waterfall; *saltillo*-tiled floors and white stucco walls give it an open, southwestern feel. Women travelers can reserve special rooms stocked with hair dryers, extra toiletries, and well-lit makeup mirrors. There are free shuttles to the airport and to the large El Con shopping center. *4550 S. Palo Verde Blvd., 85714, tel. 602/746–1161 or 800–HOLIDAY. 299 rooms with bath. Facilities: pool, sauna, whirlpool, 2 restaurants, cocktail lounge. AE, D, DC, MC, V.*

★ **The Lodge on the Desert.** Although the ambience is that of an exclusive inn, prices at this little hotel, established 50 years ago, are very reasonable. The place has retained the old-fashioned feel of a Mexican hacienda: The adobe architecture is accented with hand-painted Mexican tile and open-beamed ceilings; fireplaces warm many of the rooms in the winter; and lush gardens make the patios feel cool and private. The property is 3 miles east of the university and within a mile of golf, racquetball, and tennis facilities. On the premises you can enjoy shuffleboard, swimming, ping-pong, and croquet; there's also an excellent library. Continental breakfast is complimentary, and the Lodge Restaurant is worth a visit even if you're staying elsewhere. *306 N. Alvernon Way, Box 42500, 85733, tel. 602/325–3366 or 800/456–5634. 40 rooms with bath. Facilities: pool, restaurant, cocktail lounge. AE, D, DC, MC, V.*

Ramada Inn Foothills. Families as well as business travelers stay in this Ramada Inn on the northeastern side of town, close to restaurants, Sabino Canyon, and mall shopping. This property has a fresh, clean feel about it: A light stucco building with rounded corners, it has an updated adobe look. Furnishings are standard motel style, but they're fairly new and more than serviceable. There's a complimentary cold breakfast buffet and complimentary cocktails in the evening. Free passes to a local health club are available, and golf and tennis facilities are nearby. *6944 E. Tanque Verde Rd., 85715, tel. 602/886–9595 or 800/228–2828. 113 rooms with bath. Facilities: pool and sauna, restaurant, cocktail lounge. AE, D, DC, MC, V.*

Inexpensive

Frontier Motel. You can recognize this small motel in the university area by its red-tile roof and carports. It's nothing fancy, but it's clean and comfortable, especially for families with children. Fourteen of the rooms have fully equipped kitchenettes; there is also a barbecue grill out by the pool and a restaurant next door. Weekly and monthly rates are available. *227 W. Drachman, 85705, tel. 602/798–3005. 20 rooms with bath. Facilities: pool, guest laundry, covered parking. AE, D, MC, V.*

★ **Hotel Congress.** Loved by many for its idiosyncratic charm, this downtown hotel is not for those who want the bland comforts of chain lodgings. Built in 1919, this property has been beautifully restored to its original western version of Art Deco style. The rooms, which vary in size, are individually furnished: All have black-and-white tiled baths and the original iron beds; some have desks and tables. Near the Greyhound and Amtrak stations and the main Sun Tran terminal, and close to downtown art galleries and restaurants, this is an excellent choice for those who don't have a car. The downside of this convenient location is noise, which is compounded on weekend nights when music from the popular Club Congress filters up to some of the rooms. Still, if you're looking for an inexpensive and memorable establishmet, you can't beat this Tucson landmark. *311 E. Congress St., 85701, tel. 602/622–8848. 40 rooms with bath. Facilities: restaurant, bar, nightclub.. AE, MC, V.*

Motel Six East. Go elsewhere if you're looking for atmosphere: Part of a no-frills chain known for low prices, this Motel Six on the eastern edge of town offers clean, comfortable, basic accommodations—nothing extra. Rooms are furnished in typical motel style, and bathrooms have no tubs—only showers. This is a good stop for families; children 18 and under stay free in their parents' room. Surprise: One small pet per room is allowed. *1031 E. Benson Hwy., 85713, tel. 602/628–1264. 146 rooms with bath. Facilities: pool. AE, D, MC, V, checks accepted if sent ahead and received 10 days before arrival date.*

Park Inn/Santa Rita. When this hotel became a Park Inn in 1991 (it had been a Days Inn during the late 1980s), it also reclaimed the name by which it had been known in Tucson for years—the Santa Rita. The property was spiffed up during the past decade—modern furnishings, hand-painted Mexican tile, and adobe walls brighten the lobby—but rooms are rather dark and drably furnished, and the place sometimes shows its age in the plumbing. Still, the hotel is conveniently located near the downtown arts district and across the street from the visitor center, and it's home to Café Poca Cosa, one of the most popular Mexican restaurants in town (*see* Dining, *above*). There's a complimentary cold breakfast buffet for guests in the morning and a free happy hour in the afternoon. *88 E. Broadway, 85701, tel. 602/622–4000. 168 rooms with bath. Facilities: beauty parlor, heated pool, sauna, restaurant. AE, D, DC, MC, V.*

Rodeway Inn Tucson North. Located in the university area, this hotel caters to business as well as leisure travelers. The basic boxy motel architecture has been adapted to local style—a stucco exterior is accented with tasteful, low-key stripes of turquoise and pink. The pool is in a nicely landscaped courtyard studded with umbrella-shaded tables. Rooms are nothing fancy, but they are adequate, and there's a handy laundry facility on the premises. *1365 W. Grant Rd., 85745, tel. 602/622–7791 or 800/228–2000. 146 rooms with bath. Facilities: pool, restaurant, cocktail lounge, coin-operated laundry. AE, D, DC, MC, V.*

Bed-and-Breakfasts

Moderate–Expensive

El Presidio Bed and Breakfast Inn. This B&B, convenient to the historic El Presidio district and other downtown attractions, offers three charming suites, one in a Victorian adobe home built more than 100 years ago, and two in separate guest houses. The Carriage House, furnished with Eastlake antiques dating from the 1880s, and the Gatehouse, done in French country style, both have private entrances off a beautiful old courtyard; antique wicker sets a summery tone for The Victorian, in the main house. All have kitchenettes well stocked with fruit and beverages, as well as private baths. Depending on your preference, the morning meal varies from a copious spread to a quick Continental breakfast. Smoking is not allowed. *297 N. Main*

Ave., 85701, tel. 602/623–6151. 3 suites with bath. No credit cards.

Moderate **Copper Bell.** The copper bell after which the property is named traveled from Germany to Tucson with the innkeepers, and it graces the front porch of their 90-year-old lava stone house. Hosts Hans Herbert Kraus and Gertrude M. Eich-Kraus restored the place, using windows, doors, and other materials imported from their native land. Not surprisingly, the house has a very European feel to it; furnishings are German antiques. Guests are made to feel welcome; the hosts cook delicious German-style breakfasts and offer complimentary tea and homemade cakes in the afternoon. Smoking is allowed only on the outdoor balcony, which affords a fine view of "A" Mountain. *25 N. Westmoreland Ave., 85745, tel. 602/629–9229. 3 rooms with private bath, 2 with shared bath, separate honeymoon suite with private bath. No credit cards.*

Inexpensive–Moderate **Casa Tierra.** Those who want a real desert experience should head out to this bed-and-breakfast on 5 acres of land near the Arizona–Sonora Desert Museum and Saguaro National Monument; for the last 1½ miles you'll be driving along a dirt road. An adobe house built by host Lyle Thompson in 1989 expressly to serve as a B&B has three guest rooms, all with private bath and kitchenettes; all look out onto a lovely central courtyard with a paloverde tree and other desert foliage and also have their own private entrances from individual back patios. The southwestern-style furnishings include Mexican *equipales* (chairs with pigskin seats), tiled floors, and viga-beamed ceilings. The delicious breakfasts prepared by Karen Thompson might include blue-corn pancakes, breakfast burritos, or oatmeal apple waffles; there's always lots of fresh fruit and baked goods to accompany them. *11155 W. Calle Pima, 85743, tel. 602/578–3058. 3 rooms with bath. Facilities: hot tub. No credit cards. Closed June–Aug.*

Guest Ranches

Very Expensive **Tanque Verde Ranch.** One of the country's oldest guest ranches, Tanque Verde sits on more than 600 beautiful acres in the Rincon Mountains between Coronado National Forest and Saguaro National Monument. There's plenty to do, from guided nature walks and trail rides to tennis and swimming. Rooms in the main ranch house or in private casitas are all furnished in tasteful southwestern style; most have patios and fireplaces. Service is relaxed but very attentive. Cookouts and indoor meals are delicious (*see* Dining, *above*). Many of the guests have been coming here for years; it's not unusual for more than two generations of a family to visit together. Rates include meals and activities. *14301 E. Speedway Blvd., 85748, tel. 602/296–6275. 70 rooms with bath. Facilities: indoor and outdoor pools, 5 tennis courts (1 lighted for night use), spa, health club, bas-*

ketball, volleyball, horseshoes, horseback riding. AE, MC, V.

Expensive **Lazy K Bar Guest Ranch.** In the Tucson Mountains, 16 miles northwest of town at an altitude of 2,300 feet, this family-oriented guest ranch will please children as well as adults. Steak cookouts are held every Saturday night, and the daily fare in the community dining room is hearty and good. As you might expect, horseback riding is a focus, with mounts available for greenhorns as well as those with experience. Riders are entertained with tales of the Old West as they explore the Saguaro National Monument on horseback. There are 23 rooms, all with private bath, situated in eight *casitas*, or cottages. The older buildings are made of Mexican Indian stucco and contain rooms with fireplaces and wood-beam ceilings. Rooms in the newer, adobe-brick buildings are larger and more modern. Rates include food and riding daily; there's a three-day minimum stay. *8401 N. Scenic Dr., 85743, tel. 602/744–3050. 23 rooms with bath. Facilities: pool, library, large-screen TV in the main lodge, BYOB bar. MC, V.*

Moderate ★ **The Triangle L Ranch.** If you have plans to tour Biosphere 2 (*see* Off the Beaten Track in Exploring, *above*), consider staying at The Triangle L, a 45-minute drive northeast of Tucson at an elevation of 4,500 feet. More like a bed-and-breakfast inn, Triangle L accommodations consist of four private cottages—all at least 75 years old and furnished with antiques—scattered about the ranch's 80 acres. Built in the late 1800s, this was one of the first guest ranches in southern Arizona in the 1920s. The cottages have housed ranch workers, visitors from the city, and even such Old West celebrities as Buffalo Bill. Birds, coyotes, javelinas, rabbits, squirrels, and other wildlifenumber among the (outdoor) guests. Hiking and sitting on the porch are activities equally favored by most visitors. A ranch breakfast of eggs, homemade breads, fresh fruit, and plenty of coffee is served daily. Smoking is restricted to outdoors. *2805 N. Triangle L Ranch Rd., Box 900, Oracle 85623, tel. 602/896–2804. 2 private cottages with bath, 2 with bath and kitchen. MC, V.*

White Stallion Ranch. If you feel as if this place is right out of the film *High Chaparral*, you won't be imagining things. Many scenes from the movie were shot on the ranch, which sits on 3,000 acres of desert mountain land. The True family—Allen, Cynthia, Russell, and Michael—has run the White Stallion for almost 30 years, and it feels like a family place, where children are welcome and large groups are easily accommodated. There are no phones or TVs in the spare but comfortable rooms. Horseback rides, a weekend rodeo, and hikes along mountain trails are just a few of the activities offered. A herd of longhorn cattle and a wide variety of birds, desert cottontail rabbits, and peacocks make their home on the grounds. Children will enjoy the petting zoo, where sheep and tiny goats gently nuzzle their visitors. *9251 W. Twin Peaks Rd., 85743, tel. 602/297–0252 or 800/782–5546. 30 rooms with bath. Facilities: pool, 2 tennis courts, shuffleboard, basketball, volleyball, horseback riding. No credit cards. Closed May–Sept.*

Resorts

Very Expensive

Canyon Ranch. Mel and Enid Zuckerman opened Canyon Ranch in 1979 on the site of the old Double U Guest Ranch, set on 70 acres in the desert foothills north of Tucson. Two activity centers include a 62,000-square-foot spa complex and an 8,000-square-foot Health and Healing Center, where dietitians, exercise physiologists, behavioral-health professionals, and medical staff counsel guests on everything from kicking the smoking habit to losing weight. Guests are pampered while they're being shaped up. The food is unobtrusively healthful, satisfying—within reason—even big appetites. Rooms are luxuriously furnished in muted southwestern tones. Groups ranging from 25 to 35 persons can be accommodated in a private 16,000-square-foot conference center. *8600 E. Rockcliff Rd., 85715, tel. 602/749–9000 or 800/726–9900 (information), 800/742–9000 (reservations). 67 standard rooms, 45 deluxe rooms, 41 luxury suites, all with bath. Facilities: 1 indoor and 3 outdoor pools, 8 tennis courts, basketball, squash, racquetball, handball, extensive workout equipment. D, MC, V.*

Loews Ventana Canyon Resort. One of the newer desert resorts, Ventana Canyon is unquestionably luxurious, but also snootier than most Tucson properties. The setting is spectacular: Expect to see desert cottontails around the 93 acres of grounds, along with hummingbirds, quail, and other birds; don't be surprised if you find yourself sharing the golf course with a cottontail or two. Rooms are modern and chic, furnished in soft pastels and light woods; each bath has a miniature TV. The center of this open, airy property is an 80-foot waterfall that cascades down the Catalina Mountains into a little lake. Four restaurants offer guests a choice of casual poolside snacks and elegant dining; the upscale Ventana serves excellent, if pricey, southwestern cuisine. *7000 N. Resort Dr., 85715, tel. 602/299–2020 or 800/234–5117. 398 rooms with bath. Facilities: 2 pools, golf course, 10 tennis courts, spa, health club, gift shops, hairdresser, cocktail lounge, disco, 4 restaurants. AE, D, DC, MC, V.*

★ **Sheraton Tucson El Conquistador.** You'll know you're in the Southwest when you step into the cathedral-ceilinged lobby of this golf and tennis resort: It has a huge copper mural filled with cowboys and cacti, as well as a wide-window view of one of the pools set against a backdrop of the rugged Santa Catalina Mountains. This friendly, relaxing place draws families and out-of-town conventioneers as well as locals, who take advantage of summer rates for the Sheraton's excellent sports facilities. Rooms, either in private casitas or the main hotel building, feature stylish light-wood furniture with tin work and pastel-toned spreads and curtains, as well as balconies or patios; some of the suites have kiva-shaped fireplaces. With its wide selection of Mexican beers and live mariachi music, The Dos Locos Cantina keeps guests from heading south of the border. Biosphere 2 is just about a 10-minute drive up the road from here. *10000 N. Oracle Rd., 85737, tel. 602/742–7000 or 800/325–7832. 438 rooms with bath. Facilities: 45 holes of golf, 31 lighted tennis courts, 11 indoor racquetball courts, riding stables, 3 outdoor pools, 2 fitness centers, sauna and Jacuzzi, bicycle rentals, volleyball, basketball, 5 restaurants, gift shops. AE, D, DC, MC, V.*

Westin La Paloma. Vying with the Sheraton and Loews Ventana for convention business, this sprawling pink resort has a full range of conference and ballroom facilities, as well as numerous opportunities for relaxation. Especially noteworthy is the 27-hole Jack Nicklaus–designed golf course, which offers guests a choice in their level of challenge. Nongolfers can indulge in many other outdoor activities, or just sit out on their private patios and watch the sun set over the saguaros. Accommodations make tasteful use of natural fabrics and copper tones. The casual Desert Garden restaurant affords wonderful views of the Santa Catalina Mountains, while the more upscale La Villa specializes in freshly imported seafood. *3800 E. Sunrise, 85718, tel. 602/742–6000 or 800/876–3683. Facilities: golf course, 12 tennis courts, racquetball, pool, 3 spas, health club, jogging and cycling trails, 5 restaurants, lounge, gift shops. AE, D, DC, MC, V.*

★ **Westward Look Resort.** As its name suggests, this resort provides its guests with a glimpse of life in the West, from the wildlife on the grounds to the characteristic pastel color scheme of the guest rooms, poolside, and restaurants. Set on 80 acres in the Santa Catalina foothills north of town, Westward Look is 45 years old but was recently completely refurbished. Either a city or a mountain view is available from the 244 well-appointed rooms spread across the grounds, traversed by golf carts driven by hotel staff to transport guests. The resort is dimly but beautifully lit at night, the better for guests to stargaze. In-room hot-beverage makers, irons and ironing boards, and refrigerators are among the many special touches. If you are traveling with others and want rooms in the same vicinity, say so when you make your reservations. *245 E. Ina Rd., 85704, tel. 602/297–1151 or 800/722–2500. 244 rooms with bath. Facilities: 3 heated pools, golf course, spa, 8 tennis courts (5 lit for night playing), cocktail lounge, 2 restaurants. AE, D, DC, MC, V.*

The Arts and Nightlife

The Arts

Tucson, known as the most cultured of Arizona's cities, is one of only 14 cities in the United States that is home to a symphony as well as to opera, theater, and ballet companies. Winter is the high season for most of Tucson's cultural activities because that's when most of the visitors come, but there's something going on all the time.

Summer is when **Downtown Saturday Night,** a year-round event, comes alive. On the first and third Saturday nights of each month (around 7–10 PM), Tucson's downtown arts district opens up its galleries, art studios, and cafés. There's dancing in the street—everything from calypso to square dancing—and musical performances ranging from jazz to gospel. Most of the activity takes place along Congress Street and Broadway (from 4th Avenue to Stone Street) and along 5th and 6th avenues, but the action radiates in all directions. For information about this event and about festivals, free workshops and classes, and performances in the downtown arts district, contact **The Tucson Partnership, Inc.** (tel. 602/624–9977); this organization also offers material on self-guided gallery and historic district walking tours.

The **Tucson Poetry Festival,** now in its 11th year, is held in early spring. A large range of poets, some internationally acclaimed—Allen Ginsberg and Amiri Baraka have been participants—come to town for three days of readings and related events. Call 602/321–2163 or 602/322–0895 for details.

The cost of attending any cultural event in Tucson will be a pleasant surprise to anyone who's accustomed to paying East or West Coast prices—symphony tickets can be purchased for as little as $5 for some concerts, and tickets to a touring Broadway musical can often be had for as little as $22. Parking is frequently free. Most of the city's cultural activity takes place either downtown in the arts district, where the Tucson Convention Center complex and the old El Presidio neighborhood are located, or at the University of Arizona. For information about events, such as performances by Ballet Arizona, at the Tucson Convention Center, call 602/791–4266. Tickets to Tucson arts and entertainment events can often be purchased through **Dillard's Box Office** (tel. 602/293–1008 [information] or 800/366–3269 [phone orders with credit cards]).

The free *Tucson Weekly*, found in most supermarkets and convenience stores, and the Friday edition of *The Arizona Daily Star* both have complete listings of what's on in town.

Music The **Tucson Symphony Orchestra** (443 S. Stone Ave., tel. 602/882–8585 [box office] or 602/792–9155 [main office]), part of Tucson's cultural scene for more than 60 years, holds concerts in the newly refurbished Music Hall (260 S. Church St., tel. 602/791–4836) in the Tucson Convention Center complex. A variety of concerts and recitals, many of them free, are offered by the **University of Arizona's School of Music** (tel. 602/621–3065); a chamber music series is hosted by the **Arizona Friends of Music** (tel. 602/298–5806) at the Leo Rich Theater in the Tucson Convention Center from October through April. The **Arizona Opera Company** (3501 N. Mountain Ave., tel. 602/293–4336), headquartered in Tucson, puts on four major productions each year at the Tucson Convention Center's Music Hall.

On Sunday evenings in late May and early summer, pack a picnic basket and head for a free concert by the **Tucson Pops Orchestra** at DeMeester Outdoor Performance Center at Reid Park. It's smart to arrive at least an hour before the music starts (usually around 7:30) so that you can position your blanket exactly where you want it. Call 602/791–4873 for the schedule.

The **Southern Arizona Light Opera Co.** (1202 N. Main Ave., tel. 602/323–7888 [east side ticket office] or 602/884–1212 [west side ticket office]) is becoming increasingly popular.

Tucson's jazz scene encompasses everything from afternoon jam sessions in the park to Sunday jazz brunches at the resorts in the foothills. The **Tucson Jazz Society** (Box 44163, 85733, tel. 602/743–3399) offers information about the many events around town.

Theater Theater groups in town include Arizona's state theater, the **Arizona Theatre Company** (tel. 602/884–8210), which performs everything from classical to contemporary drama at the Temple of Music and Art (330 S. Scott St., tel. 602/622–2823 [tickets]) from November through May; it's worth coming just to see the beautiful, newly restored Spanish Colonial/Moorish–style theater. The drama department at the University of Arizona (tel. 602/621–1162) also offers productions of all styles and periods through the **Studio Theatre Series** and through the **University Theatre.** The **a.k.a. theatre** (125 E. Congress St., tel. 602/623–7852) specializes in avant-garde productions, and **Invisible Theatre** (1400 N. 1st Ave., tel. 602/882–9721) presents contemporary plays and musicals.

Nightlife

If Tucson doesn't have the huge selection of bars and clubs available in some major cities, there's something here to suit nearly every taste. Even if you can't two-step, it's worth stopping into one of the many local country-and-western bars; a number of the clubs offer free dance lessons and the crowd is friendly to city slickers and cowpokes alike. Most of the major resorts have night spots that offer late-night drinks and sometimes dancing.

Rock/Variety **Club Congress** (311 E. Congress St., tel. 602/622–8848) is the main venue in town for cutting-edge rock bands. At the **Cushing Street Bar and Restaurant** (343 S. Meyer Ave., tel. 602/622–7984) the focus is on blues, though live jazz and rock acts are also booked. The **Chicago Bar** (5954 E. Speedway Blvd., tel. 602/748–8169) features reggae on Wednesday and Thursday nights, rocking blues on Friday and Saturday nights. Nearby **Berkey's** (5769 E. Speedway Blvd., tel 602/296–1981) has live music—Motown, R&B, and blues—six nights a week. During the school year, cars line the drive of the Loews Ventana Canyon resort, where the **Flying V Bar & Grill** (tel. 602/299–2020, ext. 5280) packs the collegiate crowd into its disco.

Jazz Of the various clubs around town, **Cafe Sweetwater** (340 E. 6th St., tel. 622/6464) is the most consistent in the quality of its jazz acts—and the food's pretty good, too.

Country and Western An excellent house band gets the crowd two-stepping nightly at the **Maverick** (4702 E. 22nd St., tel. 602/748–0456). On Sunday night **The Cactus Moon** (5470 E. Broadway Blvd., tel. 748–0049) has a terrific all-you-can-eat buffet for $2 and free dance lessons. It's worth a drive to the **Wild Wild West** (4385 W. Ina Rd., tel. 602/744–7744), the Southwest's largest country-and-western nightclub, with a rotating bar, two dance floors, pool tables, and video games.

Southeastern Arizona

The southeastern corner of Arizona is a mix of ghost towns, rugged rock formations, dense, deep forests, and mountain mining towns. It's the site of Chiricahua National Monument, one of Arizona's best-kept secrets, and a paradise for birders, hikers, and antiquers—and anyone who has an interest in frontier history. Many consider this to be Arizona's most scenic region.

Much of this area is part of **Cochise County,** named in 1881 in honor of the chief of the Chiricahua Apache. Cochise waged war against troops and settlers for 11 years, but he was respected by Indian and non-Indian alike for his integrity and leadership skills. Today Cochise County is dotted by small towns, many of them much smaller—and all much tamer—than they were in their heyday. It's hard to imagine now, but Tombstone, headquarters for most of the area's gamblers and gunfighters, was once bigger than San Francisco. Today it's strictly a tourist town, with the wildest visitor usually being a six-year-old traveling with Granny and Gramps on a winter vacation from North Dakota.

The area's terrain ranges from the rugged forests of its mountains to the desert grasslands of Sierra Vista. Cochise County is home to six and part of the seventh—including the Huachucas, Mustangs, Whetstones, and Rincons—of the 12 mountain ranges that compose the 1.7-million-acre Coronado National Forest.

The loop tour suggested below covers the highlights of the region and should take at least two days; three days would offer a more leisurely trip, perhaps with some hiking and an excursion across the border from Douglas to the pleasant town of Agua Prierta in Mexico. If your time is more limited, consider taking a day trip through Texas Canyon to Tombstone and Bisbee, or one via Willcox to Chiricahua National Monument.

Numbers in the margin correspond to points of interest on the Southeastern Arizona map.

From Tucson, head east on I–10 for approximately 63 miles, where you'll see signs telling you that you're enter-
1 ing **Texas Canyon.** The rock formations here are exceptional—the huge boulders appear to be delicately balanced against one another. This is a good place to stop for lunch; there are covered picnic tables and rest room facilities here.

Texas Canyon is also the home of the **Amerind Foundation** (the name is derived from the contraction of the words "American" and "Indian"), founded by the amateur archaeologist William Fulton in 1937 to learn about the Native American cultures. Take Exit 318 off I–10 and continue southeast for 1 mile until you reach the turnoff to the Amerind Foundation, a research facility and museum housed in a beautiful Spanish-style structure built between 1930 and 1959.

Visitors to the museum are given an overview of Native American cultures of the Southwest and Mexico through well-designed rotating displays of archaeological materials, crafts, and photographs. The museum store is well stocked with books on history and Native American cultures, as well as items created by Native American craftspeople. The adjacent Fulton-Hayden Memorial Art Gallery offers an eclectic but interesting assortment of art (mostly from the Southwest) collected by William Fulton. The beautiful natural setting and the quality of the exhibits at the foundation make a visit here a delightful as well as an educational experience. *Dragoon, tel. 602/586–3666. Admission: $3 adults, $2 senior citizens and children 12–18, children under 12 free. Open daily 10–4, closed national holidays. Summer hours may be shorter, so call before you go if you're visiting between mid-May and Sept. 1.*

From the Amerind Foundation, return to I–10 and backtrack 12 miles to **Benson,** once the hub of the Southern Pacific Railroad and a stop on the Butterfield Stagecoach route, but now a fairly sleepy little town. As you go through Benson on I–10, watch for Ocotillo Road, Exit 304. It's worth a detour for the **Singing Wind Bookshop** (Ocotillo Rd., tel. 602/586–2425), located about 3 miles out of town on a ranch. It's a good idea to call before you drive out here be-

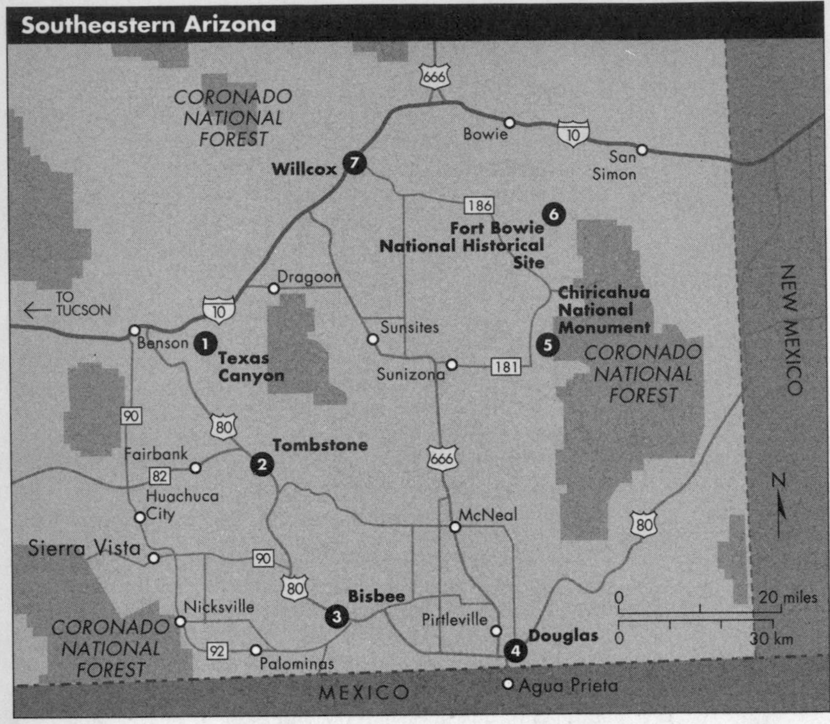

cause the shop's proprietress runs it in her spare time (she runs the ranch, too) and doesn't always keep regular hours. The unlikely location houses an excellent collection of books on Arizona wildlife, history, and geology.

Time Out For a good green-chili burrito or a patty melt, stop in at the **Horseshoe Cafe** (154 E. 4th St., tel. 602/586–3303), which has occupied its current site on Benson's main street for more than 50 years. The neon horseshoe on the ceiling, the macramés of local cattle brands, and the large Wurlizter jukebox all give this casual restaurant and lounge a unique western character.

At Benson you'll pick up U.S. 80. Drive 24 miles south, 2 through some rolling hills, to **Tombstone.** Headquarters of many of the West's rowdies in the late 1800s, Tombstone grew on the site of a wildly successful silver mine, that was discovered in 1877 by prospector Ed Schieffelin, who had been cautioned that "all you'll find there is your tombstone." He struck one of the West's richest veins of silver in the tough old hills and gave the town its name as an ironic "I told you so" to his detractors. The mine itself he called the Lucky Cuss, figuring that, indeed, he was one.

The promise of riches attracted all kinds of folks, including the outlaw type. Soon gambling halls, saloons, and houses of prostitution sprang up all along Allen Street. In the 1881 version of "Family Feud," the Earp family and Doc Holliday battled to the death with the Clanton boys at the famous shoot-out at the OK Corral. Over the past 100 years or so, scriptwriters and storytellers have done much to rewrite the exact details of the confrontation, but it's a fact that the town was indeed the scene of several gunfights in the 1880s. On Sundays, visitors are treated to replays of some of these on Allen Street.

Tombstone still gives visitors a taste of what Arizona was like in its cowboy heyday, though it verges on being a tourist trap, with its staged shoot-outs along the main street, fronted by board sidewalks. But it's good fun, and fans of the Old West's legends will enjoy it.

As you enter Tombstone, stop at **Boot Hill Graveyard,** where the victims of the OK Corral shoot-out are buried; it's on the northwestern corner of town, facing U.S. 80. The commercialism of the place may turn you off (you enter through a gift shop that sells novelty items in the shape of tombstones), but the grave markers are fascinating, and the site is one of the town's highlights.

Once you've bought your tombstone-shaped yard sign, drive into town (less than 3 miles) on U.S. 80. About a block south of the highway and parallel to it is **Allen Street,** the main drag. It's only a few blocks long, but here you'll find most of what Tombstone has to offer: several eateries, museums (not the kind likely to be taken seriously by historians), and curio shops. Many of the buildings still bear bullet holes from their livelier days, and some of the remaining artifacts are interesting—including the **original printing presses** for the town's newspaper, the *Tombstone Epitaph* (9 S. 5th St., tel. 602/457–2211), founded in 1880 and still publishing. Two dollars will admit you to **The Bird Cage Theater** (6th and Allen streets, tel. 602/457–3421). The displays in this former music hall, where Caruso, Sarah Bernhardt, and Lillian Russell—among others—performed, are dusty and chaotic. If you poke around, however, you can find such treasures as the 1881 Black Moriah hearse that brought all the victims of the OK Corral shoot-out—and everyone else who died in Tombstone—to the Boot Hill cemetery. Those whose tastes tend toward the horticultural—or who just need a break from gunfighting lore—might want to shell out $1.50 to see the **World's Largest Rosebush** at the Rose Tree Inn Museum at 4th and Toughnut streets (Toughnut runs parallel to Allen Street, one block south). The Lady Banksia rosebush found its way to Tombstone from Scotland in 1885 as a wedding gift, and today it covers 7,000 square feet. If it's not the world's largest, it's certainly a contender.

Once you've had your fill of Tombstone, take U.S. 80 for 24 miles south to Bisbee. The drive here is a scenic one, climbing another 1,000 feet in elevation to a final elevation of more than a mile (5,490 feet).

3 **Bisbee** was once a mining boomtown, and when the mines closed in 1975, the city went into a predictable decline. However, it was rediscovered in the early 1980s by burned-out city dwellers and revived as a kind of artists colony/place-to-do-your-own-thing. The permanent population is a mix of retired miners and their families, aging hippie jewelry makers, and enterprising young restaurateurs and antiques dealers. The three rather disparate groups seem to get along fine—Bisbee is that kind of place.

When you drive through Mule Mountain Tunnel on U.S. 80, you'll be getting close. You'll see the pretty, compact town hugging the steep mountainside on your left. If you want to head straight into town, get off at Brewery Gulch interchange. You can park here and cross under the highway, taking Main or Commerce or Brewery Gulch streets, all of which all here.

Another option is to continue driving on U.S. 80 about a quarter of a mile to where it intersects with AZ 92. Pull off the highway on the right into a gravel parking lot, where a short, typewritten history of the **Lavender Pit Mine** can be found attached to the hurricane fence surrounding the area (Bisbee isn't big on formal exhibits). The hole left by the copper miners is huge, with piles of lavender-hued "tailings," or waste, creating mountains around it. Arizona's largest pit mine yielded some 94 million tons of copper ore out of more than 280 million tons of raw materials before the town's mining activity came to a halt nearly 20 years ago. If you're interested in buying jewelry made from Bisbee Blue, the pretty turquoise stone still extracted from Lavender Pit, walk across the parking area toward the mountains to the right of the **Bisbee Blue shop.**

For a real lesson in mining history, however, you need to take the **Copper Queen mine tour.** The mine is less than a half-mile to the east of the Lavender Pit, across U.S. 80 from downtown at the Brewery Gulch interchange. (If you're claustrophobic, sit this one out at one of Bisbee's many restaurants. Although there is plenty of ventilation in the mine, it's dark and close in here. Note, too, that the tour might be scary for very small children.) Tours are led by one of Bisbee's several retired copper miners, who are wont to embellish their official spiel with tales from their mining days. They're also very capable, safety-minded people (any miner who survives to lead tours in his older years would have to be), so don't be concerned about the dog tags (literally—they're donated by a local veterinarian) issued to each person on the tour. They're just precautionary, in case of a problem.

The tours, which depart daily at 9, 10:30, noon, 2, and 3:30 (you can't enter the mine at any other time), last anywhere from 1 to 1½ hours, and visitors go into the shaft via a little open train, like those the miners rode when the mine was active. Before you climb aboard, you're outfitted in miner garb—a yellow slicker and a hard hat that runs off a battery pack strapped to your waist. You may want to wear a sweater or light coat under your slicker because the temperature in the mine is a brisk 47°F on the average. You'll travel by train thousands of feet into the mine, up a grade of 30 feet (not down, as many visitors expect). The slicker will keep you protected from the occasional drips and sprinkles—natural seepage from the ground. 1 Dart Rd., tel. 602/432-2071. Admission: $7.50 adults, $3.25 children 7–11, $1.50 children 3–6, children under 3 free. Open daily. Closed Thanksgiving and Christmas.

Right across the street from the mine, in Queens Plaza, is the **Mining and Historical Museum,** housed in the old redbrick Phelps Dodge general office (Phelps Dodge was the operator of the town's copper mines). The museum is one filled with old photographs and artifacts from the town's mining days, and explores other aspects of the first 40 years of Bisbee's history, from 1887 to 1920. It's fun to walk out of the museum and view those same buildings you've just seen depicted inside. *Queens Plaza, tel. 602/432-7071. Admission: $3 adults, $2 senior citizens, children under 18 free. Open daily 10–5. Closed Christmas and New Year's Day.*

Behind the museum is the venerable old **Copper Queen Hotel** (*see* Lodging, *below*), built some 100 years ago. It has housed the famous as well as the infamous: "Black Jack" Pershing, John Wayne, Teddy Roosevelt, and mining executives from all over the world made this their home away from home. It's a good establishment if you plan to be here overnight, and it's at least worth a visit to look at the historical photographs and framed mementos all over the walls. There are checks for lodging, stock transfers, and correspondence relating to other business transactions that took place more than a century ago (check out the ones by the public telephones in the lobby).

The Copper Queen is adjacent to **Brewery Gulch,** today a short street running north and south (walk out the front door of the Copper Queen, make a left, and you'll be there within about 20 paces) that's largely abandoned and lined with boarded-up storefronts. In the old days, the brewery housed there allowed the dregs of the beer that was being brewed to flow down the street and into the gutter.

Time Out **Café Maxie** (tel. 602/432-7063), in #2 Copper Queen Plaza, once the Phelps Dodge General Mercantile Store and now the town's convention center, is a good place for homemade soups and sandwiches. The eclectic menu reflects the background of the owners, Steve and Ida Jensen—he's German, she's Italian. Brightly colored parachutes are suspended from the ceiling, creating a festive, airy atmosphere. Take a trip upstairs to the rest rooms for a view of the lobby down below, with its rich copper (what else?) light fixtures and handrails.

From Bisbee, continue southeast on U.S. 80 until you reach
4 **Douglas,** on the U.S.–Mexico border. The town was founded in 1902 by James Douglas to serve as the copper-smelting center for the mines in Bisbee. Before then, the site was the annual roundup ground for local ranchers, Mexican and American—among them John Slaughter who was the sheriff of Cochise County after Wyatt Earp. Both Douglas's house and Slaughter's ranch have been turned into museums and are worth a visit, but the must-see in town is the **Gadsen Hotel** (*see* Lodging, *below*), built in 1907. The lobby boasts a solid white Italian marble staircase, two authentic Tiffany vaulted skylights, and a 42-foot stained-glass mural. Neither Douglas nor Agua Prieta across the way in Mexico fits the stereotypes of border towns: both are clean, pleasant places. **Agua Prieta** offers well-priced Mexican goods, and shopping here involves neither haggling nor hassling.

After touring Douglas, get back on U.S. 80 in the direction of Bisbee. It's less than a half-mile to the turnoff for U.S. 666; go north on this road for about 41 miles until you reach the intersection with AZ 181, where signs will direct you to Chiricahua National Monument, approximately 10 miles away.

The vast fields of desert grass you've passed during most of the drive are suddenly transformed into a landscape of forest, mountains, and striking rock formations as you enter
5 the 12,000-acre **Chiricahua National Monument.** Dubbed the "Land of the Standing-Up Rocks" by the Chiricahua Apache, who lived in the mountains for centuries—and, led by Cochise and Geronimo, tried for 25 years to prevent white pioneers from settling here—this is an unusual site for a variety of reasons. The vast outcroppings of volcanic rock worn by erosion into strange pinnacles and spires are set in a forest where autumn and spring occur at the same time; because of the particular balance of sunshine and rain in the area, in April and May visitors will see brown, yellow, and red leaves co-existing with new green foliage. Summer in Chiricahua National Monument is exceptionally wet: From July through September, there are thunderstorms nearly every afternoon. In addition, few other areas in the United States have such a variety of plant, bird, and animal life; along with the plants and animals of the Southwest, the Chiracahua Mountains also host a number of Mexican species. Deer, coatimundis, peccaries, and lizards live among the aspen, ponderosa pine, Douglas fir, oak, and cyprus trees—to name just a few. This a natural mecca for bird watchers, and hikers have more than 17 miles of scenic trails, ranging from a half-mile to 13 miles long. At the visi-

tor center, you can purchase a brochure describing the trails for 10¢; free lists of the mammals, snakes, and birds in the region are also available, and rangers frequently conduct interpretive walks. *Chiricahua National Monument, Dos Cabezas Route, Box 6500, Willcox, AZ 85643, tel. 602/824–3560. Entry fee: $3 per car. Visitor center open daily 8–5.*

In Chiricahua National Monument, AZ 181 turns into AZ
186. Continue north on this road for about 5 miles; you'll see
signs directing you to the well-maintained gravel road lead-
6 ing to Bowie and the **Fort Bowie National Historical Site,** in
the Dos Cabezas (Two-Headed) Mountains. A ranger station here is open daily from 8 AM until 5 PM. Admission to the
site is free.

The fort and the nearby **Butterfield stage stop** played important parts in Arizona's history. The stage stop, in the heart of Chiricahua Apache land, was a crucial link in the journey from East to West in the mid-19th century. Chief Cochise and the stagecoach operators ignored one another until sometime in 1861, when hostilities broke out between U.S. Cavalry troops and the Apache. After an ambush by the chief's warriors at Apache Pass in 1862, U.S. troops decided a fort was desperately needed in the area, and Fort Bowie was built within weeks. There were skirmishes for the next 10 years, followed by a peaceful decade; then renewed fighting broke out in 1881. Geronimo, the new leader of the Indian warriors, finally surrendered in 1886. The fort was abandoned eight years later and fell into disrepair.

In order to get to the fort from the ranger station, you must take a 1½-mile unpaved footpath. Today the site is virtually in ruins, and there is no showcase museum or visitor center (though there are picnic grounds and rest rooms). Instead, there is an eerie silence in this place, where the last of Arizona's battles between Native Americans and U.S. troops was fought.

When you get back to the gravel road, take it another 6
miles north until you reach Bowie, where you'll pick up I-
10. If you take it west for 15 miles, you'll arrive at the turn-
7 off for the town of **Willcox.** With fewer than 4,000 residents,
Willcox is a major cattle-shipping center; its downtown
looks like an Old West movie set. An elevation of 4,167 feet
renders the climate here moderate in summer and a bit chilly in winter. Apple pie fans from all over Arizona know this
little town, located in an apple-growing area, as headquarters; enterprising Willcox cooks bake pies for customers as
far away as Phoenix.

Stay on the I-10 frontage road and follow the signs to the historical district. Here you'll find the **Rex Allen Arizona Cowboy Museum,** set up as a tribute to Willcox's most famous native son, cowboy singer Rex Allen. He starred in several rather average cowboy movies during the '40s and

'50s for Republic Pictures, but he's probably most famous as the friendly voice that narrated Walt Disney nature films. *155 N. Railroad Ave., tel. 602/384–4583. Admission: $3, $5 per family. Open Mon.–Sat. 10–4. Closed Sun., Thanksgiving, Christmas, and New Year's Day.*

Less than a block down the street is the **Willcox Commercial Store.** Established in 1881, it's the oldest retail establishment in Arizona that's still operating in its original location; locals like to boast that Geronimo used to shop here. Today it's a clothing store, with a large selection of western wear.

As you leave town, stop at **Stout's Cider Mill** (it's on the frontage road to I–10—roll down your windows and follow the aromas of apples and nutmeg). Adjacent to Stout's, the **Museum of the Southwest** focuses on the life of the cowboy and the Native American in the late 1800s and early 1900s; the Cowboy Hall of Fame salutes the Arizona cattlemen. *1500 N. Circle I Rd., tel. 602/384–2272. Admission free. Open Mon.–Sat. 9–5, Sun. 1–5.*

Time Out For a piece of pie or a taco plate, make a stop at the **Plaza Restaurant** (in Willcox at Exit 340, off I–10, tel. 602/384–3819). It's open 24 hours and is popular with locals as well as long-distance travelers—there's a gas station in the parking lot.

To return to Tucson from Willcox, take I-10 west for 78 miles. It's an easy drive, unless you're doing it in the summertime toward the end of the day. You're best off waiting until the sun has gone down and out of your eyes.

Dining and Lodging

Bisbee *Dining*

El Zarape Café. Decorated with the Mexican ponchos for which it was named, El Zarape isn't for sophisticates. But this small, family-run place is friendly and homey, and the food is fine. Try the chimichangas: They're light, crisp, and worth every calorie. Combination plates are also a good bet. *46 Main St., tel. 602/432–5031. No reservations. Dress: informal. No credit cards. Closed Sun.; lunch only. Inexpensive.*

Golden China Chinese Cuisine. Though it may seem odd to find a good-quality Chinese restaurant in an old mining town, Bisbee once drew its share of Chinese immigrants, and the Golden China, in an old stone building on Brewery Gulch, is one of their legacies. Interesting Oriental art objects are scattered throughout the dining room, and a fountain trickles down one wall. The food isn't fancy, but it's good. Shrimp Szechuan-style can be spiced to your liking, and such Cantonese basics as sweet-and-sour pork are well prepared. The use of MSG is optional. *15 Brewery Gulch, tel. 602/432–5888. No reservations. Dress: informal. MC, V. Inexpensive.*

Stenzel's. Although this small, attractive restaurant, set in a wooden cabin off the side of the road, is touted by locals for its seafood specialties, they're not really Stenzel's strongest suit. The barbecued ribs and grilled chicken breast are fine, however, and the fettuccine Alfredo is outstanding. There's a decent wine list, and this is a good place to try the excellent Electric ale brewed locally. *207 Tombstone Canyon, tel. 602/432–7611. Reservations advised for dinner. Dress: casual. No credit cards; personal checks accepted. Closed Tues.; dinner only weekends. Moderate.*

★ **The Wine Gallery Bistro.** A favorite of many of the Yuppie residents in town, this cozy little place, located on two levels of another of Bisbee's venerable old buildings, features an excellent wine list, focusing on California bottles. Tasty homemade soups and sandwiches are served at lunchtime, a good range of pastas, fish and poultry, and vegetarian entrées at dinner. Try the cranberry-pecan chicken, a wonderful blend of fruit and nuts served over succulent white meat. *41 Main St., 602/432–3447. Reservations accepted. Dress: informal. MC, V. Closed Sun. and Mon. Moderate.*

Lodging

★ **Copper Queen Hotel.** Built by the Copper Queen Mining Company (which later became the Phelps Dodge Corporation) at a time when Bisbee was the biggest copper-mining town in the world, this hotel in the heart of downtown Bisbee is almost 100 years old. The rooms are tiny and the walls are thin, but there's a Victorian charm about the place. All around are framed receipts for room rent, mining purchases, and other boom-days memorabilia. Guests over the years have included a host of wild and crazy prospectors as well as more respectable types. Today's visitors are also a varied lot, as likely to include a film producer scouting locations as a retired snowbird from Minnesota or a family from Phoenix. *11 Howell Ave., Drawer CQ, 85603, tel. 602/432–2216 or 800/247–5829. 43 rooms with bath. Facilities: pool, dining room, saloon. AE, MC, V. Moderate.*

Greenway House. The best of the B&Bs in town, Greenway House is immaculate and has some charming rooms, but lacks the warmth one expects from this type of lodging. Built in 1906, the house is in the historic Warren district, where executives of the Calumet and Arizona Mining Company lived. All the rooms have baths with robes and hair dryers. In each there is also a fully equipped kitchen area, where most of the trappings for breakfast are left the night before; fresh blueberry muffins are delivered outside the door at 7 AM. Room No. 5, with its wooden sleigh bed and matching dresser and armoire, perhaps comes closest to recapturing the original feel of the house. Smoking is not permitted inside. *401 Cole Ave., Bisbee 85603, tel. 602/253–3325. 5 rooms, 3 suites, 2 of them in separate carriage house, all with private bath. AE, MC, V. Moderate–Expensive.*

Tombstone
Dining

Longhorn Restaurant. Like most of the places in town, this one has been rigged up for the city slickers, so they'll get an idea of what it was like to grab some grub about 100 years ago in these here parts. Set up to look like an old saloon, the Longhorn is decorated with posters and artifacts from Tombstone's wilder days. Burgers, sandwiches, and the usual middle-of-the-road American food are available here. Service is very efficient. *Allen and 5th Sts., tel. 602/457-3405. No reservations. Dress: informal. MC, V. Inexpensive.*

Nellie Cashman's Boarding House Restaurant. Billed as "Tombstone's Oldest Restaurant," Nellie Cashman's is part of a restored 1879 building that's a cross between Spanish style and Old West. It's a cheerful place, with lots of plants and flowered tablecloths—and of course Nellie Cashman memorabilia. The restaurant came under new ownership in 1992; the focus now is on burgers, with a variety of hearty steak and chicken entrées for dinner. There are plans for expansion to an outdoor terrace. *5th and Toughnut Sts., tel. 602/457-2212. No reservations. Dress: informal. MC, V. Inexpensive.*

Lodging

Adobe Lodge Motel. This is a little strip motel located downtown. It's not out of the ordinary—beige-carpeted, beige-walled rooms—but it's inexpensive and close to the boardwalk (code name for the old-fashioned sidewalks of downtown). *505 E. Fremont St., 85638, tel. 602/457-2241. 15 rooms with bath. MC, V. Inexpensive.*

The Best Western Look-Out Lodge. Overlooking Boot Hill on U.S. 80, this little motel provides basic lodging without frills. The office closes at 10 PM, so be sure to arrive before then (and make your telephone calls before then, too). It's fairly clean, but the noise from highway trucks can be bothersome to the light sleeper. The innkeeper is friendly and sympathetic to the tired traveler, offering coffee and muffins in the lobby every morning. *Hwy. 80 West, Box 787, 85638, tel. 602/457-2223 or 800/528-1234. 40 rooms with bath. AE, D, DC, MC, V. Inexpensive–Moderate.*

Index

Personal Itinerary

Departure *Date*

Time

Transportation

Arrival *Date* *Time*

Departure *Date* *Time*

Transportation

Accommodations

Arrival *Date* *Time*

Departure *Date* *Time*

Transportation

Accommodations

Arrival *Date* *Time*

Departure *Date* *Time*

Transportation

Accommodations

Personal Itinerary

Arrival *Date* *Time*

Departure *Date* *Time*

Transportation

Accommodations

Arrival *Date* *Time*

Departure *Date* *Time*

Transportation

Accommodations

Arrival *Date* *Time*

Departure *Date* *Time*

Transportation

Accommodations

Arrival *Date* *Time*

Departure *Date* *Time*

Transportation

Accommodations

Personal Itinerary

Arrival *Date* *Time*

Departure *Date* *Time*

Transportation

Accommodations

Arrival *Date* *Time*

Departure *Date* *Time*

Transportation

Accommodations

Arrival *Date* *Time*

Departure *Date* *Time*

Transportation

Accommodations

Arrival *Date* *Time*

Departure *Date* *Time*

Transportation

Accommodations

Personal Itinerary

Arrival *Date* *Time*

Departure *Date* *Time*

Transportation

Accommodations

Arrival *Date* *Time*

Departure *Date* *Time*

Transportation

Accommodations

Arrival *Date* *Time*

Departure *Date* *Time*

Transportation

Accommodations

Arrival *Date* *Time*

Departure *Date* *Time*

Transportation

Accommodations

Personal Itinerary

Arrival *Date* *Time*

Departure *Date* *Time*

Transportation

Accommodations

Arrival *Date* *Time*

Departure *Date* *Time*

Transportation

Accommodations

Arrival *Date* *Time*

Departure *Date* *Time*

Transportation

Accommodations

Arrival *Date* *Time*

Departure *Date* *Time*

Transportation

Accommodations

Personal Itinerary

Arrival *Date* *Time*

Departure *Date* *Time*

Transportation

Accommodations

Arrival *Date* *Time*

Departure *Date* *Time*

Transportation

Accommodations

Arrival *Date* *Time*

Departure *Date* *Time*

Transportation

Accommodations

Arrival *Date* *Time*

Departure *Date* *Time*

Transportation

Accommodations

Personal Itinerary

Arrival *Date* *Time*

Departure *Date* *Time*

Transportation

Accommodations

Arrival *Date* *Time*

Departure *Date* *Time*

Transportation

Accommodations

Arrival *Date* *Time*

Departure *Date* *Time*

Transportation

Accommodations

Arrival *Date* *Time*

Departure *Date* *Time*

Transportation

Accommodations

Name

Address

Telephone

Name

Address

Telephone

Name

Address

Telephone

Name

Address

Telephone

Name

Address

Telephone

Name

Address

Telephone

Name

Address

Telephone

Name

Address

Telephone

Name

Address

Telephone

Name

Address

Telephone

Name

Address

Telephone

Name

Address

Telephone

Name

Address

Telephone

Name

Address

Telephone

Name

Address

Telephone

Name

Address

Telephone

Addresses

Name

Address

Telephone

Name

Address

Telephone

Name

Address

Telephone

Name

Address

Telephone

Name

Address

Telephone

Name

Address

Telephone

Name

Address

Telephone

Name

Address

Telephone

Name

Address

Telephone

Name

Address

Telephone

Name

Address

Telephone

Name

Address

Telephone

Name

Address

Telephone

Name

Address

Telephone

Name

Address

Telephone

Name

Address

Telephone

Addresses

Name

Address

Telephone

Name

Address

Telephone

Name

Address

Telephone

Name

Address

Telephone

Name

Address

Telephone

Name

Address

Telephone

Name

Address

Telephone

Name

Address

Telephone

Name

Address

Telephone

Name

Address

Telephone

Name

Address

Telephone

Name

Address

Telephone

Name

Address

Telephone

Name

Address

Telephone

Name

Address

Telephone

Name

Address

Telephone

Addresses

Name

Address

Telephone

Name

Address

Telephone

Name

Address

Telephone

Name

Address

Telephone

Name

Address

Telephone

Name

Address

Telephone

Name

Address

Telephone

Name

Address

Telephone

Name

Address

Telephone

Name

Address

Telephone

Name

Address

Telephone

Name

Address

Telephone

Name

Address

Telephone

Name

Address

Telephone

Name

Address

Telephone

Name

Address

Telephone

Notes

Fodor's Travel Guides

U.S. Guides

Alaska

Arizona

Boston

California

Cape Cod, Martha's Vineyard, Nantucket

The Carolinas & the Georgia Coast

Chicago

Disney World & the Orlando Area

Florida

Hawaii

Las Vegas, Reno, Tahoe

Los Angeles

Maine, Vermont, New Hampshire

Maui

Miami & the Keys

New England

New Orleans

New York City

Pacific North Coast

Philadelphia & the Pennsylvania Dutch Country

San Diego

San Francisco

Santa Fe, Taos, Albuquerque

Seattle & Vancouver

The South

The U.S. & British Virgin Islands

The Upper Great Lakes Region

USA

Vacations in New York State

Vacations on the Jersey Shore

Virginia & Maryland

Waikiki

Washington, D.C.

Foreign Guides

Acapulco, Ixtapa, Zihuatanejo

Australia & New Zealand

Austria

The Bahamas

Baja & Mexico's Pacific Coast Resorts

Barbados

Berlin

Bermuda

Brazil

Budapest

Budget Europe

Canada

Cancun, Cozumel, Yucatan Penisula

Caribbean

Central America

China

Costa Rica, Belize, Guatemala

Czechoslovakia

Eastern Europe

Egypt

Euro Disney

Europe

Europe's Great Cities

France

Germany

Great Britain

Greece

The Himalayan Countries

Hong Kong

India

Ireland

Israel

Italy

Italy's Great Cities

Japan

Kenya & Tanzania

Korea

London

Madrid & Barcelona

Mexico

Montreal & Quebec City

Morocco

The Netherlands Belgium & Luxembourg

New Zealand

Norway

Nova Scotia, Prince Edward Island & New Brunswick

Paris

Portugal

Rome

Russia & the Baltic Countries

Scandinavia

Scotland

Singapore

South America

Southeast Asia

South Pacific

Spain

Sweden

Switzerland

Thailand

Tokyo

Toronto

Turkey

Vienna & the Danube Valley

Yugoslavia

Special Series

Fodor's Affordables

Affordable Europe

Affordable France

Affordable Germany

Affordable Great Britain

Affordable Italy

Fodor's Bed & Breakfast and Country Inns Guides

California

Mid-Atlantic Region

New England

The Pacific Northwest

The South

The West Coast

The Upper Great Lakes Region

Canada's Great Country Inns

Cottages, B&Bs and Country Inns of England and Wales

The Berkeley Guides

On the Loose in California

On the Loose in Eastern Europe

On the Loose in Mexico

On the Loose in the Pacific Northwest & Alaska

Fodor's Exploring Guides

Exploring California

Exploring Florida

Exploring France

Exploring Germany

Exploring Paris

Exploring Rome

Exploring Spain

Exploring Thailand

Fodor's Flashmaps

New York

Washington, D.C.

Fodor's Pocket Guides

Pocket Bahamas

Pocket Jamaica

Pocket London

Pocket New York City

Pocket Paris

Pocket Puerto Rico

Pocket San Francisco

Pocket Washington, D.C.

Fodor's Sports

Cycling

Hiking

Running

Sailing

The Insider's Guide to the Best Canadian Skiing

Fodor's Three-In-Ones (guidebook, language cassette, and phrase book)

France

Germany

Italy

Mexico

Spain

Fodor's Special-Interest Guides

Cruises and Ports of Call

Disney World & the Orlando Area

Euro Disney

Healthy Escapes

London Companion

Skiing in the USA & Canada

Sunday in New York

Fodor's Touring Guides

Touring Europe

Touring USA: Eastern Edition

Touring USA: Western Edition

Fodor's Vacation Planners

Great American Vacations

National Parks of the West

The Wall Street Journal Guides to Business Travel

Europe

International Cities

Pacific Rim

USA & Canada